UNITED NATIONS SANCTIONS AND INTERNATIONAL LAW

The Graduate Institute of International Studies

Volume 1

United Nations Sanctions and International Law

Edited by

Vera Gowlland-Debbas

With the assistance of Mariano Garcia Rubio
and Hassiba Hadj-Sahraoui

Kluwer Law International
The Hague / London / Boston

A C.I.P. Catalogue record for this book is available from the Library of Congress.

ISBN 90-411-1603-6

Published by Kluwer Law International,
P.O. Box 85889, 2508 CN The Hague, The Netherlands.

Sold and distributed in North, Central and South America
by Kluwer Law International,
101 Philip Drive, Norwell, MA 02061, U.S.A.
kluwerlaw@wkap.com

In all other countries, sold and distributed
by Kluwer Law International, Distribution Centre,
P.O. Box 322, 3300 AH Dordrecht, The Netherlands.

The Graduate Institute of International Studies
132, rue de Lausanne, Case postale 36,
CH-1211 GENEVA 21, Switzerland,
tel. 41-22-908-5700; fax 41-22-908-5710

Layout and camera-ready copy:
Anne-Marie Krens – Tekstbeeld – Oegstgeest – The Netherlands

Printed on acid-free paper

01-0702-150 ts

Kluwer Law International incorporates the publishing programmes of
Graham & Trotman Ltd, Kluwer Law and Taxation Publishers,
and Martinus Nijhoff Publishers.

Printed in the Netherlands.

TABLE OF CONTENTS

FOREWORD xi
LIST OF ABBREVIATIONS xiii

INTRODUCTION
UN Sanctions and International Law: An Overview
Vera Gowlland-Debbas 1

KEYNOTE ADDRESS
The Concept of Sanction in International Law
Georges Abi-Saab 29

PART I: SANCTIONS – THEORETICAL ISSUES 43

SANCTIONS AND THE INTERNATIONAL LEGAL SYSTEM 45

Chair: *Rosalyn Higgins*

1 Quelques remarques sur l'évolution de la pratique des sanctions décidées par le Conseil de sécurité des Nations Unies dans le cadre du Chapitre VII de la Charte
Pierre-Marie Dupuy 47

2 The Relationship between Sanctions and Countermeasures
James Crawford 57

LIMITS TO THE POWERS OF THE SECURITY COUNCIL AND THE QUESTION OF ACCOUNTABILITY 69

Chair: *Abdul G. Koroma*

3 International Law Limits to the Security Council
Nicolas Angelet 71

4 Judicial Review of Sanctions
John Dugard 83

ASSESSING ALTERNATIVES TO COLLECTIVE ECONOMIC SANCTIONS 93

Chair: *Georges Abi-Saab*

5 Unilateral versus Collective Sanctions: An American's Perception
Andreas Lowenfeld 95

6 La responsabilité pénale individuelle, alternative aux sanctions collectives?
Alain Pellet 105

7 Regional Enforcement of Community Objectives
Bruno Simma 117

PART II: SANCTIONS AND HUMANITARIAN ISSUES 123

8 Opening Remarks: Sanctions and Human Rights Law
Jochen A. Frowein 125

SANCTIONS AND HUMAN RIGHTS LAW 129

Chair: *Jochen A. Frowein*

9 Sanctions and Economic, Social and Cultural Rights
Andrew Clapham 131

10 Interpreting the Humanitarian Exceptions through the Sanctions Committees
Gian Luca Burci 143

11 UNICEF and the Sanctions Committee – Lessons Learned from Iraq
Jean Dupraz 155

SANCTIONS, HUMANITARIAN ISSUES AND MANDATES 165

Chair: *Geneviève Burdeau*

12 Les sanctions peuvent-elles se heurter à des normes concernant le système des Nations Unies lui-même?
Marie-José Domestici-Met 167

13 UN Sanctions – the ILO Experience
Janelle Diller 197

14 UN Sanctions – Dilemmas for UNICEF
Karin Landgren 205

15 UN Sanctions and ICRC's Mandate
Michele Kuhn 211

SANCTIONS AND HUMANITARIAN LAW 221

Chair: *Christian Dominicé*

16 La compatibilité des sanctions du Conseil de Sécurité avec le droit international humanitaire
Djamchid Momtaz 223

17 La compatibilité des sanctions du Conseil de Sécurité avec le droit international humanitaire – commentaire
Luigi Condorelli 233

18 Sanctions and International Humanitarian Law – commentary
Marco Sassòli 241

PART III: IMPLEMENTATION OF SECURITY COUNCIL SANCTIONS RESOLUTIONS 251

SANCTIONS AND PRIVATE RIGHTS 251

Chair: Jean-Michel Jacquet

19 Implementation of Security Council Resolutions taken under Chapter VII in Germany
Jochen A. Frowein 253

20 Les effets juridiques des résolutions du Conseil de sécurité sur les contrats privés
Geneviève Burdeau 267

SPECIAL PROBLEMS FOR IMPLEMENTING STATES 289

Chair: *Erik Suy*

21 Regional Interface between Security Council Decisions and Member States Implementation: The Example of the European Union
Daniel Bethlehem 291

22 Enforcing the Economic Embargo at Sea
Alfred H. A. Soons 307

23 Consultation under Article 50 of the United Nations Charter – the Experience of the Middle East
Bisher H. Al-Khasawneh 325

24 The Position of States Specially Affected by Sanctions in the Meaning of Article 50 of the United Nations Charter – The Experience of Eastern Europe
Wladyslaw Czapliñski 335

25 Implementation of Sanctions – The Experience of Africa
Tunguru Huaraka 349

26 Mise en œuvre par un Etat non membre des Nations Unies – le cas de la Suisse
Mathias-Charles Krafft 361

PART IV: THE FUTURE OF SANCTIONS 369

Chair: *Ismat Kittani*

27 The Impact of United Nations Sanctions on Economic Development, Human Rights and Civil Society
A. Amir Al-Anbari 371

28 Alternatives to Economic Sanctions
Christine Chinkin 381

29 Contrainte légale et violence illégale en droit international: fondements de la distinction
Monique Chemillier-Gendreau 393

PART V: ANNEXES 403

LIST OF DOCUMENTS 405

FOREWORD

The papers in this volume were first presented at the Colloquium on 'United Nations Sanctions and International Law' organised by the Graduate Institute of International Studies and its Programme for the Study of International Organisation(s) (PSIO) and held at the Hotel Intercontinental, Geneva, from 23-25 June 1999.

The Colloquium was organised within the framework of an eighteen-month project on sanctions co-ordinated by Professor Vera Gowlland-Debbas and funded by The Thyssen Foundation, The United Nations University, The Swiss Federal Department of Foreign Affairs, The Swiss Federal Department of Defence, Civil Protection and Sports, and the Tokyo Club.

This Project is in two parts. The first consists of the organisation of a Colloquium on Sanctions, the results of which are published in this current volume and focus on the general legal issues arising from the adoption by the Security Council of non-military sanctions under Chapter VII of the Charter. The second, which spans an eighteen-month period of research, is centred on a comparative national survey of the legal issues relating to the implementation and enforcement of Security Council Sanctions under Chapter VII of the Charter. It is undertaken by a number of prominent academics and legal experts around the world and some of the preliminary results were presented at the Colloquium. The final results of this research will appear in a separate publication.

The Graduate Institute of International Studies would like to reiterate its thanks to the sponsors of the project for their invaluable support. Thanks also are due to Dr. Daniel Warner, Executive Director of the Program for the Study of International Organization(s) (PSIO), who was responsible for the excellent organisation of the Colloquium and the overall administration of the project. A special word of thanks also to Mrs. Elisa Krahenbuhl for her invaluable contribution to the coordination and secretarial tasks of the project. The Institute also wishes to thank all the student assistants who contributed to the successful organization of the Colloquium.

LIST OF ABBREVIATIONS

AVR	*Archiv des Völkerrechts*
AFDI	*Annuaire français de droit international*
AJIL	*American Journal of International Law*
BYIL	*British Year Book of International Law*
CJTL	*Columbia Journal of Transnational Law*
CMLR	Common Market Law Reports
CMLRev	*Common Market Law Review*
DAI	*Documents d'actualité internationale*
EJIL	*European Journal of International Law*
GA Res.	General Assembly Resolution
ICJ Reports	International Court of Justice, Reports of Judgments, Advisory Opinions and Orders
ICLQ	*International and Comparative Law Quarterly*
ILC	International Law Commission
ILM	*International Legal Materials*
ILRM	*Irish Law Reports Monthly*
JDI	*Journal du droit international*
JRMP	*Jugoslovenska revija za meǒunarodno pravo*
PolYBIL	*Polish Yearbook of International Law*
RBDI	*Revue belge de droit international*
Recueil CIJ	Recueil des arrêts, avis consultatif et ordonnances de la Cour Internationale de Justice
Recueil des Cours	Collected Courses of the Hague Academy of International Law
Rés. AG	Résolution de l'Assemblé générale
Rés. CS	Résolution du Conseil de sécurité
RGDIP	*Revue générale de droit international public*
RSDIE	*Revue suisse de droit international et de droit européen*
RTNU	Recueil des traités des Nations Unies

SC Res.	Security Council Resolution
UNCIO	United Nations Conference on International Organization
UN Doc.	United Nations Document
UNTS	United Nations Treaty Series
Va.J.Int'l L	*Virginia Journal of International Law*
YBILC	Yearbook of the International Law Commission
ZaöRV	*Zeitschrift für ausländisches öffentliches Recht und Völkerrecht*

INTRODUCTION

UN SANCTIONS AND INTERNATIONAL LAW: AN OVERVIEW

Vera Gowlland-Debbas[■]

INTRODUCTION

The first resort to mandatory sanctions in the history of the United Nations was in December 1966 when first selective and then comprehensive measures were adopted by the Security Council under Article 41 of the Charter against the racist minority regime of Southern Rhodesia. This was followed subsequently only by a mandatory arms embargo adopted in 1977 against South Africa. The reactivation of the Security Council at the beginning of the last decade however, has resulted, since the invasion of Kuwait by Iraq on August 2, 1990, in increasing use of its powers under Chapter VII of the Charter.

The Council's determinations under Article 39 of the Charter that there exists a threat to the peace, or breach of the peace (though so far not act of aggression), have served as the basis for the adoption of wide-ranging mandatory measures under Chapter VII, against a number of state and non-state entities: Iraq (1990), the former territory of Yugoslavia (1991), the Federal Republic of Yugoslavia (Serbia and Montenegro) (1992), the Bosnian Serb party (1993), Somalia (1992), Libya (1992), Liberia (1992), Haiti (1993), UNITA (Angola) (1993), Rwanda (1993), Sudan (1996), Sierra Leone (1997) and, again, the Federal Republic of Yugoslavia(1998).

It is not only the frequency, but the reconceptualization of a threat to the peace, as well as the types of measures adopted which are striking, and in this respect the Security Council has certainly taken some innovative paths, surely never dreamed of by those who framed the Charter at San Francisco. It is enough to reflect on the wide range of the measures adopted. The Council has qualified

■ Professor of Public International Law, Graduate Institute of International Studies, Geneva.

the acts of states and non-state entities as illegal and invalid; it has imposed arms embargoes, selective as well as comprehensive economic, financial and diplomatic measures, including suspension of communications. It has authorised resort to military action (the case of Iraq), as well as authorized states and regional organizations to resort to force for limited purposes, such as to enforce economic sanctions at sea, to protect UN so-called safe areas, to facilitate the delivery of humanitarian aid, to defend UN peacekeeping forces, to reinstate democratically elected regimes, and to enforce peace settlements. In the case of Iraq it went far in assessing reparations due after the military conflict in Kuwait by establishing a UN Compensation Commission, imposing a "technical demarcation of boundaries" between Iraq and Kuwait and drawing up what has been termed a virtual peace treaty in which it imposed sweeping disarmament measures on Iraq. It has ordered states to extradite nationals (the case of Libya). It has established two international criminal tribunals for the prosecution of individuals, one for Yugoslavia and one for Rwanda.

The mandatory measures adopted by the Security Council under Chapter VII which are regulated by Article 25 of the Charter (under which states 'agree to accept and carry out the decisions of the Security Council") have not only resulted in the temporary suspension of the subjective legal rights of the state against which they are applied (though sometimes with irreversible effects), but also, as distinct from those "horizontal" reactions within a bilateral context which injured states are entitled to take, they create a vertical relationship between the Organization and implementing state. The implications for the subjective rights of Member states and, arguably, non-Member states, are therefore also far-reaching.

The web of Security Council sanctions measures, some of which have remained in force over a long period of time (those against Iraq have been in place for over a decade) have also had far-reaching implications for the rights of the civilian population which has been targeted, as well as affecting private rights within implementing states.

The current debate over the legitimacy and long-term effects of economic sanctions on states and their populations makes it imperative to re-evaluate this instrument and the broader peace maintenance function of the Security Council in the light of current community concerns. The Colloquium on "United Nations Sanctions and International Law" sought to address this debate by examining some of the legal issues which arise from the proliferation of Security Council non-military sanctions. The papers which were presented are reproduced in this book which is organised in four parts. Part One addresses the theoretical issues by focussing on: 1) The place of sanctions in the international legal system; 2) the limits to the powers of the Security Council and the question of accountability; and 3) an assessment of the alternatives to collective economic sanctions. Part Two looks at the relationship between sanctions and humanitarian issues, examining the relationship between: 1) Sanctions and human rights law; 2) sanctions, humanitarian issues and mandates; and 3) sanctions and humanitarian law. Part Three focuses on implementation by states of Security Council sanctions resolutions by examining: 1) Sanctions and private rights; and 2) special problems for implementing states. Part Four looks ahead in addressing the future place of sanctions in the international legal system.

The contributions in this book represent a diversity of views and perspectives. Rather than presenting an overview or summary of their contents, I prefer to let them speak for themselves. The following therefore are my introductory remarks at the Colloquium and reflect my personal views on these issues.[1]

Sanctions and the International Legal System

While the role played by the political organs of the UN in the *progressive development* of international law received in the past much attention from scholars, particularly in relation to the contribution of General Assembly declaratory resolutions to the customary law or treaty-making process – one has only to think of the pioneering work of Judge Rosalyn Higgins[2] – what may be perceived as the evolving function of the Security Council within the international legal system in the *enforcement* of international law has been largely discounted until fairly recently. This has been due in large part to the paralysis of the Charter's enforcement mechanisms in a cold war environment,

1 These remarks draw extensively from the following articles in particular: Vera Gowlland-Debbas, "Security Council Enforcement Action and Issues of State Responsibility", (1994) 43 ICLQ 55-98, and id., "The Functions of the United Nations Security Council in the International Legal System", in *The Role of Law in International Politics. Essays in International Relations and International Law*, Michael Byers (ed.) (Oxford, 2000), pp. 276-313.

2 Rosalyn Higgins, *The Development of International Law by the Political Organs of the United Nations* (London, 1963).

as well as to the argument that these constituted political and security arrangements and not concern with international law enforcement.

The title of the Colloquium which has been retained in this book merits therefore some justification. It has already been stated that the term sanctions is not to be found in the Charter although it has been used in the past to designate the measures provided for under Articles 5 and 6 relating to suspension and expulsion of states from the Organization, as well as under Article 19 of the Charter relating to the suspension from voting in the General Assembly as a consequence of arrears in Charter contributions. More recently however the term has begun to be used in conjunction with the enforcement powers of the Council under Chapter VII and has moreover crept into the vocabulary of Council resolutions (e.g. the preamble of res.665 (1990) on Iraq) as well as the practice of Member states.

The title "United Nations Sanctions and International Law" is therefore based on two assumptions: that the term sanctions can be used as a term of art in this context, and that it is possible – at least for purposes of a meaningful analysis – to relocate the enforcement function of the Security Council and the legal consequences it entails within the general international legal order. This means that while Charter legality remains of primordial importance, it is necesary to go beyond the confines of the United Nations Charter to examine the latter's relationship with conventional and general international law.

As international lawyers know, the concept of sanctions lies at the heart of fundamental debates on the nature and function of international law. Sanctions are of course linked to the general problem of compliance inherent in the prescriptive nature of any legal order. But what are sanctions? There are of course some commonly agreed elements to the definition: they constitute legal consequences following on a violation of a legal obligation, they infringe the subjective legal rights of the party against whom they are directed, and they are measures which amount to a dispensation of the sanctioning state from a legal obligation, or in other words, a circumstance excluding wrongfulness. But agreement seems to end here. A survey of the major philosophical and legal approaches to the question – natural law theorists, John Austin, Hans Kelsen, Herbert Hart and beyond – have shown the wide differences of views as regards the concept of sanctions in international law, the form they take, their content, conditions for their application and their purpose.

For example, do sanctions constitute the essence or characteristic of a legal norm without which it would not be law? In other words, can we conclude, in Austinian terms, that law is nothing but the command of the sovereign based on the power to inflict punishment, or with Hans Kelsen that law is "the primary norm, which stipulates the sanction" [3] Or, rather, should one not consider sanctions, in the words of Cavaré, to be only a means provided by the social order the purpose of which is "de faire disparaître, dans toute la mesure possible, le trouble apporté à l'ordre juridique et social par la violation de la règle", while at the same time drawing the separation between Sanction and Law?[4] Again, are sanctions an indispensable component of a legal system and hence of international law or are there different bases of obligation? Are sanctions necessary for ensuring the effectiveness of the law, and what is the role played by legitimacy? Is the purpose of sanctions law-enforcement, or punishment? Moreover, to some commentators true legal sanctions are non-existent in the absence of third party procedures or a centralized system to determine whether reactions to alleged violations of international law are indeed legitimate.

I will go no further since Georges Abi-Saab addresses many of these issues in his Keynote Address. I only wish to say that the traditional concept of sanctions has undergone certain mutations in international law. In his Hague *General Course*, Ian Brownlie warned us that if we "search for a species of butterfly which, it is believed, has certain characteristics, though it has not yet been found", we will bypass and hence ignore all the butterflies we notice during our search "as not corresponding to the model searched for".[5] We should heed his warning and keep an open mind.

The Relationship between Sanctions and International Responsibility

It is true that in a system in which the obligations of one State are opposed to the subjective rights of another, reactions to violations of international law

3 Hans Kelsen, *General Theory of Law and State* (Translated by Anders Wedberg) (Cambridge, Mass., 1945), p.61.

4 Louis Cavaré, "Les sanctions dans le cadre de l'ONU" (1952) 80 *Recueil des Cours* 191 at 195-197.

5 Ian Brownlie, "International Law at the Fiftieth Anniversary of the United Nations. General Course on Public International Law" (1995) 255 *Recueil des Cours* 9 at 23.

have taken decentralised and unpredictable forms. But we can point to certain developments away from this traditional structure.

Sanctions in the framework of the ILC draft articles on state responsibility

The progressive institutionalisation of international society has had an impact not only on the structure and normative content of international law, but also on its enforcement. At the same time, the on-going codification by the International Law Commission of the law of State Responsibility in the form of its Draft Articles, has resulted in a linkage between institutionalized measures and state responsibility: 1) Sanctions are now an integral part of the law of State Responsibility – the latter being defined as *all* the legal consequences of a violation of international law and not just the duty to make reparations (thus compromising between a view focused only on reparations and one focused only on sanctions as that of Hans Kelsen). 2) The term "sanctions", as a term of art, has been reserved (initially by the Special Rapporteur Roberto Ago and subsequently confirmed by Gaetano Arangio-Ruiz) for centralised mechanisms within the aegis of international organizations. In the words of the ILC commentary to Article 30 on countermeasures (which it is important to emphasize was intended to serve as an umbrella concept covering both unilateral countermeasures and sanctions) sanctions are "reactive measures applied by virtue of a decision taken by an international organization following a breach of an international obligation having serious consequences for the international community as a whole, and in particular ... certain measures which the United Nations is empowered to adopt, under the system established by the Charter, with a view to the maintenance of international peace and security".[6] 3) The exercise of unilateral countermeasures has been seriously circumscribed by means of procedural and substantive limitations (Articles 48 to 50 of the Draft Articles). 4) The concept of obligations protecting the fundamental interests of the international community has been reinforced and the notion of injured state broadened through the introduction of the concept of international crimes (Articles 19 and 40 of the Draft Articles).

Artricle 19 is after all only the reflection in the field of state responsibility of an emerging and irreversible trend that juxtaposes alongside the traditional conceptual legal framework based largely on a network of bilateral and contractual relations between atomistic states, one that is based on objective community

6 (1979) *YBILC*, vol.II (Part Two), p.121.

interests. I hasten to add that while the concept of international community in this context may not necessarily correspond to the Weberian conception of a society tending towards a higher degree of integration, with shared values and a feeling of solidarity, it has become a very real legal construct, if not a legal fiction, by which a social grouping is attributed rights and obligations, and one which points to a novel development in the legal system which has already been recognised in the law of treaties (in the form of the concept of *jus* cogens) and the law of claims (obligations *erga omnes*). Interestingly, what has amounted to a hierarchisation, or fragmentation, of the monolithic framework of international law norms once so decried by Prosper Weil, has paradoxically promoted a view based on its unity or universality. In his *Cours général*,[7] Professor Weil has himself written: "Quelle que soit la connotation que l'on entend lui conférer, la réference à la communauté internationale tend à substituer à la société international atomisée et fractionnée ... la vision d'une communauté unie et solidaire ... ..(qui) met l'accent sur ce qui rassemble plutôt que sur ce qui sépare. La référence à la communauté internationale dépasse l'éffet de style et de mode: derrière le glissement sémantique se profile une évolution dans la conception même du système international."

If the international legal system is moving towards the recognition of community interests, the question is whether it is, or should be, moving also towards the creation of international institutional responses to violations of such core norms. While it is clear that the development of centralised responses to violations of norms of concern to the international community as a whole can only lie outside an eventual treaty on State responsibility the relationship between the Draft Articles and Charter mechanisms for international peace and security becomes evident.

The absence of sanctions in the framework of Chapter VII of the Charter
What I would like in particular to highlight here is the way in which extensive and discretionary powers granted to an elitist, political United Nations organ whose primary responsibility is the maintenance of a political conception of international ordering – i.e. the maintenance of international peace and security – may be viewed also as collective responses to violations of fundamental legal norms, with all the legal consequences which ensue for the sanctioned state.

7 Prosper Weil, "Le droit international en quête de son identité. Cours général de droit international public," (1992) 237 *Recueil des Cours* 9 at 309.

The link between Charter mechanisms for peace maintenance and the concept of legal sanction may appear to be tenuous. Unlike the system instituted by the League of Nations under Article 16(1) and 16(2) of the Covenant which had marked a radical departure in international law by sanctioning infringements of the specific obligation of Member states not to have recourse to war except under the conditions specified in the Covenant, Chapter VII measures were not originally intended to be limited in their application to cases of non-compliance with pre-existing obligations. The purpose of enforcement action we have classically been told, "is not: to maintain or restore the law, but to maintain, or restore peace, which is not necessarily identical with the law".[8]

The mandatory decisions of the Security Council under Chapter VII, are the outcome of political considerations, not legal reasoning, nor are its proceedings subject to judicial procedures. That its reactions to events can be neither automatic nor impartial is an intended result of the way its competence and powers are delimited in the Charter.

The Council was deliberately given wide discretionary powers in: 1) its determination of what constitutes a threat to the peace (which is nowhere defined); 2) its choice of responses following a determination under Article 39, for the Charter does not appear to require the Security Council to match the gravity of the situation – threat to the peace, breach of the peace or act of aggression – to a rising scale of severity of the response, since it is not *explicitly* required to adopt the measures provided for under Chapter VII in any order.

As a result of this selective and to a large extent arbitrary process (it may be noted that Article 1(1) of the Charter associates justice with the peaceful settlement of disputes and not with peace maintenance), the Security Council has been as much under fire for going too far – as during the period immediately following the invasion of Kuwait by Iraq – as for being ineffectual – e.g. during the more depressing stages of the Bosnian or Kosovo crisis, or of Israeli occupation of Palestinian territory.

Sanctions and state responsibility in the practice of the Security Council

However, a legal construction can be made of the Council's discretionary determinations under Article 39, and its resulting actions – in other words, of

8 H.Kelsen, *The Law of the United Nations* (London, 1950), p.294.

what are in fact random and discretionary exercises of police powers. This construction serves to illustrate the way in which law operates in the selection and transformation of political decisions into legally significant elements or acts with definitive and far-reaching legal consequences, which escape the ambit of political processes and in turn set new constraints on political action. Although the Council is not *required* to react to violations of international law, its practice – in the form of contingency decisions which are the outcomes of political activity – produces recognisable legal patterns which change the legal positions, not only of states, but also of individuals, engendering legal consequences and making possible new normative expectations.

A number of the Security Council resolutions adopted under Chapter VII contain all the legal elements which are familiar to international lawyers when they deal with the responsibility of states for breaches of international law:

First, the mandatory measures adopted by the Security Council under Article 41 have in numerous cases, been based not only on a finding of fact but also on one of law. Determinations under Article 39 have thus been linked to alleged breaches of international law, the violation becoming therefore a constituent element of the threat to or breach of the peace.[9] These breaches have been imputed to particular legal entities, state but also non-state entities (such as UNITA in Angola or the Bosnian Serbs). Moreover, beginning with the case of Southern Rhodesia in 1966, the Council has singled out breaches of those norms that are now considered to be fundamental. The concept of international peace and security has thus acquired a meaning that extends far beyond that of collective security (envisaged as an all-out collective response to armed attack), to one in which ethnic cleansing, genocide and other gross violations

9 For some examples, see on Iraq: SC res.661, 664, 667 and 670(1990)) (invasion and occupation of Kuwait, but also violations of the law on diplomatic and consular relations, treatment of third State nationals, human rights and humanitarian law); on Libya: Res.748 (1992) (inter alia for failure to renounce on terrorism); on Yugoslavia: SC Res. 713, 752, 757,770, 787(1992), 819, 820 (1993), 836(1993), 1160 and 1199 (1998) (territorial gains or changes brought about through the use of force, massive and systematic violations of human rights and fundamental freedoms – including those of ethnic minorities and the practice of "ethnic cleansing" – grave breaches of international humanitarian law, including deliberate impeding of delivery of food and medical supplies to the civilian population); on Somalia: 794 (1992) and 837 (1992); on Rwanda: 935 (1994) (violations of international humanitarian law and in the case of the latter, genocide).

of human rights, including the right to self-determination, as well as grave breaches of humanitarian law, including those encompassed within a state's own borders, are considered component parts of the security fabric.

Moreover, the measures which follow this qualification of state and non-state acts have the effects of legal sanctions, in the sense that they deny all legal effects to the illegal acts of the entity against which they are applied, and also result in the forcible temporary suspension of its subjective legal rights.

Thus the Council has qualified the acts of states and non-state entities as illegal and invalid (including even private transactions, such as property transactions in Bosnia). This is an operation of law based on legal determinations which have what the Court has called, in its *Namibia* Opinion "operational design" in the sense of entailing definitive and far-reaching legal effects.[10] The Council has called for collective non-recognition, for refusal of municipal law benefits such as domestic application of the laws or acts of the sanctioned entity in domestic courts, or the grant of immunity. The right to conduct diplomatic relations with other states has been suspended. It has also called for exclusion from participation in international organizations, cultural relations and sports.[11]

The sanctioned state's trading relations have been severed – with the imposition of arms or petroleum embargoes, and other selective or comprehensive economic, financial and diplomatic measures. Its means of communication – by air, sea or land – has been interrupted. The Council has authorized the seizure of its modes of transportation. States have also been called on to freeze funds and other financial resources of the targeted states and to prohibit financial and other services[12] The Council has also as has been stated, authorised the use of military force for limited, as well as wide-ranging purposes.

---

10 *Legal Consequences for States of the Continued Presence of South Africa in Namibia (South-West Africa) Notwithstanding Security Council Resolution 276 (Advisory Opinion)*, ICJ Reports, 1971, p.50.

11 See, for Southern Rhodesia : SC Res.216, 217 (1965), 277 (1970) and 423 (1978); Iraq: SC Res. 662, 670 (1990), 706 and 712 (1991); former Yugoslavia: SC Res.777 (1992), 820 and 821 (1993).

12 For select sanctions resolutions, see for Iraq: SC res. 661, 670 (1990) and 1137 (1997); Yugoslavia: SC res.713 (1991), 757, 787 (1992),820,942 (1993), 1160 (1998); Somalia: SC res.733 (1992); Libya: SC res.748 (1992) and 883 (1993); Liberia: SC res.788 (1992), Haiti: SC res.841 (1993); Rwanda: SC Res. 918 (1994); Sudan: SC Res.1054 (1996); Sierra Leone: SC Res.1132 (1997) (the list is not exhaustive).

Since findings of illegality have formed in practice a constituent part of Council determinations, it is evident that peace could not be restored without putting an end to the violation. Council resolutions have therefore included calls for the cessation of the acts in question, such as withdrawal from occupied territory, an end to violations of human rights or humanitarian law, or the renunciation of terrorism. The Council has determined responsibility and imposed reparations (in the context of State responsibility, the establishment of the Compensation Commission on Iraq points to a number of interesting developments),[13] which effectively amount to the sequestration of the natural resources of a country.[14] It has called for guarantees of non-repetition going in certain cases beyond pre-existing legal obligations, such as the submission of Iraq, under Resolution 687, to the destruction, removal or rendering harmless of its nuclear, chemical and biological weapons, the 'technical' demarcation of its boundary with Kuwait and the establishment of a demilitarised zone.

However, the question of the purpose or object of sanctions measures is closely linked to the problem of when and how sanctions are to be lifted and who is competent to pronounce on the achievement of the objectives. In practice, the definition of a return to legality and hence the conditions for restoration of international peace have proved to be elastic, particularly in the case of Iraq in which to the initial objectives defined in SC Res.660 (1990) of unconditional withdrawal of Iraqi forces from Kuwait were grafted a second set of objectives requiring Iraq to comply with all resolutions of the Council, in particular SC Res.687 (1991). This raises the serious problem of termination of sanctions

13 Following a determination of Iraqi liability "for any direct loss, damage, including environmental damage and the depletion of any natural resources, or injury to foreign Governments, nationals and corporations as a result of Iraq's unlawful invasion and occupation of Kuwait" (SC Res. 687 of 1991), the Council for the first time established a compensation mechanism to serve as a comprehensive framework for dealing with Iraqi liability. This has included the creation of a fund to be financed out of a determined percentage of Iraqi oil export revenues (SC Res. 705 and 706 (1991)) and the establishment of a Compensation Commission to administer this fund. However, unlike other claims tribunals, in which responsibility has first to be determined, the issues here are only the damage suffered by the claimant and the causal connection between this damage and the invasion and occupation of Kuwait. SC Res. 986 (1995), 1111 and 1129 (1997) authorised states to permit the import of specified amounts of Iraqi petroleum and petroleum products; by Resolution 1284 (1999) the Council lifted the ceiling on revenues earned by oil exports.

14 Michael Reisman, "The Constitutional Crisis in the United Nations," (1993) 87 *AJIL* 83 at 88-9.

of which the case of Iraq, which has been subjected to sanctions for the last decade, is again the most poignant illustration. The Security Council has thus opened itself out to accusations of using sanctions for the infliction of punishment, in the sense of the creation of irreversible damage to the target state concerned. To terminate sanctions, however, means that the same consensus has to prevail within the Council on termination as did on adoption which means that even one or two permanent members of the Security Council can prevent this from happening.

Security Council action under Chapter VII has also contributed to the process of institutionalising individual criminal responsibility. This was first touched on in the cases of Southern Rhodesia, Iraq and Somalia, but put into effect by the creation of the International Criminal Tribunals on Yugoslavia and Rwanda.[15] A link has thus been established between threats to international peace and security and the core crimes giving rise to individual criminal responsibility under international law. Indeed in countering the argument that the Security Council could not create criminal liability or prosecute physical persons, the Appeals Chamber of the Yugoslavia Tribunal, in the *Tadic Case*,[16] upheld the view that the legality of its creation rested on Article 41 of the UN Charter – its establishment thus constituting one measure the Security Council could itself impose under Chapter VII (as opposed to those measures it called on Member states to carry out). The Rome Statute for the establishment of an International Criminal Court further engages the Security Council in this process, for though it will have its own treaty basis it embeds the Council's discretionary determinations under Article 39 within the Court's procedures, with potentially important implications for the legal position of individuals, for under the Rome Statute, the Council has been given powers of referral and deferral of the Court's jurisdiction, as well as a potential role in the determination of the crime of aggression.

15 For Yugoslavia: SC Res.808(1993) and 827 (1993); for Rwanda: SC Res.955(1994).

16 International Tribunal for the Prosecution of Persons Responsible for Serious Violations of International Humanitarian Law Committed in the Territory of Former Yugoslavia since 1991, *The Prosecutor v. Dusko Tadic a/k/a/ "Dule"*, Decision on the Defence Motion for Interlocutory Appeal on Jurisdiction, 2 October 1995.

THE ACCOUNTABILITY OF THE SECURITY COUNCIL

This exercise of the powers conferred upon the Council under Chapter VII raises a very serious problem of accountability of the activities of a political organ of the United Nations which is currently being debated at length. In this context, two major issues will be debated: the first relates to the existence of legal constraints on Security Council action; the second, a separate issue, that of third party scrutiny of the Council's activities.

The legal constraints on Security Council action

Seen from the perspective of the legal system, the Security Council's authority emanates from the Charter and legal obligations suppose legal accountability. It is by virtue of an operation of law, not of fact, that the Member states agree to carry out the Council's decisions and to subject their international agreements to the overriding effects of the Charter. In the words of the ICJ, the "political character of an organ cannot release it from the observance of the treaty provisions established by the Charter when they constitute limitations on its powers or criteria for its judgment".[17] In the *Lockerbie Case (Preliminary Objections),*[18] *Judge ad hoc* Sir Robert Jennings, who dissented strongly from the rest of the Court's conclusions concerning jurisdiction and admissibility, nevertheless stated in connection with the Security Council:

> "The first principle of the applicable law is this: that all discretionary powers of lawful decision-making are necessarily derived from the law, and are therefore governed and qualified by the law. This must be so if only because the sole authority of such decisions flows itself from the law. It is not logically possible to claim to represent the power and authority of the law, and at the same time, claim to be above the law.
>
> ...
>
> I therefore wholly agree with the Libyan argument that the Security Council decisions and actions should in no wise be regarded as enjoying some sort of "immunity" from the jurisdiction of the principal judicial organ of the United Nations; though I ought perhaps to add that the United Kingdom argument made no such claim."

17 *Admission of a State to the United Nations,* ICJ Reports, 1948, p. 65.

18 *Case Concerning Questions of Interpretation and Application of the 1971 Montreal Convention Arising from the Aerial Incident at Lockerbie (Libyan Arab Jamahiriya* vs. *United Kingdom) (Libyan Arab Jamahiriya vs. United States of America) (Preliminary Objections),* Decision of 27 February 1998, Dissenting Opinion of Judge Jennings.

While it is the Charter that sets both procedural and substantive limits, the latter in the form of the purposes and principles of the United Nations, limits are also set by the international legal system as a whole. The rules governing treaty law also govern the Charter's relationship with rules of customary international law, including peremptory norms from which treaties may not derogate, as well as its relationship with general principles of law such as the doctrine of abuse of rights arising from failure by states to exercise (discretionary) rights in good faith and with due regard to the consequences of such exercise.

The question of judicial review

It remains the case that the existence of legal constraints on the activities of political organs is independent of the question as to whether there is third-party review of such activities. The search for applicable constitutional and legal restraints on the Security Council also involves, therefore, an examination of the relationship between the Security Council and the International Court of Justice. In this context, it is usual to discuss their relationship in terms of the relationship between judicial and political bodies. This is however insufficient for analysis in the context of judicial review, for their relationship here should be viewed as one between two distinct instrumental processes available to states within the *legal* system for attaining much the same ends, i.e. a return to a situation of legality through judicial settlement procedures on the one hand, and institutionalised sanctions on the other.

The question of judicial review of the legality of Council resolutions is at issue in the *Lockerbie* case. If by this term is meant a constitutional process of judicial review, with compulsory effect, it is clear that no analogous procedure is to be found in the structure of the United Nations. Few would dispute however the fact that the Court can exercise some form of judicial control indirectly when the question is posed incidentally before it and in its past jurisprudence, the Court has asserted its competence both to interpret United Nations resolutions in the light of the Charter and to make judicial pronouncements concerning the legality and validity of United Nations resolutions with respect to their conformity with the constituent instrument. While it may be true that the qualification of the Security Council of a situation under Article 39 of the Charter in itself cannot be questioned *as a basis for the Council's actions under Chapter VII in the fulfilment of its own functions,* there is no reason to suppose that the ICJ could not exercise its right to protect the law of the Charter should the finding itself or the choice of measures be patently contrary to the procedural or substantive requirements of the Charter, to the principle of good faith, or to peremptory norms. Moreover, to the extent that such qualifications have been linked to findings of breaches of fundamental norms, then these secondary findings can only be declaratory and not constitutive of the legal situation. Finally, a determination of an act of aggression is clearly a matter of international law and the ICJ has not considered itself in the past debarred from such finding.

The political limits and the question of alternatives

Some mention must also be made here of the political limits, including the recent efforts within the General Assembly and its subsidiary bodies – Sixth Committee and Special Committee on Charter reform – to provide guidelines for the adoption and implementation of Council sanctions, as well as to call for Council transparency.[19]

The alternatives to collective sanctions in the form of unilateral and regional responses to the enforcement of Community objectives also have to be seriously assessed, particularly in the light of the recent NATO-Kosovo action.

THE LIMITS SET BY HUMAN RIGHTS AND HUMANITARIAN LAW

It is in particular the limits set by human rights and humanitarian law that is examined here. It must not be forgotten that the purposes and principles of the United Nations which bind the Security Council underline not only the primary goal of peace maintenance, but also reflect the human rights, humanitarian, economic and social concerns of the United Nations. It is also important to remember that these purposes and principles are dynamic and must be interpreted not as they stood in 1945, but as they exist today. The human rights component, for example, includes recently emphasized economic, social and cultural rights, such as the right to food, to health, and to a decent standard of living.

19 See, e.g, GA Res. 51/193 in which it "[e]ncourages the Security Council to provide special reports in accordance with Articles 15 and 24 of the Charter", and GA Res. 49/58, 50/51, 50/58E and 51/208, inviting an examination of the special economic problems confronting States in carrying out sanctions, under Article 50 of the Charter. This has led to a series of reports, such as from the Secretary-General and the Special Committee on the Charter of the United Nations and on the Strengthening of the Role of the Organization, on means of improving the mechanisms and criteria concerning the implementation and lifting of sanctions (see e.g. A/50/361, A/50/423 and A/51/356).

It is in this sense that General Comment No. 8, adopted by the Committee on Economic, Social and Cultural Rights in 1997, reminds the permanent members of the Security Council of their joint and several responsibilities under the Covenant. While Article 103 of the Charter could be said to override the provisions of any international agreement, including human rights treaties, with the exception of those rights that have attained the status of *jus cogens*, as well as to exonerate implementing states from responsibility for treaty breaches, such human rights treaties may be said to give effect to the broad purposes of the United Nations and hence to bind the UN organs as such.

It should be pointed out that concern has been expressed by subsidiary organs, such as UNICEF, specialised agencies such as WHO and FAO, or non-governmental organizations such as the International Committee of the Red Cross, over the compatibility of sanctions with peacetime human rights as well as the humanitarian law of armed conflict, and with respect to the suffering of the civilian population, in particular vulnerable groups such as women, children the disabled and the elderly who are often the primary victims of sanctions application.[20]

---

20 See e.g. United Nations Department on Humanitarian Affairs: Report by Claudia von Braunmühl and Manfred Kulessa, *The Impact of UN Sanctions on Humanitarian Assistance Activities* (Berlin, December 1995); World Health Organization: *The Health Conditions of the Population in Iraq Since the Gulf Crisis* (WHO/EHA/96.1, March 1996), and, the work of the Inter-Agency Standing Committee on the Humanitarian Impact of Sanctions established pursuant to General Assembly resolution 46/182 (e.g. its Statement to the Security Council (S/1998/147, 23 February 1998)). Since the Colloquium was held, UNICEF published in August 1999 its first surveys since 1991 of child and maternal mortality in Iraq (UNICEF, *The Iraq Child and Maternal Mortality Survey Report 1999* (CF/DOC/PR/1999/29)). Because of the conditions in Iraq and the inadequacy of the oil for food programme, Hans von Sponek resigned as co-ordinator of humanitarian relief to Iraq in 2000, as did his predecessor Denis Halliday in 1998. See also the Security Council's 4120th meeting of 24 March 2000 focussing on the humanitarian situation in Iraq (Press Release SC/6833), the Report of the Secretary-General submitted pursuant to Council requests in resolutions 1284 (1999) and 1281 (1999) on the humanitarian needs in Iraq (Doc.S/2000/208),and text of Secretary-General Kofi Annan's statement to the Council (Press release SG/SM/7338, SC/6834): "Let me conclude by saying that the humanitarian situation in Iraq poses a serious moral dilemma for this Organization. The United Nations has always been on the side of the vulnerable and the weak, and has always sought to relieve suffering, yet here we are accused of causing suffering to an entire population. We are in danger of losing the argument, or the propaganda war – if we haven't already lost it – about who is responsible for this situation in Iraq – President Saddam Hussein or the United Nations".

The importance of respect for fundamental humanitarian principles had been stressed as early as the League of Nations, as evidenced in the League Assembly's debates on the implementation and amendment of Article 16 of the Covenant relating to economic sanctions.[21] Such concern, therefore, has a long history – and numerous debates over this issue had been waged at the time of the sanctions against Southern Rhodesia. That there is awareness in the Security Council of the limits placed by humanitarian law is illustrated by SC Res. 666 on Iraq, which in singling out the need to pay particular attention to the more vulnerable categories of civilians, i.e. children under 15 years of age, expectant mothers, maternity cases, the sick and the elderly, brought it more in conformity with the 1949 Fourth Geneva Convention relating to the rules on the provision of humanitarian relief and to different categories of protected persons.

The humanitarian exceptions which are included in sanctions resolutions (in particular foodstuffs "in humanitarian circumstances" and medical supplies) are also meant to address this question, but one of the problems lies with their scope. Their inconsistency is highlighted by the fact that the Iraqi sanctions for example did not include humanitarian exceptions extending to educational equipment, publications and news materials which figured in the Rhodesian sanctions. One can easily gauge the serious effects on a country's infrastructure and its future generations of an embargo on educational materials lasting for over a decade. Another problem lies in the inconsistency and lack of transparency of interpretation of such exceptions in the Sanctions Committees. But there is also the question of the difficulties of processing thousands of applications through the Sanctions Committees.

Such difficulties have been underlined by the "oil for food" programme established by the Council in 1995 as a temporary measure to provide for the humanitarian needs of the Iraqi people, in the context of the sanctions regime, which allows Iraq to use part of the proceeds of its oil sales[22] for humanitarian goods for the Iraqi people. Its inadequacy has been underlined by the Secretary-General who has expressed his concern with many of the "holds" on contract applications imposed by members of the Sanctions Committee on Iraq which, he stated, have a direct negative impact on the humanitarian programme and

21 League of Nations, Reports and Resolutions on the Subject of Article 16 of the Covenant, 13 June 1927, pp.11 ff.

22 See *supra,* n.13.

on the rehabilitation of Iraq's infrasctructure most of which he said was in "appalling disrepair".[23]

Issues have also arisen in respect of the compatibility of sanctions implementation with the mandates of international bodies. The Specialized Agencies whose relationship with the UN is based on coordination and cooperation, as well as on their respective relationship agreements, have been faced with the problem of integrating UN sanctions decisions into their own constituent framework. Subsidiary organs of the UN, such as UNICEF and UNHCR, have had to reconcile, on the one hand, the undoubted obligation to respect the mandatory decisions of the Security Council, and on the other their duty to uphold the humanitarian and apolitical nature of their mandates. The hybrid status of the ICRC as a neutral and impartial humanitarian organization has also raised issues in respect of its relationship to UN Security Council decisions and more particularly, to the need to process requests for humanitarian assistance through the Sanctions Committees.

Implementation of Sanctions by States

The effects of Security Council decisions on international obligations

Sanctions resolutions affect the relationship between Charter law and other rules of international law, for implementing economic sanctions may require the suspension of existing international treaties – such as trade treaties or civil aviation agreements – on the basis of Article 103 of the Charter which upholds Charter obligations over other international agreements. Article 103 may be seen thus as amounting to a dispensation for implementing states from the performance of their conventional obligations under international law.

Security Council measures have also, on the basis of authorizations to states, resulted in the temporary suspension of (non-imperative) rules of customary international law. Such measures as interception, forcible search and even arrest of third-party ships on the high seas were once characterised by Arthur Goldberg, the US representative to the Security Council, as "one of the gravest and most far-reaching proposals that has been made to this Council ... we are asked ... to put our sanction upon what will be a rule of international law –

23 Secretary-General Kofi Annan's statement to the Council (Press release SG/SM/7338, SC/6834).

that when this Council acts vessels on the high seas can be arrested and detained in the interest of the international law which we will be making here today ..." While Lord Caradon stated: "Without the authority of the Security Council ... our government has to face defiance of the United Nations with its hands tied". They were both speaking in April 1966 during the debate preceding the adoption of the so-called Beira resolution (SC Res. 221 (1966)).[24] Moreover, such enforcement has involved, in the case of sanctions against Yugoslavia a variety of organizations such as the EU, NATO, OSCE, and WEU.

Domestic Implementation of Sanctions

As has been said, Security Council decisions are mandatory on all Member states under Article 25 of the Charter. Since it is important to ensure that there are no cracks in the universal implementation of sanctions, no state has yet been dispensed by the Security Council from this implementation even though the Council has that discretion under Article 48 (1).

The effectiveness of Security Council decisions on sanctions depends of course on the effects of sanctions on the sanctioned entity, but it also is dependent on effective compliance by those who are called on to implement the measures. The latter requires making these resolutions operative against individuals, which in turn is dependent on the effective implementation, application and enforcement of the decisions of the Security Council within the domestic order by national legislative, executive, administrative and judicial bodies in accordance with each state's constitutional and legal requirements. This raises the problem of collaboration between two autonomous legal orders and underlines the importance of a comparative study of national practice from an international law perspective.

As opposed to the obligation to fulfil in good faith obligations flowing from treaties and the consequent incurring of State responsibility for failure to do so, which is clearly a matter for international law, the mechanisms by which states incorporate international law into their domestic system is largely left by international law to be regulated by municipal law. While some measures required by the Security Council are measures which can be taken at the official level, such as the severance of diplomatic relations, and in theory do not pose problems, the majority require domestic implementation. Moreover, Security

24 SCOR, 21st yr., 1276th mtg., para.21; 68 and 69, respectively.

Council sanctions decisions have generally been regarded as non-self-executing treaty obligations, hence not directly applicable to individuals. These decisions therefore impact heavily on domestic law, entailing complex problems of implementation and introducing a new conundrum into the traditional relationship between international and domestic law.

I want to touch on only some of the salient issues here.

Enabling legislation

At the time the Charter was signed, only a handful of states adopted permanent enabling legislation to provide for automatic compliance with UN Security Council decisions. This constituted little improvement on the situation existing at the time of the Abyssinian crisis of 1935; the Committee set up by the League to coordinate sanctions against Italy, while recognizing that this was a matter falling within the exclusive competence of each state, had then reminded Members of their duty to adopt the necessary measures in order to ensure respect for their international obligations. The situation improved only slightly after the adoption of sanctions against Southern Rhodesia.

States therefore have continued to resort to all kinds of *ad hoc* bases for such measures ranging from governmental decrees to various trade and emergency laws. For some states, the issue has been made more complex by the interposition of the European Community, for EC regulations have implemented UN sanctions in respect, for example, of Iraq, Libya, Federal Republic of Yugoslavia and Haiti. This in turn has raised issues such as that of the legal basis for exercise of EU competence, the interplay between European Community and domestic legislation in sanctions implementation and the way in which the interposition of the Community has impacted on such implementation.

The effects on private rights and extraterritorial application

The decisions of the Security Council relating to sanctions have extensive effects on private contractual rights and require control of the activities of private parties, even extraterritorially, which may be at variance with the constitutional or general legal order of the Member state concerned.

In the first place, they are to apply "notwithstanding any contract entered into or any licence granted before the date of the resolution". This raises a number of issues in relation to the scope of such provisions (for they cover diverse commercial transactions), the problem of non-retroactivity, the legal effects of such provisions – nullity or temporary suspension of the execution of the contracts? – and the question of compensation for unfulfilled contracts, for at the international level, this may not be claimed as the Decision of 6 March 1992 taken by the Governing Council of the United Nations Compensation Commission makes clear (at least for purposes of the Iraqi situation).

In the second place, in seeking to enforce sanctions against evasions by multinationals operating world wide, Security Council resolutions clearly require states to adopt legislation with extraterritorial reach. States are to prohibit, *inter alia*, any activities that promote or are calculated to promote the sale or supply of prohibited items "by their nationals or from their territories"; and the "shipment in vessels or aircraft of their registration or under charter to their nationals". This entails what is a novel element in international law discernible in some recent treaties: the introduction of a duty – and not only, as traditionally was the case, a right – to exercise state control over private activities both at home and abroad. Now in the past, not only has extraterritorial application of laws not been considered a duty on states, but extensive extraterritorial claims by states in application of unilateral economic policies were met by accusations of intervention in domestic jurisdiction. The exercise of extraterritorial jurisdiction to give effect to multilateral treaty obligations in theory therefore poses a different set of problems.

An interesting claim to enforce Security Council resolutions unilaterally (i.e. without specific authorisation from the Security Council) and extraterritorially against private third parties is to be found in the United States Kennedy-d'Amato Act of 1996 imposing economic sanctions on foreign persons engaging in specified transactions with Iran and Libya, one of the purposes of which is expressly stated to be, *inter alia*, that of seeking compliance by Libya with its obligations under Security Council resolutions 731, 748 and 883.[25]

Difficult problems arise also today from the non-territorial nature of financial and banking transactions.

---

25 United States: Iran and Libya Sanctions Act of 1996, (1996) 35 *ILM* 1273 at Sec.3.

Application by domestic courts: interpreting and solving conflicts between Security Council decisions and domestic legislation.
A number of issues have arisen before domestic courts relating to sanctions implementation.

The first is the problem of conflicts between international law and domestic law. Unlike the situation under Article 103, which upholds the primacy of Charter obligations over international agreements, the Charter is silent with respect to the internal law of Member states. The fear that states would plead provisions of their domestic legislation in order to escape their obligations under the Charter had in fact been expressed at the San Francisco Conference, and Belgium had proposed, though unsuccessfully, an amendment to prevent such claims being made.[26]

It is clear however that where conflicts between municipal law and international law have been dealt with on the *international* plane, such conflicts have been resolved both in state practice and by international tribunals on the basis of the primacy of international law, which naturally includes Charter law. This is consecrated by a number of judicial and arbitral decisions, from the 1872 *Alabama Claims* Arbitration to the 1988 *PLO Missions Case*,[27] as well as by conventional international law (see art.27 of the 1969 Vienna Convention on the Law of Treaties).

The situation under domestic law depends of course on the law of the forum. Domestic courts bound by their own rules may not always uphold the primacy of international law in cases of conflict for the consequences will depend on the place attributed to international law in the national system. I will illustrate this with examples from the case of Southern Rhodesia.

One problem that arises is that of conflict between Security Council decisions and constitutional provisions of implementing states. In the Southern Rhodesian crisis certain proposals, namely severance of postal, telegraphic, radio and other means of communication, the barring of nationals from entry onto their territory, or the prohibition of insurance on the lives of passengers, were stated by certain

---

26 3 UNCIO Docs., pp.342-343.

27 See respectively, Moore, 1 International Arbitrations, p.656; Applicability of the Obligation to Arbitrate under Section 21 of the United Nations Headquarters Agreement of 26 June 1947, ICJ Reports, 1988, pp.34-35.

states to be impossible to implement on the basis that these would be barred by constitutional provisions relating to fundamental freedoms, including freedom of information and freedom of movement. I should add that in recent years, it is surrender of persons to the International Criminal Tribunals which has resulted in conflicts with constitutional provisions.

In the decision *United States v. Steinberg* concerning a potential conflict between SC Res.277 relating to non-recognition and the Constitution of the United States, the US court had stated: "This country has a continuing obligation to observe with entire good faith and scrupulous care all of its undertakings under (the United Nations Charter), including support of the resolutions adopted by the Security Council. Of course, a treaty ... .cannot run counter to the provisions of the Constitution of this country. Therefore, the government ... could not choose between respecting the constitutional rights of a citizen and adhering to the provisions of a treaty".[28]

But even where treaties are "the law of the land", the application of the rules of precedence may equally give rise to problems. Such problems arising from resolution of conflicts between Security Council decisions and ordinary legislation is well illustrated by the case of *Diggs v. Shultz* resulting from the initiation of legal action in 1972 to halt the resumption by the United States of importation of chrome from Rhodesia under the umbrella of the Byrd amendment despite the existence of a prohibition under a Security Council resolution. The United States Court of Appeals, although finding that the law authorizing such imports showed "blatant disregard, of our treaty undertakings", nevertheless referred to the "constitutional power of Congress to set treaty obligations at naught' and concluded that "under our constitutional scheme, Congress can denounce treaties if it sees fit to do so, and there is nothing the other branches of government can do about it"[29] The Court also rejected the contentions of the appellants that commitments to the United Nations have more force than an ordinary treaty.

Sanctions implementation has also raised the question of the extent to which domestic courts can interpret and eventually control the legality of Security

28 *United States v. Steinberg* (478 F. Supp.29). See Whiteman, *Digest of US Practice*, pp. 436-437.

29 United States. Decision of the Court of Appeals for the District of Columbia, *Diggs v. Shultz,* October 31, 1972 ((1972) 11 *ILM* 1252).

Council decisions (though naturally for domestic application purposes only). As sanctions implementation becomes increasingly more complex, so will multiplication of domestic court decisions and a widening of the possibility of divergent interpretations. An interesting illustration of the problem of interpretation in domestic courts is the decision of the Irish High Court in the case of *Bosphorus Hava v. Minister for Transport,*[30] relating to the impounding by the Irish authorities of an aircraft registered in Turkey and leased by a wholly-owned Turkish company from Yugoslav Airlines. The Court, in reaching the conclusion that the Irish authorities were not empowered to impound the aircraft in the circumstances, held that while United Nations resolutions did not form part of Irish domestic law, SC Res.820 had provided the genesis for the relevant provisions of the EEC Council regulation. Nevertheless, it summarily dismissed the Sanctions Committee decision that the aircraft fell within the terms of Resolution 820, since the latter's unexplained conclusion could be of no value to the Court. In its interpretation, the Irish Court also balanced private and public interest, stating that: "it is clear that the regulations are not intended to punish or penalise peoples or countries who have not in any way caused or contributed to these tragic events". On the contrary, the Court of Justice of the European Communities based itself on a different teleology. It considered that implementation by the EC of Security Council sanctions was in the pursuit of a particularly fundamental general interest of the international community, namely the ending of a state of war and of the massive violations of human rights and humanitarian law in Bosnia-Herzegovina and that this should be taken into account by national courts.[31]

Another problem arising before domestic courts relates to matters of cognisance. The Security Council's call on states not to grant certain municipal law benefits which are normally regulated by the municipal law of states and not by international law, such as non-cognizance of acts in domestic courts (SC Res.277) or denial of rights inherent in government status, i.e. right to sue or to sovereign immunity (see SC Res. 712 in connection with petroleum and petroleum products

30 *Bosphorus Hava Yollari Turizm Ve Ticaret Anonim Sirketi v. Minister for Transport, Energy and Communications,* Ireland and the Attorney General and TEAM Aer Lingus Ltd, Irish High Court 1993, No.352JR of 21 June 1994 ((1994) 2 *ILRM* 551).

31 See Opinion of Advocate General F.V. Jacobs, delivered on 30 April 1996 and Judgment of 30 July 1996, Court of Justice of the European Communities, Case C-84/95: *Bosphorus,* Reports of Cases before the Court of Justice and the Court of First Instance, Part I, Court of Justice, 1996-7, paras.2 and 64-69. See also Judgment of 27 February 1997, Case C-177/95: *Ebony Maritime.*

under Iraqi title subject to SC Res.706), raises the problem of the separation of powers between executive and judicial bodies. While in some systems the opinion of the government in matters of cognisance and interpretation is binding, which makes application of such provisions possible, where there is such separation, courts in applying international law have usually acted in complete independence from the executive branch of the government.

Economic and Financial Difficulties Arising from Sanctions Implementation
Council decisions override pleas of force majeure or necessity from states – neighbouring states or significant trading partners of the target state – which may suffer major disruptions to trading patterns as a result of sanctions implementation. This may in some cases entail economic and financial losses far greater than those faced by the targeted state itself, yet the only recourse of such states is a right to consult the Council under Article 50 of the Charter. This problem was first raised during the Rhodesian crisis in the case of neighbouring African states or enclaves of South Africa, but the examples since have been numerous – including that of Jordan, and of those states in Eastern Europe which have suffered losses from the disruption of freedom of navigation on the Danube. Article 50 is in fact not a remedy since it merely provides for a right to consult the Security Council for any state confronted with special economic problems as a result of measures decided on by the Council and does not include compensation. The large number of countries which subsequently invoked Article 50 led to a series of recommendations by the Sanctions Committees, the highlighting of the problem by the Secretary-General in his *Agenda for Peace*[32] and efforts made by the General Assembly to address the problem. In practice the Security Council has acknowledged the requests of affected states and called upon other Member states and relevant international institutions to review their programmes of technical and financial assistance, and some assistance has been meted out to selected states. But a set of measures involving the UN system and institutionalized relief or compensation mechanisms has yet to be devised.

32 See S/21786, S/22021 and Add.1 and 2, and B. Boutros-Ghali, An Agenda for Peace, 1992. SC Res.748(1992) on Libya and SC Res.757(1992) on Yugoslavia make explicit reference to Article 50.

It should be said that if a state does not respect the sanctions measures, the consequences of such responsibility may well be determined by the Security Council.[33]

The problem of Switzerland as a non-Member state with a status of permanent neutrality

The Council had not hesitated in the past to call on non-Member states (relying on Article 2(6)of the Charter) even though these have no obligations as third parties. The problem of third parties to the Charter is of course by now moot were it not for the position of Switzerland. In the case of Southern Rhodesia, although Switzerland would have been on firm ground in basing its position solely on its status as a non Member, the official Swiss statement chose to stress the position of Switzerland as a permanently neutral state in deciding that Swiss-Rhodesian trade would remain at the level of the *courant normal*. The case of Switzerland therefore addresses important issues that had originated as far back as the League of Nations concerning the compatibility between a status of permanent neutrality and membership in such universal organizations, particularly in situations in which non-military sanctions are nevertheless applied against the background of an armed conflict (it will be noted that Austria, as a UN member and permanently neutral state, had, while reserving its position of principle, agreed to implement Security Council resolutions on Southern Rhodesia). The position of Switzerland has been substantially modified since and it has adopted sanctions in recent cases, including against Iraq, Yugoslavia and Haiti, which have proved to be very similar to those requested by the Council. It has also had to enact special federal legislation to provide for Switzerland's cooperation with the international tribunals on Yugoslavia and Rwanda. This has increasingly confirmed the view that while the United Nations cannot purport to bind non-Member states, these for political reasons and reasons of public policy cannot ignore or act counter to such decisions. The views expressed by the Swiss Federal authorities have clearly reflected the attitude that a permanent neutral non-Member state can no longer adopt a position of absolute impartiality by ignoring *authorised* collective action (see recent Swiss attitude *vis-a-vis* NATO action in Kosovo) when taken in the interests of international peace and security or the enforcement of universal human rights.

33 See SC Res.670(1992), para.12, on Iraq.

Sanctions implementation therefore leads to some interesting theoretical conclusions on the extent of the growing permeability between two legal orders, not only in terms of substance or normative content, but also, in view of their considerable impact on private and individual rights, of legal subjects. This raises the extent to which traditional solutions to the way in which international law and domestic law interrelate, including those proffered by monist or dualist theories, adequately address the emerging framework of an international legal order that juxtaposes an objective international law based on Community interests alongside subjective and bilateral relations between states.

CONCLUSION

I would personally like to state the following. On the one hand, the development of the concept of fundamental community norms logically calls for centralised and institutionalised mechanisms to ensure their respect and enforcement. This logic comes, not from the application of domestic analogies, but from the need, in a heterogeneous world, to avoid unilateral or even regional decisions which affect the interests of the international community as a whole.

On the other hand, in view of the trend in international law to constrain unilateral responses, one must define the outer boundaries of collective responses, so as to avoid giving the possibility to states of escaping the limits imposed by international law by hiding behind the corporate veil. Moreover, in the words of the French representative to the Security Council, the effects of the current application of comprehensive and long-standing sanctions "should lead the Council to question, in the future, the effectiveness and consequences of broad, indiscriminate sanctions that hurt civilian populations exclusively and whose human cost clearly exceeded the political benefits that the Council could expect".[34]

But it is also important to reassess the place and ethics of sanctions in an international legal system which is giving increased importance to the individual. For developments in international law enforcement have also taken off in another direction, in moving towards the institutionalisation of individual criminal responsibility. This pierces another corporate veil: the fiction of the

34 See the Security Council's 4120th meeting of 24 March 2000 focussing on the humanitarian situation in Iraq (Press Release SC/6833).

monolithic state and the traditional position that it is responsible for all acts imputable to it which are committed within its territory. This is a development that, in certain cases, may well be preferable to holding entire populations accountable for the acts of their leaders, as the International Military Tribunal at Nuremberg recognised some time ago.

But in the final analysis, no legal system can depend on coercion alone, as the concluding panel which examines the future of sanctions and its alternatives underlines. Sanctions, therefore, have to be seen within the context of the international legal system as a whole as well as in the context of the evolution of international society and the functions that we as a result would like international law to perform.

Although references to justice in the Charter were kept separate from the peace maintenance function, the Council's efforts at enforcement by means of sanctions adopted under Chapter VII of a category of norms which can be termed humanitarian (in the broad sense), as well as ethical, have resulted, in the longer term, not only in modifications of the legal position of states, but also in changed legal expectations. As a result, the Council's actions cannot, without falling into contradictions, continue to be based on the premise that security concerns must prevail over longer-term considerations of justice, or encroach on the very values that its practice has served to promote. Moreover, legitimacy is a means of ensuring effectiveness in the longer-term.

The shift we have been witnessing in recent years from longer-term so-called "peace building" – the creation of the human rights, economic and social conditions for peace – to day-to-day "peace maintenance", from participation by a representative organ in the development of international law to that of an elitist organ in the enforcement of international law, must not obscure the fact that the development of an objective international law based on Community interests requires the participation of, and recognition by, the international community as a whole.

KEYNOTE ADDRESS

THE CONCEPT OF SANCTION IN INTERNATIONAL LAW

Georges Abi-Saab▪

"Sanction" is one of the great conundra of legal theory. The term can simultaneously carry a positive connotation, as when we speak of the "legal sanction" of a title or a normative proposition, in the sense of conferring on it the legitimacy and dignity of law; but at the same time, in fact most of the time, it also carries the negative connotation of a penalty or punishment of deviant behaviour. And it is particularly in this negative sense that the problem of "sanction" has always been at the centre of the theoretical debates over the nature, structure and functions of international law, if not over the reality of its existence as a legal order.

Part of the confusion that surrounds these debates arises from the fact that the protagonists often use the term proceeding from different premises or conceptions of sanction without expliciting them. Moreover, from time to time, new terms suddenly emerge, like parasitical plants, purporting vaguely to cover, in all or in part, the same ground as old concepts, such as "counter measures" in relation to sanctions (on which more later), thus adding to the confusion.

My modest purpose in what follows is to examine critically the constellation of terms and concepts that revolve around those of "sanction", with a view to identifying the hard-core (at least, my conception of it), and situating the satellites in relation to it, to see whether we can chart their respective roles and ambits in contemporary international law.

▪ Professor of International Law, Graduate Institute of International Studies, Geneva.

I THE MANIFOLD MEANINGS OF "SANCTION"

First of all we have to identify the different meanings of "sanction", and its place in the international legal system. Note that I am speaking here of "sanction" in general and in the singular, while in other contexts we speak of sanctions in particular and in the plural; a subtle distinction which is pregnant with ambiguity, but which will become clearer as we proceed.

In the final analysis, the meaning of "sanction" within any legal system depends on what we understand by law. If we follow the positivists, starting with Austin who defines law as "command backed by threats", via his successors, whether the voluntarists such as Anzilotti or the normativists, viz. Kelsen who describes law as a "coercive order"[1] – especially if we situate this vision within the atomistic and purely inter-State representation of the classical system of international law, (according to which the State is the master-player in international relations and the only subject and organ of international law) – if we accept and proceed from these premises, then we are inexorably led to consider or identify sanction in international law with all means of coercion available to States, the archetypes being war and reprisals; a purely material or forcible vision of sanction. Moreover, according to this school of thought, sanction is a consubstantial element of law – not only of the legal system as a whole, but of every rule or norm taken individually – without which they do not qualify either as a legal system or as a legal rule or norm.

If, on the other hand, we consider that the existence of the legal order – and *a fortiori* of each legal rule or norm taken individually – does not rest ultimately and exclusively on coercion, and that social ordering has other main-springs than sheer coercion, while not totally ignoring it, we reach a different meaning and role of sanction.

To this end, we can take one of two routes. We can follow H.L.A. Hart who, cogently and eloquently demonstrates in his *magnum opus* "The Concept of Law"[2] that sanction, in the narrow sense of almost exclusively material or physical coercion, is not an essential element of law, neither of the legal system as a whole, nor of each rule taken individually. He provides many examples

1 Hans Kelsen, *The Pure Theory of Law*, (translation of the 2d German edition by Max Knight) (Berkeley, 1970), p. 30.

2 H.L.A.Hart, *The Concept of Law* (Oxford, 1961).

of rules, and even of whole branches of law, such as constitutional law, where such an element is lacking, but which are generally perceived and followed by the subjects of the system as law.[3]

Alternatively, we can adopt a much broader concept of sanction, which goes beyond physical or material coercion, corresponding to that of the great Italian legal philosopher Santi Romano[4] and his institutionalist theory of law; though foreshadowed a millennium earlier by the Muslim jusrisconsults who spoke of "the guarantee of the rules" (*Damman-ul-ahkham*), and not of their sanction.

This broad *lato sensu* concept of sanction comprises all the means and guarantees that the legal system can muster in order to ensure its "normative integrity", *i.e.* the conformity of social conduct with its normative prescriptions; in other words, its efficiency and credibility as a legal system. These means can be preventive or corrective; purely legal or coercive. They can also be positive (inducive) or negative (punitive); whence the importance, as a positive sanction, of the benefits of collaboration, and of the exclusion therefrom as a negative sanction within the international law of cooperation, in terms of the famous classification of international law by Wolfgang Friedmann into "the law of co-existence" and "the law of co-operation".

According to this concept, which I share, sanction *lato sensu* or generically speaking is an attribute of the legal system as such and not of every legal rule or norm in isolation. It partakes of the institutional component of the legal system (or what Hart calls its "secondary rules"); and its typical manifestation is purely legal, namely the regime of responsibility or the legal consequences that the system attaches to conducts at variance with its normative prescriptions.

It is true that at the end of the spectrum we reach "enforcement", or what in French is called *exécution forcée*, *i.e.* forcible execution through the organs of the legal system, such as a forcible eviction. But such enforcement through coercive measures is an ultimate step and an "exceptional limiting case", which is not always attainable, even in municipal law. And, of course, it can only be taken on the basis of a decision of a legally competent organ and by an equally competent organ of the legal system.

---

3 *Ibid.* p. 80.
4 Santi Romano, *L'ordre juridique*, (traduction de la 2è éd. par Lucien François et Pierre Gollut) (Paris, 1975).

This last hypothesis provides us with the elements of definition of sanctions *stricto sensu* (in contrast to the generic meaning I have been discussing until now), which can be then formulated as "coercive measures taken in execution of a decision of a competent social organ, *i.e.* an organ legally empowered to act in the name of the society or community that is governed by the legal system". Coercive measures taken individually by States or groups of States outside a determination and a decision by a legally competent social organ, whatever the label they are given (war, reprisals, counter-measures, quarantine, humanitarian intervention, etc.), obviously do not fall within this definition. They are manifestations of "self-help" or "private justice", and their legality is confined to the very narrow limits within which "remnants" of "self-help" are still admitted in contemporary international law. But if we want to give a complete picture of the means and guarantees available in the international legal system to ensure its normative integrity, we cannot totally ignore these means of private justice in a far from perfectly integrated international community.

The over-all purpose of sanction, as I said, is to ensure the normative integrity of the legal system, that is the translation of the normative prescriptions of its rules into social conduct (whether we describe that as respect, compliance, application, implementation or otherwise). Such a translation can take two routes (the choice of terms is necessarily subjective):

1. An endogenous or internal route, through the *direct application* of the rules by the subjects of the legal system, by internalising these rules, which are after all addressed to them, and modulating their conduct according to their prescriptions. Here the rule is absorbed and followed directly by the subject without the intermediation of an organ of the legal system. This is why I object to Kelsen's characterization of the State as a subject and organ of the international legal system at the same time. For, even when the same subject acts as an organ, he has to put on another hat or distinctive sign, be it a notional one, the passing through an organ having precisely for purpose to exteriorize the manner in which the rules are applied and to give it, through following a certain procedure, an external representation or stance.

In this modality of implementation through the direct application of rules, the inducive or positive features of sanction play a major role, without neglecting, however, the deterrence effect of the negative or punitive side of it. It does not raise problems unless the conformity of this direct application with the normative prescriptions of the rule is contested by another subject of the system; that which may lead to the other modality of implementation.

2. An exogenous or external (ultimately forcible) route, through the *execution* or *enforcement* of the rules by the social organs of the legal system; but exceptionally, in the primitive systems of private justice, by the other subjects of the legal system acting individually, in their own name.

It is to this type of forcible implementation or execution (evoking the Austinian or Kelsenian version of material or physical coercion) that the concept of sanction is usually associated. But before examining the legal status of its two varieties (social and individual) in contemporary international law, a few words are in order on the legal consequences the legal system attaches to the violation of its norms, which necessarily precede and open the way to enforcement.

II THE EXCLUSIVELY LEGAL CONSEQUENCES OF VIOLATING THE LAW

These consequences are produced and exist exclusively in the legal universe. Still, they partake of the concept of sanction *lato sensu*, as part of the means deployed by the legal system to bring deviant conduct back to a pattern consistent with its normative prescriptions. Moreover, they provide the executory title on the basis of which resort to enforcement can be had, while determining the content and limits of the remedy that can thus be obtained. They can be classified in three categories, according to their finality and the subjects to whom they are addressed:

1. Legal consequences not foreseen by the author of the violation or which in any case he would not have willed or wanted, when committing the act or omission constituting the violation. These consequences include first and foremost the international responsibility of the subject.[5] They also provide the

5 Some authors do not consider responsibility as partaking of "sanction", such as Jean Combacau, *Le pouvoir de sanction de l'ONU: Etude théorique de la coercition non militaire* (Paris, 1974), p. 44, who argues that as State responsibility does not interrupt the normative chain, but merely transform the contents of the obligations, creating new legal relations between the parties, it continues to treat the State whose responsibility is thus engaged as a party to a normative relation (be it a new or transformed one) and not as a target of a coercive measure, which is the essence of sanction according to him. This position proceeds from the narrow concept of sanction associating it exclusive-

executory title for any collective or individual measures of enforcement permitted in contemporary international law that may be taken against the author of the violation;

2. Consequences that deny or neutralize the legal effects the author of the violation intended to produce by his act or omission. This is the sanction of nullity for violations (*i.e.* non observance) of the conditions of validity of legal acts. But it can also take the form of grounds for abrogation, termination or withdrawal from synallagmatic agreements validly concluded, in case of non performance or violation by the other party. One should mention also in this context the "*exceptio non adempleti contractus*" (invoking negative reciprocity in case of non-execution of a contract), as well as the concept of "set-off", which is based on a positive version of the same *rationale* (although it operates automatically, *ipso jure*, and can be assimilated in some of its legal effects to an enforcement measure);

3. Legal consequences *vis-à-vis* third parties, such as denying or neutralizing all the legal effects of the act or omission constituting the violation in the international community in general. As far as legal acts are concerned, this effect falls under the preceding category. An agreement which is null and void does not exist not only between the parties, but also, and *a fortiori*, *erga omnes*. The same with unilateral legal acts which are not in conformity with the legal rules applicable to them, such as the delimitation by a State of its maritime zones of national jurisdiction: they cannot produce the legal effects intended by their authors *vis-à-vis* the other subjects of international law in general, whether we analyze this technically in terms of invalidity or of non-opposability.

In practice, however, this category of consequences *vis-à-vis* third parties goes beyond the mere neutralisation of the effects of defective legal acts. It is associated mainly with tortious acts which constitute not only a violation of international law, but a particularly serious or qualified breach falling within the category of "crimes of States" provided for in Article 19 of the Draft Articles on State Responsibility adopted in first reading by the International Law Commission in 1980.

---

ly with coercion. Be that as it may, responsibility ascribes to the subject new obligations constituting a negative value for him, against (or in any case irrespective of) his will. It thus corresponds to the negative version of the concept of sanction *lato sensu*. Moreover, it can open the way to the application of coercive enforcement measures.

These violations give rise to a triangular relation of responsibility (and not merely a bilateral one, as in the case of non qualified responsibility), between the active subject and two passive subjects: the direct victim of the act (of aggression for example), and the international community as a whole, which globally and through each of its members has a direct legal interest and *locus standi* to defend the common value or interest protected by the violated rule or norm. The rules envisaged here are generally *jus cogens* or at least of the type that creates *erga omnes* obligations for States, and entitles all other States, even those that are not directly affected by the violation, to react legally against their violations (and to some extent even obliges them to do so).

These three types of legal consequences that law attaches to the violation give rise to new legal relations in terms of rights, obligations and licences. These in turn serve as legal basis to enforcement or "forcible execution" measures that can be taken by the international community or its members acting individually in order to implement these new rights and obligations ensuing from the violation.

Are these enforcement or forcible execution measures part of "sanction", or is it, on the contrary, the "sanctions" that are part of these measures? The answer to this question depends on the definition we adopt of "sanction". If it is the *lato sensu* definition, it would then include all the means used to ensure the normative integrity of the system, *i.e.* which increase the probabilities of compliance with its rules, whether preventive or corrective. We have then to conclude that all means of execution, including forcible execution or enforcement measures are part of sanction. But if, by contrast, we proceed from the definition *stricto sensu* of sanctions as those coercive measures which are taken in implementation of a decision by a competent social organ to face up to the violation, then such sanctions would be a species of enforcement or forcible execution measures.

In this respect it is necessary to recall that the different means deployed by the legal system in case of violation can serve other purposes, in addition to that of sanction *lato sensu*, such as "reparation" (for injuries caused by the violation, a kind of "civil responsibility"), "punishment" (evocative of criminal responsibility) or deterrence (by setting the example). But above and beyond these intermediate, ancillary objectives, the prominent purpose of all these means remains the guarantee of the conformity, or the highest degree of conformity, of social conduct with the normative prescriptions, or the rapid rectification of the deviant pattern of conduct in this direction. That is what counts above all from the point of view of the legal system; the other, mediate, purposes, however important they may be, are only accessory to it. This is the crucial element in evaluating these means to which I shall now briefly turn.

III Enforcement or Forcible Execution Measures available to States Acting Individually (uti singuli): Variations on the Theme of "Counter Measures"

These are the remnants of the archaic institutions of "private justice" or "self-help" which are still admitted in international law. Some of these institutions, such as self-defence, exist even in the most developed legal system, for reasons of efficiency and economy of functions. But their scope in international law has been traditionally much wider.

First of all, it is necessary to situate these means in relation to "counter-measures", a term that was suddenly propelled on the scene of international law at the end of the seventies by a series of successive transplantations: originating in American strategic studies, used by analogy in commercial policy circles, via which it entered into the formulation of the US legal position in the Arbitration concerning the *Air Services Agreement of 27 March 1946 between the USA and France,* whose award of 9 December 1978[6] uses the term apparently for the first time in a formal international law instrument. It is probably via the members of the ILC who participated in this arbitration as arbitrators or counsel that the term found its way into the Draft Articles on State Responsibility adopted by the Commission in 1979,[7] and the following year in the judgement of the ICJ in the *Teheran Hostages* case,[8] the ultimate legal consecration (or sanction!) of the term and the concept.

This ready use of the term by decision-makers, judges and arbitrators, reflects a concern to avoid being tied down with too constraining legal classifications where all that was required for decision was an indication that the act or measure under consideration was taken in reaction to a legal violation. The term can thus be used generically and indifferently to signify a legally admis-

6 UN, *RIAA*, vol. 18, p. 458 (para. 81).
7 (1979) *ILCYb.*, vol. II, p. 128 (art. 30).
8 ICJ Reports, 1980, p. 3.

sible reaction, whether the violation is merely alleged or has been the object of a "determination" by a competent social organ, whether the responsibility arising from it is contractual or delictual (tortious); whether the reaction is individual *uti singuli* or collective and institutional, and finally whether the reaction does not constitute in itself a violation of international law or it would have constituted such a violation had it not been in response to another violation.

The innovation, if there is one, is not so much in the content of the concept (which straddles several venerable old notions, such as reprisals and retortion), but in the change in perspective and approach; in its dynamic representation of the matter as a process or a sequence of movements rather than in terms of intemporal normative propositions; that which sheds new light on the modalities, the finalities, and the immediate and not so immediate legal consequences of these movements, and makes us see them in a sequential and global perspective.

If everybody understands and accepts this generic sense of counter measures – as covering all the reactions permitted in international law to illegality *i.e.* to the violation of its norms – this is because thus understood, the concept has a useful explicative function. But precisely because of its generic and comprehensive character it has to abandon all claims to being operational. For once we try to examine the conditions it has to fulfil, apart from the prior violation to which it is reacting, we have to identify the particular species of counter measures we are considering, as at that level, conditions can widely vary from one species to another.

Yet, there is no general consensus on confining the use of the term "counter measures" to its generic meaning. This presents a double danger. The first is lending itself to manipulation by those who would intentionally use the generic term instead of the particular specific category they really mean in order to by-pass one of the conditions required by the specific category. The other danger is that of confusion, as a concept of variable geometry according to the context or author.

Thus, Professor Ago used initially in his Draft Article 30 the term "sanction" to cover at the same time (as a justification excluding responsibility) the reactions of States acting individually or *uti singuli* and the social reactions, taken in application of a decision or recommendation of a competent social organ (international organization).

The discussions in the Commission revealed, however, that for a good part of the members the term "sanction" has acquired a more specific meaning in contemporary international law, limiting it only to the second type of reactions; which led to its substitution by "counter measures" in order to cover both. Yet, for Ago, followed by the Commission, "counter measures" do not include "retortion" as it does not involve acts which would have been *per se* illegal, but for their being a reaction to a violation, and which in consequence do not need to be "justified" or "exonerated". By contrast, major writers, such as Schachter, Virally and Leben, consider that counter measures include retortion. Still, some of these very authors, *e.g.* Virally, exclude from counter measures, sanctions *stricto sensu i.e.* those in application of "social" decision by a competent organ, limiting them to the reactions of States *uti singuli*.

Thus the common denominator is reduced to good old "reprisals" (including its sub-species: the *exceptio non adempleti contractus*, negative reciprocity and reprisals in kind). But if it is mere reprisals, was it worth the trouble?[9]

In any case, reprisals have been greatly restricted. Historically moulded after its prime example, armed reprisals which were usually taken in last resort with an afflictive or punitive intent, the legal institution of reprisals almost lost its *raison d'être* with the prohibition of the use of force in the UN Charter. It had to readapt to its secondary, non-forcible uses and manifestations, basically in the economic field, which also led to the readaptation of its legal functions and finality, to become a mere interim measure for the protection of rights, or as a source of pressure to bring the other party to accept a procedure of settlement (*i.e.* measures which are reversible rather than afflictive and irretractable).[10]

---

9 One of the fortunate, though unintended side-effects of the interest aroused by the concept of "counter-measures" is that it inspired several young internationalists to write excellent doctoral thesis on the subject. See D. Alland, *Justice privée et ordre juridique international: étude théorique des contre-mesures en droit international public* (Paris, 1994); L.-A. Sicilianos, *Les réactions décentralisées à l'illicite. Des contre-mesures à la légitime défense* (Paris, 1991); L. Boisson de Chazournes, *Les contre-mesures dans les relations internationales économiques* (Paris, 1993).

10 See Boisson de Chazournes, *ibid.*

Be that as it may, measures of "self-help" or "private justice" are dangerous and controversial. They are always suspect as they are based on "self-interpretation" – both as to the materiality of facts and the requirements of the law as well as to the proportionality of the response – in contrast to sanctions *stricto sensu*.

IV Sanctions stricto sensu

As defined above, these are coercive measures taken against a target State or entity in application of a decision by a socially competent organ. Three elements stand out in this definition:

1. "Coercive measures" involve coercion whether armed or not, material (military, economic) or moral (condemnation, censure) or purely legal (loss of status, suspension or expulsion from membership of an international organization, though these may have material consequences).

"Coercive" also means taken against the will of the target State at least without its consent; the ultimate purpose being, as with all forcible execution or enforcement measures, precisely to bend its will in order to bring it back to a conduct compatible with legal prescriptions. It is as a target and not as a party in a legal relation that these measures are aimed at it.

2. These measures are taken against, *i.e.* at the detriment of the target State, involving a deprivation or a loss (a negative value) in relation to its prior situation, a diminution of its material or moral patrimony.

3. They are taken in application of a decision or recommendation of a competent social organ. They thus fall outside or beyond the measures of "private justice". This is because such a decision must be based on a "finding" and not on a mere "contention" or "allegation" resulting from the "self-interpretation" of the situation by the other party. Moreover, this "determination" must be accompanied by a "decision", ordering or recommending the measures to be taken on the basis of this finding. Such measures are thus a function of the degree of institutionalisation of international law, because they depend on the existence of a conventional framework providing for such organs. They are special regimes of sanctions, whose legal profile and modalities vary with the organization.

However, the advent of general purpose organizations during this century and their efforts to contain war through their systems of collective security, produced a generalized model of sanctions for each period. But the degree of institutionalisation and particularly of the centralisation of the decisions relating to sanctions is not the same in the two general systems of the League of Nations and the United Nations. These decisions take place at three levels: determining the occurrence of the violation; deciding what measures to be taken in response and executing these measures.

The Covenant of the *League of Nations*, having prescribed in its article 10 the obligation of Member states "to respect and preserve as against external aggression the territorial integrity and existing political independence of all Members of the League", established in article 16 its system of collective security. According to the first paragraph, "should any Member ... resort to war in disregard of ... articles 12, 13 or 15 [prescribing the procedures for the peaceful settlement of disputes], it shall *ipso facto* be deemed to have committed an act of war against all other Members [who] undertake immediately", *i.e.* automatically, to apply to it all the economic sanctions. Moreover, pursuant to paragraph 2, the Council may recommend the taking of further measures, including military ones.

This apparently clear and simple system proved to be much less so in practice. The "automatic application" of economic sanctions in case of aggression was considered too strenuous by many Member states. The controversy soon arose as to the instance competent to make the prior determination. A Committee of Jurists charged with interpreting the Covenant on this point, interpreted it retrogressively, by invoking the 19th century doctrine of interpreting in favour of sovereignty, while ignoring the new institutional context of the League, thus leaving the determination to each State individually rather than to the decision of the Council. A State which did not want to apply economic sanctions in implementation of its obligation under article 16/1 could simply determine for itself that there was no aggression (as did three States in the case of Italy's invasion and colonisation of Ethiopia!). Other (including military) measures could be recommended by the Council, but the decision was left to Member states, as was the implementation of all measures. In other words, as it came out in practice, there was no centralization of decision on any of the three levels in the League of Nations; that which explains the pitiful results of the only attempt to impose sanctions (but only economic ones) on Italy and which served as a telling lesson to the drafters of the UN Charter.

The Charter of the *United Nations* does much better. It centralizes the decision at the three levels. It is the Council that *determines* "the existence of any threat to peace, breach of peace or act of aggression" (art. 39). And it is also the Council, and the Council only, that *decides* "what measures shall be taken in accordance to articles 41 and 42, to maintain or restore international peace and security" (that is what went wrong in the Kosovo crisis). Moreover, according to the initial design of the Charter, there would have been a UN army, constituted pursuant to the procedure of article 43, under the direct operational command of the Council, to *execute* the military sanctions of article 42 (economic sanctions, by necessity, have to be executed by States, though coordinated and monitored by the Council).

In practice, this model was never applied in totality. Centralization at the third level of *execution* failed to materialize. A hybrid model progressively developed since the early fifties, first in Korea, then labeled as "permissive enforcement". It separates the two first levels of the determination and the decision – which have been described (politically) as "collective legitimization" – from the level of execution. The UN not disposing of the needed resources to undertake "collective action", would leave the execution of its decisions in this field to those Member states who volunteer to do it.

Ideally, this hybrid model can fulfil a useful function, by putting individual resources in the service of common ends. But it carries with it the danger of diverting the collective framework and purpose to serve unavowed individual ends of the States who take the action, rather than the other way around (the syndrome of the tail that wags the dog). Moreover, the pathological developments of this practice of "contracting-out"[11] since the end of the cold war, clearly demonstrate that the more "permissive" (*i.e.* the larger and vaguer) the "authorization", as in the case of the Gulf War, the greater are the ambiguities that surround the action taken under it, and the dangers of its "high-jacking" to serve ends other than those for which it was given. In other words, we may end up having measures taken *uti singuli* disguised in the garb of sanctions *stricto sensu*, a *mélange des genres* which goes against both the spirit and the letter of the law.

11 For an excellent recent study of this subject, see D. Sarooshi, *The United Nations and the Development of Collective Security. The Delegation by the UN Security Council of its Chapter VII Powers* (Oxford, 1999).

PART I

SANCTIONS – THEORETICAL ISSUES

Sanctions and the International Legal System

Chair: *Rosalyn Higgins*
Judge, International Court of Justice

QUELQUES REMARQUES SUR L'ÉVOLUTION DE LA PRATIQUE DES SANCTIONS DÉCIDÉES PAR LE CONSEIL DE SÉCURITÉ DES NATIONS UNIES DANS LE CADRE DU CHAPITRE VII DE LA CHARTE

Pierre-Marie Dupuy▪

Le Conseil de sécurité des Nations Unies n'est, en droit, ni un procureur, ni un juge mais simplement le gardien de la paix internationale. Il dispose, pour ce faire, par détermination du chapitre VII de la Charte de l'Organisation, du 'monopole de la violence légitime'.

Organe essentiellement politique, la Charte l'investit de compétences légales. Elle lui confère aussi la légitimité nécessaire à l'exercice de ces compétences au nom de la communauté des Etats membres, laquelle correspond pratiquement, aujourd'hui, à la communauté internationale 'dans son ensemble'. Il a d'autant plus besoin de cette légitimité selon la Charte qu'à la restriction de sa composition (quinze membres dont cinq sont 'plus égaux que les autres') correspond l'universalité de sa fonction.

Elle lui ménage enfin, sur la base de son article 39, un pouvoir d'appréciation discrétionnaire de l'opportunité de constater une rupture de la paix ou une 'menace à la paix internationale'; cette dernière expression n'a, au demeurant, d'autre acception que celle qu'il décidera, au cas par cas, de bien vouloir lui donner. Libre d'agir face à certaines situations qu'il jugera relever de la sécurité collective, il pourra tout aussi bien ne rien faire face à d'autres dont le simple bon sens suffirait pourtant à persuader qu'elles sont beaucoup plus dangereuses pour la paix internationale que bien des évènements auxquels il aura pourtant

▪ Professeur à l'Université Panthéon-Assas (Paris 2), Directeur de l'Institut des Hautes Etudes Internationales de Paris.

V. Gowlland-Debbas (ed.), *United Nations Sanctions and International Law,* p. 47-55.

décidé de réagir, reprenant implicitement la vielle formule régalienne, 'parce que tel était son bon plaisir'.

Tout ce qui précède est bien connu. Si on croit un peu utile de le rappeler, c'est parce que la pratique riche à défaut d'être toujours cohérente du Conseil de sécurité au cours de la dernière décennie du siècle écoulé a incité beaucoup à voir en lui une sorte de promoteur universel de l'ordre public, au double sens du terme : celui de la sécurité collective, mais également celui des valeurs et principes d'*ordre public*, au sens où l'on désigne par là les règles fondamentales hors du respect desquelles il ne saurait y avoir de vie collective dans une société ordonnée.

Pour ce faire, à partir du mois d'août 1990, à l'occasion de l'invasion du Koweït par l'Irak, le Conseil de sécurité a pris ce qu'il est couramment convenu d'appeler des 'sanctions'. Or, si on lit le chapitre VII de la Charte, on y trouvera abondamment mention des 'mesures' mais, jamais, de 'sanctions'. Si le langage commun a retenu ce terme, c'est pourtant qu'il y a à cela des raisons. Elles découlent de la pratique, naturellement empirique, et non d'abord du droit, étranger à cette appellation. Pourtant, ces raisons concrètes paraissent aussi inspirées par des considérations où la politique s'enrichit elle-même de considérations juridiques.

Deux d'entre elles peuvent notamment expliquer ce gauchissement des 'mesures' en 'sanctions' dans le langage courant. D'abord, les *situations* auxquelles ces mesures réagissent résultent souvent elles-mêmes d'une atteinte au droit. C'est particulièrement, mais pas seulement, le cas à propos des 'ruptures de la paix internationale'. Ensuite, la *réaction* que constitue la mesure elle-même, surtout lorsqu'elle est décidée et pas seulement recommandée par le Conseil, s'apparente en effet à une sanction juridique, tant par sa forme que par sa finalité. Par la forme, parce que la sanction vise un ou plusieurs Etats en les désignant ainsi comme étant à l'origine de la situation menaçant ou atteignant la paix internationale; ceci place *de facto* cet Etat dans la posture d'un responsable. Par la finalité, ensuite, parce que l'action du Conseil vise le rétablissement de la situation qui prévalait antérieurement à l'initiative du fauteur de troubles; cela donne au phénomène des allures de *restitutio in integrum*, dont on sait que le but est précisément de rétablir l'ordonnancement juridique qui prévalait avant que la commission d'un fait illicite international vienne lui porter atteinte. On ajoutera que le contexte politique souvent assez émotionnel dans lequel interviennent par la force des choses les 'sanctions' prises par le Conseil de sécurité facilite, notamment dans la presse, le recours à un vocable dont la forte connotation pénale frappe les esprits. Il faut enfin rappeler que, les juristes eux-mêmes n'étant pas toujours d'accord sur la définition technique de la sanction, il s'agit décidément d'une appellation non contrôlée.

Cette relative mais certaine indétermination de concept explique que, dans une période caractérisée un temps par la surchauffe du système de la sécurité collective (en particulier de 1990 à 1995), bon nombre de mesures prises par le Conseil pour la réalisation d'une conception très élargie du maintien de la paix et de la sécurité internationale aient contribué à accroître l'équivoque de la pratique des 'sanctions' qu'il prenait.

L'usage accru du concept, appuyé sur une invocation explicite du chapitre VII, s'est ainsi trouvé associé des actions de types variés. Ceci devait donner lieu à des tendances contrastées, puisque les 'sanctions' ainsi prises par le Conseil se trouvaient tour à tour ou, parfois même, simultanément, spécifiées comme telles (I), ou bien tout au contraire, fondues dans un ensemble de mesures plus larges (II), avant même d'être mises à l'écart pour qu'on leur substitue à nouveau, comme avant 1990, des actions unilatérales prises en dehors de l'ONU alors même qu'elles visaient le rétablissement de la paix comme le respect de certains principes jugés fondamentaux par leurs auteurs (III).

I Spécification des mesures en sanctions

Le premier phénomène notable, à partir du début de la crise du Golfe (août 1990) jusqu'au cœur de la crise bosniaque (1994-95), c'est-à-dire durant la période d'entente suffisante entre les membres permanents pour que le chapitre VII soit efficacement utilisé, c'est celui de la pratique de mesures plus ou moins inspirées par le catalogue de celles énoncées à l'article 41 de la Charte (coercition non militaire) et destinées à organiser la réaction de la communauté internationale à l'atteinte à certains principes cardinaux.

L'action contre l'Irak commence ainsi par un retour aux sources et une innovation. Le premier est précisément constitué par le recours effectif à l'éventail des 'mesures' de l'article 41, dont l'effectivité sera d'ailleurs contrôlée par un 'comité des sanctions' constitué par le Conseil et comportant la même composition que lui. L'innovation est réalisée par le fait que le destinataire de ces sanctions, l'Irak, est lui-même désigné par le Conseil, dès sa résolution 661, comme engageant sa responsabilité internationale vis-à-vis du reste de la communauté internationale, ce qui, en soi, outrepasse les fonctions de cet organe telles que rappelées au début de la présente communication. On constate ainsi que le retour aux sanctions, oubliées depuis celles que le Conseil avait prises à l'encontre de l'Afrique du Sud et de la Rhodésie à la fin des années soixante, s'accompagne déjà d'un dépassement du rôle que confère la Charte au Conseil, puisqu'il n'a pas en principe à charge de prononcer de constat d'illicite imputable à l'un des Etats membres. En agissant comme il l'a fait vis-à-vis de l'Irak, il visait non seulement la situation crée par l'Irak mais cet Etat lui-même. Il s'investissait ainsi lui-même d'une sorte nouvelle de fonction quasi judiciaire.

Par la suite, l'affirmation de son rôle de défenseur de la légalité internationale s'accentuera, dans la 667 terminant l'affaire du Golfe, puis dans les résolutions prises à l'encontre de la Libye (Res. 748), de la Yougoslavie (Res. 751), d'Haïti (940), ou du Rwanda. Le Conseil s'appuie sur le chapitre VII pour prendre des décisions obligatoires pour tous les Etats membres; il prend des sanctions qu'il qualifie comme telles; il prononce l'illicite, 'dénonce', 'condamne' et manifeste ainsi que les mesures qu'il prend sont bel et bien, au sens le plus accepté du terme, des sanctions, puisqu'elles réagissent à l'illicite en exerçant sur son auteur des pressions concrètes destinées, non sans connotation pénale politiquement entretenue, à l'amener à mettre un terme à ses infractions au droit international. Les sanctions prises sont effectivement contrôlées par un comité créé à cet effet; c'est à nouveau le cas, après l'Irak, pour les Etats issus de l'ancienne Yougoslavie. Elles sont constituées en particulier par des mesures d'embargo, de plus ou moins grande ampleur suivant la gravité avérée de l'illicite à l'origine de la situation attentatoire à la paix ou de l'effet recherché. L'embargo vise les communications aériennes lorsqu'il s'agit de réagir à l'appui allégué de la Libye au terrorisme ayant entraîné la destruction en vol de deux aéronefs civils. Il porte sur le commerce et la vente d'armes dans le cas des anciens membres de la République fédérale socialiste de Yougoslavie.

II DILUTION DES SANCTIONS

Les sanctions dont l'énoncé précède ne furent que très rarement prises isolément. Elles constituaient au contraire, dès l'affaire du Golfe, un élément, certes déterminant, dans un train de mesures de tous ordres au sein desquelles il n'est pas toujours aisé de les distinguer.

Le Conseil de sécurité met en place un dispositif de contrainte qui visera tour à tour l'Irak, la Yougoslavie ou Haïti pour faire triompher une conception large de la paix.

Comme on l'a expliqué par ailleurs, il ne se contente plus de camper dans le domaine, en principe balisé par le chapitre VII, de la sécurité collective *stricto sensu*. Il s'aventure, du moins durant la première partie de la décennie écoulée, dans le champ de la promotion de la paix telle qu'elle était plutôt en charge, par détermination de la Charte, de l'Assemblée générale. On sait l'étape importante que constitua à cet égard l'Agenda pour la paix préparé par le Secrétaire général des Nations Unies, qui distinguait entre maintien, restauration et promotion de la paix.

C'est également ainsi que seront constitués les deux tribunaux pénaux '*ad hoc*'. Destinés à juger les responsables individuels de crimes contre l'humanité *lato sensu*, ces nouveaux organes judiciaires tirent les conséquences de l'accumulation d'actes illites organisés ou rendus possibles par des Etats, même s'ils sont accomplis par des particuliers. On pourrait trouver là une parenté avec des sanctions au sens classique du terme, mais il paraît bien difficile de les y assimiler.

Il en va *a fortiori* de même lorsque le Conseil prend des actions de type humanitaire pour venir en aide aux populations sinistrées par les conflits internes (Somalie, Bosnie) ou internationaux et l'on peut *a fortiori* faire la même observation à propos des mesures adoptées pour garantir les conditions nécessaires au retour à la démocratie en Haïti.

Les sanctions *stricto sensu*, en tant que mesures affectant la situation matérielle ou juridique d'un Etat membre en vue de l'amener à respecter ses obligations selon la Charte sont les parties prenantes d'un dispositif normatif diversifié dont les finalités élargies dépassent le cadre classique du maintien de la paix. Le chapitre VII cesse ainsi d'être exclusivement l'instrument normatif de la sécurité collective. Il devient aussi le moyen pour le Conseil, alors au sommet de sa gloire, de veiller au respect des droits de l'homme, des principes cardinaux du droit humanitaire, voire à l'instauration des conditions nécessaires à la légitimité démocratique des pays affligés par la guerre civile ou l'autoritarisme de juntes militaires.

Tout cela n'a cependant qu'un temps. C'est précisément dès la fin de l'année 1994, au moment où l'autorité des Nations Unies se délite à raison des incertitudes du mandat mal défini des casques bleus de la FORPRONU en Bosnie, que le Conseil de sécurité va être progressivement mis sur la touche, pour être finalement écarté, avec le reste de l'Organisation, de la négociation des accords de Dayton, en 1995, censés ramener la paix dans les Balkans.

III Substitution aux sanctions de mesures unilatérales collectives extérieures à l'Organisation

Au sens strict, on sort ici du sujet assigné à cette communication, puisqu'il s'agit tout au plus d'une 'non pratique' du Conseil de sécurité. Comment, pourtant, parler de l'évolution du droit du maintien de la paix en juillet 1999 sans évoquer la récente crise du Kosovo ? D'autant qu'à y regarder de près, c'est précisément parce que l'intervention humanitaire des alliés s'est déroulée sous l'égide de l'OTAN qu'on n'a jamais cessé de parler des Nations Unies.

On l'a fait soit pour souligner l'illégalité de l'action des pays occidentaux en dehors de l'Organisation mondiale, soit, au contraire, et tant bien que mal, pour trouver dans les dernières résolutions du Conseil de sécurité avant l'éclatement de la crise un mandat à vrai dire bien incertain. La France, en particulier, parce qu'elle était soucieuse de ne pas constituer un précédent susceptible de ruiner rapidement l'autorité des Nations Unies en matière de maintien de la paix, a plusieurs fois, par la voie du Premier Ministre ou du ministre des affaires étrangères, souligné que les résolutions 1199 et 1203 du Conseil de sécurité avaient été prises dans le cadre du chapitre VII.

Aucune d'entre elles, pourtant, ne comporte d'habilitation à prendre des sanctions sous forme de coercition militaire à l'égard de la Yougoslavie si cette dernière ne respectait pas, avant un certain délai, les engagements pris par elle à l'égard de Monsieur Richard Holbrooke, considéré *de facto* comme le représentant de la communauté internationale. La résolution 1199 se contente de constater en début octobre 1998 que la situation au Kosovo constitue une menace à la paix internationale; elle fait référence à la possibilité qu'aurait le Conseil d'envisager la prise éventuelle de mesures destinées au maintien et à la restauration de la paix; elle ne détermine pour autant aucune mesure concrète. Quant à la 1203, prise à la fin du même mois, elle entérine les deux accords conclus par Richard Holbrooke, mais sans davantage habiliter les Etats membres à prendre les mesures de coercition militaire du type de celles prévues à l'article 42. En janvier 1999, Kofi Annan rappellera, comme s'il était déjà résigné à l'inéluctable, que 'normalement, une résolution du Conseil de sécurité est requise pour recourir à la force'.

Durant la même période, l'opinion est couramment exprimée, notamment par certains diplomates émanant des membres permanents du Conseil de sécurité, que la seule référence au chapitre VII établie dans une résolution du Conseil suffirait à habiliter ses membres au recours à la force, en cas de persistance de la situation visée.

On perçoit toute la distance qui sépare une telle opinion de la pratique antérieure du même organe, celle inaugurée précisément durant la crise du Golfe avec la résolution 678. Cette dernière ne se contentait pas d'une simple référence au chapitre VII. Elle la comportait mais pour habiliter ensuite explicitement les Etats membres à prendre toutes les mesures requises (ce qui couvrait le recours à la coercition non militaire) si la situation créée par l'Irak perdurait au-delà d'une certaine date. Dans les deux résolutions d'octobre 1998 précitées, tout au contraire, une telle habilitation expresse fait défaut. Qui plus est, l'attitude de deux des membres permanents, la Russie et la Chine, durant l'opération entreprise par les pays de l'OTAN au Kosovo, caractérisée par le veto à l'égard de toute résolution d'habilitation au recours à la force, interdit qu'on puisse voir dans la pratique une consécration de la thèse exprimée par des diplomates occidentaux. La seule référence au chapitre VII dans une résolution du Conseil ne suffit pas à habiliter les Etats membres à recourir à la force, fut-ce à l'égard d'un Etat persistant dans une atteinte à la paix internationale.

Il paraît également très hasardeux de tenter de voir dans le texte de la résolution 1244 qui clôt la période de recours à la force un aval donné à l'action des Etats membres de l'OTAN. Tout au contraire, si la résolution adoptée le 10 juin 1999 après d'âpres négociations entre les membres du Conseil commence par affirmer 'la responsabilité principale du Conseil de sécurité pour le maintien de la paix et de la sécurité internationale', c'est bien pour rappeler quel est le droit commun.

La suite de la résolution mettra en place un dispositif au sein duquel on sait que l'ONU retrouve une place centrale. Ainsi, d'une certaine manière, il y a une symétrie parfaite entre l'affaire de la Bosnie et celle du Kosovo. La première commence par l'affirmation de la toute puissance du Conseil de sécurité et finit par la mise à l'écart de l'ONU. La seconde, à l'inverse, commence en substituant à la paralysie du Conseil une action extérieure à l'Organisation mondiale mais elle se termine par le retour à la case départ, celle selon laquelle le maintien de la paix internationale est du ressort principal (et, par conséquent, non exclusif) de l'ONU.

Si l'on veut tenter de trouver une justification juridique de l'intervention humanitaire des pays de l'OTAN au Kosovo tout en restant dans le cadre de la Charte de l'ONU, il semble que la seule voie, au demeurant, bien étroite, qui s'offre à l'analyste consiste à observer que l'article 2§4 n'établit pas une interdiction générale de recours à la force. Il l'interdit seulement 'soit contre l'intégrité territoriale ou l'indépendance politique de tout Etat, soit de toute autre manière incompatible avec les buts des Nations Unies'. La dernière hypothèse citée n'est certainement pas vérifiée dans le cas considéré. Au contraire, c'est bien la Yougoslavie qui violait outrageusement les buts de l'Organisation et les pays membres de l'OTAN qui tentaient d'en faire triompher le respect. La seconde hypothèse n'est pas forcément réalisée non plus. Les alliés n'ont jamais prétendu désirer porter atteinte à l' 'indépendance politique' de la Yougoslavie. Ils ont tout au contraire rappelé à plusieurs reprises que le peuple yougoslave devait lui-même déterminer la nature de ses institutions politiques même s'il est vrai qu'ils l'on également incité à désavouer le régime de Slobodan Milosévitch. Il paraît en revanche beaucoup plus difficile de prétendre que la vague des bombardements massifs déclenchée par les forces de l'OTAN n'ait pas abouti à affecter l'intégrité territoriale de la Yougoslavie, dans la mesure, en particulier, où le Kosovo est aujourd'hui soustrait à l'administration des autorités de Belgrade. Il est cependant notable que la résolution 1244 réaffirme 'l'attachement de tous les Etats membres à la souveraineté et à l'intégrité territoriale de la République fédérale de Yougoslavie et de tous les autres Etats de la région, au sens de l'Acte final d'Helsinki et de l'annexe 2 à la présente résolution'. Ce sont, à la suite, les points 5 et 8 de l'annexe 2 qui prévoient l'instauration d'une 'autonomie substantielle' qui tienne compte de 'l'intégrité territoriale de la République fédérale de Yougoslavie'.

L'autre façon de rechercher une justification juridique à l'intervention humanitaire internationale au Kosovo se situe dans le cadre du droit international général. Elle consiste à rappeler que les principes mis en cause et bafoués par le comportement du régime de Belgrade présentent un caractère impératif, qui ne saurait supporter nulle exception.

Mais ceci est une autre histoire, qui se heurte pour l'instant à d'autres précédents bien difficiles à rendre compatibles avec cette argumentation.

Celui de la première comme de la seconde guerre de Tchéchénie vient bien entendu le plus spontanément à l'esprit...

2

THE RELATIONSHIP BETWEEN SANCTIONS AND COUNTERMEASURES

James Crawford[■]

I THE NOTION OF A "SANCTION" IN INTERNATIONAL LAW

Professor Abi-Saab has defined a sanction as a coercive response to an internationally wrongful act authorised by a competent social organ. It may be inferred from that definition that a "competent social organ" is not an individual state acting in its own right, or even a small group of states so acting. Instead it seems to refer to some competent social organ authorised to act on behalf of a collective interest, such as, for example, the Security Council.

But some care is needed here. The term "sanction" is not used in the United Nations Charter, and subject to one possible qualification, the Security Council, though it authorises coercive responses, does not impose "sanctions" in the strict sense. Its powers are described not in terms of responses to internationally wrongful acts but to situations which it characterises as threats to or breaches of the peace. As Pierre-Marie Dupuy has pointed out, these threats or breaches do not necessarily entail internationally wrongful conduct. Indeed they may involve conduct which is exclusively within the domestic jurisdiction of the "target" state (see article 2 (7)). Moreover the response to them is authorised in virtue of their character as threats to or breaches of the peace and not in virtue of their character as internationally wrongful acts. So the Security Council

■ Whewell Professor of International Law; Director, Lauterpacht Research Centre for International Law, University of Cambridge; International Law Commission Special Rapporteur on State Responsibility. My thanks to Pierre Bodeau for his assistance with this comment.

V. Gowlland-Debbas (ed.), *United Nations Sanctions and International Law*, p. 57-68.

is – with one exception – not specifically authorized to impose sanctions as Professor Abi-Saab has defined them. It is not specifically authorized to adjudicate on wrongful conduct and to respond to it in its character as such.

In recent practice, this distinction has been obscured if not confounded. In a number of cases (notably concerning Iraq) the Security Council has apparently taken Chapter VII action in virtue of its qualification of conduct as internationally wrongful. Moreover it has established bodies such as the United Nations Compensation Commission with a view to obtaining something which it is impossible to distinguish from restitution and compensation as those terms are used in the law of state responsibility.

It is true that in the case of aggression the Security Council is specifically authorised to determine that there has been an internationally unlawful act of a certain kind, and to respond accordingly. Unlike threats to or breaches of the peace, the concept of aggression seems to be in principle legally defined, however much in practice it has escaped authoritative definition.[1] A determination under article 39 of the Charter that there has been an act of aggression entails what amounts to a binding judgment by an international executive organ. We may wish to say that the Security Council's action against Iraq, and in particular its action in establishing the United Nations Compensation Commission,[2] is justified on the basis of an implicit (and factually justified) finding of aggression by Iraq against Kuwait. That might help to limit the scope of the "precedent" set by the relevant resolutions. On the other hand, it ignores two facts. First, the Security Council has never actually qualified conduct as aggression, even when it would have been justified in doing so. Secondly the powers of the Council under Chapter VII are no differently expressed in the case of aggression than they are in cases of threats to or breaches of the peace. Perhaps the Security Council does not judge conduct as aggression because it has no need to do so?

---

1 GA Res 3314 (XXIX) of 14 December 1974 on the Definition of Aggression notoriously avoids the major difficulties. Under Art 2, the first use of force contrary to Charter Art 2 (4) is aggression unless the Security Council otherwise determines. But this is not a definition, and its effect is to reverse the veto.

2 See SC Res 687E (1991); 692 (1991), 706 (1991), etc.

II COUNTERMEASURES IN THE DRAFT ARTICLES ON STATE RESPONSIBILITY (1996)

I turn to the question of countermeasures in the law of state responsibility, which has been the subject of continuing discussion in the International Law Commission.[3] What is the relationship between countermeasures and sanctions as defined above?

Special Rapporteur Roberto Ago, who was responsible for the basic conceptions underlying the Draft Articles, had to face this question directly. Did state responsibility involve in its essence a series of secondary legal obligations in the framework of restitution and compensation, or was it essentially concerned, as Kelsen and some others thought, with a form of sanction in response to an internationally wrongful act? Ago thus faced an older doctrinal controversy of an entrenched kind, with two well defined views. He resolved it, as so often such controversies are resolved, by adopting elements of both views – by having, as it were, something of both worlds.[4] He conceived state responsibility as concerned with reparation in the general sense – restitution, compensation, etc. – *and* as a form of sanction. Countermeasures in effect sanction the failure to cease internationally wrongful conduct and to provide reparation, and they do so even where the wrongfulness is strictly bilateral, i.e. where it arises exclusively between an injured state and a state responsible for internationally wrongful conduct *vis-à-vis* the former state.

The only provision on countermeasures which Judge Ago actually proposed was article 30. In its first version this read:

> The international wrongfulness of an act not in conformity with what would otherwise be required of a State by virtue of an international obligation towards another State is precluded if the act was committed as the legitimate application of a sanction against that other State, in consequence of an internationally wrongful act committed by that other State.[5]

---

3 For a review of the state of play see J. Crawford, *Second Report on State Responsibility* (A/CN.4/498/Add. 4, 6 July 1999), and for an account of the debate so far see *ILC Report, fifty-first session* (1999) (A/54/10, Suppl. No 10), Ch. V, paras. 426-453.

4 See commentary to Article 1 of the Draft Articles on State Responsibility as adopted on first reading, in (1973) *YBILC,* vol. II, pp. 173-176, especially paras. (5) and (10).

5 Ago, Eighth Report, (1979) *YBILC,* vol II, part 1, p. 47.

Although this formulation did not use the term "countermeasure", it clearly covered countermeasures and it further implied that countermeasures might be taken by way of sanction or punishment for wrongful conduct. In its reformulation of the proposal, the ILC was more reserved.[6] The term "sanction" was dropped and replaced by "measure". The title of the article became "Countermeasures in respect of an internationally wrongful act",[7] indicating that the legitimate measures to which article 30 applies are considered as countermeasures. But nonetheless the breadth of Ago's original conception was retained. Article 30 as adopted on first reading read:

> The wrongfulness of an act of a state not in conformity with an obligation of that state is precluded if the act constitutes a measure legitimate under international law against the other state in consequence of an internationally wrongful act of that other state.

Thus countermeasures were considered as "legitimate" if taken in response to an internationally wrongful act. Their wrongfulness was precluded to the extent that they were a legitimate response to such an act.

Article 30 had two further features. First, it did not define in what circumstances countermeasures are "legitimate" under international law.[8] So it left entirely to one side the question to what extent countermeasures are legitimate in any given case. Secondly, it referred to countermeasures in indefinite terms, that is, as an act of state A not in conformity with an obligation of state A towards state B and carried out in consequence of an internationally wrongful act of state B. That is a broad conception of countermeasures.

To an extent these features are now addressed in Part 2. First, a serious effort is made in articles 47-50 to define the circumstances in which countermeasures may be legitimate, and to impose limitations on the taking of countermeasures to prevent abuses.[9] Secondly, the approach taken to countermeasures is an

---

6 See the plenary debate in (1979) *YBILC*, vol. I, pp. 171 (para. 8) and 175.

7 For the commentary to the article, see (1979) *YBILC*, vol. II, part 2, pp. 115-122. Ago's proposed title had been "Legitimate application of a sanction".

8 Note the use of the word "legitimate", well before Professor Franck popularised it: see T. Franck, *The Power of Legitimacy Among Nations* (Oxford, 1990).

9 In the *Case concerning the Gabčikovo-Nagymaros Project*, the International Court referred to these limitations with general approval: see ICJ Reports, 1977, p. 3 at 55 (para. 83). It added a useful clarification to the principle of proportionality by its

instrumental rather than a punitive one. Countermeasures are measures taken not with a view to the punishment of the state which committed the internationally wrongful act, but with a view to ensuring that the state ceases the internationally wrongful act (if it is a continuing act) and provides reparation. Countermeasures are seen as instrumental to obtaining reparation in the broad sense. To this extent Professor Arangio-Ruiz's conception of a countermeasure, as embodied in Article 47, is narrower than that implied by article 30. Conduct is not a (potentially legitimate) countermeasure merely because it is taken in consequence of an internationally wrongful act: it must be taken in response to an internationally wrongful act and with a view to obtaining reparation.

In the *Case concerning the Gabčikovo-Nagymaros Project*, the Court took this one step further. It referred, in passing, to "one other condition for the lawfulness of a countermeasure, namely that its purpose must be to induce the wrongdoing state to comply with its obligations under international law, and that the measure must therefore be reversible".[10] This is a useful clarification, and like Part 2 of the Draft articles it leaves questions of punishment or reprisal to one side.

Notwithstanding this instrumental approach, countermeasures – as defined in article 47 – seem to satisfy two of the requirements for sanctions laid down by Professor Abi-Saab. They are measures taken in response to an internationally wrongful act and they are, or may well be, coercive in their effect. But they do not meet his further requirement, since they are taken not by a "competent social organ" but by an individual state injured by the act in question. The injured state is acting in its own right and on its own account. It is attempting to vindicate, by measures otherwise unlawful, what the ILC's commentaries repeatedly refer to as its "subjective" rights. I suppose we might say that an individual state lawfully (or legitimately) imposing countermeasures is acting as a "competent social organ". But it is doing so only indirectly, if at all: it may be acting quite selfishly and without any regard for the interests and views of other states. The Draft Articles presently draw no distinction between a state acting solely in its own interest and one acting in some more general interest.

---

statement that "the effects of a countermeasure must be commensurate with the injury suffered, taking account of the rights in question": *ibid.*, p. 56 (para. 85).

10 *Ibid.*, pp. 56-57 (para. 87). To similar effect see J. Crawford, "Countermeasures as Interim Measures", (1994) 5 *EJIL* 65.

To complete the picture let me refer to some other aspects of countermeasures as articulated in the Draft articles adopted on first reading. First of all, article 39 reserves entirely the question of actions taken pursuant to the Charter. The whole question of Chapter VII action falls outside the scope of the Draft articles. Countermeasures and Charter action are now seen as distinct domains. Secondly, however, countermeasures may be taken in respect of collective violations, even though there is no coordination of the action to be taken. This can be clearly seen if one reads articles 47-50 in light of the general definition of "injured State" in article 40. Any state so defined may take countermeasures, and it may do so to enforce its own view of what is required, under international law, by way of reparation for an internationally wrongful act.[11] This is understandable where "subjective" rights are concerned – that is to say, rights specific to the state taking countermeasures. But it is more problematic when the state is complaining of a breach of an obligation in the performance of which it has a general interest common to all or many states. Article 40 identifies a number of cases where this will be so, e.g. breaches of general human rights, and so-called "international crimes" of states. But it seems odd to equate the breach of such obligations with violations of the subjective rights of individual states, e.g. under a bilateral treaty.

The tendency to treat solidary obligations, i.e. obligations held in common to all or many states, as if they were bundles of individual obligations is reminiscent of the older view of the multilateral treaty as a "bundle" of bilateral treaty relations.[12] But the whole point of the Court's dictum in *Barcelona Traction* was to distinguish some few solidary obligations of a general character from

---

11 Of course a state cannot take countermeasures merely because it asserts or believes there has been a breach of international law: the test is an objective one. See Art 47 and commentary: *ILC Report, forty-eighth session* (1996) (A/51/10, Supp. No.10), pp. 154-158. But different views can be taken on many consequential questions: whether restitution or compensation is appropriate, whether and what measures of satisfaction should be made, etc., and it is idle to suggest that these matters are legally predetermined. The point is that if all or many states can take countermeasures independently, they are each apparently entitled to assert and to enforce their own reasonable views on these questions. State A may settle for compensation to the injured party; state B may insist on restitution. There is no way in the Draft Articles as they stand of resolving such conflicts between states which are equally defined as "injured".

12 See K. Marek, "Contribution à l'étude de l'histoire du traité multilatéral" in *Festschrift für Rudolf Bindscheidler* (Bern, 1980) pp. 17, 24.

the normal run of bilateral obligations.[13] To disaggregate solidary obligations at the threshold of their potential application seems pointless and self-defeating.

A further and perhaps related tendency is to equate solidary obligations with "objective" *rights* under international law, such objective rights as may be entitled to respect from all. There are many such rights, for example those associated with territorial sovereignty, yet these seem to have nothing to do with the special category of solidary obligations referred to by the Court in *Barcelona Traction*. A state which has sovereignty over a given territory is the holder of what may be called a "subjective" right (or a bundle of such rights), even though such a right is held as against the world. Traditional international law had such conceptions, yet seemed to have no need for a category of "*erga omnes* obligations".

Both tendencies can be seen in the dissenting opinion of Judge Weeramantry in the *East Timor* case. Seeking to escape from the dilemma presented in that case by the *Monetary Gold* principle,[14] he asserted that:

> An *erga omnes* right is, needless to say, a series of separate rights *erga singulum*... These rights are in no way dependent one upon the other. With the violation by any state of the obligation so lying upon it, the rights enjoyed *erga omnes* become opposable *erga singulum* to the state so acting.[15]

But this confuses the assertion of a legal right with the procedural conditions required for its implementation. The problem was to determine that state B, Australia, had infringed the right and, on a certain view of the matter, it had only done so if state A, Indonesia, had first infringed it. A more direct approach

13 ICJ Reports, 1970, p. 32 (paras. 33, 34).

14 See ICJ Reports, 1954, p. 16. The *Monetary Gold* decision stands for the proposition that an international court cannot decide on a breach of an international obligation by state B if that breach is consequential upon, and requires the determination of, a prior breach of obligation by state A and state A is not a party to the proceedings and has not otherwise authoritatively been held to have breached the obligation. *Cf. Certain Phosphate Lands in Nauru*, ICJ Reports, 1992, p. 240. In *East Timor*, Australia was in the position of state B; Indonesia, not a party to the proceedings, was in the position of state A.

15 *Case Concerning East Timor*, ICJ Reports, 1995, p. 90 at 172; see also ibid., pp. 214-216.

to the *Monetary Gold* problem seems to have been required in that case, or a more subtle one.[16]

III POSSIBLE APPROACHES TO COUNTERMEASURES AND SANCTIONS: THE ILC'S SECOND READING

Clearly the question of countermeasures or other collective action taken in response to a breach of solidary obligations needs further thought. Indeed it is one of the most difficult questions facing the ILC in its remaining work on state responsibility,[17] and it may be useful therefore to say something briefly about the issues which will arise as the second reading progresses.

The essential problem will have already become clear. In the modern world it is impossible to think of state responsibility exclusively in a bilateral way, or simply to reduce the effect of multilateral obligations to bilateral ones, as Judge Weeramantry sought to do in the passage just quoted. The Draft Articles strikingly demonstrate this in article 40, which defines "injured state" in a very broad way. The inspiration was, no doubt, the famous and wholly unnecessary *dictum* of the International Court in the *Barcelona Traction* case.[18] But on the occasions when the International Court has been concerned with obligations to the international community as a whole, for example in the *Second South West Africa* cases or in the *East Timor* case, it has been much more reticent about those obligations than it was in *Barcelona Traction*. It may be that the nearer you come to obligations *erga omnes*, the more reticent you become about them.

16 A more direct approach would have been to say that obligations *erga omnes* require each of the states to further compliance with the obligation, so far as lies in their power and irrespective of compliance by other states. The implications of such an approach for self-determination are intriguing, especially since self-determination is often paired with the principle of non-intervention in internal affairs. A more subtle approach would have been to rely on the principle that a state may not recognise the acquisition of sovereignty resulting even from a lawful use of force, whereas the *Monetary Gold* principle is only applicable to cases of unlawful conduct.

17 As noted by S. Rosenne, "Some Reflections *Erga Omnes*" in A Anghie & G Sturgess (eds), *Legal Visions of the 21st Century: Essays in Honour of Judge Christopher Weeramantry* (The Hague, 1998) p. 509.

18 *Ibid.*, pp. 509-510.

Reticence hardly seems an option, however, for the ILC in its work on state responsibility. And the problem is exacerbated if we think of the notion of "international crimes of state". If there are "crimes of state" in the proper sense of the word, there must presumably be sanctions in the proper sense of the word as well, i.e., in the narrow and strict sense given by Professor Abi-Saab. But the Draft Articles having, with a flourish, announced the concept of international crimes of state in article 19, when one gets to the consequences of the crimes in Part II the mountain appears to have divided and produced a mouse. The consequences are trivial, they are poorly defined, and they are not specific to the most serious violations of the most serious norms (even if we can get agreement on what these are).[19]

The ILC has set aside Article 19 for the time being pending further consideration.[20] Instead it is looking carefully to see whether there are ways in which the notion of peremptory norms and the closely associated notion of obligations to the international community as a whole can be reflected in the Draft Articles, independently of the qualification of conduct as "criminal". While it remains to be seen whether that will be achieved, there is provisional agreement on including compliance with norms of *jus cogens* in Chapter V of Part 1 of the Draft Articles as a circumstance precluding wrongfulness.[21] That will be a significant step, of equivalent importance in the field of responsibility to the inclusion of Article 53 in the Vienna Convention on the Law of Treaties. It is true that the vehicle of *jus cogens* has rarely, if ever, left the garage of Article 53,[22] and the same may be predicted for the proposed Article 29 *bis* of the Draft Articles on State Responsibility. The legal consequences of peremptory norms in most cases may well be less direct and more subtle than outright invalidity or the suppression of one obligation by another. It is, still, something to have two garages.

Another issue is whether the Draft Articles should deal with countermeasures at all. A number of states (numbering among them certain states which are accustomed to taking countermeasures) take the view that the definition of

19 See J. Crawford, *First Report on State Responsibility* (A/CN.4/490/Add. 1 to 3, May 1998), especially para. 51 and the consideration of different alternatives in Add. 3.

20 See *ILC Report, fiftieth session* (1998) (A/53/10, Suppl.No.10), p. 147, para. 331.

21 See *ILC Report, fifty-first session* (1999) (A/54/10.Suppl.No.10), paras. 316-318.

22 To adopt a metaphor of Ian Brownlie's: *cf.* A Pellet, "Can a State Commit a Crime?" (1999) 10 *EJIL* 425, 428.

countermeasures in Part II is unnecessary and counterproductive. All that is needed is the recognition that countermeasures preclude wrongfulness.[23] This would be an acknowledgment of the *lex lata*, but a very discreet one: a statement *that* there is *lex lata* without any attempt to say *what* it is. But this does not seem a desirable approach. For example it would be difficult to support a statement in Article 33 that necessity may preclude wrongfulness without going on to specify under what conditions it does so,[24] and the same surely applies to countermeasures. Indeed it applies *a fortiori*, since countermeasures are much more often invoked than necessity. Thus the ILC has decided that it will not attempt to reformulate Article 30 in Part I until it has decided whether countermeasures will remain in Part II. If countermeasures are left out of Part II and we revert to a conception of state responsibility as exclusively concerned with reparation and not at all concerned with countermeasures, then those countermeasures which preclude wrongfulness in Chapter V of Part I should be more precisely defined.[25]

This brings us back to the question how countermeasures are to be conceived. As the Court affirmed in its valuable discussion of countermeasures in the *Gabčikovo-Nagymaros* case, countermeasures ought to be seen as instrumental. That is, they are part of a process of obtaining cessation and reparation for wrongful conduct; they do not involve freestanding rights.[26] It is significant that the international community has moved away from the classical terminology of reprisals and towards the notion of countermeasures as temporary, reversible steps taken in response to, and for particular purposes in relation to, prior internationally wrongful conduct. This idea is already reflected in Part 2 and there are good reasons for maintaining it in the "dynamic" context of that Part, rather than limiting it to the "static" context of Part 1.

A remaining problem is that of collective countermeasures. It may be that the law of collective self-defence is not well defined in state practice. But the Court

---

23 See among others comments by the United States and the United Kingdom (Doc. A/CN.4/488, pp. 83-84 and 116-117).

24 The tendency of Government comments on Article 33 was that this should spell out the conditions for invocation of necessity in detail and with rigour: see J. Crawford, *Second Report on State Responsibility* (A/CN.4/498/Add.2, 30 April 1999), para. 282.

25 See J. Crawford, *Second Report on State Responsibility*, (A/CN.4/498/Add.4, 6 July 1999), particularly paras. 33-36 and *ILC Report, fifty-first session* (1999), paras. 438-441 and 448.

26 See *supra*, n. 9.

clarified it to a degree in the *Nicaragua* case, in particular by requiring that measures of collective self-defence be taken at the request of the injured state (the state which is the subject of the armed attack).[27] That must be right in principle, whatever difficulties there may be in the injured state expressing its consent.

The notion of collective countermeasures is more obscure and unstudied. Whatever the position with self-defence, it cannot be limited to interstate relations, as the law of self-defence is normally limited. The interests being protected are wider and more diffuse. In particular they concern not only the interests of states but also those of human groups and individuals, and this creates significant questions of representation which do not normally arise in the context of the interstate use of force.[28] A key point of the definition of the injured state in Article 40 is that it opens up the system to major forms of collective countermeasure. Under the existing text, many states are defined as injured in relation to a single wrongful act and all of those states are apparently entitled severally to take countermeasures under Part II. So every state in the world, in response for example to a breach of fundamental human rights, or many states in the world, in response to a breach of certain multilateral conventions, may be entitled to take countermeasures, and to do so on their own separate account. How the principle of proportionality operates in that situation, what the constraints are on collective countermeasures, is very uncertain.

Again we see that ideas of state responsibility have developed within the matrix of bilateral relations and so-called "subjective" rights. But there must be a more differentiated approach to responsibility than this. Formulations which may be appropriate to classical bilateral responsibility are not necessarily appropriate for solidary obligations, especially obligations to the international community as a whole. Article 40 is a clear illustration: it fails to distinguish the two categories, and yet it seems that the way forward must involve a distinction between them. Accepting, on the basis of the *Barcelona Traction* dictum, the proposition that there is a legal interest of states at large in respect of violations of certain obligations, to conceive that legal interest in the same way as the

27 *Case Concerning Military and Paramilitary Activities in and Against Nicaragua (Merits)*, ICJ Reports, 1986, p. 14 at p. 120 (para. 232).

28 As noted by Judge Vereshchetin in his separate opinion in the *East Timor* case, ICJ Reports, 1995, p. 90 at 135-8.

subjective rights of an individual state in a bilateral relationship with another state seems a fundamental error. It has the effect, among others, of turning human rights first into collective state rights, and then into individual state powers of reaction, and of doing so *a priori* – which is all rather problematic.

Thus there is an important task ahead in dealing with collective countermeasures. What happens if a collective countermeasure is taken when the state which is most directly affected does not want that countermeasure to be taken, or is satisfied with the situation on the basis of some lesser form of reparation? To what extent are third states entitled to intrude on a dispute settlement process, in respect of a breach of a norm of community interest, which is in fact of primary concern to another state? These questions you might think go well beyond the law of state responsibility. But just as the law of the Charter has been, as it were, flowing up the rivers of state responsibility in ways previously unforeseen, so the process may be happening in reverse.

Limits to the Powers of the Security Council and the Question of Accountability

Chair: *Abdul G. Koroma*
Judge, International Court of Justice

3

INTERNATIONAL LAW LIMITS TO THE SECURITY COUNCIL

Nicolas Angelet▪

I INTRODUCTION

There is a widespread view amongst practitioners and scholars of international law that the Security Council's action under Chapter VII of the Charter must be kept within bounds so as to protect the legitimate interests of individual Member States. In the same vein, the international law limits to the Security Council are frequently related to the International Court of Justice's power of judicial review.

However, the scarcity of jurisdictional links hampers the development of a constitutional system protecting the interests of individual Member states through judicial review. In these circumstances, the major power of control lies with the Member states themselves. The Organization of African Unity's refusal further to apply the United Nations economic sanctions against Libya,[1] and the subsequent adoption of Security Council Resolution 1192 (1998), testify to the effectiveness of such control.

As a consequence, it also appears to be in the Security Council's *interest* to base its decisions on the principles and rules of international law, so as to foster the acceptance of these decisions by the 'target' entity (the entity whose behaviour constitutes a threat to international peace and security), as well as

▪ Avocat at the Brussels Bar; Research Fellow at the International Law Center, Université libre de Bruxelles; Lecturer, Université libre de Bruxelles.

1 Doc. AHG/Dec. (XXXIV) of 10 June 1998.

V. Gowlland-Debbas (ed.), *United Nations Sanctions and International Law*, p. 71-82.

by the United Nations Members in general.[2] This is the more so in view of the Security Council's failing procedural legitimacy and the problems concerning its composition, which limit the Council's capacity to generate legitimate decisions on the basis of a discretionary power.[3]

This has a number of important consequences. Whether it really is in the Security Council's interest to base its decisions on international law also depends on whether international law is flexible enough to allow the Security Council to carry out its duties for the maintenance of international peace and security. Further, if this is the case, the Council must also be *seen* to rely on the rules and principles of international law.

II The Principle of Proportionality

A first limit to the Security Council's discretion under Chapter VII of the Charter flows from the proportionality principle, according to which the Council's action must be appropriate and necessary for the achievement of its stated purposes (typically, the removal of a threat to the peace), and may not affect other interests to an extent which is disproportionate to the advantage obtained or pursued.[4] At the very least, the Security Council may not take any action which is unnecessary for the removal of a threat to the peace.

2 See also R. Higgins, "The Place of International Law in the Settlement of Disputes by the Security Council", (1970) 64 *AJIL* 3.

3 *Cf* Th. Franck, *The Structure of Impartiality* (New York, 1968), pp. 168-169 and *The Power of Legitimacy Among Nations* (New York, Oxford, 1990), pp. 61 and 64. See also K. Doehring, "Der Verlust der Autorität des Rechts als Problem der aktuellen Rechtsentwicklung", in T. Stein (ed.), *Die Autorität des Rechts* (Heidelberg, 1985), pp. 79-80.

4 See *i.a.* M. Bothe, "Les limites des pouvoirs du Conseil de sécurité", in R.J. Dupuy (ed.), *The Development of the Role of the Security Council – Peace-Keeping and Peace-Building, Workshop of the Hague Academy of International Law* (The Hague, 1992), pp.135-136. *Cf* however R. Higgins, "International Law and the Avoidance, Containment and Resolution of Disputes – General Course on Public International Law", *Recueil des Cours* (1991-V), pp. 296-298; V. Gowlland-Debbas, "Security Council Enforcement Action and Issues of State Responsibility", (1994) 43 *ICLQ* 62, whose analysis however relates to the proportionality between the offence reacted against and the reaction itself, rather than to the question whether the means are reasonably related to the aims pursued.

This principle is reflected in Article 42 of the Charter, which provides that, "Should the Council consider that measures provided for in Article 41 *would be inadequate or have proved to be inadequate*, it may take such action by air, sea, or land forces as may be *necessary* to maintain or restore international peace and security". The Council also calls upon States to use such measures "commensurate with the specific circumstances as may be necessary" to achieve the Council's objectives,[5] and Members of the Council insist on the "reasonable and proportionate" character of a given measure.[6]

Admittedly, the proportionality principle only allows for a limited protection of the legitimate interests of the target State or entity. The application of the proportionality principle is based on a largely subjective appreciation of the facts of any particular case, as well as of its likely evolution. Further, the Council's power to determine the existence of a threat to the peace, and thus, to choose and to concretize the objectives of its action, often makes it possible for the Council to pre-determine the outcome of the proportionality test: while the creation of an international criminal tribunal might be regarded as unnecessary or counter-productive for the purpose of halting an ongoing armed conflict, the same measure can hardly be criticized if it is presented as a measure of post-conflict peace-building.

This is not to say, however, that the proportionality principle cannot reinforce the legitimacy of Security Council decisions. Indeed, the principle can often be concretised on the basis of other rules of customary and conventional international law. In the Haitian case, for example, the Sanctions Committee considered the issue of shipment of goods belonging to diplomatic and consular missions in Haiti, as well as personal effects of the personnel of such missions, and declared that the sanctions against Haiti "should not apply to the functioning of foreign diplomatic and consular missions in Haiti, which remain subject to the Vienna Conventions on Diplomatic and Consular relations, so that their normal functioning would remain unimpeded".[7] While this exception to United Nations economic sanctions is presumably based on the proportionality principle, its existence as well as its scope are equally determined by rules of conventional international law. This increases the normative density of the proportionality

5 SC Res. 787 (1992) of 16 November 1992, para. 12.
6 See *e.g.* S/PV.3117 of 2 October 1992, p. 3-4/5.
7 UN Doc. SC/5862 of 15 June 1994.

principle, and thus compensates for the Security Council's lack of procedural legitimacy.

The Sanctions Committee's ruling, however, also indicates that international law limits to the powers of the Security Council do not always determine the drafting of the Council's resolutions. They may be implied, and appear at a later stage, either in the Sanctions Committees or in the implementing measures taken by the Member states. What is more, such implied limits may remain hidden for ever. In a future case, the Council or the Committee might refuse to grant the exemption for diplomatic missions in the sanctioned State. In that case, no limit to the Council's discretionary power would appear from the decision taken. However, the decision not to grant the exemption should, and probably would be based on a comparison between the Haiti case and the case at hand, and in this reasoning, the Vienna Conventions on diplomatic and consular relations would still have a central role to play. The limit to the Council's discretion would thus be in the production process, rather than in the product itself.

The Council possibly relies on international law more frequently than it appears to do. This is, in a way, reassuring, but also problematic to the extent that these hidden limits to the Council's discretion fail to contribute to the legitimacy of its decisions. If the major power of control lies with the Member states, the Security Council must also be *seen* to rely on the rules and principles of international law.

III THE PRINCIPLES AND PURPOSES OF THE UNITED NATIONS

A second constitutional limit to the Council's powers stems from Article 24 of the Charter, which provides that in discharging its duties the Council shall act in accordance with the Purposes and Principles of the United Nations. This provision limits the Council's discretion in the determination of the objectives of its action, or in other words, in respect of the decisions which may be addressed to the target State or entity. But it equally limits the Council's discretion in respect of the enforcement measures, *i.e.*, in respect of the decisions addressed to the Member states under Article 41 of the Charter and of the authorizations for States to take military action.[8]

This limit to the Council's discretion notably applies in respect of fundamental human rights, which have become an integral part of the law of the Charter well beyond the terms of Article 1, paragraph 3 of the Charter.[9] In the case concerning *Legal consequences for States of the continued presence of South Africa in Namibia (South West Africa) notwithstanding Security Council Resolution 276 (1970)*, the International Court of Justice thus declared:

> "To establish ... and to enforce, distinctions, exclusions, restrictions and limitations exclusively based on grounds of race, colour, descent or national or ethnic origin which constitute a denial of fundamental human rights *is a flagrant violation of the purposes and principles of the Charter.*"[10]

Again, in the case concerning the *United States diplomatic and consular staff in Tehran*, the Court judged that

> "Wrongfully to deprive human beings of their freedom and to subject them to physical constraint in conditions of hardship is in itself *manifestly incompatible with the principles of the Charter of the United Nations*, as well as with the fundamental principles enunciated in the Universal Declaration of Human Rights."[11]

This bypass is, admittedly, not indispensable in respect of the peremptory norms of human rights law, which may also be considered as binding upon the Security Council on the basis of the principle *nemo plus juris transferre potest quam*

---

8 *Cf* Professor Dominicé's analysis, according to which the authorization to use force creates a "horizontal" relationship between the UN and the 'target' State, so that the military forces acting on behalf of the United Nations are bound to comply with customary international law: see Chr.Dominicé, "Le Conseil de sécurité et le droit international", (1996) *JRMP* 198-200.

9 See also T. Meron, *Human Rights and Humanitarian Norms as Customary Law* (Oxford, 1989), p. 82, referring to L. Sohn; *Restatement of the Law Third, Foreign Relations Law of the United States* (1987), Para. 701, Comment (d).

10 *Legal consequences for States of the continued presence of South Africa in Namibia (South West Africa) notwithstanding Security Council Resolution 276 (1970)* (Advisory Opinion), ICJ Reports, 1971, p. 57, para. 131 (emphasis added). See also *ibid.*, para. 129.

11 *Case concerning United States diplomatic and consular staff in Tehran, Judgment,* ICJ Reports, 1980, p. 42, para. 91 (emphasis added).

ipse habet, or by reason of the very nature of *jus cogens*. The concretization of the Charter Principles could however also be relied upon in respect of other rules of international law which are not peremptory in nature. In Resolution 667 (1990), for instance, the Security Council considered that Iraq's violations of diplomatic inviolability and immunity

> "strike at the root of the conduct of international relations in accordance with the Charter of the United Nations".[12]

This indication that the Security Council considers diplomatic inviolability and immunity to be part of the principles of the United Nations, is further confirmed by the Security Council Presidential Statement made following the bombing of the Chinese embassy in Belgrade by NATO forces. In that Statement,

> "The Council, *bearing in mind the Charter of the United Nations*, reaffirms that the principle of the inviolability of the diplomatic personnel and premises must be respected *in all cases in accordance with internationally accepted norms*."[13]

Even though this Statement does not expressly address the issue of Security Council powers, the reference made to the United Nations Charter, and even more so, the statement that diplomatic inviolability must be respected "in all cases", are bound to limit the Council's power to set aside diplomatic inviolability on the basis of Chapter VII of the Charter.

This is not to say that diplomatic inviolabilities and other rules and principles which are part of the 'law of the Charter' cannot in any way be affected by Security Council decisions under Chapter VII. Rather, the setting aside of such rules must be in accordance with the "internationally accepted norms" referred to in the Presidential Statement of 14 May 1999. The question will thus be whether the situation giving rise to the Council's action justifies any limitation in the enjoyment of conventional or customary rights in accordance with the applicable law, including the law of treaties, the law of state responsibility, or general principles of law. It should not lightly be presumed that this body of rules hampers the Security Council in performing its duties under the Charter. If, for instance, the law of diplomatic relations prevents the Council from deciding that a diplomat violating a United Nations arms embargo shall be

12 SC Res. 667 (1990) of 16 September 1990, preambular para. 6.
13 UN Doc. S/PRST/1999/12 of 14 May 1999 (emphasis added).

prosecuted in the receiving State, this can hardly be regarded as an obstacle to the maintenance of international peace and security. Rather, the law of diplomatic relations indicates that the declaration *persona non grata* and the severance of diplomatic relations "are, by their nature, entirely efficacious"[14] to guarantee the effectiveness of an arms embargo in the face of an abuse of diplomatic privileges and immunities.

IV Decisions Addressed to the 'Target' State or Entity

A third limit to Security Council powers flows from the scope of Chapter VII itself, as further defined in Chapter I of the Charter. It relates to the decisions which the Council may address to the 'target' State or entity – although the issue may equally arise in the absence of an explicit decision addressed to the 'target' State or entity. This limit to the Council's powers is thus narrower than the previous one, insofar as it does not concern the decisions requesting or authorizing the Member states to take coercive measures.[15] On the other hand, it has a wider scope than the limit previously analysed, to the extent that it equally relates to rules of international law which are not part of the Principles of the United Nations or the 'law of the Charter'.

The draft version of Chapter VIII B (which later became Chapter VII of the Charter) adopted by the Great Powers at Dumbarton Oaks would have made it possible for the Security Council to settle disputes and situations by means of compulsory decisions.[16] This draft was, however, amended at the Conference of San Francisco so as to deprive the Council of that power. This resulted in Article 39 of the Charter, which *i.a.* provides that the Council "shall make recommendations, or decide what measures shall be taken in accordance with Articles 41 and 42, to maintain or restore international peace and security". The reference to Articles 41 and 42 was added to indicate that the Council would not be entitled to address compulsory decisions to the 'target' State so as to settle the dispute or situation. Rather, the coercive measures were to pave

14 *Case concerning United States Diplomatic and Consular Staff in Tehran, Judgment,* ICJ Reports, 1980, para. 86.

15 On this cardinal distinction between decisions enunciating coercive measures and injunctions addressed to the State threatening international peace and security, see Dominicé, "Le Conseil de sécurité", *supra* n. 8, in particular p. 202 ff.

16 *UNCIO*, vol. 3, Doc. 1 G/1, p. 14-15.

the way to a settlement on the basis of Chapter VI of the Charter. This was expressly confirmed by the report of Committee 3/III,[17] as well as by the United States and United Kingdom representatives at the Conference.[18]

This also led to a rephrasing of Article 2, paragraph 7 of the Charter: the draft providing that the principle of non-intervention "shall not prejudice the application of Chapter VIII, Section B"[19] was amended so as to limit the exception's scope to "the application of enforcement measures under Chapter VII". Further, this is not contradicted by Article 1, paragraph 1 of the Charter, which provides that one of the purposes of the United Nations is:

> "to take effective collective measures for the prevention and removal of threats to the peace etc., and to bring about by peaceful means, and in conformity with the principles of justice and international law, adjustment or settlement of international disputes and situations".

The reference to the principles of justice and international law only appears in the second part of the paragraph, which relates to the peaceful settlement of disputes and situations. The requirement does not apply to the collective measures taken by the Council to prevent or remove threats to the peace. However, this was only intended not to restrain the Council in its policing task, and did not in any way empower the Council to impose new obligations on a State threatening international peace and security. The Rapporteur of Committee I/1 thus declared:

> "(..) the Organization should (..) promptly stop any breach of the peace or remove it. *After that, it can proceed to find a just adjustment or settlement of the dispute or situation.* When the Organization has used the power given to it and the force at its disposal to stop war, *then it can find the latitude to apply the principles of justice and international law*, or can assist the contending parties to find a peaceful solution.
>
> The concept of justice and international law can thus find a more appropriate place in context with the last part of the paragraph dealing with disputes and situations.

---

17 *UNCIO.*, vol. 12, p. 507, Doc. 881 III/3/46 of 10 June 1945, at p. 6. See also *UNCIO*, vol. 12, p. 162, Doc. 1027 III/2/31 (1) of 16 June 1945.

18 *UNCIO*, vol. 6, p. 25, Doc. 1006 I/6 of 15 June 1945, at p. 14 (United Kingdom). See also *UNCIO*, vol. 6, p. 29-30, same Doc., p. 18-19 (United States).

19 *UNCIO*, vol. 3, p. 623, Doc. 2 G/29 of 5 May 1945, at p. 2.

> (..) *There was no intention to let this notion lose any of its weight or strength, as an over-ruling norm of the whole Charter.*"[20]

In the view of the authors of the Charter, the Security Council's power to take 'quasi-judicial' decisions would thus be limited to the hypothesis of agression. The terms of the Charter however allow for a slightly different view, enlarging the Security Council's power to take 'quasi-judicial' decisions. This enlargement is indispensable in view of the fact that the Council's action under Chapter VII of the Charter frequently involves peremptory norms of international law (other than the prohibition of agression), the application of which cannot be made subject to the agreement of the States concerned in the context of Chapter VI of the Charter. Apart from that, the enforcement of international law may be regarded as a necessary means of maintaining international peace and security, in particular when a settlement under Chapter VI of the Charter would cause undue delays or would weaken a conventional or customary regime which is itself essential for the maintenance of international peace and security.

The fundamental principle, however, remains that the Security Council may not create new obligations for the target of its action under Chapter VII of the Charter. The Council may, in other words, act as a law-enforcing body, but not as a legislator. This is not contradicted by Article 103 of the Charter, which provides that in the event of a conflict between the obligations of the Member states under the Charter and their obligations under any other international agreement, their obligations under the Charter shall prevail. Article 103 only comes into play in the face of "obligations of the Member states under the Charter". These obligations are defined elsewhere in the Charter, and *i.a.* depend on its Chapters I and VII defining the powers of the Security Council.

This limit to the Council's discretion has important consequences in respect of the appreciation of facts and the rules concerning evidence. Generally speaking, the Council's powers under Chapter VII may be resorted to on the basis of a limited knowledge of the facts. It may be based on prognoses, as in the case of a threat to the peace, or on the basis of a limited knowledge of the facts, as when the Council determines the existence of a breach of the peace without identifying the culprit. Quasi-judicial decisions must, on the contrary,

---

20 *UNCIO*, vol. 6, p. 453-454, Doc. 944 I/1/34 (1) of 13 June 1945 (emphasis added). See also *UNCIO*, vol. 6, p. 22, Doc. 1006 I/6 of 15 June 1945.

be based on the rules of evidence prevailing under general international law, and many Security Council decisions could be criticized in this respect.[21]

This is not to say that the principles and rules of international law set undue limits to the Security Council's action for the maintenance of the peace. In respect of the enforcement of primary rules of international law, the doctrine of abuse of rights, on which the Council relied as soon as 1951 to condemn Egypt's blockade of the Suez Canal,[22] may play an important role. The existence of a threat to international peace and security can, indeed, often be related to an abuse of rights. The prohibition on abuse of rights thus makes it possible for the Security Council to take account of the legitimate interests of the international community, but also limits the Council's discretion in various ways. First, a State may not be presumed to abuse its rights. As a consequence, unless an abuse of rights is duly substantiated, the Security Council should respect the target State's rights under customary or conventional international law. This may make it easier for Members of the Council to resist the Western Permanent Members sponsoring a resolution, whose *de facto* persuasive force may affect the Council's legitimacy as much as the veto right. Further, under the abuse of rights doctrine, the Council will have to investigate whether the rights relied upon by the 'target' State may be exercised in a way which is compatible with the rights of the other States concerned (or in other words, with the requirements of international peace and security), and conversely, whether the other States' rights (or international peace and security) may be maintained without affecting the target State's rights under customary or conventional international law. The abuse of rights doctrine would thus substantially limit the Council's discretion, without however affecting its capacity to take efficient action to restore or maintain international peace and security.

Finally, the Security Council may also enforce secundary rules of public international law under Chapter VII of the Charter. While this entails the creation

21 See, *e.g.*, the statements made on the legal status of the boundary treaty between Iraq and Kuwait of 1963. The Indian representative stated that Iraq and Kuwait "both took the precaution to register their agreement with the United Nations" (S/PV.2981, p. 78), while the U.S. representative declared that the agreement was registered by Kuwait only (*loc. cit.*, p. 84/85-86). Other, more crucial points were not even addressed. Likewise, the debates on the adoption of Resolutions 1044 (1996) and 1054 (1996) requesting the Sudan to extradite alleged terrorists ignore international legal standards relating to the burden of proof: see S/PV.3627, *i.a.* p. 4 (Sudan) and 14 (United States).

22 See SC Res. 95 (1951), paras. 5-7.

of 'new' obligations for the target State, such obligations nevertheless flow from the application of international law. Failing an agreement between the States concerned, the form and amount of reparation may be settled by an international tribunal, and there is thus no reason why the Security Council, which is entitled to enforce primary rules of international law, would not have the power to apply the law of State responsibility.[23] This offers an adequate basis for many of the measures taken in Resolution 687 (1991) concerning Iraq. A number of them may, more specifically, be regarded as guarantees of non-repetition. Again, this figure allows the Security Council to take post-conflict measures for the purpose of maintaining and restoring international peace and security. It limits the Council's discretion without affecting its ability to carry out its duties for the maintenance of international peace and security.

This, of course, merely means that the Security Council is *competent* to take binding decisions for the purpose of settling disputes and situations in accordance with international law. Another question is whether the Council as a political organ is also *qualified* to do so, or in practical terms, whether the Council is able to render *authoritative* decisions on questions of a legal nature. Article 36, paragraph 3 of the Charter, which requests the Council to take into consideration that legal disputes should as a general rule be referred by the parties to the International Court, indicates that the Council's qualification in this field is rather limited. The Council can however solve this problem without losing control over its agenda by requesting advisory opinions to the International Court of Justice or, what may be more feasible in political and practical terms, by delegating the decision-making on specific legal issues to qualified subsidiary organs or by openly taking expert advise.

V CONCLUSION

In conclusion, international law limits the Security Council's powers in many ways, without however affecting the efficiency of its action. International law

---

23 See however *contra*: G. Gaja, "Réflexions sur le rôle du Conseil de sécurité dans le nouvel ordre mondial – A propos des rapports entre maintien de la paix et crimes internationaux des Etats", (1993) 97 *RGDIP* 308; B. Graefrath, "Iraqi Reparations and the Security Council", (1995) 55 *ZaöRV* 13 and 18; and in more cautious terms, Chr. Dominicé, "Le Conseil de sécurité et l'accès aux pouvoirs qu'il reçoit du Chapitre VII de la Charte des Nations Unies", (1995) 5 *RSDIE* 420-421.

itself makes it possible to take account of the special circumstances which the Council often invokes to justify its action under Chapter VII of the Charter. What international law requires is a reasoned approach, based on generally recognized legal authority. In view of the Security Council's failing procedural legitimacy and the problems concerning its composition, making reference to legal principles which are accepted by all the United Nations Members is the best means for the Council to foster the legitimacy of its decisions.

4

JUDICIAL REVIEW OF SANCTIONS

John Dugard▪

The question whether the International Court of Justice (hereinafter ICJ) may review resolutions of the Security Council adopted under Chapter VII of the UN Charter has recently received attention in *Lockerbie (Provisional Measures)*[1] and *Application of the Genocide Convention (Provisional Measures).*[2] In the former case the ICJ was called upon to decide whether Security Council resolutions under Chapter VII[3] directing Libya to surrender the persons allegedly responsible for the bombing of PanAm Flight 103 over Lockerbie to the United States or the United Kingdom precluded the ICJ from finding that Libya was entitled to try its own nationals in terms of the Montreal Convention on aerial sabotage. In the latter case the question was raised whether a Security Council resolution[4] imposing an arms embargo on Bosnia might be reviewed on the ground that it impaired the right of self-defence against a genocidal aggressor.

It is not surprising that the power of the ICJ to review Chapter VII resolutions of the Security Council has only recently been raised before the Court. During the Cold War so few resolutions were adopted under Chapter VII that there was

---

▪ Professor of Public International Law, University of Leiden; Emeritus Professor of Law, University of the Witwatersrand; Member of the International Law Commission.

1 *Case Concerning Questions of Interpretation and Application of the 1971 Montreal Convention Arising from the Aerial Incident at Lockerbie* (Libya v UK), ICJ Reports, 1992, p.3.

2 *Case Concerning the Application of the Genocide Convention* (Bosnia and Herzegovina v Yugoslavia), ICJ Reports, 1993, 3, p.325.

3 Sc Res. 731, 748 (1992).

4 Sc Res. 713 (1991).

V. Gowlland-Debbas (ed.), *United Nations Sanctions and International Law*, p. 83-91.

little incentive to consider this matter. The increase in the number of such resolutions adopted in the last decade has, however, encouraged debate over the question and prompted states to raise the subject before the ICJ. The perception on the part of some states that the Security Council is governed and directed by an unrepresentative elite has probably fuelled this new interest in judicial review. Considerations of this kind ensure that demands for judicial review of Security Council actions will grow. There is, moreover, a new factor to be reckoned with: the emergence of powerful non-governmental organizations (NGO's) determined to use the ICJ to advance their goals – as illustrated by the role of NGO's in the advisory proceedings before the ICJ on *The Legality of the Threat or Use of Nuclear Weapons*.[5] Public interest lawyers in domestic societies are bolder and more innovative than "hired" lawyers. They know that the key to success, the furtherance of the cause they espouse, is judicial review. There is no reason to believe that the new international public interest Bar will behave differently.

Of course it is open to the ICJ to simply assert that there is no power of judicial review of Security Council resolutions under Chapter VII. Certainly there is judicial precedent for this position. In its Advisory Opinion in the case concerning *Certain Expenses of the United Nations (Article 17, paragraph 2, of the Charter)*, the Court declared:

> "In the legal systems of States, there is often some procedure for determining the validity of even a legislative or governmental act, but no analogous procedure is to be found in the structure of the United Nations. Proposals made during the drafting of the Charter to place the ultimate authority to interpret the Charter in the International Court of Justice were not accepted."[6]

Again, in its Advisory Opinion on *Legal Consequences for States of the Continued Presence of South Africa in Namibia (South West Africa) notwithstanding Security Council Resolution 276 (1970)*, the Court reiterated that:

> "Undoubtedly, the Court does not possess powers of judicial review or appeal in respect of the decisions taken by the United Nations organs concerned."[7]

5 ICJ Reports, 1996 (I), p.226.
6 ICJ Reports, 1962, p.168.
7 ICJ Reports, 1971, p.45.

These dicta are premised on the silence of the UN Charter on judicial review and on the *travaux préparatoires*, which saw a Belgian proposal for review rejected. Most recently, Judge Schwebel has stated, in his dissenting opinion in *Lockerbie (Preliminary Objections)*:

> "It does not follow from the facts that the decisions of the Security Council must be in accordance with the Charter, and that the International Court of Justice is the principal judicial organ of the United Nations, that the Court is empowered to ensure that the Council's decisions do accord with the Charter. To hold that it does so follow is a monumental *non sequitur*, which overlooks the truth that, in many legal systems, national and international, the subjection of the acts of an organ to law by no means entails subjection of the legality of its actions to judicial review....[8] The Court is not generally so empowered, and it is particularly without power to overrule or undercut decisions of the Security Council made by it in pursuance of its authority under Articles 39, 41 and 42 of the Charter to determine the existence of any threat to the peace and to decide upon responsive measures to be taken to maintain or restore international peace and security."[9]

In my view this approach – total rejection of judicial review – is unlikely to prevail. There are too many contrary arguments in favour of judicial review; arguments that are likely to gather momentum as the Security Council adopts more Chapter VII resolutions and the United Nations remains incapable of addressing the problem of legitimacy over the composition of the Security Council. These arguments include the failure of the Charter to exclude the competence of the ICJ to "compete" with the Security Council as it does in respect of the General Assembly in Article 12 of the Charter; the inevitable ambiguity of *travaux préparatoires*; and the limits placed on the powers of the Security Council in Articles 1 and 24 of the Charter, which require the Council to secure the maintenance of international peace and security "in conformity with the principles of justice and international law". The Security Council has interpreted the Charter liberally to give itself implied powers – notably in respect of peacekeeping and peace enforcement where the Council appears to have created a new Chapter – Chapter VI½ – to authorize its actions. There is no reason why the ICJ should not follow this example in respect of its own powers.

8 (1998) 37 *ILM* 627.
9 *Ibid.* 625.

Clearly there are limits on the powers of the Security Council. It is not above the law. This is made clear by Judge *ad hoc* Sir Elihu Lauterpacht in the *Application of the Genocide Convention (Provisional Measures)*:

> "The concept of *jus cogens* operates as a concept superior to both customary international law and treaty. The relief which Article 103 of the Charter may give the Security Council in case of conflict between one of its decisions and an operative treaty obligation cannot – as a matter of simple hierarchy of norms – extend to a conflict between a Security Council resolution and *jus cogens*. Indeed, one only has to state the opposite proposition thus – that a Security Council resolution may even require participation in genocide – for its unacceptability to be apparent."[10]

Once this is accepted it is a short step to the finding that the Court is the appropriate body to determine whether the Council has exceeded its powers. This is borne out by the dissenting opinion of Judge Fitzmaurice in the 1971 Advisory Opinion on *Namibia* when he stated:

> "These limitations on the powers of the Security Council are necessary because of the all too great ease with which any acutely controversial international situation can be represented as involving a latent threat to peace and security, even where it is really too remote genuinely to constitute one. Without these limitations, the functions of the Security Council could be used for purposes never originally intended, – and the present case is a very good illustration of this: for not only was the Security Council not acting under Chapter VII of the Charter (which it obviously could not do – though it remains to be seen by what means and upon what grounds the necessary threat to, or breach of the peace, or act of aggression will be determined to exist); – not only was there no threat to peace and security other than such as might be artificially created as a pretext for the realization of ulterior purposes, – but the whole operation, which will not necessarily end there, had as its object the abrogation of the Mandatory's rights of territorial administration, in order to secure (not eventually but very soon) the transformation of the mandated territory into, and its emergence as, the sovereign independent Sate of 'Namibia'. This is what is declared in terms, not only in Resolution 2145 itself, but also in the subsequent Assembly Resolution 2248 (S-V) of 1967, specifying June 1968 as the intended date of transfer, – and this is par excellence the type of purpose, in

10 *Supra* n. 2, ICJ Reports, 1993, at 440.

> promoting which, the Security Council (and *a fortiori* the Assembly) exceeds its competence, and so acts *ultra vires*."[11]

Probably the best evidence for the proposition that the powers of the Security Council are subject to judicial review is the decision of the Appeals Chamber of the International Criminal Tribunal for the Former Yugoslavia (ICTY) in *Prosecutor v Tadic (Jurisdiction)*[12] in which it was held that the Tribunal could consider whether it had been lawfully established by the Security Council. In finding that it had been lawfully established the Tribunal held that the situation in the Former Yugoslavia did constitute a 'threat to peace" within the meaning of Article 39[13] and that the establishment of the ICTY was an appropriate measure not involving the use of force under Article 41 for the restoration of peace.[14]

Finally there is the domestic law analogy. Many domestic courts have exercised powers of judicial review without express constitutional licence where it is clear that there are limits on the exercise of legislative or executive power.[15] The decision of the US Supreme Court in *Marbury v Madison* is testimony to this.[16]

I THE JUDICIAL DECISION AS AN EXERCISE IN CHOICE

It is trite that the judicial decision is an exercise in choice where there are tenable arguments for and against a particular proposition. Where there are compelling arguments in support of both propositions it is not uncommon for a court, national or international, to seek a *via media*. In the present case there are persuasive arguments that have been, and may be, raised for and against judicial review of Security Council resolutions. It is not unlikely therefore that the ICJ will seek to reach some Solomonic compromise. My prediction is that the ICJ will choose to exercise judicial review, but subject to severe restraints.

11 *Supra* n.7, at 294, para 116. See too the dissenting opinion of Judge Gros, *ibid* 340, para 34; and the dissenting opinion of Judge Bedjaoui in *Lockerbie (Provisional Measures), supra* n.1 at 152-3.
12 (1996) 35 ILM 35.
13 *Ibid* at 43, para 30.
14 *Ibid* at 44-45, paras 32-40.
15 See José E Alvarez, "Judging the Security Council", (1996) 90 *AJIL* 1, particularly at n. 81.
16 5 US (1 Cranch) 137 (1803).

The debate therefore shifts from *whether* the Court will exercise judicial review to *how much.*

In predicting *how much* review will be exercised it is necessary to distinguish between two types of Security Council action: first, the decision that a particular situation constitutes a threat to the peace under Article 39 in respect of which some sanction should be imposed; and, secondly, the nature of the sanction selected. In the first case one may speak of *substantive* review and in the second of *incidental* review.

(a) Substantive Review

I suspect that the ICJ will balk at the idea of reviewing findings under Article 39 and the decision to impose Chapter VII measures.[17] Where the Security Council clearly acts in bad faith, and its decisions amount to an abuse of right, the Court should interfere[18] but in practice this is unlikely to happen. The composition of the Council and the veto power ensure a diversity of opinion likely to obstruct such a manipulation of power. (In this respect the Security Council differs from national executives in which, frequently, only one political party is represented.) In any event it would not be improper for the Court to give the Council a wide "margin of appreciation"- as the European Court of Human Rights does in respect of national executives – in respect of its decision that international peace is threatened and that some sanction should be imposed.

(b) Incidental Review

The ICJ is more likely to exercise judicial review in respect of the kind of measures adopted by the Security Council to restore international peace. This was precisely what the ICTY did in *Tadic* when it examined the appropriateness of the establishment of the Tribunal as a measure to restore international peace.[19]

Here considerations of proportionality might be examined by the Court. If a particular form of sanctions results in injury to innocent civilians or causes

17 See the statement of Judge *ad hoc* Sir Elihu Lauterpacht in the *Application of the Genocide Convention (Provisional Measures), supra*, n. 10, at 439, para 99.

18 See *supra*, n.11; Vera Gowlland-Debbas "The Relationship between the International Court of Justice and the Security Council in the Light of the *Lockerbie* Case", (1994) 88 *AJIL* 643, especially at n. 105-110.

19 *Supra,* n.12-14.

serious harm to the environment and has no discernible impact on the targeted delinquent regime, would it be improper for the Court to say that the measures taken are disproportionate to the goals to be achieved?

Presumably the Security Council has the competence to override rules of customary international law. But the question may be asked whether this competence extends to norms of *jus cogens*[20] or to fundamental institutional principles, such as that of *aut dedere aut judicare* in the context of extradition.

It is indisputable that the Security Council has a fact-finding power under Article 39. But at times the Council assumes a judicial role. For instance, in Resolution 687 of 3 April 1991, the Council, acting under Chapter VII, decided that Iraq

> "is *liable under international law* for any direct loss, damage, including environmental damage and the depletion of natural resources, or injury to foreign governments, nationals and corporations, as a result of Iraq's unlawful invasion and occupation of Kuwait."[21]

Is this appropriate? Surely it would be more appropriate for the Court to make such a decision?

Here too the Security Council should be given a "margin of appreciation". For example, it would not have been appropriate for the ICJ to review the decision of the Security Council to move from economic sanctions to force against Iraq in 1990/1991.[22] However, there are, as I have suggested, circumstances in which a "margin" test should not be allowed to protect the Council from review.

II Predicting the Court's Behaviour

International Court judges do not like being subjected to appraisal and prediction in terms of the tenets of the school of American legal realism.[23] Both the political nature of their task and the method of their election suggest, however,

20 See *supra*, n.10.
21 Para 16 (emphasis added).
22 Sc Res 678 of 29 November 1990.
23 See the present author's attempt at such an analysis in "The Nuclear Tests Cases and the South West Africa Cases: Some Realism about the International Judicial Decision", (1976) 16 *Virginia Journal of International Law* 463.

that such a jurisprudential analysis is appropriate. Certainly it would contribute to a greater transparency about the functioning of this Court.

The ICJ is not an activist Court. There are good reasons for this, particularly the fact that in contentious proceedings the parties before it are sovereign states. Thus it is unlikely to adopt an activist approach to judicial review of Security Council action.

There are sound policy reasons for judicial restraint. If judicial review of Security Council action becomes the vogue, desirable community action may be irreparably delayed while the target state challenges the lawfulness of that action. Where, for example, the Council authorizes states to use force to urgently avert a humanitarian catastrophe it would be disastrous to encourage judicial review. A warning of this danger is given by Judge Schwebel in his dissent in *Lockerbie (Preliminary Objections)*.[24]

Judges of the International Court consciously or subconsciously reflect national positions and as national positions toward the Security Council change it is not unlikely that these new attitudes may be adopted by judges. Today there is a growing disenchantment among some states, particularly developing states, with the composition and actions of the Security Council. Rightly or wrongly, they perceive the Security Council to be unrepresentative and subject to the dictates of a powerful elite. Judges from these countries may believe that a legitimate function of the Court is to exercise judicial review of Security Council action in order to protect the majority of states against the minority – the reverse of the inspiration for judicial review in domestic societies where review is exercised to protect the minority against majoritarianism.

Failure to hold out some prospect of judicial review to disenchanted states may prompt them to refuse to comply with Security Council measures. Indeed there are suggestions that this may already be happening in the case of Iraq. This is a policy consideration in favour of review.

That judicial review of Security Council action is theoretically possible seems irrefutable. Whether it is desirable, and if so in what circumstances, are ques-

24 *Supra* n. 8, at 625. See too Marcella David, "Passport to Justice: Internationalizing the Political Question Doctrine for Application in the World Court", (1999) 40 *Harvard International Law Journal* 81, particularly at notes 174-184.

tions that admit of no easy answers. The subject is, however, high on the agenda of international law and one that seems bound to challenge the International Court in the years ahead.

Assessing Alternatives to Collective Economic Sanctions

Chair: *Georges Abi-Saab*
Honorary Professor, Graduate Institute of International Studies

5

UNILATERAL VERSUS COLLECTIVE SANCTIONS: AN AMERICAN'S PERCEPTION

Andreas F. Lowenfeld[■]

There is no doubt that the United States has been the strongest proponent of economic sanctions since World War II – in connection with the Cold War in its various shapes: in response to terrorism as directed from Libya, Iran, Syria, perhaps Afghanistan, and other countries; in response to suppression of democracy, as in Haiti and Yugoslavia; and in response to forbidden arms build-up, as in Iraq.

Successive United States administrations have preferred to implement sanctions on a multilateral basis, both to have the cover of a collective decision and to reduce the opportunity for evasion, but the United States has not hesitated to act alone when consensus could not be achieved. For instance, when Iranian "students" took over the American embassy in Teheran in November 1979 and seized more than 50 hostages, the United States sought collective sanctions through the UN Security Council. When the Soviet Union, which had abstained in December 1979 on an earlier Security Council resolution *deploring* the continued detention of the hostages, vetoed a resolution calling for economic sanctions pursuant to Articles 39 and 41 of the UN Charter, the United States imposed a trade embargo anyway, after a short delay.

Similarly, and at almost the same time, the United States sought Security Council approval of sanctions against the Soviet Union for its invasion of Afghanistan. When that resolution was vetoed – as must have been expected –

■ Herbert and Rose Rubin Professor of International Law, New York University School of Law.

V. Gowlland-Debbas (ed.), *United Nations Sanctions and International Law*, p. 95-103.

the United States sought allies for its program of sanctions, including a grain embargo and a boycott of the 1980 Moscow Summer Olympics.

I Sanctions Without Security Council Approval

Whatever one may think of these programs as a matter of policy, I believe two conclusions can be drawn from the vantage point of a lawyer. *First*, the suggestion that economic sanctions are unlawful unless approved by the Security Council (or by a regional organization such as the OAS) is obsolete, if indeed it was ever sound. True, Article 16 of the OAS Charter of 1948 (Article 19 in the 1967 version) provides that

> No State may use or encourage the use of coercive measures of an economic or political character in order to force the sovereign will of another State and obtain from it advantages of any kind.

But quite apart from the fact that this provision appears only in a regional agreement, sanctions have become sufficiently common – and often better than the alternatives – to have become tolerated (not to say accepted) as a tool of foreign relations, even without approval by the Security Council.

Second, the fact that the Security Council has expressly considered a program of sanctions but failed to adopt it – whether because of a veto or because of failure to achieve the required majority – does not alter the first conclusion. Other states are not, of course, required to impose sanctions not decided upon by the Security Council, but neither are they precluded from doing so, as for example the members of the European Community did (with varying degrees of intensity) *vis-à-vis* Iran in the spring of 1980.

II Sanctions Pursuant to Chapter VII of the UN Charter

As is well known by the experts, but not so well understood by press and public, UN sanctions can be authorized in two ways, by recommendation or by decision. In either case, Article 39 requires that the Security Council must first determine the existence of a "threat to the peace, breach of the peace, or act of aggression," – words that have come to mean whatever situations can command an affirmative vote of the Council – without differentiation between internal and trans-border conflicts.

(a) Recommended Sanctions
I take it that if the Security Council makes a *recommendation* to states to impose economic sanctions against a state or territory, as happened for example with regard to Rhodesia after UDI from November 1965 to December 1966, any action taken by a Member state to carry out the recommendation is authorized, and (if it is within the scope of the recommendation) cannot constitute a violation. I believe this is true even if, for instance, Patria and Xandia have a trade agreement, the Security Council recommends a trade embargo against Xandia, and Patria, contrary to the provisions of the trade agreement, prohibits trade by its citizen with Xandia or its nationals. If Xandia raised a claim against Patria under a dispute settlement provision in the trade agreement and Patria relied on the Security Council resolution for its defense, I believe Patria would prevail. This follows, in my submission, from the supremacy of the Security Council resolutions under Chapter VII, even though, because the resolution was not mandatory, - i.e., did not create an obligation – Article 103, the Supremacy Clause of the Charter, would not, by its terms, be applicable. On the other hand, if Patria, whether in reliance on the trade agreement or for any other reason, chose not to implement the sanctions, it could not be faulted on legal grounds.

Furthermore, if Patria had a law like §5 of the American United Nations Participation Act, the effect of the recommendation to impose sanctions would be that only those measures could be implemented that were authorized by independent legislation. Thus for the United States, as was shown in the instance of Rhodesia, export controls could be imposed, pursuant to the Export Control Act of 1949, but import controls and financial controls could not be imposed until the Security Council, by a *decision*, required such action.

(b) Mandatory Sanctions
If the Security Council *decides*, by the required majority, that all Member states shall stop all trade with the target state, or shall cease to export petroleum products or weapons to that state or shall prevent air traffic with the target state, we speak of mandatory sanctions. I would have thought that there can be no doubt – no legal doubt, that is – that such a resolution overrides all other obligations, including existing international agreements and private contracts, unless, of course, the resolution calling for the sanctions has a future starting date or contains an exemption for existing contractual arrangements, as was

the case, for example, in the arms embargo mandated by the Security Council against South Africa in 1977. That conclusion would seem to me to follow from the combination of Article 103 of the Charter and Article 25, which provides that the Members of the United Nations agree to accept and carry out the decisions of the Security Council, in contrast to resolutions or recommendations of the Security Council or recommendations of the General Assembly, none of which are subject to a comparable requirement. I say it could "seem to follow," because several recent sanctions resolutions of the Security Council, for instance those against Iraq at the end of the Gulf War, against Yugoslavia in 1992, and against Haiti in 1994 contain provisions – i.e., decisions – that

> all States ... shall take the necessary measures to ensure that no claim shall lie at the instance of the authorities in [the target state] or of any persons or body [in that state] or of any person claiming through or for the benefit of such person or body in connection with any contract or other transaction where its performance was affected by reason of the measures imposed by this resolution and related resolutions.

Do mandatory resolutions of the Security Council that do not contain such a paragraph not prevail over existing contracts? What about states that do not enact the implementing legislation apparently called for by the quoted text? I would hope that national governments and courts conclude that once a mandatory resolution under Article 41 has been adopted by the Security Council, no additional measures are necessary, and I am quite sure this is true under United States law. I am less sure than I used to be about other states, or, as we have heard here, about the European Community. Of course the question is not solely a legal one. The doubt about the answer reflects the continuing ambivalence about economic sanctions in general, and the answer in particular cases may well reflect the degree of support in different states for the sanction at issue.

How mandatory is a mandatory sanction anyway? For example in response to the failure by Libya to cooperate with the investigation of the terrorist bombing of Pan Am Flight 103 over Lockerbie, the Security Council decided in 1992 that all states shall suspend all air traffic between their territories and Libya until the Libyan government complied with prior demands of the Security Council to furnish information and surrender the persons suspected of having carried out the crime. With a few exceptions, the resolution held, until the suspects were turned over to Scottish authorities in the Netherlands in the beginning of 1999. But suppose that, say Italy or Greece or Egypt had continued to maintain air traffic with Libya. Would Italy or Greece or Egypt now be subject to sanctions?

In theory the answer is yes. I know of no case, however, in which a state that failed to obey a mandatory sanction resolution has itself been subjected to a sanction.

In the early 1970's, during the height of the aircraft hijacking epidemic, some 70 states adopted the Hague Convention for the Suppression of Unlawful Seizure of Aircraft, which obligated all state parties to arrest and prosecute or extradite persons in their territories believed to have committed or aided in the commission of the offense of aircraft hijacking. The United States tried to follow up the Hague Convention with another convention to impose sanctions – such as suspension of air service – on states that did not comply with the Anti-Hijacking Convention, for example by giving shelter to an alleged offender. The attempt failed to win any substantial support. Subsequently, the G-7 industrial countries, meeting in Bonn in 1978, did adopt a Declaration along these lines, but though aircraft hijacking and terrorist attacks continued, the Bonn Declaration has never been invoked to interrupt air communications with a delinquent state.

I do not suggest that a state that ignores or defies a mandatory sanction resolution of the Security Council can do so cost-free. An instructive illustration is the case of Jordan before and during the Gulf War with Iraq in 1990-91. Jordan continued to trade with Iraq despite the UN sanctions, and generally supported the Iraqi position. No sanctions were imposed – or even proposed – against Jordan, but when Jordan applied under Article 50 of the Charter for assistance to make up the damage to its economy attributable to the embargo against Iraq, the states that might have supported extra economic aid to Jordan were – I think justifiably – unsympathetic. To come back to the earlier example, if Italy or Greece or Egypt had continued air service to Libya while the rest of the world had shut such service down pursuant to a Security Council decision under Article 41 of the Charter, they would almost certainly have been made to pay in some way, but not by the kind of sanctions here under discussion. In short, defined in terms of punishment for non-compliance, "mandatory" UN sanctions have the character more of soft than of hard law. In some countries, including the United States and the United Kingdom, they bring extraordinary powers into effect; in other countries, they serve to give impetus to a government's action, without subjecting its decision-making to the domestic political process. Mandatory sanctions do not ensure that 180 Member states actually perform as the Security Council has ordered.

III Territorial and Extraterritorial Enforcement of Sanctions

When the sanctions in question are imposed or authorized by the Security Council, the question of extraterritorial jurisdiction generally does not arise; the sharp controversy arises when the policy of the host country of the branch or subsidiary and the country where the parent company is domiciled – the United States in the typical case – are different, as is true at present with regard to trade with Iran, Libya, and Cuba, and has been true in the past with respect to China, the Soviet Union, and other states. It is at that point that claims of sovereignty, policy, and legal doctrine come together.

Discussion of extraterritorial jurisdiction nearly always concerns the United States, and is by no means limited to economic sanctions. Indeed many of the controversies between the United States and Europe about the reach of American law have arisen from application of US antitrust law, or from efforts to obtain discovery, American style, from parties whose headquarters – and information – are located in Europe. Still, an important element of what Professor Schlosser called the *Justizkonflict* has been the application of American economic sanctions to subsidiaries of US-based corporations established in Europe, and also in Canada. The *Fruehauf* case of 1964-65, involving an effort by the US government to impose its embargo on trade with China on the French subsidiary of a US-based company comes to mind, as does the American effort in 1981-82 to punish the Soviet Union for the imposition of martial law in Poland by requiring European companies to cease work on construction of the Siberia-Western Europe natural gas pipeline.

(a) The Question of Links

I have been writing about this subject for more than thirty years, but only a few remarks will have to suffice here. *First*, hardly anyone objects to a regulation or order that applies to all citizens of the ordering state, wherever they happen to be at a given time. If the United States prescribes that no US citizen may trade with Cuba or North Korea or Iraq without a special license, no one could contend that US citizens residing in Paris or Rome are exempt, or that the sovereignty of France or Italy is infringed by application of the prohibition to them. The controversy turns on whether the same principle should apply – directly or by analogy – to corporations. Are Coca Cola/Spain or General Motors/Germany or Mobil/UK not still American, Philips/North America not Dutch, Nestlé not Swiss – regardless of where a particular unit of the multilateral enterprise is established or incorporated?

I don't find this proposition as unreasonable as many others do, particularly when it is clear that the major decisions are made in Atlanta, Detroit and New York, in Eindhoven and Vevey, not at the seat of the subsidiary. Nor do I find the distinction between a branch and a subsidiary very persuasive in this context. The question remains whether the link between the parent corporation, clearly subject to the territorial jurisdiction of the state imposing the sanction, and the member of the multinational enterprise established in another country, is sufficient to support application of a prohibition by the sanctioning state to the foreign unit – branch or subsidiary.

What links, then, should suffice between the sanctioning state and the establishment abroad to which an embargo or similar restraint is sought to be applied? I think "ownership or control", as in the typical US regulation under the Treaty with the Enemy Act or its successor statute, the International Emergency Economic Powers Act (IEEPA) is legally sufficient, but as the ALI Restatement of Foreign Relations Law states, should be resorted to only in exceptional circumstances and only when essential to implementation of a program to further a major national interest of the state exercising jurisdiction – i.e., not as the ordinary or routine extent of a domestic regulation. The resort by the United States in 1982 in the *Pipeline* case to the link of commercial technology licenses between American companies such as General Electric and non-American companies such as the French firm Alsthom-Atlantique was unjustified, and therefore, as I see it, the attempt by the US government to impose its regulations on such companies and to punish them for non-compliance was exorbitant and unlawful. Though no court has directly so held, I believe the history of the US pipeline regulations, which were withdrawn under pressure from the European Community and its Member states, supports my conclusion.

(b) The Helms-Burton Act

This brings me, if only briefly, to the current focus of controversy, the so-called Helms-Burton Act, adopted by the US Congress and signed reluctantly by President Clinton in 1996. The object of the legislation is to deter commercial relations – trade and investment – between Cuba and firms in Europe, Canada and Latin America. The United States, of course, cannot regulate such firms directly (assuming they are not subsidiaries of US firms), and the legislation does not purport to do so. But, says Helms-Burton, if a firm "traffics" in property that once belonged to US nationals and was confiscated by the Cuban government since January 1, 1959, it risks litigation in the United States and exposure in the first instance to damages equal to the property in question, and if the trafficking continues, to treble damages. Thus if, say, an English company purchases sugar from a Cuban state enterprise and the English company also does business in the United States and accordingly is amenable to the judicial jurisdiction of a US court, it would be liable under the Act to a US national who could show that some of the company's purchases consisted of sugar grown on the plantation that the plaintiff once owned.

There are a good many defects with Helms-Burton, which I have discussed elsewhere. For present purposes, and putting aside the merits of the American embargo against Cuba, I want to stress only that the attempt to impose American policy judgments on nationals of friendly foreign states is not only unwise but in my view is a violation of international law. I do not accept the distinction between a purported prohibition, as in the *Pipeline* case, and the threat of litigation and heavy damages, as under Helms-Burton. In both cases, an acceptable jurisdictional link between the United States and the person whose actions are sought to be controlled is absent and therefore the effort to affect those actions is an exorbitant exercise of jurisdiction.

I am glad, for several reasons, that the attempt by the European Union to bring Helms-Burton before a WTO dispute settlement panel was deflected, essentially by an undertaking by President Clinton to continue to issue waivers deferring effectiveness of the provisions of Helms-Burton that I have described. I hope the lesson of the unacceptability of Helms-Burton sinks in, and that this lesson is understood to have legal content, not just to reflect political resentment.

IV Conclusion

I want to conclude with two remarks about sanctions in general. First, sanctions are supposed to hurt. They are supposed to deter, they are supposed, if possible, to change conduct, and they are supposed to express outrage, as over the suppression of freedom in Poland in 1981-82, the ouster of an elected president in Haiti in 1991-94, ethnic cleansing in the former Yugoslavia in the 1990's, apartheid in South Africa for many decades, aggression and build-up of weapons of mass destruction in Iraq from 1990 on. One hopes that sanctions will hurt the government of the target state more than its population. Most UN sanctions have sought to achieve this, at least in part, by exempting food shipments from a trade embargo. We know, however, that such efforts are only partly successful. Everyone is hurt as a consequence of a program of sanctions, particularly if the program is implemented on a collective basis, such as one ordered by the UN Security Council. If that gives pause – and indeed it should – it is necessary, nevertheless, to consider the alternatives. Sanctions are a middle ground, as the drafters of Article 41 of the UN Charter understood, between resort to military force and "business as usual". As recent events in Kosovo – and also in several countries in Africa – have shown, sanctions are often too late and too slow. But the alternatives – doing nothing and applying force – may well be even more unattractive in a still dangerous world.

6

LA RESPONSABILITÉ PÉNALE INDIVIDUELLE, ALTERNATIVE AUX SANCTIONS COLLECTIVES?

Alain Pellet[■]

Le sujet qui m'a été imparti implique que soit mises en perspective les sanctions collectives d'une part et la responsabilité pénale des individus, au moins celle des dirigeants étatiques, d'autre part. Considérer qu'il s'agit là d'une "alternative" est, *a priori*, une idée un peu singulière et, à vrai dire, dangereuse: non seulement la mise en œuvre de la responsabilité des dirigeants n'est pas une alternative aux sanctions, mais encore, elle ne doit certainement pas l'être. L'admettre, ce serait justifier l'inaction de la communauté internationale organisée et faire apparaître les juridictions pénales internationales comme des alibis ou l'expression tardive de la mauvaise conscience des Etats, ce dont de bons esprits n'ont d'ailleurs pas manqué d'accuser les tribunaux pénaux internationaux pour l'ex-Yougoslavie et pour le Rwanda.

À mes yeux, la responsabilité pénale des individus ne peut en aucun cas apparaître ni de près ni de loin comme une alternative aux sanctions collectives ce qui ne veut pas dire, bien sûr que les deux phénomènes sont dépourvus de tous liens. Bien au contraire ils sont complémentaires et il existe une sorte de partage des tâches entre le Conseil de sécurité et les florissantes juridictions pénales internationales, peut-être même d'ailleurs plus largement entre le Conseil de sécurité et les juridictions internationales tout court, à commencer par la Cour internationale de Justice, voire même les juridictions nationales. Et cette complémentarité doit aller en s'approfondissant dans la société internationale: de même que, dans l'Etat, les fonctions de police et de justice sont à la fois

■ Professeur, Université de Parix X-Nanterre; Directeur du CEDIN; Membre et ancien Président de la Commission du droit international.

V. Gowlland-Debbas (ed.), *United Nations Sanctions and International Law,* p. 105-116.

bien distinctes, au moins dans les Etats de droit, de même cette "séparation des pouvoirs" constituerait un pas en avant vers l'instauration d'une "société internationale de droit", même s'il faut se méfier des rapprochements trop poussés entre la société internationale et son droit d'un côté, les droits nationaux de l'autre.

En premier lieu donc, *la responsabilité pénale individuelle n'est pas, ne peut pas être, et ne doit pas être, une alternative aux sanctions collectives.*

Ces institutions juridiques relèvent des fonctions différentes, font appel à des moyens distincts et doivent, ou devraient – si les mots ont un sens, notamment le mot "juridiction" – demeurer nettement séparées.

Avant de le montrer, il n'est peut-être pas totalement inutile de s'attarder quelques instants sur des problèmes de définition, en tout cas en ce qui concerne les sanctions. On l'a souvent dit, le mot "sanction" n'apparaît pas dans la Charte.[1] Le Chapitre VII est intitulé "Action en cas de menace contre la paix, de rupture de la paix ou d'acte d'agression", et cette action se traduit par des constatations (art. 39) qui peuvent déboucher sur des recommandations ou des décisions sur les mesures provisoires (article 40) ou définitives (articles 41 et 42) qui doivent être prises, impliquant ou non l'emploi de la force armée.

Davantage même, cette "action", ces "mesures", n'ont certainement pas pour objet, pour objet premier en tout cas, de faire respecter le droit fût-il international. La Charte n'est guère ambiguë: le droit international est un objectif très vague dont les peuples des Nations Unies se proclament dans le préambule résolus à créer les conditions nécessaires à sa mise en œuvre. Il contribue à l'ajustement ou au règlement "de différends ou de situations de caractère international susceptibles de mener à une rupture de la paix", au terme de l'article 1er, paragraphe 1, mais le but premier, fondamental sinon exclusif des Nations Unies, est de maintenir la paix et la sécurité internationales.

Le droit international est, dans la vision la plus optimiste des choses, un moyen parmi d'autres pour y parvenir, un moyen qui peut être écarté le cas échéant, aux termes tout à fait nets de la Charte, comme le montre de façon presque caricaturale l'article 94 sur la mise en œuvre des arrêts de la Cour internationale

1 V. par exemple Jean Combacau, *Le pouvoir de sanction de l'O.N.U. – Étude théorique de la coercition non militaire* (Paris, 1974), p. 1.

de Justice.[2] Les mesures que le Conseil de sécurité peut être amené à prendre contre des Etats ne visent donc pas à assurer le respect du droit international, mais ce qui est assez différent, à maintenir la paix et la sécurité internationales, si elle peuvent l'être par le droit, tant mieux – on peut postuler qu'il y aura une coïncidence entre l'un et l'autre, mais c'est loin d'être une évidence.

La responsabilité pénale des individus poursuit un tout autre objectif. Il s'agit cette fois de sanctionner au sens propre du terme les manquements au droit, au droit international s'il s'agit de la responsabilité internationale, qui sont commis par les individus.

Les tribunaux pénaux internationaux qui ont été créés, tout comme la future Cour pénale internationale qui va l'être, ont, me semble-t-il, une triple fonction: une fonction préventive, il s'agit, par la menace d'une sanction effective, de dissuader les auteurs des "crimes les plus graves qui touchent l'ensemble de la communauté internationale" et "ne sauraient", pour reprendre les termes du préambule du Statut de la CPI, "rester impunis"; ils ont une fonction répressive et ne peuvent intervenir concrètement qu'une fois le crime commis; et ils ont une fonction symbolique, ils portent le témoignage de la communautarisation, encore balbutiante, mais tout de même appréciable de la société internationale. Et c'est ce que disait déjà en 1946 le Tribunal militaire international de Nuremberg: "Le Statut [annexé à l'Accord de Londres] ne constitue pas l'exercice arbitraire par les nations victorieuses de leur suprématie, il exprime le Droit [avec un D majuscule] international en vigueur au moment de sa création, il contribue par cela même au développement de ce Droit".[3]

Autre antinomie entre les deux termes de notre sujet, elle aussi fondamentale, les "sanctions" – le mot doit être mis entre les guillemets – du Conseil de sécurité, comme celles qui sont décidées ou infligées par des organisations régionales, concernent des Etats, alors que, par hypothèse, la responsabilité pénale vise des individus qui peuvent être, mais qui ne sont pas forcément, des représentants de l'Etat, à commencer par des chefs d'Etat.

---

2 Article 94, paragraphe 2: "Si une partie à un litige ne satisfait pas aux obligations qui lui incombent en vertu d'un arrêt rendu par la Cour, l'autre partie peut recourir au Conseil de sécurité et celui-ci, *s'il le juge nécessaire, peut* faire des recommandations ou décider des mesures à prendre pour faire exécuter l'arrêt" (italiques ajoutées).

3 Jugement du 1er octobre 1946, p. 491.

Je voudrais d'ailleurs ouvrir sur ce point une parenthèse qui porte sur un sujet qui m'est cher[4]: on pourrait se demander si la véritable alternative aux sanctions collectives ne serait pas la responsabilité pénale internationale des Etats plutôt que celle des individus, fussent-ils des dirigeants étatiques. Après tout, le célèbre article 19 du projet de la Commission du Droit international sur la responsabilité des Etats nomme "crimes" les violations par un Etat d'une obligation internationale essentielle pour la sauvegarde des intérêts de la communauté internationale. Malgré mon attachement très fort à la distinction entre crime et délit – mon attachement à la chose, pas vraiment à la terminologie retenue par la CDI –, ma réponse à cette interrogation est fermement négative. Malgré ce vocabulaire pénaliste, la responsabilité internationale des Etats n'est ni civile ni pénale. Au surplus, les conséquences qui s'attachent à la distinction entre crimes et délits et à la notion même de crime sont clairement de nature non pénale, non criminelle, et la sanction qui en résulte n'est pas, en principe au moins, de nature répressive, même si les récents événements du Kosovo traduisent un "frémissement répressif".

En revanche, il existe des liens étroits entre la notion de crime international de l'État et la responsabilité pénale des individus, au moins lorsque ceux-ci ont agi en tant que dirigeants gouvernementaux. À ce titre, ils sont couverts par l'immunité de juridiction de l'Etat et c'est parce que celui-ci a, par eux, commis un crime que le voile étatique peut être percé. L'une des conséquences du concept de crime, totalement oubliée par le projet d'articles de la CDI,[5] est, en effet, la "transparence" de l'Etat grâce à laquelle la responsabilité des individus par l'intermédiaire desquels il a agi (ou qui ont agi par son intermédiaire?) peut être recherchée sans qu'ils puissent se retrancher derrière leurs fonctions officielles.

Cette parenthèse refermée, revenons aux différences fondamentales qui caractérisent d'une part les sanctions et d'autre part la responsabilité pénale des individus. Les sanctions ne sont pas prononcées sur la base du droit existant.

---

4 V. not. Alain Pellet, "Vive le crime! Remarques sur les degrés de l'illicite en droit international" *in* C.D.I., *Le droit international à l'aube du XXIème siècle – Réflexions de codificateurs* (New York, 1997), pp. 287-315 et "Can a State Commit a Crime? Definitely, Yes", (1999) 10 *EJIL* 425-434.

5 *Cf.* les articles 51 à 53.

La Libye s'en est suffisamment plainte dans l'affaire de *Lockerbie*.[6] Elles sont prononcées sur la base de déterminations faites en opportunité par le Conseil de sécurité en fonction de considérations politiques. Au contraire, la responsabilité pénale des individus est gouvernée par deux principes fondamentaux, de nature éminemment juridique: *nullum crimen, nulla poena, sine lege*. Comme on l'a écrit, le droit de la Charte, et d'abord le droit des sanctions, est un droit d'exception. Le Conseil de sécurité pratique une politique d'engagement sélectif en fonction de la faisabilité.[7] Au contraire, les tribunaux pénaux internationaux font passer, en tout cas devraient faire passer, le rouleau compresseur du droit sur les herbes folles de la *Realpolitik*.

Ceci bien sûr ne va pas sans tension comme l'ont montré les récents événements du Kosovo, avec la mise en accusation par le Procureur du TPI d'un Milosevic avec lequel, *Realpolitik* oblige, on n'hésite pas, tout de même, à signer un accord qu'on présente comme un accord d'adhésion; mais la résolution 1244 adoptée par le Conseil de sécurité le 10 juin 1999 ne s'en félicite pas moins de l'adhésion de la Yougoslavie, représentée par son Président, à cet accord, tout en rappelant, quelques paragraphes plus loin, "la compétence et le mandat du Tribunal pénal international pour l'ex-Yougoslavie".

Même embarras dans le Statut de la Cour pénale internationale, on crée une juridiction qui peut, aux termes de l'article 1er de son Statut "exercer sa compétence à l'égard des personnes pour les crimes les plus graves ayant une portée internationale"; mais, au mépris des principes juridiques les mieux établis concernant l'indépendance des tribunaux par rapport aux pouvoirs politiques, on glisse dans le Statut des dispositions que je considère comme proprement scélérates, et d'autant plus absurdes qu'elle sont probablement inapplicables. Je pense surtout à l'article 16, pudiquement intitulé "Sursis à enquêter ou à poursuivre", qui, en clair, permet au Conseil de sécurité – pourrait lui permettre, si les conditions pouvaient en être réunies – d'empêcher les poursuites contre les auteurs de ces mêmes crimes du moins jusqu'au jour où ces criminels ou présumés criminels seront "lâchés" par le Conseil de sécurité lorsqu'il n'aura

---

6 V. *Recueil CIJ,* 1992, ordonnances des 14 avril 1992, pars. 35 et 38, pp. 14 et 125 et arrêts du 27 février 1998 sur les *Exceptions préliminaires*, pars. 23 ou 50, *Recueil CIJ*, 1998, pp. 18 et 28 et pars. 22 et 49, Recueil CIJ, 1998, pp. 123 et 134.

7 Cf. Jean-Marc Sorel, "L'élargissement de la notion de menace contre la paix" *in* SFDI, Colloque de Rennes, 1994, *Le chapitre VII de la Charte des Nations Unies* (Paris, 1995), pp. 49-51.

plus besoin d'eux pour s'acquitter de sa responsabilité principale en matière de maintien de la paix et de la sécurité internationales.

C'est que les sanctions d'un côté, la responsabilité pénale de l'autre, relèvent décidément de philosophies profondément différentes qui excluent que la responsabilité pénale puisse constituer une quelconque alternative à celles-là. Les sanctions relèvent de la *Realpolitik*, c'est-à-dire d'une politique de puissance faiblement encadrée par le droit, qui ménage une large appréciation au Conseil de sécurité. Les tribunaux pénaux internationaux relèvent peut-être, pour leur part, comme on l'a dit, de la "*global morality*"; sûrement en tout cas exclusivement de la sphère du droit.

Cela étant, *il n'en existe pas moins une complémentarité certaine, et probablement utile, entre les sanctions et la responsabilité pénale.*

Cette complémentarité, sans doute plus intéressante pour les juristes que la prétendue alternative que cette dernière offrirait aux premières, tient d'abord à ce que la mise en œuvre de la responsabilité pénale individuelle peut être un alibi à l'absence des sanctions. Elle peut être aussi un prolongement ou un complément des sanctions. En outre et en troisième lieu, il existe une sorte de partage des tâches entre les tribunaux pénaux internationaux d'une part et le Conseil de sécurité d'autre part.

Le premier de ces points n'appelle pas de longs commentaires. La création des deux tribunaux *ad hoc* le prouve: la mise en place d'une juridiction pénale internationale peut être, c'est tout à fait évident, la traduction de la mauvaise conscience de la communauté internationale. On laisse des génocides se commettre en Bosnie-Herzégovine ou au Rwanda sous les yeux de forces de maintien de la paix, trop faibles de toutes façons pour pouvoir empêcher les massacres, quand on ne les retire pas purement et simplement, puis on crée un tribunal pour se donner bonne conscience.

Je tiens cependant à nuancer ceci. Je n'ai pas de doute sur le fait qu'il y a du vrai dans cette analyse. J'ai été associé d'assez près à la création du Tribunal pour l'ex-Yougoslavie et je ne peux malheureusement pas démentir complètement cette analyse. Mais, je crois qu'il faut reconnaître aussi qu'il y a eu de la part des promoteurs du Tribunal, au moins de certains d'entre eux, la conviction sincère que le jugement des responsables de génocide, bosniaque ou rwandais, était indispensable pour panser, si faire se pouvait, les blessures engendrées par les crimes commis et le désir de lutter contre une insupportable impunité.

Par ailleurs, et l'évolution du Tribunal pour l'ex-Yougoslavie le montre bien, il faut bien voir aussi que la créature échappe à son créateur. Même s'il a été au départ en partie une juridiction alibi, le Tribunal de La Haye a su asseoir sa légitimité d'une manière que je crois exemplaire. Pas plus que celui d'Arusha, il ne peut faire oublier l'échec des sanctions ou des opérations de maintien de la paix, mais, dans la sphère qui est celle des deux tribunaux, ils s'acquittent comme ils peuvent, mais finalement plutôt bien que mal, de leur fonction propre. Du coup, on peut penser que, dans certains cas, les initiatives prises par les tribunaux (ou par le Procureur qui fait partie du Tribunal *lato sensu*) ont, finalement, tout bien pesé, plutôt gêné les puissances alliées que cela ne les a aidées. Tel est le cas, par exemple, de l'initiative de Mme Arbour de mettre en accusation M. Milosevic.[8]

Cette dissociation entre les sanctions et la responsabilité pénale sera encore plus manifeste avec la Cour pénale internationale dont la création se sera faite en dehors du Conseil de sécurité même si personnellement, je le dis au passage, j'eusse préféré qu'elle ait été décidée par l'Assemblée générale plutôt que par une conférence diplomatique, mais cela est une autre histoire. Il reste que, même dans le cas de la Cour, on peut penser que son action prolongera le cas échéant les sanctions décidés par le Conseil de sécurité qui, agissant en vertu du chapitre VII de la Charte, pourra saisir le Procureur[9]; mais ce n'est que l'un des modes possibles de saisine de la Cour et, dans tous les cas, le Procureur demeurera maître des poursuites et la Cour se prononcera en toute indépendance. *Mutatis mutandis*, le même phénomène s'est produit avec les Tribunaux de Nuremberg et de Tokyo, dont il est tout à fait erroné de prétendre qu'ils ont rendu une "justice de vainqueurs", même s'ils ont été créés par les vainqueurs. Mais cela est, bien sûr, beaucoup plus frappant encore s'agissant des tribunaux *ad hoc*. Dans l'affaire bosniaque, le processus est très parlant. Dans un premier temps, le Conseil de sécurité décide des sanctions économiques. C'est la longue série des résolutions, qui commence avec la 713 de septembre 1991. Dans un deuxième temps, en même temps qu'il aggrave les sanctions économiques, le Conseil affirme la responsabilité individuelle des auteurs des crimes de guerre et des violations graves du droit humanitaire; il le fait pour la première fois

8 V. l'acte de mise en accusation du 24 mai 1999 (IT-99-37-I).
9 Article 13.c) du Statut de la CPI.

de manière nette dans la résolution 764 de juillet 1992. Troisième temps: le Conseil crée une commission chargée d'enquêter sur ces crimes, par la résolution 780 d'octobre 1992, à peu près au moment où il se décide enfin à mettre en œuvre des sanctions militaires, par les résolutions 770, 781 et surtout par la résolution 787 du 16 novembre. Enfin, quatrième temps, il crée le Tribunal pénal international par les résolutions 808 et 827 du 10 février et du 25 mai 1993. Le parallélisme est ici très frappant, mais c'est un parallélisme, ce n'est pas une alternative et il serait abusif de prétendre que l'on a pensé que la création du Tribunal pouvait relever les Etats de l'obligation d'essayer de faire quelque chose.

Mais les relations entre sanctions et création des tribunaux ne se bornent pas à cette coïncidence dans le temps. Elles s'étendent aussi aux fondements juridiques des unes et des autres. Certes, la création du Tribunal n'est pas en soi une sanction, mais, comme ce que l'on a coutume d'appeler "sanctions", ce n'en est pas moins une "mesure" au sens de l'article 41 de la Charte (c'est d'ailleurs pour cela que le terme sanction fait problème[10]), qui repose, s'agissant de l'ex-Yougoslavie et du Rwanda, sur le Chapitre VII de la Charte alors même que, à la demande de la Chine et de la Russie – déjà! –, celui-ci n'est pas visé par la résolution 808; mais il l'est expressément dans la résolution 827. Quoique l'on en ait dit[11] c'est un fondement juridique vraisemblable, globalement acceptable; il n'en reste pas moins que si le Conseil de sécurité n'avait pas pris la précaution de constater que les violations graves du droit humanitaire en Yougoslavie ou au Rwanda constituaient une menace contre la paix, il n'aurait pu, en droit, créer les tribunaux *ad hoc*, alors que, pour sa part, l'Assemblée générale pourrait le faire dans tous les cas, mais sans pouvoir obliger juridiquement les Etats à coopérer avec les juridictions qu'elle viendrait à créer.

Il est bien évident que cette identité de fondement aux sanctions, d'une part, et à la responsabilité pénale individuelle, d'autre part, en tous cas à la création des tribunaux, ne se retrouve pas s'agissant de la Cour pénale internationale parce qu'elle va être créée par un traité. Il est d'autant plus intéressant de relever

10 V. *supra*, p. 106.

11 V. not. Gaetano Arangio-Ruiz, "The Establishment of the International Criminal Tribunal for the Former Territory of Yugoslavia and the Doctrine of Implied Powers of the United Nations" *in* F. Lattanzi (ed.) et E. Sciso (dir.), *Dai Tribunali penali internazionali* ad hoc *a una Corte permanente* (Naples, 1996), pp.31-45.

que l'alinéa 3 du préambule du Statut de Rome reconnaît que des crimes d'une telle gravité, ceux que la Cour est appelée à punir, "menacent la paix, la sécurité et le bien-être du monde", ce qui montre sinon une identité de fondement juridique qui n'existe pas ici, au moins une proximité frappante dans les objectifs poursuivis.

Enfin – et pour en terminer avec cette revue un peu plate de la problématique du sujet qu'il m'a été demandé de traiter –, il convient de mettre l'accent sur la complémentarité des fonctions, presque le partage des tâches qui existe entre les sanctions, d'une part, et la responsabilité individuelle, d'autre part, ou, si l'on préfère, entre le Conseil de sécurité et, le cas échéant, les organisations régionales, d'une part, et les juridictions pénales internationales, d'autre part, une complémentarité qui joue dans les deux sens et dont je me bornerai à énumérer brièvement les principales manifestations.

En premier lieu, le Conseil de sécurité soit, dans le cas des tribunaux *ad hoc*, définit la compétence des juridictions qu'il a créées, soit peut être à l'origine des poursuites après avoir constaté l'existence au moins d'une menace contre la paix comme le prévoit l'article 13.c) du Statut de la CPI, alors même que la Cour n'est pas un organe des Nations Unies, même si elle leur est liée par un accord.[12]

Deuxièmement, plus conjoncturellement, le Conseil de sécurité peut aussi contribuer à définir le droit de référence applicable par ces juridictions actuelles ou futures. Le fait que le Conseil de sécurité ait donné compétence au TPI et au TPR pour condamner les auteurs de génocides perpétrés en ex-Yougoslavie et au Rwanda, ne constitue peut-être pas un critère décisif au point de vue juridique, mais c'est, à mon avis, un argument extrêmement fort malgré tout pour permettre de considérer qu'il s'est effectivement agi de génocides. Et les tribunaux ne s'y sont d'ailleurs pas trompés que ce soit dans la mise en accusation de Karadzic et de Mladic par le Tribunal de La Haye en 1996[13] ou

12 *Cf.* l'article 2 du Statut.

13 *Cf.* l'examen de l'acte d'accusation dans le cadre de l'article 61 du Règlement de procédure et de preuve, *Karadzic et Mladic*, IT-95-5-R61 et IT-95-18-R61, 11 juillet 1996, pars. 84 et 92-95; v. aussi IT-95-2-R61, 20 octobre 1995, par. 34 et les actes d'accusation dans les affaires, *Meakic* (IT-95-4-I), *Karadzic et Mladic* (IT-95-5-I et IT 95-18-I), *Sikirica* (IT-95-8-I) et *Jelisic* (IT-95-10-I).

dans l'ensemble des décisions du Tribunal pour le Rwanda.[14] De même, je vois mal comment la définition de l'agression par un futur amendement au Statut de la CPI pourra éviter de faire référence au pouvoir de qualification du Conseil de sécurité, même si cela politiquement déplaît à beaucoup.

Troisièmement, un jour ou l'autre, le problème se posera inévitablement de juger les membres d'une force militaire de maintien de la paix pour des crimes internationaux définis dans le Statut de la CPI et peut-être dans ceux des tribunaux, ce que le détestable article 124 du Statut de la CPI ne peut pas et, d'ailleurs ne se propose pas, d'empêcher indéfiniment.[15] Au demeurant, quelles que soient les critiques qu'encourt cette disposition, il faut bien reconnaître qu'il y a là un vrai problème car il n'est pas du meilleur goût de juger sur les mêmes bases ceux qui commettent un génocide ou une agression et ceux qui risquent leur vie pour empêcher que ces crimes soient commis. Ceci dit, ces derniers n'en doivent pas moins être jugés s'ils ne s'acquittent pas de leur mission et, plus encore, si, à l'occasion de celle-ci, ils se rendent coupables de crimes de guerre ou complices de crimes qu'ils pouvaient éviter.

Pour sortir de ce dilemme, la meilleure solution consisterait probablement à créer une juridiction spéciale, ayant compétence pour juger les infractions (et pas seulement les crimes les plus graves) commises par les membres des forces de maintien de la paix. Ceci serait d'autant plus logique qu'il s'agit d'agents internationaux dont le statut implique (ou devrait impliquer) qu'ils ne sont pas soumis à la juridiction (dans les deux sens du terme) des États aux forces armées desquels ils appartiennent mais à celle de l'Organisation au nom de laquelle ils agissent; ceci est "essentiel" "afin de garantir l'indépendance de l'agent et, en conséquence, l'action indépendante de l'Organisation elle-même".[16] On

---

14 V. les premiers arrêts du TPR dans les affaires *Akayesu* (ICTR 96-4-T, 2 septembre 1998), *Kabamda* (ICTR 97-23-T, 4 septembre 1998) et *Kayishema et Ruzindana* (ICTR 95-1-T, 21 mai 1999).

15 Aux termes de l'article 124, "un État qui devient partie au présent Statut peut déclarer que, *pour une période de sept ans à partir de l'entrée en vigueur du Statut à son égard*, il n'accepte pas la compétence de la Cour" en ce qui concerne les crimes de guerre (italiques ajoutées). Nulle part il n'est prévu que cette déclaration peut être renouvelée; et il ne pourrait en aller ainsi que si le Statut était modifié en ce sens – on peut espérer qu'il n'en sera rien même si la rédaction actuelle résulte probablement d'une inadvertance.

16 *Cf.* CIJ, avis consultatif, 11 avril 1949, *Réparation des dommages subis au service des Nations Unies*, Recueil CIJ, 1949, p. 183.

peut cependant craindre que le "souverainisme" exacerbé des principaux pourvoyeurs de casques bleus, à commencer par la France, ne se satisfasse pas d'une telle solution, la seule juridiquement correcte pourtant, qui traduirait, concrètement, le fait que les membres des forces de maintien de la paix sont censés être à la disposition de la communauté internationale dans son ensemble, et ne pas relever, sauf en matière disciplinaire, de l'État qui les met à la disposition des Nations Unies.

Quatrièmement, enfin et à l'inverse, les sanctions peuvent être et finiront sans doute un jour par être un moyen d'assurer concrètement la mise en œuvre de la responsabilité pénale des individus responsables des crimes internationaux les plus graves.

À l'heure actuelle, on a tendance à voir au fond la responsabilité pénale comme un prolongement des sanctions, mais un jour, qui n'est peut-être pas si lointain maintenant, viendra où un Etat qui ne s'acquitterait pas de ses obligations à l'égard des juridictions pénales internationales pourrait se voir infliger des sanctions de ce fait. En particulier on peut fort bien envisager une opération de police internationale, impliquant, le cas échéant, l'emploi de la force pour arrêter les auteurs des crimes les plus graves. Et, après tout, l'affaire des *sub poena* devant le TPI et surtout le mandat même de la K-FOR, constituent des illustrations encore timides mais assez claires de cette possibilité. Dans son arrêt du 29 octobre 1997, la Chambre d'appel du TPI a rappelé que "[l]e Conseil de sécurité a établi le Tribunal international au titre du chapitre VII de la Charte des Nations Unies dans le but de poursuivre les personnes présumées responsables de violations graves du droit international humanitaire commises sur le territoire de l'ex-Yougoslavie. Le corollaire logique de la manière dont le Tribunal international a été créé est qu'à chaque fois qu'un Etat ne respecte pas son obligation au titre de l'article 29 du Statut, l'empêchant ainsi de remplir la mission que lui a confiée le Conseil de sécurité, le Tribunal international est en droit d'informer le Conseil de sécurité de ce non-respect".[17] Quant à la résolution 1244, elle exige que tous les intéressés, y compris la présence internationale de sécurité, apportent leur entière coopération au Tribunal international

17 IT-95-14-AR 108bis, par. 33.

pour l'ex-Yougoslavie.[18] S'ils ne le font pas, on peut imaginer que la K-FOR intervienne.

Lorsque cette évolution, sera achevée on sera passée d'une société internationale anarchique à une communauté internationale de droit. La responsabilité internationale ne sera évidemment pas devenue une alternative aux sanctions, mais la police internationale sera au service du droit et de la lutte contre l'impunité. Evidemment, parlant au futur plutôt qu'au conditionnel j'ai peut-être chaussé des lunettes roses. Je concède qu'il reste pour en arriver là bien du chemin à parcourir, mais contrairement aux grincheux, aux pessimistes professionnels, je ne puis m'empêcher de voir dans les mutations formidables de la société et du droit internationaux de la dernière décennie, au moins des petits pas dans cette direction.

18 *Cf.* le paragraphe 14: "Le Conseil de sécurité (...) *agissant* (...) en vertu du chapitre VII de la Charte des Nations Unies, (...) 14. Exige que tous les intéressés, y compris la présence internationale de sécurité, apportent leur entière coopération au Tribunal international pour l'ex-Yougoslavie".

REGIONAL ENFORCEMENT OF COMMUNITY OBJECTIVES

Bruno Simma[■]

I think it is best if I cut what I have to say down to a few remarks which might seem to be a bit incoherent but I hope that they will address the main issues that come to mind when we think about Kosovo, international law and the UN Charter. So, I am going to skip what I wanted to say about the uneasy relationship between regional organizations and the United Nations in Chapter VIII – that tension between the text of the Charter that repeats the priority of the Charter expressed in Article 103 and the actual state of affairs that could be characterised as a constant tug-of-war between regional organizations and the universal organization.

Let me turn at once to the problem of enforcement action. If you look at Chapter VIII, Article 53, you will see that the question of enforcement comes up there in a double context. On the one hand, enforcement is mentioned in the context of the Security Council utilising regional agencies for the enforcement of its decisions – this is not the alternative that I am going to address. I am going to discuss the other thing that Article 53 has to say about enforcement action by regional organizations, that is paragraph 1 of the Article which outlines the need for authorisation from the Security Council in situations where regional organizations are taking enforcement action without a Security Council mandate. I think that if you look at the history of regional organizations – I have to say of course that regional organizations in that context actually boil

■ Professor of International and European Community Law, University of Munich; Affiliate Overseas Professor, University of Michigan Law School, Ann Arbor; Member of the International Law Commission.

V. Gowlland-Debbas (ed.), *United Nations Sanctions and International Law*, p. 117-122.

down to the OAS – you see that this is a long history of attempts to circumvent the requirement of prior authorisation by boiling down the action, by calling it "peacekeeping" rather than enforcement, etc. I would say that the case of the Dominican Republic of 1965 is very telling in that regard.

In regard to authorisations, there are various possibilities. One question could be whether it would be admissible for the Security Council to issue a general authorisation and I think that the answer has to be no. If one had the time, one could qualify this and say that if the Security Council ever considered issuing such a general authorisation, that authorisation would have to be extremely sophisticated and extremely detailed.

The next question is, can there be something like a tacit authorisation, and here I think the answer has to be a clear and unequivocal no. There were voices in the 1960s, 1970s and again in the context of Kosovo according to which the following scenario could be seen as a tacit authorisation – that is a valid authorisation – namely the regional agency going ahead with no Security Council censure of that action, and that could be seen as a tacit authorisation or approval. But this attitude is to me a sort of legal trick because in view of the veto, of course, such a censure would never occur as the history of the OAS amply demonstrates.

On the contrary, I would take the view that there is the possibility for the Security Council to render an implicit authorisation, I think that this is possible. The majority of the literature is very cautious and I think that there is good reason to be cautious, the cases are to be handled with the utmost care – particularly if I add the qualifier *ex post facto* to the qualifier implicit. So the question would be "can there be something like an explicit authorisation *ex post*"? I think that there can, but the question really has to be approached on a case by case basis. In the presence of Judge Koroma, I will not enter into the details of the Liberia case but the dominant view about what happened with ECOWAS and ECOMORG is probably that what ECOMORG did there did not really amount to enforcement in that narrow sense of robust military engagement, that is at least what I got from reading the sources. I think on the other hand, that there were elements of an implicit authorisation *ex post* present in the Liberia case. Of course, what one has to keep in mind is that if it is a case, in the abstract, where there is a lack of enthusiasm in the rest of the world, particularly among the countries that are militarily capable – and that lack of enthusiasm will of course translate itself into inaction or inertia in the Security

Council – then it would be easier for me to admit that if something happens à la Liberia that could amount to an implicit authorisation *ex post.*

Let me just mention in passing that the scenario of inaction of the Security Council was hotly debated at the San Francisco Conference, some states – guess who? – proposing that in such a case there should be freedom of action for regional agencies, but that proposal was refused. Another interesting proposal made in 1945 was that in case of enforcement action within the ambit of Article 53, the veto power should only be made available to members of that regional agency.

Now, on the basis of these few words, let me turn to Kosovo. You are all probably very familiar with the facts and so I can be very brief. I would characterise the NATO approach as an attempt to latch onto what the United Nations Security Council did in the months preceding the decision of NATO in October last year to threaten the use of force. So the NATO approach was that of an organization – one can of course debate whether NATO can be considered a regional organization – as closely as possible following the logic of and expressly linking its action to the precedent Security Council efforts. If you look at the NATO communiqué of early October 1998, you will see that every effort is made to make NATO appear as the natural enforcer of the line of Security Council action. Thus, NATO was able to argue that the Security Council had already determined that the situation was a threat to the peace and that all they were doing was to counter that threat to the peace. To this was, of course, added the argument of humanitarian necessity. So, I think that if one had to characterise the NATO action, one could say that it was a sort of an agency without authority. Or, as German lawyers would say, a *Geschäftsführung ohne Auftrag*. But that doesn't keep me from labelling the NATO activity as a breach of international law, and in a paper that I published in March 1999,[1] I said that it was illegal but due to NATO trying to extrapolate the Security Council direction, it was only a thin red line that separated NATO action from legality.

The next question would be, did the Security Council authorise or legitimate the NATO threat *ex post*. Again, in that paper, I sketched the interesting fact that just a couple of days after Richard Holbrook had concluded the agreements in mid-October, you had the Security Council stepping in again in Resolution

1 "NATO, the UN and the Use of Force: Legal Aspects", (1999) 10 *EJIL* 1-22.

1203 condoning and quite warmly welcoming the result of an agreement which, according to international law, had probably been brought about in violation of the Charter. There was also a Presidential statement by the Security Council which also welcomed the action of the Contact Group following Resolution 1203. I took the view then, and I still stick to it, that this could not be seen as an authorisation *ex post* in view of the attitudes of the Permanent Members of the Security Council, especially, of course, the attitude of Russia and China. Then followed the use of force by NATO and the question now is, does Resolution 1244 amount to an *ex post* authorisation – after all, it welcomes the general principles of a political solution that were found and the acceptance by the FRY of these principles. In the light of the circumstances, I think that 1244 cannot be seen as healing the illegality with effect *ex tunc*. I think that 1244 is a very realistic, pragmatic, forward-looking resolution and that the Permanent Members and all the other Members of the Security Council have good reasons to shy away from looking back because looking back could turn them into the same state in which those people who tried to look back at Sodom and Gomorrah ended up. So, better not to look back; let us make a sort of break and hope that in the future things will be legal. That is my reading of 1244.

However, whatever we say, we cannot deny that there is a lacuna in the Charter system which is due to the emergence of human rights concerns as considerations that may grow just as, if not more, compelling than the security concerns that were embodied in Article 2 (4) in 1945. I think that we have to do something about that. Some authors have already discerned a certain trend which would change the handling of Article 53 situations. This trend could be described as follows: you have a regional agency seizing the Security Council but the Council is unable or unwilling to act. But there is no implicit Security Council denial of the existence of a humanitarian crisis – or if the Security Council issues a determination that that humanitarian crisis constitutes a threat to the peace, the better. The next step would be for the regional agency to act on the basis of collective decisions arrived at in conformity with the purposes and principles of the United Nations Charter. The regional agency would claim the legitimacy of these measures, firstly on the basis of congruity with the purposes and principles of the Charter and secondly, because the decisions taken are collective decisions, maybe even unanimous decisions. My personal view on that trend would be that, at best, in circumstances such as the Kosovo case, that would get you to that thin red line. However, one has to take the consequences into consideration. Let me just quote to you from an American source about what the possible consequences could be if Kosovo turned out to be a precedent for future cases: "Under such a scenario, the organization in danger of sliding into irrelevance seems to be not NATO but the United Nations. In a political variant of free-market competition, the UN Security Council risks disappearing as a serious security body as the genuinely powerful prefer to work through a more convenient instrument. All that the Security Council can offer is 'legitimacy' in the view of some Western governments – and NATO may provide the desired multilateral covers with less obstruction."[2]

Let me conclude my presentation with a few words on a new phenomenon, or at least new for international lawyers. Until now, we have been speaking of regional organizations as enforcers of Security Council decisions or as enforcing human rights in lieu of the Security Council. Let me just say a few words on the involvement of some agencies in the decision-making of the Security Council – of course there has been talk about a European Security Council, of a European regional committee within the Security Council, etc. What I have found fascinating over recent weeks has been the role that the G8 (or the G7 plus one) has played in bringing about the solution – or hopefully the solution – to the Kosovo crisis. Of course, there is very little that I can say about the G7 plus one, or the G8, by way of legal observation, so let me just make a few more loose remarks. To subsume the G8 under Chapter VIII or regional agencies, you have to employ a very relaxed concept of regional organizations – you could say, well the G8 comprises the region where the money is and I think that compared to other definitions of "regions" that I have found in the literature, this is not really a very exuberant definition. If you look at 1244 and if you compare it to the G8 decisions, you will see that the Security Council did little more than to put the UN logo on top. The G8 regards itself as "an instrument of crisis management", "a clearinghouse both for the UN Security Council and the OSCE". It stresses that it is not a competitor for the UN but rather, a kind of "fire brigade" – this is the official self-understanding of the G8. As I see it from the sidelines, it appears to be a very cosy institution, an institution of "wellness" for its members. Just think of Russia and what Joschka Fischer said: "the issue is that of taking Russia back into the boat". Of course, I personally feel better in a boat than swimming around, even though I have to say that Russia has not been taken aboard definitively. At the June 1999 meeting, it was decided that Russia would be a member of G8 with regard to foreign policy and security matters whereas in relation to economic matters,

2 Jeffry Laùrenti, "NATO, the U.N. and the Use of Force", Background paper prepared for the United Nations Association of U.S.A. (1999), p.3.

the G7 plus one principle would apply – that is, that Russia would be taken aboard but dropped into the water again as the case may be. So much about the "wellness" of Russia. But let me talk about my own country, Germany feels great in the G8 because it has been frustrated about not getting into the Security Council but it is in the G8 and if the G8 does to the Security Council what it did in relation to Resolution 1244 then that is wonderful. My guess is that Japan will have similar thoughts. I guess that Canada also finds charming an expression used for the G8 which is "the little Security Council" – four permanent members already aboard; only China feels very uncomfortable about the G8 construction. My final question is, if the G8 has such a constructive impact upon Security Council decision-making as it certainly had in relation to Kosovo, isn't that an important step towards Security Council reform? We cannot deny that Security Council reform is overdue. One really sees the truth of the statement that if a problem only becomes sufficiently pressing a solution will be found, whether that solution is channelled into legal instruments and avenues or finds another way and overcomes any legal hurdles that may exist. But does this not imply a marginalisation of the UN Charter? That is the question. I think that one can have a slightly positive view on this – after all, in the Kosovo instance, the G8 brought the matter back to the UN Security Council. What is wrong with informal preparations of formal decisions? What is the difference between a superpower or the hyper-power providing the texts that are then approved or the G8 providing the text – I would certainly prefer eight States doing so. My view would be that what we see happening with regard to the G8 does not necessarily imply a weakening of the legal institutions which will then take the formal decision. After all, that is what is happening in national parliaments – probably even in Switzerland – that you have informal factions and alliances, or political party leaders getting together. My thesis would be – a thesis which is hopefully a bit provocative – that it was precisely the work of the G8 that brought the handling of the Kosovo crisis back to the Charter and constitutionality and therefore the G8 mechanisms deserve a friendly reception by what my friend Alain Pellet would call "les nations unistes".

PART II

SANCTIONS AND HUMANITARIAN ISSUES

8

OPENING REMARKS: SANCTIONS AND HUMAN RIGHTS LAW

Jochen A. Frowein[■]

Human rights form part of International Law. The International Court of Justice has recognised that the fundamental rights of the human person create obligations *erga omnes* which must be respected by all states. It should not be permissible to put into question the binding force of human rights as principles of present day international law with legal force, also for the United Nations Security Council.

International law has in fact in the second half of the 20th century rediscovered the dignity of the individual human being as last value for all law, including international law. A certain constitutionalisation of the international legal order has taken place. A hierarchy of norms is now also recognised in international law.

Sanctions against the state for violations of international law, particularly for breach of the fundamental norm prohibiting the use of force, are part of the collective security system of the United Nations. To a growing extent gross and flagrant violations of human rights are no longer seen as only human rights violations but also as a possible threat to the peace which can trigger the application of Chapter VII of the United Nations Charter.

■ Dr. jur., Dr.jur.h.c., M.C.L., Professor of International Law, Director of the Max-Planck-Institute for Comparative Public Law and International Law; former Vice-President of the European Commission of Human Rights.

V. Gowlland-Debbas (ed.), *United Nations Sanctions and International Law*, p. 125-128.

Economic sanctions under article 41 of Chapter VII create an important tension in international law. While the state and the state machinery having acted in violation of article 2 ? 4 of the Charter are the target of sanctions under Chapter VII, it is in fact the most vulnerable part of the population which will be the victim. This has been shown very clearly in the case of Iraq.

It should be mentioned in our context that Chapter VII sanctions can go as far as the use of armed force as article 42 shows.

Humanitarian law is of course directly applicable to this use of armed force. In addition, human rights treaties may be applicable, as article 15 of the European Convention on Human Rights clearly shows which stipulates that even in emergency cases no derogation from article 2, except in respect of deaths resulting from lawful acts of war, are permissible. This is clear evidence for the applicability of the Human Rights Convention also in armed conflict.

In addition to rules of humanitarian law it would seem to be possible to bring cases concerning the use of force under, e.g. the European Convention on Human Rights.

In this context it should be mentioned that positive obligations to remove dangers for the civilian population may be the result of article 2 of the European Convention on Human Rights. I would be of the opinion that there is a clear obligation for NATO Member states to remove the cluster bombs in Kosovo which create an enormous danger to the population.

Reports show that in Iraq the food and health situation, particularly for young children, is very dramatic indeed. It is also clear that there is a very limited access to clean water.

It should be accepted that there is an obligation under human rights provisions, particularly the International Covenant on Civil and Political Rights, to remove as far as possible these consequences. Indeed, the Security Council has shown that it is fully aware of that problem.

It seems to be of great importance to increase the awareness of lawyers in general concerning the issue of sanctions and human rights. Court proceedings in Member states may be one possibility to achieve that result.

As somebody who as a German school boy of ten years has seen the efforts of feeding the German population, particularly school children, after the Second World War one would like to express the view that similar efforts must be made for innocent young people in Iraq.

Sanctions and Human Rights Law

Chair: *Jochen A. Frowein*
Professor of International Law
Director, Max-Planck-Institute for Comparative Public Law
and International Law

9

SANCTIONS AND ECONOMIC, SOCIAL AND CULTURAL RIGHTS

Andrew Clapham[■]

Three questions come to mind when the topic of UN sanctions and economic, social and cultural rights are raised in the context of international law. First, can the UN impose sanctions in response to violations of economic, social and cultural rights? Second, can the UN be held responsible for violations of economic, social and cultural rights as a result of a decision to impose sanctions? Third, and perhaps this is the most complex problem, under what circumstances are those Member States of the Security Council that approve the adoption of mandatory sanctions responsible for violations of economic, social and cultural rights?

Let us turn to the first question. When considering the list of countries on which sanctions have been imposed by the Security Council in the last decade one finds the Security Council acting either in response to apartheid, to armed conflict, or in the case of Libya in regard to a dispute over the handing over of suspects for the Lockerbie bombing. If apartheid had not been centred on race discrimination but had simply denied part of the population, for whatever reason, their basic economic, social and cultural rights would the Security Council have had the power to impose mandatory sanctions? As we know, the Charter is clear that for the Security Council to decide to call on Members to interrupt economic relations or means of communications the Council has to determine the existence of a threat to the peace, breach of the peace, or act

■ Associate Professor of Public International Law, Graduate Institute of International Studies, Geneva.

V. Gowlland-Debbas (ed.), *United Nations Sanctions and International Law*, p. 131-141.

of aggression before it decides on the measures to maintain or restore international peace and security.

Could massive violations of economic, social and cultural rights lead to mandatory sanctions imposed by the Security Council? This may actually be a moot question as one could argue that the famine and humanitarian crisis in Somalia was simply a massive violation of the economic right to food. Even if sanctions are imposed in the context of armed conflict the factions may have as a primary tactic the systematic denial of food to various sectors of the population. Although such economic, social and cultural rights are not cited as the reason for the sanctions, they may indeed be at the heart of the sense of obligation engendered in the international community which triggered action under Chapter VII of the Charter. The fact that the crisis revolves around the denial of economic, social and cultural rights has important implications for any effective response. It is to miss the point if the international response is to study reports of torture and disappearance when the seeds of future instability lie in the denial of economic, social and cultural rights.

But before we leave this question we should decide if there is really scope to be more honest about the causes of crisis and the triggers for intervention. In 1992 the Security Council Summit, buoyed by the recent victory over President Saddam Hussein in the Gulf, felt ready to elaborate on their understanding of the trigger condition of a threat to international peace and security. In an important passage adopted at the level of Heads of State and Government they stated:

> the absence of war and of armed conflicts between States does not alone guarantee international peace and security. Other non-military menaces to peace and security can be found in the instability which exists in economic, social, humanitarian and environmental areas. It is incumbent upon all Members of the United Nations Organization, acting within the appropriate organs, to attach the highest priority to the solution of these problems.[1]

It seems then that there is an adequate legal base to consider imposing mandatory sanctions as a response to violations of economic, social and cultural rights that lead to the sort of instability that has an international dimension.

1 "Statement by the President of the Security Council on Behalf of the Council", Security Council Summit Meeting, 3 January 1992, UN Doc. S/23500.

As serious social or economic instability usually leads to migration and people leaving their country in search of work abroad the international dimension is almost inevitably present.

This is not to suggest that sanctions will always be the most appropriate response. We are only concerned here to clarify that when discussing early warning and prevention strategies with regard to threats to international peace and security it may be much more pertinent to consider violations of economic, social and cultural rights as well as reports of massacres and disappearances. In fact we may even have to move beyond a traditional human rights approach and tackle phenomena which do not fit neatly under the rights rubric. Corruption and financial scandals may now be seen as critical factors which can destabilize the population or even trigger a humanitarian crisis (consider Albania and Zaire in 1997). In fact the root of the instability may even be foreign commercial interests which have fragmented society and thrown up new power bases outside the influence of the state authority (consider Liberia, Sierra Leone and Angola in 1997).[2]

Turning to our second question: does the UN as a legal entity have international duties with regard to economic social and cultural rights violations which might flow from a sanctions decision? This is not the place to discuss whether the relevant Security Council decision can be subject to judicial review. The question of review and justiciability should not alter the issue of responsibility which flows from international legal personality. As is well known the UN has limited international legal personality in order to fulfill its functions. The International Court of Justice has stated that the UN "is a subject of international law and capable of possessing international rights and duties, and that it has capacity to maintain its rights by bringing international claims."[3] In this case the Court was concerned with a claim by the UN for the killing of its Chief negotiator Count Bernadotte. But once we accept the possible existence of rights and international claims we also have to accept the reality of duties and international responsibility. What are the international duties in this case? Of course the UN is not a party to any human rights treaty. The question then turns on customary international law. Is the UN bound by customary international human rights law?

2 I have explored some of these issues in *Human Rights and the Prevention of Humanitarian Emergencies*, (UNU/WIDER Working Paper 2001 (forthcoming)).

3 *Reparations for Injuries Case*, ICJ Reports, 1949, p. 174 at p. 179.

The obvious analogy is with international humanitarian law. For some time the UN has been grappling with the problem of which international humanitarian law standards to apply in the context of peace-keeping operations. The position has become much clearer in recent years. In a contribution to a symposium on "Humanitarian Action and Peace-Keeping Operations" two key members of the UN's Legal Office stated: "The Geneva Conventions which have by now been widely accepted as part of customary international law are binding upon all States, and, therefore, also upon the United Nations, irrespective of any formal accession."[4] Turning to the customary international law of human rights we can include the right not to be arbitrarily deprived of the right to life, the right to minimum sustenance, and the right to public assistance regarding health care and education as customary international law.[5] More generally one can add the right not to be subjected to inhuman and degrading treatment.

The question then arises can the Security Council choose to violate these rights in order to achieve international peace and security. No one has yet suggested that military forces have the right to commit war crimes in order to achieve a return to international peace. The attacks are justified as attacks on legitimate targets. Civilian casualties are dismissed as "collateral damage". It has been put forward by Reisman and Stevick that international law suggests that the framework for deciding the legitimacy of military action in time of war be applied to any determination of the legality of UN sanctions. In other words

---

4 Daphna Shraga and Ralph Zacklin "The Applicability of International Humanitarian Law to United Nations Peace-keeping Operations: Conceptual, Legal and Practical Issues", *Symposium on Humanitarian Action and Peace-keeping Operations* (22-24 June 1994) (ICRC), 39-59 at 47. The authors include the normal disclaimer that the views in the paper do not necessarily reflect the views of the Office of Legal Affairs or of the United Nations.

5 For a detailed discussion see O. Schachter *International Law in Theory and Practice* (Dordrecht, Boston, 1991), Ch XV, and B. Simma and P. Alston "The Sources of Human Rights Law: Custom, Jus Cogens, and General Principles", (1992) 12 *Australian Year Book of International Law* 82. See also General Comment no. 8 of the UNESCRC: "given the status of economic, social and cultural rights of vulnerable groups as part of general international law, as evidenced, for example, by the near-universal ratification of the Convention on the Rights of the Child and the status of the Universal Declaration of Human Rights" (at para. 8). Note the reference to general international law is probably intended to suggest that human rights principles do not need to pass the traditional tests for determining the emergence of customary international law. Rather they might also spring from peremptory norms or general principles of law. See Simma and Alston (infra).

five principles should guide the Security Council when imposing mandatory economic sanctions: that highly coercive sanctions be based on lawful contingencies (in our case on approval by the UN SC), that the sanctions be necessary and proportionate, that they reasonably maximize the distinction between combatants and non-combatants, that they be periodically assessed, and that relief be provided to injured third parties.[6]

The problem with this approach is that it is prisoner to the shifting concepts of proportionality and necessity. Which sanctions are necessary for the goal of getting President Saddam Hussein to change his mind about co-operation with the UN? How much suffering is proportionate for avoiding the alleged threat of the use of chemical weapons by Iraq? In some ways these are tests that are even more subjective than the tests applied in the laws of war. They certainly allow for a great deal of subjective assessment from the powers that drive the Security Council's sanctions regime.

An alternative approach can be found in the General Comments of the UN Economic Social and Cultural Rights Committee. In May 1999, in its latest General Comment on the Right for Food the Committee stated:

> 37. States parties should refrain at all times from food embargoes or similar measures which endanger conditions for food production and access to food in other countries. Food should never be used as an instrument of political and economic pressure. In this regard, the Committee recalls its position, stated in its General Comment No. 8, on the relationship between economic sanctions and respect for economic, social and cultural rights.

To take an analogy from international humanitarian law, using food as an instrument of pressure is like targeting medical transportation or undefended localities. Absolutely forbidden even if an argument can be made about necessity or proportionality. In fact even international humanitarian law states quite clearly: "Starvation of civilians as a method of warfare is prohibited." (Protocol I Article 54(1)). The Committee refers us back to its earlier comment on sanctions. In that comment the Committee referred to the Security Council's sanctions regime and the need to "distinguish between the basic objective of applying political and economic pressure upon the governing élite of a country to

6 M. Reisman and D. Stevick, "The Applicability of International Law Standards to United Nations Economic Sanctions Programmes", (1998) 9 *EJIL* 86-141

persuade them to conform to international law, and the collateral infliction of suffering upon the most vulnerable groups within the targeted country." The comment refers to the inclusion of humanitarian exemptions designed to permit the flow of essential goods and services for humanitarian purposes but goes on to explain how these exemptions are very limited in scope. "They do not address, for example, the question of access to primary education, nor do they provide for repair for infrastructures which are essential to provide clean water, adequate health care, etc." The comment points out that insufficient attention is being paid to the impact of sanctions on vulnerable groups and calls for the injection of a human rights dimension into deliberations on the issue of sanctions.

We only need consider one report on Iraq by UNICEF to realize the extent of the impact on children. The UNICEF representative for Iraq stated in October 1996: "Around 4,500 children under the age of five are dying here every month from hunger and disease". The Information sheet goes on to explain that:

> "According to Iraqi Government figures, cases of severe malnutrition increased substantially and the percentage of underweight children in Baghdad alone has risen from 7 per cent in 1991 to 29 per cent in 1995 – an increase of 400 percent. The decline leaves the children of a once prosperous nation suffering from malnutrition on a level with those in Mali and Northern Sudan – two of the poorest countries in Africa."[7]

Having concluded that the UN itself is bound by relevant human rights law in this field we need not speculate too long on which jurisdictions could adjudicate a claim against the UN for violating economic, social and cultural rights. The UN cannot be a defendant in the International Court of Justice in such a case and it is almost certain that international law would demand that the UN be afforded immunity from jurisdiction where the question was the effect of sanctions. Indeed even if international human rights law seems to have overridden concerns about immunity in the case of General Pinochet and President Milosevic, it remains supportive of the importance of functional immunity for international organizations at the national level.

In the *Case of Beer and Regan* v. *Germany* in the European Court of Human Rights, the Court saw that the "attribution of privileges and immunities to

7 PR/GVA/96/035, 4 October 1996.

international organizations is an essential means of ensuring the proper functioning of such organizations free from unilateral interference by individual governments." (At para 63, Judgement of 18 February 1999). But for us to overly concentrate on questions of legal responsibility and justiciability is to miss the point. Once we accept that the UN has obligations in this field we can design procedures to ameliorate the violations. For example the sanctions mechanism to be based within the UN Secretariat suggested by Secretary-General Boutros Boutros-Ghali in his supplement to his *Agenda for Peace*[8] could report to the Economic, Social and Cultural Rights Committee (or ECOSOC) on the human rights impact assessments which were built into the design of the sanctions regime, the actual impact on these rights, and the steps that are being taken to minimize any violations of economic, social and cultural rights. As the General Comment points out, all five permanent Members of the Security Council have signed the Covenant on Economic, Social and Cultural Rights. It is difficult to see why those States would want to do anything that would defeat the object and purpose of this treaty even if they are not bound in law to fulfill all the obligations in it. Apart from the obligation of these signatories and the obligation of the Parties to the Covenant to engage in international assistance to achieve the realization of the rights in the Covenant, we should remember that nearly all the States targeted under UN sanctions are States Parties to this treaty: Angola, Iraq, Libya, Somalia, Yugoslavia all have international obligations under this treaty.

Let us now turn to our last question and ask whether indeed there is room to discuss the responsibility of Member States of the Security Council for the results of the Council's sanctions. We have argued that the UN may be responsible for violations of customary international law in this area. But holding Member States responsible for the actions of international organizations is not obvious in international law. So far most of the cases and scholarly writing have concentrated on the dissolution of international organization and the question of whether the Member States should be liable for the debts of the organization. The lack of convincing international legal authority in this area has led some scholars to fall back on policy considerations. In a thorough examination of the question, the Institut de Droit International canvassed all

8 A/50/60-S/1995/1, 3 January 1995 at para. 75. Among other things this mechanism was to "assess, at the request of the Security Council, and before sanctions are imposed, their potential impact on the target country and on third countries;" and "to monitor application of the sanctions."

possible perspectives on the issue. The rapporteur, Judge Rosalyn Higgins had the following preliminary conclusion:

> "By reference to the accepted sources of international law, there is no norm which stipulates that Member states bear a legal liability to third parties for the non-fulfilment by international organizations of their obligations to third parties."[9]

Turning to questions of policy she weighed on the one hand the "efficient and independent functioning of international organizations, and second, the protection of third parties from undue exposure to loss and damage."[10] She was concerned that "If members know they are potentially liable for contractual damages or tortious harm caused by the acts of an international organization, they will necessarily intervene in virtually all decision-making by international organizations." This concern mirrors the concern shown by the European Court of Human Rights in the *Beer and Regan case* referred to earlier. Higgins suggests that third parties can be protected through insurance and *ad hoc* guarantees from Members. But if we consider the policy issues surrounding our problem of the human rights impact of sanctions the parameters are rather different. It is not a question of a Member State interfering in the decision-making process of the organization but rather fifteen Member States creating the policy of the organization. The question is not really about quantifiable contractual or tortious harm but rather about violating fundamental human rights. And the possibilities for third parties to protect themselves from these violations are almost non-existent. It makes no sense to say that the civilian population can rise up and overthrow the leader who has engaged the wrath of the Security Council Members. Nor is it credible to simply blame the leader of the targeted state for the human rights violations which the civilian population are being subjected to.

Although the majority of members of the Institut shared the view of the rapporteur that "there was no rule of international law providing for the liability of states members for the defaults of international organizations," and that "Any liability could only be determined by reference to the particular provisions governing the operation of specific international organizations," a minority stressed that there was no rule saying that there was no liability. For some the question is the function of the organization. Where the functions are governmental rather than commercial then States retained a financial responsibility.

9 (1995) *Annuaire de l'Institut de droit international* at 287.
10 *Ibid.* at 288.

Although the final resolution states that "there is no general rule of international law whereby states members are, due solely to their membership, liable concurrently or subsidiarily, for the obligations of an international organization of which they are members" the minority view was accommodated through the inclusion of an exception. The exception which was accepted by the majority reads:

> "In particular circumstances, members of an international organization may be liable for its obligations in accordance with a relevant general principle of international law, such as acquiescence or the abuse of rights."

It would not be appropriate to continue to try to adapt the debate over non-fulfilment of obligations by international organizations to our subject. Because the debate at the Institut took place against the obligations of Member States of the Tin Council for its debts, it is hard to really draw conclusions about the obligations of Member States for the acts of international organizations more generally. We suggest here that some continuing separate responsibility for Member States continues in the context of the UN and the Security Council and that this is particularly the case with regards to human rights obligations.[11] Suffice it to say that there is plenty of scope to argue that States Parties to the Economic, Social and Cultural Rights Covenant, such as the UK and France, that have openly explained their policy towards inter-governmental decision-making at the UN as based on the importance of protecting human rights around the world, could be legitimately questioned about their obligations under the Covenant as they arise from their decision-making in the Council. In fact as permanent Members and as Members of the European Union they are obliged

---

11 In a discussion of the Security Council and the rule of law Brownlie concludes: "Even if the political organs have a wide margin of appreciation in determining that they have competence by virtue of Chapter VI or Chapter VII, and further, in making dispositions to maintain or restore international peace and security, it does not follow that the selection of the modalities of implementation is unconstrained by legality. Indeed when the right of individuals are involved, the application of human rights standards is a legal necessity. Human rights now form part of the concept of international public order and the International Court, in dictum supported by 12 judges, has asserted that the obligations of States deriving from the "basic rights of the human person" are obligations *erga omnes.*" [*Barcelona Traction* case (Second Phase), ICJ Reports, 1970, p. 3 at p. 32.] This discipline is no less applicable when Member states are discharging their responsibilities as members of the Security Council." I. Brownlie, "The Decisions of Political Organs of the United Nations and the Rule of Law" in R. St. J. Macdonald (ed), *Essays in Honour of Wang Tieya* (Dordrecht, Boston, 1993), pp. 91-102 at 102.

under Article 19(2) of the Treaty on European Union to "in the execution of their functions, ensure the defence of the positions and the interests of the Union, without prejudice to their responsibilities under the provisions of the United Nations Charter." Considering that one of the objectives of the Union's common foreign and security policy is identified in the Treaty as developing and consolidating democracy and the rule of law, and respect for human rights and fundamental freedoms, it seems clear that at least these two States have responsibilities, not only under customary international law and the Covenant, but also under EU law.

In fact the European Court of Human Rights, in the *Beer* case mentioned earlier has sent a clear message that not only will they judge any immunity granted to an international organization for conformity with the human rights guarantees in the Convention, but they also seem to have indicated that they could be prepared to lift the organizational veil where a government seemed to be hiding behind an international organization in breach of that government's international human rights obligations.

> 57. The Court is of the opinion that where States establish international organizations in order to pursue or strengthen their cooperation in certain fields of activities, and where they attribute to these organizations certain competences and accord them immunities, there may be implications as to the protection of fundamental rights. It would be incompatible with the purpose and object of the Convention, however, if the Contracting States were thereby absolved from their responsibility under the Convention in relation to the field of activity covered by such attribution. It should be recalled that the Convention is intended to guarantee not theoretical or illusory rights, but rights that are practical and effective.

Again it is not necessary here to speculate on how to hold Members of the Council to account in a court of law, or even what would happen in a clash between the European Convention and a State invoking Article 103 of the UN Charter. But having identified the international legal framework, the moral and political case for discussing responsibility of Council members for human rights violations which result from sanctions becomes much more pressing. If we move from the language of the "disastrous"[12] effects of sanctions to the language of "human rights violations" we change the way we see the same problem. Some violations will not always be predictable. But, as the general comment

12 See the UNICEF Information Sheet (*supra*).

shows, it is the current methodology for designing and monitoring sanctions which is faulty. We do not need to conclude that sanctions law simply trumps human rights law. If we want to start to take human rights seriously in the context of sanctions, we could start to include hard questioning when Security Council members come before the human rights treaty bodies. Inserting a sanctions dimension into the world of human rights monitoring could be just as fruitful as inserting a human rights dimension in the design and monitoring of sanctions.

10

INTERPRETING THE HUMANITARIAN EXCEPTIO]
THROUGH THE SANCTIONS COMMITTEES

Gian Luca Burci■

It has become customary for economic and similar sanctions imposed by the UN Security Council under Chapter VII of the Charter to provide for exceptions allowing the supply of certain materials and items, or the performance of certain transactions, activities or services, to satisfy "humanitarian" or "civilian" needs of the population of the target country. The first major precedent in this sense is paragraph 3 (d) of resolution 253 (1968), under which the prohibition to supply commodities and products to Southern Rhodesia excluded medical and educational items and, in humanitarian circumstances, foodstuffs.

After a hiatus of more than 20 years, humanitarian exceptions (as they are commonly referred to) have been introduced in various forms into all sanctions programmes established by the Security Council, with the obvious exception of embargoes on the supply of weapons. Thus, paragraph 3 (c) of resolution 661 (1990) which imposed sanctions against Iraq, excludes "supplies intended strictly for medical purposes, and, in humanitarian circumstances, foodstuffs" from the prohibition to sell or supply "commodities or products" to Iraq. Moreover, paragraph 4 of the resolution allows "payments exclusively for strictly medical or humanitarian purposes and, in humanitarian circumstances, foodstuffs". With the exception of the special programme referred to as "oil-for-food" launched by resolution 986 (1995), the current terms of allowed transactions with Iraq are provided for in paragraph 20 of resolution 687 (1991), which

■ Senior Legal Officer, Office of the Legal Counsel, World Health Organization. The opinions expressed are exclusively those of the author and do not necessarily reflect those of the World Health Organization.

V. Gowlland-Debbas (ed.), *United Nations Sanctions and International Law*, p. 143-154.

exempts "foodstuffs notified to the Committee established by resolution 661 (1990) or, with the approval of that Committee ... materials and supplies for essential civilian needs and financial transactions related thereto". The economic sanctions imposed against the Federal Republic of Yugoslavia (hereafter "Yugoslavia") by resolutions 757 (1992), 760 (1992) and 820 (1993) provided for humanitarian exceptions couched in similar terms. In the case of Haiti, the prohibition to sell or supply commodities and products to that country, set out in resolution 917 (1994), excluded "supplies intended strictly for medical purposes and foodstuffs"; other commodities and products "for essential humanitarian needs", as well as petroleum or petroleum products, with the approval of the competent Sanctions Committee; and other items at the specific request of the legitimate authorities overturned by the coup of 1991. The same resolution, as in the case of Southern Rhodesia, also unconditionally exempted "trade in information materials ... needed for the free flow of information". Finally, resolution 748 (1992), which imposed limited financial and trade sanctions as well as a flight embargo against Libya, makes an exception to the latter in paragraph 4 (a) if "the particular flight has been approved on grounds of significant humanitarian need by the Committee" established by the same resolution.

The Security Council, normally with the same resolution imposing sanctions, also establishes a committee composed of all the Council's members at any given time (the "sanctions committees"). The operation of the humanitarian exceptions is, in general, subject to some form of vetting or monitoring by these committees. The need for a case-by-case vetting reflects the legal scheme followed by the Council: the sanctions entail a total prohibition to perform certain activities, unless individual exceptions are granted on proved humanitarian or other specified grounds. The committees usually discharge the tasks of advising the Council on how to improve the effectiveness of the sanctions, advising States at their request on the scope of their obligations, investigating and reporting to the Council violations of the sanctions, and regulating humanitarian exceptions. In the latter area, the committees generally have to approve individual exceptions to the sanctions at the request of states or international agencies, and have on occasion issued elaborate guidelines advising states about the scope of the exceptions and the modalities to be followed by requestors.

Sanctions committees are political/administrative bodies whose practice and procedures can be quite complex, prone to politicization and at times bewildering to the observer.[1] They meet in private sessions, thus the records of their meetings and their working documents are mostly restricted and beyond public scrutiny. The committees have until recently nurtured the secrecy of their proceedings as essential to ensure the effectiveness of their role.[2] Decisions of the Committees are addressed to their requestors by a confidential communication, normally without further publicity or circulation. Decisions are remarkably laconic and generally do not provide any justification. Largely for political reasons, key members of the committees have always claimed the importance of a case-by-case approach to requests for advice or exceptions, to the cost of inconsistencies within and between sanctions regimes.[3] This attitude, and the virtual lack of any mechanism of accountability, have generated a rather haphazard and unpredictable jurisprudence, which sometimes reflects shifting political attitudes by individual members against the target State. Another distinguishing feature of the committees' work is decision-making by consensus. This gives a virtual veto to every member, but in practice ensures the leverage of the main sponsors of the sanctions, which can block requests for exceptions to an otherwise complete ban. The politicization of the committees explains the prevalence of the "symbolism of power" over considerations of pragmatism and viability: besides the aspects just referred to, some committees have shown a tendency to micromanage the implementation of control and monitoring measures, as well as a reluctance to delegate authority for managing or overseeing administrative or operational details. It can also be argued that the sanctions committees are an example of "split personality", combining enfor-

1 An incisive introduction to the Iraq Sanctions Committee is provided in M. Koskenniemi, "Le comité des sanctions (créé par la résolution 661 (1990) du Conseil de sécurité)", (1991) 37 *AFDI* 119-137. For a thorough analysis of the practice of the Yugoslavia Sanctions Committee, see M. Scharff, J. Dorosin, "Interpreting UN Sanctions: The Rulings and Role of the Yugoslavia Sanctions Committee", (1993) 19 *Brooklyn Journal of International Law* 771-827.

2 This practice, which has been widely criticized by states, international agencies and scholars, has been improved by some recent decisions of the Security Council, under which, for example, the Chairperson of each Committee has to brief other delegations and correspondents about the highlights of each meeting. See most recently UN Doc. S/1999/92 of 29 January 1999, "Note by the President of the Security Council: Work of the Sanctions Committees". Since 1996, moreover, sanctions committees have begun to report regularly on an annual basis to the Security Council on their activities.

3 It is not infrequent that two requests by the same government to supply the same item to the same end-user for the same purpose, are approved the first time and rejected the second. This is probably also due to the high volume of requests that flood the committees and on oversights on the part of staff of members' delegations.

cement functions with the regulation of humanitarian exceptions. In this regard, the construction of what represents "humanitarian" or "civilian" needs, and the practical modalities of how to address them, assumes a crucial importance to define the median line between considerations of international security and the safeguard of basic needs and rights of the civilian population of the target State.

The basic approach of the sanctions committees to the definition of "humanitarian circumstances" and "humanitarian" or "essential civilian" needs, and the related political and conceptual difficulties emerge clearly from the debates held in the Iraq Sanctions Committee between September 1990 and the end of the Gulf War. The approach followed by the 661 Committee has been implicitly adopted by other sanctions committees and thus constitutes an important precedent. As noted above, resolution 661 (1990) allowed the supply of foodstuffs "in humanitarian circumstances", implicitly to be determined by the Committee. During a paralysing debate, which originated from the request of some States to provide food to their nationals stranded in occupied Kuwait and was then broadened to the general issue of supplying food to Iraq, Cuba and Yemen took the position that access to food was a basic and inalienable human right. Humanitarian circumstances thus existed by definition, without further determinations by the Committee. The majority of the Committee, however, rejected this position and settled for an overall approach based on a number of explicit or implicit criteria, set out by the Council in resolution 666 (1990) of 13 September 1990. Since it proved impossible to agree on an objective definition of humanitarian needs, the Committee would rely on reports from third parties, normally international agencies, and the supply of foodstuffs would be subordinated to conditions and modalities which would ensure its delivery to the intended beneficiaries and its non-diversion. There was no recognition of an unconditional right of a population to relief from the effects of sanctions directed against its government. Rather, the Committee implicitly accepted a threshold of suffering and hardship to be determined at the discretion of the Committee as not incompatible with human rights or humanitarian law criteria, and only above which humanitarian relief would be allowed. The discourse in the Committee was reminiscent of the parameters of humanitarian law, e.g. those of Article 23 of the Fourth Geneva Convention and Article 70 of its

Protocol I, rather than of reliance on the normal parameters of human rights law.[4]

The hard lessons learnt from the paralysing debates in the Iraq Sanctions Committee led to resolution 687 (1991), and the subsequent resolutions on Yugoslavia, Haiti and Libya. These allowed the provision of medical supplies and foodstuffs, but subjected the supply of other commodities or products, or the performance of services or flights, to approval by the sanctions committees. The approach followed by the committees, especially in the initial period of their activity, is remarkably uniform. The common trend was to consider immediate, acute and short-term needs for essential items and products, akin to the provision of relief in military conflicts or in case of disaster relief. The approval of those items and products depended on the requests received by the Committees, which played a largely passive role. The committees considered individual requests in isolation and case-by-case. There was no attempt to encourage the prioritization or consolidation of supplies, so as to create synergies and maximize the impact on civilians. There was also extreme reluctance, for political reasons as well as to avoid manipulations by the target States, to assign the monitoring or assessment of the situation of the population to international agencies. Such an overall approach cannot effectively address the essential needs of a civilian population in the medium- to long-term, and the dramatic deterioration of conditions of life in Iraq and Haiti are testimony to the inadequate functioning of humanitarian exceptions as managed by the committees.[5] Following is an overview of some of the main elements of the practice of the sanctions committees.

---

4 It is for these reasons that General Comment No. 8 of 4 December 1997 by the Committee on Economic, Social and Cultural Rights is particularly relevant. See UN Doc. E/C.12/1997/8. The Committee unambiguously rejects the contention that the provision of the Covenant could be "inoperative, or in any way inapplicable" solely because economic sanctions have been imposed against a State. By strongly arguing that the international community remains responsible for ensuring the protection of at least the "core content" of the economic, social and cultural rights of the people of the target State (paragraph 7), the Committee aimed at overcoming the apparent dichotomy between human rights and "humanitarian law-like" considerations as applicable to states under sanctions.

5 It was precisely to address the inherent inadequacy of the functioning of the humanitarian exception that the Security Council, as early as August 1991 by resolutions 706 (1991) and 712 (1991), launched the so-called "oil-for-food" programme, in order to allow Iraq

I Items Falling Within the Humanitarian Exceptions

The open-ended nature of the terms used by the Security Council and the case-by-case approach favoured by all sanctions committees have made it impossible for the latter to arrive at an agreed definition or listing of categories of items, products and transactions considered "humanitarian", or of general substantive guidelines for the screening of applications. For example, an attempt in 1992 by the non-aligned members of the Iraq Sanctions Committee to designate categories of items and products to be transferred from the no-objection to the notification procedure failed after protracted negotiations. The only outcome was a vague gentleman's agreement to consider favourably applications to supply those items and products, which was soon forgotten.[6] The practice of the sanctions committees, however, especially those on Iraq and Yugoslavia, allows the identification of a number of categories of items for which approval was, in principle, granted: food production equipment; agricultural products (with the partial exception of fertilizers and pesticides for their dual-use potential); materials for sanitation and water purification; clothing; soaps and detergents; educational materials; religious objects; health-related materials (e.g. ambulances) beyond strictly medical supplies which are normally exempted from the sanctions.[7] The sanctions committees were probably more successful

---

to sell a limited amount of oil under UN supervision and to destine the revenues to finance humanitarian supplies to that country as well as a number of UN activities. While the initial plan was extremely stringent and proved unacceptable to Iraq, a "softened" version adopted by resolution 986 (1995) was finally accepted by Iraq in May 1996 and implemented as from December of the same year. An even summary description or analysis of the oil-for-food programme, however, would be out of place in the context of the present contribution, which is thus limited to the other examples of humanitarian exceptions.

6 See UN Doc. S/1996/700 of 26 August 1996, containing the first substantive report of the 661 Committee to the Security Council since 1990, in particular paragraph 43. The gentleman's agreement concerned the following categories of supplies: medical equipment; packaging material for medical supplies and foodstuffs; clothing; supplies for babies and infants; soaps; animal feed and animals and eggs for breeding or hatching purposes; agricultural seeds; supplies and materials for primary and secondary education; spare parts and materials for water treatment and sewage plants; and storage facilities for grain and foodstuffs.

7 General Assembly resolution 51/242 of 15 September 1997, adopted on the basis of the work of a Sub-Group of the Working Group on an Agenda for Peace, which also dealt with UN sanctions, states that "Basic or standard medical and agricultural equipment and basic or standard educational items should also be exempted; a list should be drawn up for that purpose. Other essential humanitarian goods should be considered

in defining negatively what cannot be considered humanitarian items and products: industrial inputs, identified in a very broad way as anything that could conceivably benefit the local industry (e.g. the supply to Iraq of raw textiles as opposed to finished clothing, or of chemical precursors to Yugoslavia as opposed to manufactured medicines); items in quantities considered excessive (e.g. two million pencils to be supplied to Iraqi schools, as opposed to only one million); dual-use items; luxury items (defined rather arbitrarily between sanctions regimes, so that whiskey would not be allowed into Iraq but was allowed into Yugoslavia). More in general, members of the committees would object to items they would consider as non-essential. They introduced as a yardstick for this purpose the distinction between humanitarian relief and development, and between satisfaction of short-term civilian needs and rehabilitation of infrastructures, even though the two are often logically and functionally inseparable. A separate mention should be made of the inconsistent treatment of information material, such as newsprint and broadcasting equipment. Whereas the Iraq Sanctions Committee always rejected their supply as non-essential items, the Yugoslavia Sanctions Committee, at the request of the US and subsequently France, allowed their supply to opposition parties in Serbia on the declared basis that they aimed at satisfying the Yugoslav people's fundamental human right to freedom of information and thus fell within the humanitarian exception.[8] Finally, all sanctions committees adopted a much more liberal policy concerning requests by humanitarian agencies such as Office of the High Commissioner for Refugees (UNHCR) or the International Committee of the Red Cross (ICRC). These came to be approved almost automatically and without particular scrutiny after initial periods of uncertainty and tensions between the Committee and humanitarian actors.

II Modalities and Conditions of Approval and Delivery

The practice of the Committees, summarized above, has developed towards streamlining and simplification. The 661 Committee, once again, pioneered

---

for exemption by the relevant United Nations bodies, including the sanctions committees."

8 See Scharff and Dorosin, "Interpreting UN Sanctions", *supra,* n. 1, pp. 791-793. In reality, those requests coincided with the 1992 presidential elections in the Federal Republic of Yugoslavia and represented an (unsuccessful) attempt by some Western states to influence their outcome by strengthening the outreach capacity of the political opposition to their President Milosevic.

a practice that was subsequently endorsed by the other committees. That Committee initially considered every request in the course of its meetings, but in view of the growing number of applications, this procedure quickly became unwieldy. The practice thus developed of the so-called no-objection procedure, under which the Secretariat would circulate all applications to the permanent missions of the Committee's members, with a deadline for placing an objection. In the absence of such an objection, the request was considered approved. A twist on this procedure consists of the so-called "holds". A delegation which needs clarifications on a request or has other concerns short of an objection, can place the request on hold, on the understanding that it will contact the requesting government or organization with a view to solving the issue. Such contacts can either lead to a removal of the hold (i.e. to an approval) or to an objection, and take place on a purely bilateral level, at the initiative of the member concerned and outside of the Committee's purview and control. This practice introduces a bilateral element that contradicts the role of the committee as a collective body and is prone to abuse; it has been routinely used by members that wanted to delay (sometimes for months) or hinder the approval of certain requests. At meetings of the Committee, the Secretariat circulates a list of all recent applications with an indication of their status and the delegations that have placed objections or holds. This gives the other members a possibility in principle to question the rationale for objections and holds which, however, cannot be challenged or overruled. The leverage granted by the rule of consensus to individual members of the Committee, and the weakening of the authority of the committees as institutions is indeed extraordinary.

Some sanctions committees, in particular those on Iraq and Yugoslavia, adopted a policy of discriminating between requests of a commercial nature by governments on behalf of their companies (companies cannot apply directly) and requests by humanitarian agencies. The Iraq Sanctions Committee, acting under the "oil-for-food programme" established by Security Council resolution 986 (1995), only cursorily examines requests by UN agencies for importation of materials into northern Iraq, whereas it subjects requests by governments to a harsher scrutiny and heavier documentary requirements. The Yugoslavia Sanctions Committee developed a particularly articulated policy concerning requests by humanitarian agencies or by governments on behalf of humanitarian NGOs, which were processed on a priority basis as of 1995. This policy was progressively implemented after an initial period of rigidity on the part of the Committee and of tensions with UNHCR, then the lead agency for humanitarian assistance in the Balkans. UNHCR was severely hindered in its operations, budgeting and planning by the intransigence of the Committee in approving on a case-by-case basis each and every consignment directed to or transiting through Yugoslavia. The Yugoslavia Sanctions Committee had to adapt its *modus operandi* to the exceptional situation it was facing, in which the civil war in Bosnia and Herzegovina and the subsequent convulsions in Croatia and Yugoslavia confronted it with humanitarian tragedies of great scope and complexity.[9] Humanitarian consignments directed to Bosnia and Herzegovina generally had to transit through Yugoslavia – which required case-by-case approval pursuant to resolution 820 (1993) – and necessitated much pre-planning on the part of the UN. Thus, in 1995 the Committee decided that consignments transiting through the Yugoslavia would be approved under the no-objection procedure, and accepted "programme applications" from international agencies, covering their consignments and transfers of funds on an annual or semi-annual basis rather than approving them case-by-case.[10] It is evident that the extent of the Committee's authority was interpreted in a flexible way by its members and allowed it to take measures which appeared to fall outside its competence under the applicable Security Council resolutions. Mention can also be made of occasional authorizations to UN agencies to use border crossing points not approved by the Committee pursuant to paragraph 23 of resolution 820 (1993).[11] The Yugoslavia Sanctions Committee, however, was also a good example of the penchant of the sanctions committees for micro-managing the modalities of delivery and monitoring the end-use of the supplies approved by them, as well as of the introduction of conditions and requirements other than those based on the objective humanitarian situation in the target country. This aspect became evident with regard to requests to supply fuel or gas to Yugoslavia or, through the latter, to Bosnia and Herzegovina. The Committee subjected such requests to strict conditions in terms of quantities and time-span of deliveries, as well as to the identification of the end-users/beneficiaries and to stringent monitoring and verification procedures by international agencies such as UNHCR and WHO. The conditions imposed by the Committee to prevent diversion of the assistance and ensure end-use by small groups identified as particularly vulnerable, were so demanding that several requests were not approved or could not be imple-

9 The evolving practice of the Yugoslavia Sanctions Committee is summarized in its third and final report to the Security Council. UN Doc. S/1996/946 of 15 November 1996, in particular paras. 68-78.

10 *Ibid.*, para. 69.

11 *Ibid.*, para. 72.

mented.[12] The Committee also conditioned the supply of heating oil and liquid gas to Yugoslavia to their being transported on the Danube rather than by road, and linked the supply of natural gas to Yugoslavia to an uninterrupted supply of the same to Sarajevo (by a pipeline that ran through Yugoslavia). Also the regulation by the Libya Sanctions Committee of medical evacuation flights from Libya appears to be an example of micro-management: besides being approved on a case-by-case basis, under guidelines issued by the Committee in 1995, evacuation flights could only be undertaken by four specified aircraft. The guidelines, furthermore, prescribed a limited number of allowed destinations in five countries and required inspection and surveillance of the aircraft by the country of destination as one of the conditions for granting approval.

III FINANCING OF HUMANITARIAN SUPPLIES AND OTHER FINANCIAL TRANSACTIONS

This is perhaps the area of greatest difficulty in the design and management of the humanitarian exceptions, and in which the solutions adopted have proved more unsatisfactory. It should be recalled that most recent sanctions regimes prohibit States from transferring funds or making available financial resources to the target State or entities incorporated in it or controlled by it. They also normally require States to freeze the assets of the target State present under their jurisdiction. The question thus arises, especially for sanctions regimes of a certain duration, how the target State can finance the purchase of its humanitarian supplies. Resolutions 661 (1990) and 687 (1991) on Iraq, as well as resolution 757 (1992) on Yugoslavia, did not prohibit the release by third states of frozen assets of the target state, and several states reportedly did unfreeze Iraqi and Yugoslav funds to finance sales by their national companies. However, the resolutions in question only authorized states to do so if they so wished. A number of countries holding large frozen amounts and with claims against the target state – for example the United States – consistently refused to unfreeze funds, thus partly frustrating the purpose of the humanitarian clauses. The trend in most recent sanctions regimes, moreover, has been towards a total freeze of the assets of the target state, putting the financing of its own humanitarian needs on an even more precarious legal footing.

12 *Ibid.*, paras. 73-75.

In the case of Iraq, for example, paragraph 11 of Security Council resolution 778 (1992) of 2 October 1992 prohibited the direct release of frozen Iraqi funds to exporters, only allowing their release into a United Nations sub-account of the escrow account established under resolutions 706 (1991) and 712 (1991) containing the first and ill-fated oil-for-food scheme. The sub-account in question was to receive funds, other than revenues from the sale of Iraqi oil, to finance the purchase of humanitarian supplies which were in principle subject to the same heavy monitoring of in-country distribution as those purchased using oil revenues. The 661 Committee, by a decision adopted in October 1991,[13] confirmed this requirement, which became very soon inapplicable in view of Iraq's refusal to implement the oil-for-food scheme. Still, the 661 Committee never revoked the requirement of in-country monitoring, making the use of the sub-account practically impossible. Resolution 778 (1992), by establishing the sub-account as the only avenue to lawfully unfreeze Iraqi funds, in reality closed that avenue. This issue, prior to the implementation of the oil-for-food scheme launched by resolution 986 (1995) which created a regular source of funds, had become a major irritant within the Committee, especially between the United States and United Kingdom on the one hand, which wanted to maintain the status quo, and France and the Russian Federation on the other hand, which favoured the elimination of an unacceptable vicious circle created for political reasons. The major perverse effect of the policy in question is that it made any release of frozen Iraqi funds automatically illegal. Still, since 1992 the Committee approved literally thousands of applications, whose source of funding was hardly ever scrutinized or challenged. By attempting to make the sanctions against Iraq more coercive and effective, the Security Council and the 661 Committee may have ironically weakened their own ability to oversee and control financial transactions with Iraq while worsening the situation of Iraqi civilians. The other major perverse effect is that this imbalance in the sanctions regimes and the manner of their implementation and management, create an inconsistency between commercial transactions, which were allowed and actually approved by the committees, and the financial transactions necessary to enable even limited trade relations, which were instead either prohibited or made almost impossible by the policy of individual states.

In conclusion, this sketchy overview of the practice of the sanctions committees shows how imperfect and politicized the system of administration of sanctions

13 UN Doc. S/23149 of 16 October 1991, in particular section III.B.

centred on the United Nations can be. Its politicization, in particular, makes the sanctions committees further instruments, in addition to the Security Council, of the policies pursued by some of their members against the target States. The sanctions committees thus appear to fall short of their potential role of administrators and regulators of United Nations sanctions regimes. They could instead bring an element of pragmatism and stability, necessary for the long-term viability of measures which are often as disruptive for the target State and its population as they are for the implementing States.[14] This state of affairs has had particularly heavy repercussions on the situation of the populations of the target States, and has strengthened doubts about the legitimacy of particularly coercive and indiscriminate sanctions regimes in the light of the UN Charter, human rights law and, by analogy, humanitarian law. While major modifications of the system as it has evolved since 1990 do not appear likely at this time, scholars, practitioners and diplomats have pointed to numerous areas for possible improvements.[15] The measures recently adopted by the Security Council,[16] if fully and consistently implemented, will play a positive role in progressively rationalizing certain aspects of the functions of the sanctions committees. A proposal that I would like to offer, in closing this contribution, is for the Security Council to delegate much more substantive authority to manage and administer humanitarian exceptions to the United Nations Secretariat, similarly to what already happens in the European Union in favour of the Commission and its Secretariat.

---

14 See also the comments and suggestions in G.L. Burci, "Do Economic Sanctions Work? A View from the United Nations", (1996) 2 *ILSA Journal of International and Comparative Law* 577-586.

15 See, for example, the insightful and constructive proposals contained in L. Minear, D. Cortright, J. Wagler, G. A. Lopez, T.G. Weiss, "Towards More Humane and Effective Sanctions Management – Enhancing the Capacity of the United Nations System", October 6, 1997, a report prepared jointly by the Watson Institute of Brown University, the Kroc Institute of the University of Notre Dame, and the Fourth Freedom Forum, at the request of the former UN Department of Humanitarian Affairs.

16 *Supra*, n. 2.

11

UNICEF AND THE SANCTIONS COMMITTEE – LESSONS LEARNED FROM IRAQ

Jean Dupraz[■]

I INTRODUCTION

On 10 December 1996, the very first day of the implementation of Security Council Resolution 986, commonly known as the Oil for Food Programme (OFFP), Secretary General Boutros-Ghali declared, "This is a victory for the poorest of the poor in Iraq, for the women, the children, the sick and the disabled". Security Council President, Mr. Paolo Fulci added, "More than 20 million innocent Iraqi civilian will be finally saved from starvation and untold suffering".

Two and a half years later, on 28 April 1999, Secretary General Kofi Annan, in his two year review and assessment of the programme stated, "Regardless of the improvements that might be brought about in the implementation of the current humanitarian programme – in terms of approval procedures, better performance by the Iraqi Government, or funding levels – the magnitude of the humanitarian needs is such that they cannot be met within the context of the parameters set forth in resolution 986. Nor was the programme intended to meet all the needs of the Iraqi people".[1]

■ Monitoring and Evaluation Officer, UNICEF.

1 In August 1999, UNICEF and the Government of Iraq released the first surveys of child mortality in Iraq since 1991. The survey in the Centre and South of Iraq, showed that under 5 mortality had risen from 56 to 131 deaths/1000 live births between 1984-1989 period and 1994-1999 period. Infant mortality in the Centre and South had also risen from 47 to 108 deaths/1000 live births during the same period. In contrast, a separate

V. Gowlland-Debbas (ed.), *United Nations Sanctions and International Law*, p. 155-163.

As great expectations turned to more realistic views, all parties involved in the implementation of the OFFP had to adapt to the most complex requirements of a unique and huge programme, often described as the most comprehensive humanitarian operation ever planned by the United Nations. Part of the learning process was the interface of humanitarian agencies with the Security Council sanctions committee (661 Committee). The interface already existed, as UN agencies had been importing goods into Iraq with sanctions committee approval since the imposition of sanctions in 1990. However, with the introduction of the OFFP and its cumbersome and lengthy procedures, the interface became much more complex.

This note illustrates the difficulties UNICEF has faced in the field to adapt itself to meet the requirements of the sanctions committee, particularly in processing of contracts. At the same time, some valuable lessons can be drawn not only in the challenges involved in the processing of contracts, but also in how UNICEF, together with all other UN agencies in the field, formulated recommendations in order to facilitate the processing of contracts by the 661 committee, and subsequently help expedite the arrival of much needed humanitarian supplies into Iraq that helped protect children and the most vulnerable from the impact of sanctions.

II THE OIL FOR FOOD PROGRAMME

It should be noted that since the Colloquium was held in June 1999, the Security Council adopted on 17 December, Resolution 1284, which in addition to extending the programme for 180 days, brought about some key developments to the OFFP. They include: (1) creation of the UN Monitoring, Verification and Inspection Commission (UNMOVIC), which replaced the Special Commission; (2) lifting of the ceiling on the revenue from petroleum sales; (3) the Sanctions Committee lists of humanitarian items, including foodstuffs, pharmaceutical and medical supplies, basic/standard medical and agricultural equipment and basic/standard educational items, would not be submitted to the Committee for approval but to the Executive Director of the Office of Iraq Programme (OIP);

---

survey carried out in the three Northern Governorates showed that under 5 mortality had decreased from 80 to 72 deaths/1000 live births between 1984-1989 and 1994-1999 period and infant mortality too had decreased from 64 to 59 deaths/1000 live births during the same period.

(4) the Committee was directed to take a decision on all applications in respect of humanitarian and essential civilian needs within two working days.

Furthermore, on 9 June 2000, the Security Council adopted resolution 1302, which extends the programme for another 180 days. Noteworthy in this resolution is the fact that it invited the Secretary-General to appoint independent experts to prepare a comprehensive report and analysis of the humanitarian situation in Iraq. Other measures include introduction of the above-mentioned accelerated procedures for the approval to the basic water and sanitation supplies.

To briefly describe the nature of the OFFP, it first of all establishes an overall exception to the prohibition of export of Iraqi oil and import by Iraq of humanitarian goods. The OFFP can also be understood as a consequence of the sanctions imposed against Iraq being general, not targeted.

Secondly, one must first recognise its magnitude. To date, over US$ 12 billion have been generated by the sale of Iraqi oil, and the Sanctions Committee processed contracts worth over US$ 7 billion. UNICEF alone would have submitted by the end of the year to the 661 Committee contracts worth a value of US$ 150 million.[2] It is a programme entirely financed by the sale of Iraqi oil. The chart below explains how funds generated are used, with two thirds destined for humanitarian purposes only.

As the chart illustrates, the 13% and the 53% accounts refer to two different geographical zones[3] and two different mandates, and, in the context of this note, two different mechanisms and ways to liase with the Security Council.

---

2 In the 180 day report of the Secretary General on 1 June 2000, he reported that total revenue during the reporting period would reach $8.4 billion. According to the Office of Iraq Programme, the total value of oil exports since the beginning of the programme stood at $29 billion as at 9 June 2000. As at 31 May 2000, contracts valued at $15 billion were received with $11.5 million worth of them approved by the Sanctions Committee. For the three Northern Governorates, UNICEF alone submitted contracts worth $215 million as at 31 May 2000.

3 The distribution of oil revenue between the Center/ South and the North follows the population distribution, 87% and 13% respectively. However, as the chart illustrates, the expense for UN compensation, administration of the OFFP & UNSCOM/UNMOVIC and the escrow account come out of the Center/South portion, leaving it with 53% of the total oil revenue.

Oil for Food Programme. Use of revenues generated by the sale of Iraqi oil.

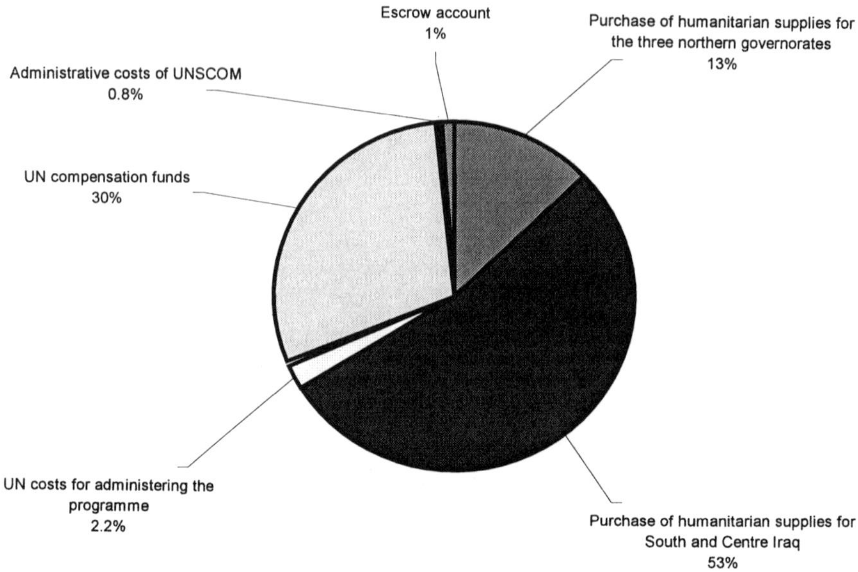

The 53% account means that 53% of the funds generated by the sale of Iraqi oil every six months is used for the purchase of humanitarian goods for South and Centre Iraq, that is 19 million people. The Government of Iraq implements the programme, i.e. it enters contracts with suppliers of its choosing, and submits, through the Office of the Iraq Programme (OIP) in NY, contracts for approval by the Security Council Committee. UN agencies are not part of the process. The UN mandate is only to observe, report and assess the implementation of the programme by the Iraqi government. The interface with the Security Council only occurs when the Sanctions Committee puts the approval of contracts submitted by the Government of Iraq on hold.

The 13% account means that 13% of the funds generated by the sale of Iraqi oil every six months is used for the purchase of humanitarian goods for the three autonomous governorates in northern Iraq, that is 3.5 million people. Here, the mandate is completely different, as the UN agencies implement the programme, submitting to the Security Council Committee, *through* the OIP, applications for approval to import goods and supplies, and procuring and delivering them. The United Nations and eight UN agencies, including UNICEF, are participating in the implementation of the programme in a wide range of sectors such as food, health and nutrition, water and sanitation, agriculture, electricity, education, rehabilitation and settlements, mine clearance and telecommunication.

III Role of the Sanctions Committee (661 Committee)

The Sanctions Committee is composed of 15 members, including the 5 permanent members of the Security Council. Any member of the Committee can put a contract on hold, submitted either by the Government of Iraq under the 53% account or by UN agencies under the 13% account. The most common reason for placing a contract on hold is the lack of information on technical specification, price and end use of the questioned items. There is no *direct* link between the Sanctions Committee and UN humanitarian agencies, as all contracts go through the OIP, as described earlier.

IV An Example of "Dual Use" Items – a field perspective

With regards to goods purchase under the 13 %, it can be said that the interface with the Sanctions Committee is smooth, in the sense that out of 550 contracts UNICEF submitted so far for approval, only three have been put on hold. In this case, reference can be made to article 48 of the UN Charter, which stipulates that the action required to carry out the decisions of the Security Council for the maintenance of international peace and security shall be carried out by the Members of the United Nations directly *and through* their action in the *appropriate international agencies* of which they are members. Thus, UN agencies should be trusted to implement their programmes in accordance with the sanctions regime requirements.

With regards to goods purchased by the Government of Iraq under the 53% account, there is much higher scrutiny that often results in contracts being put on hold by the Sanctions Committee.

A good example to illustrate this scrutiny and, therefore, the difficulties encountered in the field, is the import by the Government of Iraq of liquid chlorine gas. Liquid chlorine gas is used as a chemical to purify water. It's the most commonly used water purification chemical in the world and the only chemical used for this purpose in Iraq. Under phase I of the OFFP, which started in December 1996 and ended in June 1997, the Government of Iraq ordered 2,750 tons of liquid chlorine to be imported in 2, 750 cylinders of 1 tonne each. Chlorine was desperately needed in Iraq, and all indicators pointed to the catastrophic situation of the water and sanitation sector. However, it took 8 months for the first cylinders to reach Iraq, in late October 1997, almost at the end of phase II, due to the fact that chlorine is considered by the Sanctions Committee as a "dual-use" item (chlorine can also be used for military purposes).[4]

UNICEF, being in charge of the observation of the water and sanitation sector, had to ascertain its ability to track each single chlorine gas cylinder delivered into Iraq in order to ensure Member states that the chlorine would be used for its intended purpose. To help obtain approval from the Committee, UNICEF developed a heavy and time-consuming tracking system, a kind of "cradle to grave" monitoring procedure for about 2, 750 cylinders scattered in 15 governorates, in over 300 water sites, benefiting 13 million people.

- Each cylinder would be engraved with a unique serial number
- Based on the serial number the following information would be provided at any given time:
  - Date and port of entry of the cylinder into Iraq
  - The exact weight of the cylinder at import
  - Date of arrival of the cylinder in Baghdad, and location of storage
  - Date of distribution of the cylinder from Baghdad to the water site
  - Name and location of the water site, in addition to the date of arrival at the site
  - The starting date of utilisation of the chlorine cylinder

4 Despite continued advocacy by UNICEF to have holds lifted on water and sanitation supplies, contracts valued at $137.63 million are on hold as at end of May 2000. Especially when the Iraqi infrastructure is in state of appalling disrepair, high number of holds continue to have direct negative impact on the humanitarian programme and on the effort to rehabilitate the country's infrastructure.

- The ending date of utilisation of the chlorine cylinder
- The location of the empty cylinder after use

While the example of chlorine is extreme, all items imported into Iraq both by the Government of Iraq or by the UN agencies are subject to a rigorous three-tier UN observation mechanism. The UN observers track all items to ensure their intended end-use and end-user and assesses the effectiveness, equitability and adequacy of the items in meeting the objectives of the programme. The observation mechanism is increasingly emphasized in the effort to reduce the number of contracts put on hold.

V IMPROVING THE PROGRAMME

What the above example of chorine also signifies is the heaviness of the procedure in contracts processing and approval and, above all, the lack of flexibility of the mechanism of the programme. In late 1997, the UN system in Baghdad developed recommendations in order to bring flexibility in the programme and to improve the processing of contracts by the Committee. Later, on 29 January 1999, the President of the Security Council, Ambassador Amorim of Brazil, referred to the work of the Sanctions Committees and ways to improve it. While the note concerned sanctions in general, articles 11 and 16 of the Note[5] reflected what UNICEF had been promoting.

- The need for the sanctions committee to monitor, throughout the sanctions regime, the humanitarian impact of sanctions on vulnerable groups, including children, and make adjustments– thus addressing the issue of flexibility of the mechanism – toward exemption mechanisms to facilitate the delivery of humanitarian assistance.

- The drawing up of a list of essential humanitarian goods that would be exempted from the Sanctions Committee approval requirement, including educational items.

---

5 UN Doc. S/1999/100. It should be noted that the Office of the Coordination for Humanitarian Affairs (OCHA) played an important role in the development of this note, following consultations with members of the IASC Technical Group of Experts on Sanctions in which UNICEF was represented.

UNICEF welcomed these proposals. On 12 February 1999, at the Security Council's Open Briefing on the Protection of Civilians, UNICEF Executive Director Carol Bellamy[6] stated:

> "We must protect children from the effects of sanctions. In the interests of children, sanctions should not be imposed without obligatory, immediate and enforceable humanitarian exemptions, along with mechanisms for monitoring their impact on children and other vulnerable groups. In all countries under comprehensive economic sanctions, the inadequacy of current provisions has resulted in alarming rates of child malnutrition, and in child and maternal mortality. [T]hese inadequacies must be addressed. We welcome the Security Council's recent call to monitor the humanitarian impact of sanctions on children and to create more efficient exemption mechanisms. We believe that child-impact assessments are central to this and should be carried out before, during and after sanctions are imposed. Humanitarian assistance represents less than 5 percent of all of the goods presented for Sanctions Committee exemptions. I would underscore the need, therefore, to develop a list of essential humanitarian goods for exemption – items that must include educational supplies."

Pursuant to the aforementioned Note by Ambassador Amorim, three panels were created on Iraq on disarmament issues, current humanitarian situation and on war-prisoners issues, respectively. A report of the panel on the humanitarian issues was submitted to the Security Council on 30 March 1999[7] which proposed three recommendations regarding the processing of contracts by the 661 Sanctions Committee:

- *Pre-approved humanitarian supplies*: "Foodstuffs, pharmaceuticals and medical supplies, as well as basic or standard medical and agricultural equipment and basic or standard educational items included in a list of exempted humanitarian supplies, pre-approved by the 661 Committee, on the basis of a proposal from the Office of the Iraq Programme (OIP), should be contracted and procured directly by the Government of Iraq without any requirement for approval or notification to the 661 Committee."

6 UNICEF Executive Director Carol Bellamy addressed the Security Council twice again in October 1999 and on 24 March 2000. On the latter occasion, the Secretary General noted that the humanitarian situation in Iraq posed serious moral dilemma for the UN, citing that the organization was increasingly being accused of causing the suffering of civilians.

7 UN Doc. S/1999/356 Annex II.

- *Other supplies:* "Goods not included in the pre-approved list of humanitarian supplies that are not dual-use items should be authorised by the 661 Committee within two business days, upon receipt of a request from the exporting State, containing a description of the goods to be exported and the agreed price, as well as the estimated time of arrival."

- *Dual-use items*: "Dual-use items should be processed under the Export/Import Mechanism as per Security Council Resolution 1051 (1996). The requests for the supply of such items, along with the evaluation and comments as per the aforementioned resolution, should be submitted to the 661 Committee for approval under the no-objection procedure."

Over a year and a half passed between the initial recommendations in the field and Security Council Resolution 1242 dated 21 May 1999. This Resolution extended the OFFP for another period of six months, and referred to the panel's recommendations in the following terms: "the Security Council expresses its *willingness to review* the recommendations of the report of the panel".[8]

VI CONCLUSION

One must recognise that delays noticed at the early stage of the OFFP between the submission of contract to the Sanctions Committee and the arrival of goods into Iraq substantially decreased in the subsequent phases of the programme. UNICEF's experience regarding the sanctions on Iraq and the Sanctions Committee has involved the complexity of the programme and the distrust between the various actors. However, it has remained a fact that the OFFP is the only existing mechanism that can be used to alleviate the suffering of the Iraqi people. As illustrated above, the UN system in implementing the OFFP in Iraq, including UNICEF, has continued to seek more flexibility in the programme, in ways that improve the processing of contracts by the Committee and in turn better address the vulnerable populations within Iraq.

8 SC Res 1284 of 17 Dec 1999 reflected the panel report and its recommendations.

Sanctions, Humanitarian Issues and Mandates

Chair: *Geneviève Burdeau*
Professor of International Law,
Université de Paris I – Panthéon-Sorbonne
Secretary-General of The Hague Academy of International Law

LES SANCTIONS PEUVENT-ELLES SE HEURTER A DES NORMES CONCERNANT LE SYSTÈME DES NATIONS UNIES LUI-MÊME?

Marie-José Domestici-Met▪

L'intitulé de cette communication peut apparaître étrange. Il n'est cependant pas le fruit d'une illusion, mais d'une interrogation particulièrement judicieuse de Vera Gowlland-Debbas qui a réparti les rôles, et dont on pourrait dire qu'elle a savamment disposé ses troupes de manière à enserrer l'embargo[1] dans un réseau de contradictions. Le terrain est étroitement jalonné. Nous sommes des enquêteurs chargés chacun d'un angle d'attaque précis, afin qu'aucune zone d'ombre ne risque d'être laissée.

Je voudrais, maintenant, situer ma recherche dans le prolongement d'une clé d'analyse essentielle évoquée par Pierre-Marie Dupuy. Ce dernier a opposé, dans le système des Nations Unies deux objectifs: l'un à moyen et long terme, concernant ce que l'on n'appelait pas encore le "développement humain" mais qu'annonçaient l'article 55 sur les droits de l'homme et le Chapitre sur le Conseil Economique et Social; l'autre à court terme, concernant le maintien de la paix et de la sécurité internationale.

▪ Professeur à l'Université d'Aix-Marseille III, Directrice du Laboratoire de Droit humanitaire et de Gestion humaine des crises.

1 En fait, une partie seulement des mesures de pression économique sont des embargos, celles qui interdisent la livraison vers le pays cible. La mesure inverse est le boycott. L'expression "Sanctions économiques" n'est d'ailleurs, elle-même, pas exempte de toute critique. Destinées à faire changer un comportement, les mesures en question s'apparentent en fait davantage à des astreintes (*cf* J. Combacau, *Le pouvoir de sanction de l'ONU. Etude théorique de la coercition non militaire* (Paris, 1974).

V. Gowlland-Debbas (ed.), *United Nations Sanctions and International Law*, p. 167-195.

Au service de ce dernier objectif ont été – sinon inventées, car elles appartiennent à l'histoire des relations internationales...au point d'évoquer la guerre de siège – du moins rendues licites, par l'article 41 de la Charte, des mesures de pression économique qui, a priori, pouvaient légitimement apparaître comme un diminutif heureux des mesures militaires prévues à l'article 42.

Or, près de cinquante cinq ans après l'adoption de la Charte, la réalité a pris un autre visage. Si le six milliardième être humain arrive dans un monde qui connait encore 800 millions de malnourris, le concept de développement humain a cependant aujourd'hui pris un contenu concret. Les instruments d'analyse sont désormais au point, l'on sait mesurer les avancées et les reculs d'un pays sur cette échelle. Et précisément, on démontre aujourd'hui scientifiquement que l'utilisation des mesures que l'on présente avec quelqu'approximation sous le terme d'embargo est hautement préjudiciable au développement humain.

Ainsi l'organisation des Nations Unies elle-même peut-elle, par l'usage du Chapitre VII, porter atteinte aux buts de l'Organisation des Nations Unies! A la contradiction substantielle des objectifs s'ajoute le choc juridique, car la finalité du développement humain s'est trouvée à l'origine d'une institutionnalisation de plus en plus dense dans l'organisation elle-même – organismes subsidiaires des Nations Unies – et à sa périphérie – Institutions spécialisées. Avec personnalité morale dans le second cas, ou sans dans le premier, l'idée essentielle demeure la même: désigner un instrument de la politique à moyen et long terme centrée sur l'être humain, et lui confier un secteur de responsabilité. *Le mot "mandat"* est ici central. Qu'il définisse la tâche d'un organisme subsidiaire – Fond ou Programme – ou d'une Institution spécialisée, il *peut être invoqué comme une limite à l'obligation de porter assistance au Conseil de Sécurité dans son action de maintien de la paix et de la sécurité internationale.* Sans annoncer la révolte des Agences humanitaires et développementalistes onusiennes contre le Conseil de Sécurité, on se doit, cependant, de prêter attention à ce qui pourrait être un réel problème juridique... et, peut-être, un réel argument contre les sanctions économiques.

Mais, si la contradiction substantielle est de plus en plus évidente, le choc juridique, lui, est aujourd'hui moins insoluble qu'il ne pouvait sembler il y a trois ans.

I Une contradiction substantielle de plus en plus évidente

La contradiction existe clairement entre certains types de sanctions et certains types de statuts:

- les sanctions économiques sont contraires au principe de non discrimination dans les échanges posé par le GATT. Certes, on est ici en présence d'un appareil normatif et institutionnel dont la position par rapport aux Nations Unies n'est pas très nettement définie.[2] Néanmoins, il est impossible de ne pas évoquer la contradiction normative, car la lutte contre le protectionnisme fait partie de la philosophie politique avec laquelle les Nations Unies se sont lancées dans la lutte contre les causes de la guerre;
- les sanctions qui gèlent les communications sont contraires aux buts poursuivis par l'OACI, l'OMI, l'UPU, l'UIT;
- et la continuation des sanctions met en cause l'oeuvre de la FAO, de l'OMS, du PNUD, de l'UNICEF, de la BIRD, de l'AID, voire du FMI, de la SFI.

La prise de conscience de cette contradiction est relativement récente; et elle est étroitement fonction des circonstances (A) et du contenu (B) de la sanction.

A. La perception de la contradiction est fonction des circonstances de la sanction

Ces dernières sont représentées par la crise à l'occasion de laquelle un pays donné devient cible des sanctions. Celles-ci sont motivées par un certain comportement (1); et l'organe sanctionnateur lance un appel, plus ou moins impératif (2). Ces deux variables commandent la perception de la contradiction.

1) Le motif de la sanction

Les premières mesures dites de "sanction économique" prises par les Nations Unies concernaient l'Afrique australe. Elles furent d'abord décidées en 1956 contre la Rhodésie du Sud qui s'était auto-proclamée indépendante, sous la conduite d'un gouvernement blanc pratiquant la discrimination raciale. Cette première utilisation de l'article 41 intervenait sur la base d'une interprétation de l'article 39. Il n'y avait pas menace matérielle à la paix, mais trouble à la conception du monde que véhiculent les Nations Unies. Avant que ces sanctions ne soient levées, en 1979, d'autres furent décidées, en 1977, à l'encontre de

2 La relation est moins étroite qu'elle ne semblait devoir l'être dans les premières années d'après-guerre, lorsqu'était en question la création de l'Organisation Internationale du Commerce.

l'Afrique du Sud que sa politique d'embargo menait à des incidents avec les "pays de la ligne de front". Le motif était ici plus proche de la notion classique de "menace à la paix".

Dans ces affaires, on a vu les Institutions spécialisées concourir aux sanctions diverses. D'un côté, on les a vu interdire leurs réunions aux Etats condamnés. Et, de l'autre, on les a vu assister les Nations Unies dans l'application de "sanctions économiques". Par exemple il leur fut demandé d'informer le Comité des sanctions de toute activité qui pourrait constituer une évasion par rapport aux mesures décidées.[3] Dans la coopération, l'OIT fut sans doute la plus zélée, puisqu'elle est allée jusqu'à adopter deux amendements constitutionnels pour pouvoir répondre aux demandes des Nations Unies.

Force est bien de reconnaître que nul ne s'est ému de ces mesures qui, aux yeux de la Communauté internationale toute entière, avaient le mérite de combattre la discrimination raciale, et à ceux du Tiers Monde celui de mettre en oeuvre le droit des peuples à disposer d'eux-mêmes.[4] Et ce manichéisme a été introduit jusque dans le Mouvement de la Croix Rouge, puisque la suspension de la Société Nationale sud africaine a été prononcée lors de la XXV° Conférence internationale de la Croix Rouge. C'est dire que l'on était loin de toute idée d'exception humanitaire. Dans cette homogénéité des comportements, il faut, toutefois, signaler le cas de l'OACI qui s'est insurgée contre les mesures demandées; nous y reviendrons en seconde partie.

Depuis ce temps, des sanctions ont été prises par les Nations Unies contre l'Irak, la Yougoslavie, la Somalie, la Libye, Haïti, le Rwanda, le Soudan, la Sierra Leone, l'Afghanistan et contre des groupes privés (FNPL de Charles Taylor, UNITA de Jonas Savimbi, Serbes de Bosnie), tandis que les Etats voisins du Burundi en décidaient contre ce dernier.

C'est dans le contexte de la Guerre du Golfe et de ses sanctions prolongées contre l'Irak qu'est née l'interrogation sur les sanctions économiques. La faute imputée à l'Irak était d'abord l'invasion du Koweit, qui fit l'unanimité contre

3 Rés. CS 253 (1968).

4 En effet, pour les Etats du Tiers Monde, bien plus que d'un problème de droits individuels, il s'agissait du parachèvement de la décolonisation par la mise à terre de gouvernements qui se trouvaient aux mains d'anciens colonisateurs ou de leurs descendants.

lui. Mais, ce qui justifie la poursuite des sanctions en avril 1991, au moment de la résolution 687, est le risque de voir l'Irak ne pas laisser l'UNSCOM faire son travail en matière de contrôle des armements. Il ne s'agit pas d'un sujet aussi sensible que l'Apartheid, d'où la faveur qui est finalement allée à l'Irak, une fois évanouïe la crédibilité de sa dangerosité.

Le cas d'Haïti, Etat pauvre parmi les pauvres, dont la population a dû payer doublement le prix d'un coup d'Etat contre son Président élu a contribué de manière non négligeable à discréditer l'embargo. Exempté de sanctions diplomatiques, le pays a été privé du pétrole qui permettait de faire fonctionner des pompes hydrauliques, ce qui a accru la vulnérabilité des populations. Mais, une seconde variable réside dans l'appel lancé en vue des sanctions.

2) La nature de l'appel aux sanctions lancé dans une crise donnée

L'organe sanctionnateur, lorsqu'il organise la machinerie destinée à maintenir ou rétablir la paix ne se sert pas du seul instrument des sanctions. Il joue de mesures positives – ou affirmatives – comme négatives. Et, dès lors, il peut n'exiger des agences humanitaires aucune activité sanctionnatrice. Ou bien il attend d'elles une activité d'assistance, en se contentant de cibler les bénéficiaires; ou bien il leur adresse une simple invitation à se montrer sévères, sans jouer dans le registre de la décision obligatoire.

a) L'assistance aux Nations Unies par l'assistance aux populations

Il n'est pas porté atteinte au mandat humanitaire, tout d'abord, lorsque les Nations Unies – dans la poursuite de l'objectif motivant les sanctions – ne demandent pas d'action purement sanctionnatrice aux agences humanitaires. Tel est le cas quand le Conseil de Sécurité ou l'Assemblée Générale se contente de leur demander une action d'un autre type, au soutien de la politique d'ensemble, par exemple d'aider les victimes de l'Etat sous sanctions. Dans ce cas, on peut parler d'assistance aux Nations Unies par l'assistance à des populations. Et *l'on se situe hors du champ d'affrontement des concepts, du champ de la contradiction substantielle entre sanctions et développement humain.*

Telle est la signification que l'on peut trouver à l'assistance que les Institutions spécialisées étaient appelées à fournir aux réfugiés fuyant la Rhodésie du Sud "blanche" ou l'Afrique du Sud et à leurs Etats d'accueil. Le Conseil de Sécurité lança de tels appels à propos de chacun des pays de la ligne de front.[5] L'Assemblée générale, quant à elle, au nom de la résolution 1514, et en traitant globalement de tous les problèmes de l'Afrique australe[6] demanda aux Institutions spécialisées d'aider les réfugiés en provenance de l'Afrique australe "blanche",[7] comme elle leur demande diverses mesures symboliques de non reconnaissance, ainsi qu'on le verra plus loin.

La conséquence est une activité "normale" pour les Institutions spécialisées, par exemple lorsque l'OIT mène, sur le territoire des Etats de la ligne de front, une activité de préparation des réfugiés à la création des petites entreprises. Mais, on ne saurait dire la même chose lorsqu'elle incite au désinvestissement et exclut l'Afrique du Sud.

Les crises récentes sont très riches d'illustrations du même type: l'accueil des réfugiés kosovars en Albanie en est un exemple très clair. Il n'y a ici rien qui participe à l'activité sanctionnatrice, même si les misères soulagées sont celles de l'adversaire de l'Etat sous embargo. Un autre exemple serait l'aide aux Kurdes irakiens, poursuivie en même temps que l'embargo contre l'Irak. Cette dernière affaire voit d'ailleurs le Conseil de Sécurité demander à l'OMS une mission qui n'est pas étrangère à l'esprit de son mandat: participer à la réflexion internationale sur la neutralisation des armes chimiques[8]

Un autre contexte encore peut retarder la prise de conscience de l'anomalie que représente la pratique des sanctions: lorsque l'institution spécialisée ou l'organisme subsidiaire a la possibilité juridique d'échapper au rôle d'agent sanctionnateur, en raison du libellé permissif de la requête d'assistance qui lui est adressée.

b) Des appels inégalement contraignants.

La possibilité d'échapper au rôle d'agent sanctionnateur existe dès que la résolution n'est pas contraignante par exemple parce que le Conseil de Sécurité

---

5 Rés. CS 253 (affaire rhodésienne) et 329 (affaire sud-africaine) pour la Zambie; rés. CS 277 (affaire rhodésienne) et 403 (affaire sud-africaine)pour le Botswana, rés. CS 402 pour le Lesotho, 403 pour le Mozambique.

6 C'est-à-dire aussi bien du refus portugais de décoloniser l'Angola et le Mozambique, que de l'apartheid sud-africain et que du gouvernement minoritaire blanc de Rhodésie.

7 *Cf* Rés. AG 2555(XXIV) et 2704 (XXV).

8 Art 8 de la résolution 687 (1991).

opte, en la circonstance, pour une simple recommandation. C'est le cas avec la résolution 232 sur la Rhodésie pour l'aspect économique des sanctions.

Un autre problème vient aussi du fait que les Etats membres des Institutions spécialisées appartiennent ou non aux Nations Unies. Lorsque la Résolution 277, pour parvenir à la non reconnaissance de la Rhodésie, appelle les Etats qui ont la double appartenance à prendre "des actions appropriées", ceci crée des obligations selon l'art 25. En ce qui concerne les Etats non membres, la résolution 253 leur demande

- de faire rapport au Secrétaire Général;
- de fournir au Comité des sanctions des renseignements sur leur commerce, les activités de leurs nationaux, les activités commerciales affectant leur territoire.

Leur participation à la lutte contre la fraude aux sanctions ne répond qu'à une simple invitation, puisque l'article 25 n'est pas applicable en l'espèce.

Il faut encore s'interesser à une autre dimension qui conditionne la perception de la contradiction entre mesures de sanctions et mandat des agences humanitaires.

B. La perception de la contradiction est fonction du contenu des sanctions

Il est vrai que les affaires d'Afrique australe ne mettaient pas les sanctions économiques au premier plan. En Rhodésie les sanctions passaient d'abord par le refus de reconnaissance. L'aspect juridique l'emportait sur l'aspect économique. Et en Afrique du Sud, on peut faire une réflexion semblable avec le refus de recevoir les pouvoirs des représentants à l' Assemblée Générale, à partir de la session de 1974 de celle-ci. Puis les sanctions portèrent sur les livraisons d'armes avant de prendre une tournure économique.

1) Les sanctions visant l'isolement.

Celui-ci peut être diplomatique ou concerner les communications physiques. Ce type de sanctions a d'abord une signification symbolique: *elles témoignent du rejet d'une politique à travers celui de son auteur.*

Il faut envisager sous cet angle l'exclusion de l'Afrique du Sud de la session de l'Assemblée générale, le refus de laisser les athlètes de l'ensemble de l'Afrique australe "blanche" prendre part à des compétitions sportives, ... En fait, ce sont des adaptations fonctionnelles:

- soit du concept d'inexistence;
- soit de certaines formes extrêmes de sanction pénale pour motif politique, au sens large – ou d'incivisme – (ostracisme, bannissement, exil...).

Les constitutions des Institutions spécialisées ne comportent pas toujours une procédure d'exclusion, et jamais de procédure de sanction pour menace à la paix. C'est pourquoi le Conseil de sécurité, ou éventuellement l'Assemblée générale, lorsqu'ils souhaitent obtenir la synergie de ces institutions leur demandent d'avoir des comportements qui, fonctionnellement, peuvent se lire en ce sens.

Les Institutions spécialisées, en effet, se voyaient demander de rompre toute collaboration avec la Rhodésie, jusque–là membre de certaines d'entr'elles en tant que territoire non autonome. Elles firent effectivement le choix de continuer à traiter avec la Grande Bretagne au sujet de la Rhodésie autoproclamée indépendante. C'est ainsi que l'UIT qui était en cours d'adoption de la Convention de Montreux, décida (après avoir reçu notification, de la part du Royaume Uni, du fait que l'autorité de la délégation rhodésienne avait cessé) d'annuler la signature de la Rhodésie qui venait d'être donnée, et de refuser tout acte de ratification ou d'adhésion qui pourrait venir de la Rhodésie. On peut aussi citer le cas de l'OMS. La Rhodésie du Sud y avait été admise comme membre associé en sa qualité de colonie britannique. Mais en juin 1970, une communication adressée au Secrétaire Général indique que, la Déclaration unilatérale d'indépendance n'étant pas légale, les relations sont suspendues. L'OMM, de même, n'accepta jamais de correspondre avec la Rhodésie, et maintint ses contacts avec le Royaume Uni. De même encore, l'UPU, dans le cadre de laquelle le territoire de Rhodésie n'apparaissait que sous le nom du Royaume-Uni; et qui ne changea jamais ce système, tant que la crise ne fut pas résolue.

En fait, la sanction de l'apartheid et de l'indépendance autoproclamée s'insère dans un mouvement plus vaste: celui de la dernière phase de la décolonisation. C'est ainsi que les résolutions 2555 et 2704 sus-mentionnées demandent aux Institutions spécialisées

- de cesser de collaborer avec la Rhodésie du Sud, le Portugal et l'Afrique du Sud;
- de faire, au contraire, participer les mouvements de libération nationale à leurs instances;
- voire même d'assister les mouvements de libération nationale dans leur combat.

Même si la Rhodésie se voyait privée de pétrole et si l'Afrique du Sud se voyait refuser ses Kruggerrand, les sanctions étaient plus significatives dans la symbolique de l'ostracisme que dans le registre économique.

2) Les sanctions concernant principalement les flux de marchandises[9]

Les sanctions économiques contre la Rhodésie ne faisaient, on l'a vu plus haut,[10] l'objet que d'une recommandation. Les sanctions économiques contre l'Afrique du Sud ont pris une forme sélective.[11] Les sanctions économiques contre l'Irak sont, elles, générales – on évoquera ensuite le "filtrage" – et obligatoires. Elles constituent les plus complètes et les plus rapidement décidées de toutes.[12] Elles ouvrent une ère nouvelle: désormais, les sanctions, plus générales, seront aussi plus systématiques.

Si les sanctions, en elles-mêmes, ne constituent pas un concept répréhensible, et bénéficient, au contraire, d'un ancrage textuel – l'article 41 de la Charte – il est cependant des textes fondamentaux du droit international dont on ressent d'emblée qu'ils ne s'accordent pas, soit avec l'esprit des sanctions, soit avec leur mise en oeuvre.

a) Les sanctions contrarient *ab initio* les normes sur le commerce international

Parce qu'elles constituent une interdiction d'entretenir des relations commerciales, les sanctions vont à l'encontre du traité du *GATT* qui condamne les entraves au commerce. C'est dès l'origine que la décision du Conseil de Sécurité qui met en place des sanctions économiques sous forme d'embargo ou de boycott est contraire à ce traité. Il est vrai que *l'activité sanctionnatrice fait l'objet d'une exemption par le traité même*, à l'article XXI c). Mais, celle-ci

9 "Limited and targeted measures generally have less severe humanitarian effects than comprehensive trade sanctions" L. Minear, D. Cortright, J. Wagler, G.A. Lopez, T.G. Weiss, "Towards More Humane and Effective Sanctions Management – Enhancing the Capacity of the United Nations Sanctions System", (étude commandée par le Département des Affaires humanitaires) octobre 1997, p. 4 (disponible sur http://www.reliefweb.int).

10 Point I, A.

11 Refus d'acheter les Kruggerrand par exemple.

12 L'invasion de l'Irak datant du 2 Août 1990, l'idée de sanctions "as a tool of peaceful settlement of disputes" fut avancée dès le 3 Août par une Note verbale des Pays-Bas, auxquels s'associait l'Australie, rédigée avant même l'invasion (A/50/322). La résolution 661 imposant les sanctions intervint le 6 Août.

est une sorte de reprise de l'article 103;[13] elle concerne les obligations des Etats membres – ce qui n'est pas notre axe de travail.[14]

b) La prolongation des sanctions, un danger pour la vie humaine.
On sait, depuis que l'on a vu fonctionner des sanctions économiques sur plusieurs années quelles peuvent être les conséquences sur le plan humain: malnutrition, déficit pondéral, courbe de croissance retardée... L'UNICEF, quant à lui, s'intéresse à l'impact social: destruction des familles sous l'effet de la misère, abandon de l'école en vue du travail des très jeunes ou de leur prostitution.

Mais le fait que la *poursuite* d'un embargo ait des répercussions négatives sur un objectif officiellement poursuivi par le système des Nations Unies peut-il avoir un impact sur la qualification de la mesure initiale? Peut-être en ce sens qu'elle n'est affectée d'aucune limite dans le temps et s'avère, de ce fait, sinon dès l'origine néfaste, du moins *dès l'origine potentiellement dangereuse pour des objectifs consacrés.*

L'observation est valable pour des objectifs consacrés par le statut de certaines Institutions spécialisées ou Fonds des Nations Unies. Mais, surtout, depuis, ces structures ont développé une dynamique très puissante en faveur de l'alimentation. Et le fossé s'est encore creusé.

b1. *Plusieurs textes de base sont dans une logique contraire à celle des sanctions.* L'Acte constitutif de la FAO est parfaitement limpide sur les objectifs. Son préambule parle de *libérer l'humanité de la faim.* Les attributions de l'organisation concernent la promotion de la recherche scientifique, technologique, l'amélioration de la production, de la mise sur le marché et de la distribution de nourriture. Et la Constitution de l'OMS confère à cette dernière le mandat de diriger et coordonner les actions visant à *permettre à tous d'atteindre le plus haut niveau possible de santé*, tout en définissant la santé comme "un état de bien-être physique, mental et social complet", plutôt que comme la simple absence de maladie ou d'infirmité. D'emblée, l'idée de rationnement apparait contraire à l'objectif poursuivi par l'organisation... L'inquiétude

13 Sous l'intitulé "Security exceptions", il dispose "Nothing in this agreement shall be construed ....c) to prevent any party from taking any action pursuant to other obligations under the UN Charter".

14 *Cf* en seconde partie, point A, introduction.

au sujet du ravitaillement, l'angoisse pour la survie n'est déja pas cet état complet de bien-être, au moins mental. La constatation se renforce, lorsque l'on parcourt la liste des responsabilités de l'OMS qui doit *promouvoir une amélioration* de la nutrition, du logement, de l'hygiène, des conditions de travail et autres aspects d'environnement. Or, la mise en oeuvre des sanctions provoque une régression, une atteinte par l'organisation-mère aux conditions minimales. A quoi sert, dès lors, l'établissement de standards pour la nourriture et les produits biologiques et pharmaceutiques? On se croirait en présence d'une gigantesque hypocrisie.

b2. Mais, surtout, *depuis quelques années, des agences des Nations Unies ont développé une dynamique en faveur de l'alimentation*, non seulement sur le plan opérationnel,[15] mais encore *sur le plan conceptuel.*

La FAO a été à l'origine d'un travail en profondeur accompli dans la lignée de l'article 11 du Pacte de 1966 sur les droits économiques et sociaux qui mentionne *la nourriture,* sans préciser ni les concepts, ni le régime juridique.[16] La Conférence Mondiale de l'Alimentation a adopté en 1974 une Déclaration Universelle sur l'*Eradication de la faim et de la malnutrition*, posant le "*droit inaliénable*" à être libéré de ces deux fléaux et affirmant que la nourriture ne devait pas être un instrument de pression politique et économique. Ces positions ont été avalisées par l'Assemblée générale lors de la session de 1974. Puis le Sommet Mondial sur l'Alimentation, en 1996, dans son Plan d'action accorde une part importante au problème conceptuel du droit à l'alimentation, son paragraphe 7.4 fixant pour objectif la clarification du contenu:

---

15 La Conférence Mondiale de l'Alimentation de 1974 établissait l'IFAD (Fonds International pour le Développement Agricole). Ayant débuté ses activités en 1978 a aujourd'hui à son actif à peu près 500 projets dans plus de 100 pays. En 1994, la FAO mit sur pieds un Programme Spécial pour la Sécurité Alimentaire qui permettra une planification par pays, en coopération avec les paysans locaux, en incorporant certaines techniques traditionnelles. Quatre ans plus tard, il était mis en place dans 36 pays, et en cours de mise au point dans une trentaine d'autres.

16 Le texte de l'article 11 est: § 1:"...le droit de toute personne à un niveau de vie suffisant pour elle-même et sa famille, y compris une nourriture, un vêtement(..) suffisants." § 2:"(...) le droit fondamental qu'a toute personne à être à l'abri de la faim (...)".

- du droit à une nourriture adéquate;[17]
- du droit fondamental à être libéré de la faim.

Le même point considère ce droit à la nourriture comme un moyen d'atteindre la sécurité alimentaire pour tous.

En vue de la "clarification" recherchée, le droit à la nourriture, qui avait déja été mentionné en 1987 par le rapporteur de la Sous-Commission contre la Discrimination raciale et pour la Protection des Minorités, est désormais entré, sous l'effet de campagnes d'un collectif d'ONG -FIAN – de plein pied dans le champ d'action des organes onusiens en charge des droits de l'homme. La Commission des Droits de l'homme a affirmé, par une résolution 97/8, que *la faim constitue une violation de la dignité humaine*. On retrouve la même affirmation, désormais rituelle, dans les résolutions 1998/23 et 1999/24. Et le Haut Commissaire des Nations Unies aux Droits de l'Homme, mandaté par le Sommet Mondial de l'Alimentation, a engagé des consultations systématiques dès 1997. On est désormais passé à une approche délibérément axée sur les "droits de l'homme" dont les différents mérites sont recensés par ces groupes de travail:

- celui de reposer sur une base juridique obligatoire et homogène d'origine internationale (les différentes constitutions nationales impliquant à un titre ou à un autre le droit à l'alimentation[18] constituent des bases hétérogènes);
- celui d'introduire la notion de responsabilité, même si le débiteur de cette dernière reste mal défini;
- et, même, celui de réconcilier l'approche économique et sociale et celle des droits civils, car la dignité humaine est en cause.

Ce processus rencontre des obstacles théoriques; mais la volonté de réussir la conceptualisation est très forte. Le processus implique de plus en plus largement les Institutions spécialisées et les organismes subsidiaires, notamment la FAO, le PAM, l'IFAID, l'OMS, l'OIT, l'UNICEF, le HCR, le PNUD et la Banque mondiale. Un document publié par la FAO sous le titre "The right to food in theory and

---

17 On notera le glissement du "'niveau de vie' englobant la nourriture" à la "nourriture" proprement dite. Quant au mot "adéquat", il est présent dès la version anglaise du Pacte. Mais il semble qu'un second glissement se soit opéré entre sa signication qualitative – équivalente à "suffisante" – et sa signification qualitative, ce qui correspond à la volonté d'affiner le "droit" envisagé.

18 On trouve les formulations les plus diverses impliquant différents débiteurs (Etat, famille, société...voire aucun débiteur mentionné), différents créanciers (enfants, personnes âgées, adolescents, handicapés), stigmatisant diverses formes de violations des droits.

in practice" et introduit par Mary Robinson, Haut Commissaire aux Droits de l'Homme, pousse fort loin les exigences.[19] Le même document précise les types de droits et obligations qui pèsent sur l'Etat en vue de la réalisation de ces droits.[20]

Tout *ce travail conceptuel rend plus choquant encore la conduite, par l'organe principal du Maintien de la Paix, des activités sanctionnatrices qui mettent en danger la nourriture* de populations coupables d'appartenir à un Etat donné...et peut-être de ployer sous le joug d'un gouvernement hostile. Pour insister encore davantage, on citera une résolution récente de la Commission des Droits de l'homme qui condamne en termes excellents les "mesures coercitives" sur la base de la Charte des Droits et devoirs économiques. On peut y lire:

> "dénonce le recours à des mesures de cette nature pour exercer des pressions politiques ou économiques sur un pays donné (...) en raison de leurs effets négatifs sur l'exercice de tous les droits de l'homme..." (§ 2) "souligne que l'adoption de mesures coercitives (...) est un des principaux obstacles à l'application de la Déclaration sur le droit au développement" (§ 3)
> ... mais force est bien d'ajouter que la résolution porte sur les mesures coercitives "unilatérales"... c'est-à-dire étatiques,[21] tandis que peuvent prospérer les mesures "conformes au droit international et à la Charte des Nations Unies" (§1).

La *contradiction* substantielle est manifeste; fort heureusement la *prise de conscience* est largement amorcée. Elle est, d'abord, apparue dans la "société civile". L'*enjeu* aujourd'hui est de savoir si elle va gagner le *monde des Nations Unies*, et permettre un changement de pratique.

---

19 *-fourniture d'aliments adéquats*, c'est-à-dire adaptés aux exigences locales, régionales et même familiales; *-culturellement acceptables -couvrant les besoins nutritionnels en quantité et en qualité -sans danger pour la santé -de bonne qualité gustative.*

20 Pour expliquer que le développement peut passer par l'économie de marché, même en ce qui concerne les droits économiques et sociaux, les malentendus sur l'interventionnisme étatique étant dissipés, ce document assure que l'Etat n'est tenu que de respecter les ressources matériellles ou humaines des individus; protéger ces droits contre les prédateurs et faciliter l'accès à la nourriture pour les personnes frappées par les catastrophes, l'âge, le chômage.

21 Résolution 1999/21.

Un premier pas a été franchi par l'Assemblée générale des Nations Unies, pour ce qui est de la *conception d'ensemble des "sanctions"*. Dans une résolution 51/242,[22] elle a proclamé: "le but des sanctions est de modifier la conduite d'une partie qui menace la paix (...) et non de punir et d'exercer une vengeance".[23] Peut-on espérer que, selon cette inspiration, le système des Nations Unies fasse en sorte *que la contradiction substantielle* entre l'objectif de maintien de la paix et celui du développement humain *ne se traduise pas en un conflit normatif* insurmontable.

II Le choc des pouvoirs normatifs n'est pas nécessairement insoluble

Aujourd'hui, la mesure du problème humain a été prise. Et alors que toutes les branches des Nations Unies axées sur l'être humain travaillent à préciser le concept de "droit à être libéré de la faim", les Institutions spécialisées et organismes subsidiaires qui s'impliquent dans cet effort devraient pouvoir se tenir à l'écart des sanctions économiques, voire les contrer, au nom de leur mandat.

Mais, en termes juridiques, le conflit ne se présente pas toujours avec la même intensité, aussi faut-il soigneusement recenser les cas de figure qui peuvent se rencontrer (A). Même dans les cas les plus aigüs, on peut encore remplacer l'affrontement par une redéfinition des rôles (B), à laquelle le système des Nations Unies commence à réfléchir pour une meilleure compatibilité des actions menées au nom de la paix avec les objectifs humains.

A. Un conflit juridique à géométrie variable

Ce conflit ne saurait trouver une solution dans l'article 103,[24] lequel concerne les engagements des Etats membres des Nations Unies.[25] Ici, ce qui est en cause est la relation entre le système central des Nations Unies et des organis-

22 Concernant le "Supplément à l'Agenda pour la Paix", et adoptée le 26 septembre 1997

23 Annexe point 5.

24 En revanche, on évoquera ci-après (point A 1) l'art 30/6 (qui correspond à l'art 103 pour les relations entre organisations internationales), dans la Convention sur le Droit des traités entre Etats et organisations internationales ou entre organisations internationales (1986).

25 On a vu plus haut (1° partie, B) que le GATT fait écho à l'article 103. L'article prive les Etats de capacité de résistance aux mesures de sanctions demandées.

mes subsidiaires ou des Institutions spécialisées dotées de la personnalité morale. Tout est fonction de l'état des relations permanentes entre les organismes concernés. S'il s'agit d'un organisme subsidiaire, l'autorité des résolutions des organes principaux des Nations Unies est à son maximum, car l'organe subsidiaire doit obéir à l'organe principal qui l'a créé(2). Mais, s'il s'agit d'une Institution spécialisée, elle est une personne morale dans une relation contractuelle avec les Nations Unies, ce qui change les équilibres (1).

1) Le cas des Institutions spécialisées: "Résolution sanctionnatrice c/ accord inter organisations"

On est en présence d'un double schéma. Avant tout, les Institutions spécialisées sont des organisations internationales. Elles sont créées par un traité constitutif, ont leurs propres membres qui coïncident ou non avec ceux des Nations Unies, leurs organes décisionnels. Selon la Charte, les relations sont à base de recommandation de l'Assemblée générale ou de l'ECOSOC (art 58, 62, 63), de rapports (art 64), mais aussi de conventions internationales (art 63); et le rôle du Conseil de sécurité n'est pas cité dans les articles qui parlent des Institutions spécialisées.

Mais cependant l'article 65, lui, prévoit que l'ECOSOC peut assister le Conseil de Sécurité. Et ce Conseil, lui-même se tient en contact avec les Institutions spécialisées, dont il est le co-contractant. De plus, à une certaine époque, des résolutions des Nations Unies ont exigé des Institutions spécialisées une synergie dans les procédures de sanctions qui va peut-être au-delà des textes.

Aujourd'hui une Institution spécialisée ne peut-elle s'appuyer sur son mandat et sur l'accord inter-organisation? Ce dernier n'a aucune raison pour organiser la méconnaissance du mandat.

a) Il importe donc, dans un premier temps, de s'intéresser à la rédaction de ces accords qui se répartissent en trois groupes.
Les Institutions financières du système des Nations Unies n'ont accepté que de "tenir dûment compte" des décisions de Conseil de Sécurité prises selon les articles 41 et 42, et de fournir des informations au Conseil de Sécurité. Il n'y est même pas question de l'Assemblée générale.

Les accords conclus avec les Nations Unies par l'UPU, l'IUT, et l'OMS sont conclus "sous réserve du mandat" de l'Institution spécialisée; c'est-à-dire qu'ils sous-entendent que les Institutions en question ne s'engagent à rien qui puisse aller à l'encontre de leur mandat.[26] En revanche ces Institutions acceptent que leurs Traités constitutifs, pour leurs membres cèdent devant la Charte, en vertu de l'article 103.

Mais il reste d'autres Institutions spécialisées. Dans leur cas, nulle exception n'est spécifiée, et ces accords comportent une formule contraignante. L'OIT (article VI[27]), la FAO (article VI), l'OACI (article VII), et l'UNESCO acceptent de fournir les informations et l'assistance que le Conseil de Sécurité peut demander pour le maintien ou le rétablissement de la paix et la sécurité. Ces Institutions spécialisées acceptent également de se soumettre aux recommandations de l'Assemblée générale.

b) Il est maintenant possible d'aller plus avant dans le montage d'un schéma de *ce qui pourrait être la résistance juridique des Institutions spécialisées aux Nations Unies.*
On signalera tout d'abord qu'à ces trois séries d'accords inter organisations s'applique l'art 30 § 6 de la Convention sur le Droit des traités entre Etats et organisations internationales ou entre organisations internationales (1986)[28] qui affirme:

> "...en cas de conflit entre les obligations découlant de la Charte des Nations Unies et les obligations découlant d'un traité, les premières prévaudront".

Faudrait-il en conclure que, quelle que soit sa rédaction, le traité ONU-Institution spécialisée ne peut servir de rempart?

---

26 Par exemple pour l'UPU: "L'Union convient de coopérer avec l'ONU et de lui prêter son concours dans la mesure compatible avec la Convention postale universelle. En ce qui concerne les membres de l'ONU, l'Union reconnaît que, conformément aux dispositions de l'article 103, aucune disposition de la Convention postale universelle(...) ne peut être invoquée comme faisant obstacle (...) à l'observation par un Etat de ses obligations envers l'ONU"(RTNU vol 19).

27 "L'OIT convient de coopérer avec le Conseil économique et social en fournissant telles informations et telle assistance que le Conseil de sécurité pourrait demander, y compris l'assistance destinée à l'application des décisions du Conseil de sécurité pour le maintien ou le rétablissement de la paix et de la sécurité internationales." (RTNU vol 1, vol 8, vol 23).

28 Pour un commentaire, cf Ph. Mamin, "La Convention de Vienne sur les accords entre Etats et organisations internationales ou entre organisations internationales", (1986) *AFDI* 454-473.

Cette conclusion serait excessivement pessimiste, car *la source formelle de la sujétion des Institutions spécialisées* n'est pas la Charte, mais le *texte des traités du troisième groupe*. Il ne s'agit donc pas de confronter la Charte et le traité inter-organisations. Il s'agit de confronter le Statut de l'Institution spécialisée – où se trouve mentionné le mandat – et la résolution du Conseil de sécurité – qui exige un comportement contraire au mandat, en cherchant si le traité inter-organisations peut renforcer le Statut pour lui donner l'avantage.

On notera ensuite que les dispositions du premier groupe de traités sus-évoqués ont permis à la Banque mondiale de ne pas mettre en oeuvre des résolutions lui demandant de refuser toute assistance au Portugal et à l'Afrique du Sud.[29] Elle évoqua, pour cela, l'interdiction pesant sur elle de mener une action politique "quelle que fut la valeur des objectifs politiques".[30]

Les dispositions des traités du deuxième groupe fournissent, elles aussi un solide ancrage.

Quant aux *accords inter organisations du troisième groupe, ceux dont le texte réserve le moins de marge de manoeuvre, ne pourraient-ils pas être lus, dans l'esprit de ceux du deuxième groupe, à la lumière du mandat?* Celui-ci permet de les interpréter dans un sens qui soit favorable aux populations sous sanctions. Et, si cette interprétation ne devait pas être retenue, ne pourrait-on mettre en cause la validité même de l'accord?

b1) L'interprétation des accords dans le sens du mandat humanitaire.

Chacun des accords qui nous intéressent est appelé à régir les rapports de deux organisations créées au nom de l'humanité, que l'une prétend débarrasser du "fléau de la guerre", tandis que l'autre doit poursuivre sur un point précis l'amélioration de la condition humaine, afin de poser les bases d'une paix plus profonde et durable. Puisque les règles d'interprétation accordent une grande importance à la *logique*,[31] il faut donc supposer que ces accords sont destinés à mettre en oeuvre les deux mandats qui résultent des deux faces de cet objectif, et non pas l'un de ces mandats au détriment de l'autre. Quant au contenu de ces mandats, lui-même aussi issu d'un traité, il s'interprétera selon les règles

29 Les faits remontent à 1966 et 1976.

30 Formule tirée de l'article IV § 3 du traité ONU-BIRD.

31 "L'interprétation, c'est la logique au service du droit" (P. Daillier, A. Pellet, *Droit International Public* (Paris, 1994), 5° éd., n° 171).

qui commandent de *donner aux mots leur sens ordinaire.*[32] On insistera donc pour la FAO sur la "libération de la faim", pour l'OMS sur l'objectif du "degré de santé le plus élévé possible". Il ne serait pas concevable que la FAO, l'UNESCO ou l'OIT s'engagent par traité à violer leur mandat. Il faut en conclure que *la réserve du mandat contenue dans le traité ONU-OMS doit être sous-entendue dans tous les traités qui ne l'énoncent pas explicitement.*

Et s'il ne pouvait en être ainsi, parce que les Institutions spécialisées en question auraient délibérément fait abandon de leur mandat, en promettant une soumission totale à de futures demandes des Nations Unies?

b2) On pourrait, alors, valablement soutenir qu'un tel traité serait nul, et celà à plusieurs titres. Curieusement, il ne serait pas impossible d'invoquer

- et une nullité relative pour défaut de capacité juridique;
- et une nullité absolue pour contrariété à l'ordre public.

On peut parler de défaut de capacité juridique, car celle des organisations internationales est "dérivée et partielle", "limitée par le principe de spécialité".[33] Selon l'art 6 de la Convention sur le droit des traités conclus entre Etats et organisations internationales ou entre organisations internationales, "la capacité d'une organisation internationale de conclure des traités est régie par les règles pertinentes de cette organisation". *L'organisation devant poursuivre la réalisation de ses objectifs, elle ne saurait avoir la capacité de s'engager à agir contre ceux-ci.* La nullité pour incapacité étant une nullité relative, *il appartiendrait aux Institutions spécialisées qui se seraient engagées à aliéner leur mandat d'invoquer elles-mêmes cette nullité.*

Il n'est pas non plus interdit de parler de *nullité absolue pour contrariété à l'ordre public.* Le mandat humanitaire d'une Institution spécialisée n'est pas la chose de cette dernière; il ne lui appartient pas de l'aliéner. On sait qu'il existe divers témoins du régime impératif des normes de droit humanitaire. L'interdiction faite aux personnes protégées par les Conventions de Genève de renoncer à "leurs droits"[34] en est un. L'interdiction de conclure des accords qui diminuent les garanties humanitaires – donc des accords dérogatoires –

32 Art 31 § 1 Convention de Vienne de 1969: "...suivant le sens ordinaire à attribuer aux termes du traité(...) et à la lumière de son objet et de son but".

33 Daillier et Pellet, *supra* n.31, n°119.

34 Art 7, 7, 7, 8 commun aux quatre Conventions

prévue par les mêmes Conventions[35] en est un autre. La mise à l'écart du principe de réciprocité dans l'hypothèse de traités humanitaires, par l'article 60 § 5 de la Convention de Vienne sur le droit des Traités, en est un troisième. De cet ensemble d'éléments, on peut induire l'existence d'un régime d'ordre public. L'exigence formelle de l'article 53 de la Convention de Vienne sur le *jus cogens* – reconnaissance par la communauté internationale des Etats dans son ensemble en tant que norme impérative – est sans doute satisfaite par ces témoins. Or, par ailleurs, le mandat de libérer l'humanité de la faim concerne directement la vie humaine. Il est tellement fondamental qu'on peut le dire d'essence humanitaire. Et du régime d'ordre public des normes humanitaires découlerait l'*impossibilité de déroger par traité au mandat humanitaire* d'une Institution spécialisée.

b3. On peut également invoquer le changement de circonstances – art 62 du "Traité sur les Traités" – en vue de plaider l'extinction du traité. L'argument serait que lorsque les traités Nations Unies-Institutions spécialisées ont été conclus, on avait des sanctions économiques une approche qui ne s'est pas confirmée. Elles ne représentaient qu'un des volets d'une stratégie d'isolement, à laquelle participait la rupture des relations diplomatiques, postales, aériennes, maritimes. Et l'on n'imaginait pas que les sanctions puissent être maintenues à travers les années et les décennies, au point d'être dangereuses pour les populations. Aujourd'hui, se serait instaurée une pratique qui s'éloigne de la désapprobation symbolique, pour se rapprocher d'une guerre d'usure. *Les accords Nations Unies-Institutions spécialisées ont été conclus dans un contexte d'effort en faveur de la paix par le développement; ils ne l'ont pas été dans celui d'une guerre de siège dirigée par les Nations Unies, caractéristique du* "Nouvel Ordre Mondial". Est-il envisageable d'invoquer un changement de circonstances "mett(a)nt en péril le développement vital de l'une des parties" ou (ayant) "entrainé une transformation radicale de la portée des obligations qui restent à exécuter".[36] Il n'est pas impossible de soutenir que désormais, ces traités demandent aux Institutions spécialisées de développer une activité qui va à l'encontre de leur mandat, ce qu'ils ne leur demandaient pas précédem-

35 Art 6, 6, 6, 7 .
36 Selon les termes de l'arrêt de 1973 sur la *Compétence en matière de pêcheries* (Recueil CIJ, 1973, pp.19 et 21).

ment,[37] de parler de "concordance rompue entre (le) contenu (du traité) et les réalités sociales nouvelles qu'il ne peut plus régir"?[38]

Ainsi, toutes les Institutions Spécialisées seraient en droit

- soit d'interpréter[39] l'accord qui les lie aux Nations Unies comme leur interdisant de prêter la main à une action qui porte atteinte à la vie, l'intégrité physique, la santé, et finalement la dignité de populations sous embargo;
- soit de soutenir que les stipulations qu'il serait littéralement impossible d'interpréter en ce sens doivent être réputées non écrites;
- soit d'invoquer l'extinction par changement de circonstances.[40]

C'est à la lumière de ce raisonnement que l'on pourrait interpréter le comportement de l'OACI qui, à l'époque de la lutte des Nations Unies pour la transformation de l'Afrique australe, a refusé d'empêcher l'atterrissage des avions portugais et de refuser des facilités de transit aux avions portugais. L'organisation avait fait valoir que ceci était contraire aux articles 5 et 6 de la Convention de Chicago. On trouve, dans cette affaire, la trace d'une conviction selon laquelle une organisation créée dans l'intérêt de l'aviation civile ne peut, en aucun cas, aller à l'encontre de cette mission, fut-ce pour satisfaire l'organe principal du maintien de la paix et de la sécurité internationale. La sécurité collective ne saurait être qu'humaine.

Mais, alors, semblable raisonnement ne peut-il être tenu lorsqu'au lieu d'une Institution spécialisée, il s'agit d'un organisme subsidiaire des Nations Unies?

---

37 En revanche, il ne semble pas que la même évolution puisse être invoquée au soutien d'un moyen d'annulation fondé sur l'erreur. Il s'agirait alors de soutenir que les Institutions spécialisées se seraient trompées (ou auraient été trompées) sur les conséquences de leur engagement. Mais la prudence de l'OMS prouve qu'il était déja possible d'être méfiant sur les conséquences de cet engagement.

38 Selon l'expression de Daillier et Pellet, *supra*, n. 31, n°207

39 Le problème de la compétence des Institutions spécialisées pour se livrer à cette interprétation ne se pose guère. L'on sait que les organes d'une organisation internationale sont compétents pour en interprêter l'acte fondateur. Il en va clairement ainsi des organes principaux des Nations Unies, puisque "la Cour internationale de justice n'hésite pas à s'appuyer sur la manière dont l'Assemblée générale et le Conseil de Sécurité interprètent la Charte" (Daillier et Pellet, *supra*, n.31, n°170).

40 On ajoutera que l'on ne trouve pas dans une des hypothèses où l'article 62 exclut le jeu de la clause *rebus sic stantibus*. Il ne s'agit ni de traité concernant une frontière, ni d'une violation du traité ou d'une autre obligation par la partie (l'Institution spécialisée) qui invoquerait cette clause.

2) *Le cas des organismes subsidiaires: Résolution sanctionnatrice c/ mandat humanitaire*

Les plus actives des institutions onusiennes dans l'urgence humanitaire sont dépourvues de personnalité internationale: l'UNICEF, le HCR et le PAM. Ce sont les organismes qui sont le plus au contact de la détresse criante. Or la complexité des crises, et l'ambition de les aborder dans leur globalité depuis que le Conseil de Sécurité n'est plus entravé par la guerre froide, font que *désormais, presque systématiquement, sont mis en oeuvre, dans une même crise, un mécanisme de maintien de la paix incluant des sanctions économiques et des mesures d'assistance.* Même si les premières sont dirigées contre la personne "Etat" – ou un groupe armé considéré comme particulièrement nuisible, et la seconde vers les êtres humains qui vivent sur le territoire, les Nations Unies peuvent difficilement jouer ce rôle de *Janus à deux visages*. Les branches humanitaires se trouvent entravées dans leur activité par le régime d'embargo, et, en tout cas retardées s'il est "filtrant" et comporte des procédures d'examen des demandes d'importation. Dans ce malaise, la diversité des statuts tend d'ailleurs à s'effacer derrière le caractère humanitaire du mandat. Les Institutions spécialisées qui "have no choice but to remain involved"[41] ne sont pas plus à l'aise dans ces procédures que les organismes subsidiaires.

Mais, alors que les Institutions spécialisées ont des arguments juridiques à faire valoir, la structure des Nations Unies proprement dites permet l'exercice d'une sorte de pouvoir hiérarchique sur les organismes subsidiaires. Même si c'est l'Assemblée générale qui a créé l'UNICEF et le HCR avec un certain mandat, l'on est dans l'hypothèse des décisions coercitives du Conseil de Sécurité, responsable principal du maintien de la paix. Elles ont valeur obligatoire. Et *un refus d'obtempérer ne peut être opposé au nom du mandat des organismes subsidiaires.*[42] Ledit "mandat", au demeurant, faute de mécanisme contractuel, ne comporte que l'aspect matériel du mandat – une mission exercée pour autrui. Les garanties qu'apporte la technique contractuelle étant absentes, il s'agit plutôt d'une fonction dont la pérénnité n'est pas garantie.

Ici, seul le thème du caractère d'ordre public de cette mission humanitaire pourrait être invoqué à l'encontre d'une décision de coercition économique. Mais, on ne saurait oublier que la décision coercitive elle-même est prise au

41 Minear, Cortright, Wagler, Lopez, Weiss, *supra*, n.9, p 5.

42 Même si le cas du PAM, créé à la fois par l'Assemblée générale et la FAO, peut mériter quelqu'examen supplémentaire.

nom d'une règle impérative – la prohibition du recours individuel à la force et la centralisation du maintien de la paix.

Pourtant, on entrevoit une issue à ce conflit de normes: *une exception humanitaire pour tout ce qui concerne l'assistance humanitaire correspondant à un mandat. Peu importe que ce dernier soit défini par la résolution qui arrête les statuts d'un organisme subsidiaire ou par le traité fondateur d'une Institution spécialisée*; l'exemption serait valable, par exemple, pour l'assistance destinée aux réfugiés ou aux enfants dont l'UNICEF assure la protection.[43] Dans les deux cas, le risque de détournement des biens à "double usage" serait, au demeurant, faible.

On entre alors dans une autre logique: celle de la mitigation des mesures de sanction grâce au mandat humanitaire de certaines branches des Nations Unies.

B. Du conflit juridique à une rédifinition des rôles

Depuis les sanctions quasi unanimement décernées aux Etats de l'Afrique australe blanche, qui remontent aujourd'hui, pour les plus anciennes à 35 ans, le climat a changé. Le système onusien lui-même s'est préoccupé de compatibiliser son volet "maintien de la paix" et son volet humain. Désormais, la sécurité collective est voulue comme une sécurité humaine. Le volet "maintien de la paix", quand bien même il impose des sanctions obligatoires, n'exige donc plus systématiquement une obéissance aveugle. L'idée s'est instaurée que les institutions spécialisées et les organismes subsidiaires – les agences humanitaires – peuvent servir à modérer les sanctions, à les rendre compatibles avec les objectifs humanitaires. Le souci de ne pas porter atteinte aux conditions d'existence des populations des Etats sous embargo est présent dans le système onusien, au moins à deux niveaux. Le premier est celui des principes: l'embargo dit filtrant est la forme de sanctions la plus fréquemment mise en place au cours de la décennie 90. Le second niveau est celui de la mise en oeuvre.

1. Une première innovation décevante: l'embargo "filtrant"

Les sanctions contre l'Irak décidées en 1990 furent les premières à comporter d'emblée l'idée d'exemption et un mécanisme d'examen de demandes en ce sens. Il implique la création systématique de Comités des sanctions qui n'ont

43 Pour l'assistance aux réfugiés et l'absence d'exemption systématique *cf* Pirkko Kourula, "International Protection of Refugees and Sanctions: Humanizing the Blunt Instrument", (1997) 9 *International Journal of Refugee Law* 255-265.

pas exactement les mêmes fonctions que celui qui traitait des mesures contre la Rhodésie et n'avait pour mission que de veiller au respect de l'embargo. Désormais, ces Comités sont en charge de la délivrance d'autorisations dérogatoires d'exportation, fondées sur l'idée que les necessités humaines priment sur celles de l'ordre mondial. Chaque Comité des Sanctions est composé de représentants des 15 Etats membres du Conseil de sécurité, généralement sous la Présidence d'un membre non permanent.

Cependant, cette mécanique de l'embargo filtrant n'est pas d'une grande efficacité humanitaire. Il n'existe pas encore d'exemption par catégorie de produit, ni par catégorie de destinataires. On sait aujourd'hui parfaitement que l'embargo irakien a fait reculer ce pays sur l'échelle du développement. L'embargo haïtien et celui de Sierra Leone que l'on pourrait dire imposés pour punir des peuples de n'avoir pas défendu, contre des coups d'Etat, des Présidents issus du suffrage universel ont frappé des populations extrêmement vulnérables. L'embargo contre la RFY n'est pas innocent, lui non plus.

Et, l'on aurait tort de croire que tous les embargos sont désormais filtrants. On a vu, au Libéria et en Sierra Léone, l'embargo frapper l'aide humanitaire elle-même, partiellement en raison de l'interférence de l'ECOMOG[44] et partiellement à dessein. Il s'agissait de mettre fin – sans mauvais jeu de mots – aux agissements de ceux qui semblaient un obstacle à la paix.

2. *Le schéma d'avenir:les agences humanitaires, chargées de modérer les sanctions*

Le recours à l'article 41 est devenu la *première forme de réponse* aux menaces à la paix; mais il s'agit encore d'une *réponse primitive*, permettant avant tout de dire que les Nations Unies ont adopté des mesures allant au-delà de la condamnation verbale, sans engager la création d'une force armée, aux paramètres toujours complexes. L'essor quantitatif des sanctions économiques ne s'est pas accompagné immédiatement du développement de services administratifs, ni d'une méthodologie.

Les choses devaient cependant commencer à évoluer à la lumière de la formule employée par Boutros Boutros Ghali, en 1995, qualifiant les sanctions

44 Force armée créée par la CEDEAO, en tant que force de maintien de la paix, mais qui s'est comportée comme un belligérant et n'a, délibérément laissé passer aucune livraison humanitaire depuis la Guinée.

d'"instrument brutal".[45] L'institution a mis assez longtemps pour amorcer une certaine maîtrise d'une machine que l'on pouvait qualifier d'emballée.

a) Depuis cette années-là, plusieurs organismes onusiens chargés de suivre la mise en oeuvre des Conventions sur les droits de l'homme se sont dressés au nom des droits qu'ils ont en charge,[46] et *plusieurs études*, dans le système des Nations Unies ou à la demande de celles-ci,[47] *ont mis en lumière différentes procédures qui permettraient de mieux gérer les sanctions pour plus d'humanité*:

- une étude de l'économie du pays-cible, avant d'arrêter le type de mesures à prendre;
- un suivi automatique et étroit des conséquences des sanctions sur l'économie et la société du pays-cible.

A partir de là, pourraient être utilisés plusieurs paramètres qui pourraient permettre un meilleur ciblage des opérations

- choix des mesures qui touchent les dirigeants plutôt que les populations qui endurent déjà la présence des premiers;
- adoption de mesures de compensation des souffrances endurées par la population du pays cible;
- programmation d'un arrêt des mesures en fonction des résultats acquis dans la poursuite de l'objectif qui les a motivées.

Les *Institutions spécialisées et les organismes subsidiaires* ont un rôle important à jouer dans cette perspective, ne serait-ce qu'à travers les *informations* qu'ils peuvent fournir sur différents paramètres:la santé (HINAP),[48] les récoltes et les perspectives alimentaires (GIEWS, FIVIMS, VAM).[49]

---

45 Supplément à l'Agenda pour la Paix, 3 janvier 1995 (Document A/50/60 – S/1995/1).

46 Comité des droits économiques, sociaux et culturels, "Commentaire général n° 8" 1997, Comité sur les Droits de l'enfant, 1998.

47 Von Braun et Kulessa, "The Impact of UN Sanctions on Humanitarian Assistance Activities", Berlin Gesellschaft für Communication Managegment Interkultur Training, décembre 1995 (étude demandée par le Département des affaires humanitaires); Minear, Cortright, Wagler, Lopez, Weiss, *supra*, n. 9; C. Bruderlein et P.Erhardy, "DHA Report on Regional Sanctions against Burundi", décembre 1997.

48 High Intelligence Network for Advanced Contingency Planning, sytème commun à l'OMS et le Center for Diseases Control and Prevention américain.

49 Global Information and Early Warning System et Food Insecurity and Vulnerability Information and Mapping System de la FAO -le second résultant du Sommet mondial

Un indicateur pluridimensionnel, HEWS,[50] a été mis au point par le Département des Affaires humanitaires.

L'ensemble de ces indicateurs peut permettre de *diagnostiquer la vulnérabilité d'un Etat cible et de suivre son évolution* pendant l'application des sanctions. Il permettrait également d'évaluer *ab initio* l'ampleur de l'aide humanitaire qui va être nécessaire pour faire que la vulnérabilité ne se transforme pas en désastre. Bien entendu, les mesures sus-évoquées sont encore largement du domaine de la prospective.

b) Mais, *déjà, certaines innovations* montrent la volonté du système des Nations Unies de faire jouer à sa branche humanitaire un rôle effectif dans la mitigation des effets négatifs du mécanisme de coercition non armée.

b1. Cette volonté s'est d'abord manifestée *in concreto* dans trois affaires. C'est ainsi qu'après le vote de la résolution 1070, le 16 août 1996, à l'encontre du *Soudan* -assortie d'une condition résolutoire: la livraison dans les 90 jours des personnes suspectées d'être impliquées dans l'attentat du Président égyptien Hosni Mubarak, le DHA enquêta sur les probables effets d'une interdiction des transports aériens à l'intérieur du Soudan dans le domaine humanitaire. Le recours à cette étude a pu être considéré comme un compromis entre les Etats pro- et anti-sanctions. Et de fait, après l'étude – qui décrivait des effets négatifs, certes, mais plus limités qu'on ne l'annonçait auparavant, les sanctions n'ont pas été mises en vigueur, comme si la fièvre était retombée.

Par ailleurs, une évaluation de la situation humanitaire fut menée par OCHA en novembre 1997 au *Burundi* que ses voisins avaient mis sous embargo en 1996. Elle releva un assez grand nombre de dysfonctions.

Enfin, on a pu remarquer, à propos de la *Sierra Leone* une certaine volonté des Nations Unies de gérer cet embargo de manière humaine – même si les conditions particulières du pays qui vivait sous "perfusion" humanitaire y ont rendu le choix même de l'embargo particulièrement choquant, et même si

de l'Alimentation de Rome, en 1966, et devant fonctionner sur une base nationale-; Vulnerability Analysis and Mapping du Programme Alimentaire Mondial – ce dernier se focalisant sur les conséquences en matière d'alimentation que peuvent avoir les catastrophes naturelles.

50 Humanitarian Early Warning System.

l'attitude de l'ECOMOG en a rendu le mécanisme d'exception inopérant.[51] En effet, formellement, la résolution du Conseil de Sécurité 1132, du 8 octobre 1997, qui établissait les sanctions prévoyait, dans ses articles 5 et 6, leur suppression. Et celle-ci fut évoquée par le Président du Conseil de Sécurité dès le 26 Février 1998, alors que la junte militaire était à peine tombée, comme une mesure qui allait intervenir aussitôt que possible. Entre temps, OCHA – le Bureau de coordination des affaires humanitaires – avait mené une mission sur place. Ironie du sort, c'est pendant cet embargo, particulièrement scandaleux à bien des égards[52] que la branche humanitaire du système des Nations Unies avait engagé la mise en place d'un processus correspondant un peu au schéma idéal esquissé ci-dessus sous le point a).

b2. Puis, a été esquissée, par les services humanitaires des Nations Unies une sorte de *théorisation* de la matière.
L'Inter-Agency Standing Committee, réuni en novembre 1997, confirma que les agences humanitaires étaient prêtes à fournir des données humanitaires, *ab initio* et en cours de sanctions. Il mit ensuite sur pied un Groupe d'experts inter-agences, avec pour mission

- d'entreprendre des missions d'évaluation;
- de faire des recommandations, sur la gestion de terrain des sanctions, comme sur l'amélioration de la méthodologie;
- et, point plus symbolique encore du rééquilibrage du système des Nations Unies, de conseiller et aider le Coordinateur des secours d'urgence, Sous-secrétaire général, dans son rôle d'"Advocacy" auprès du Conseil de Sécurité.

Et le Sous-secrétaire général a présenté une synthèse presque militante de la matière aux donateurs,[53] puis fait présenter un rapport complet sur une humanisation qui amènerait en même temps un gain d'efficacité.[54] Désormais, est en vue une réforme des exemptions, par opérateur et par produit, ainsi

51 *Cf* M. J. Domestici-Met, in *Les Nations Unies et les sanctions économiques*, Rencontres d'Aix en Provence (Paris, 1999).

52 *Cf* les paroles du Président Kabbah, évincé par le coup d'Etat, et de son entourage, justifiant l'embargo par le fait qu'il fallait punir la population de ne pas l'avoir soutenu (cité in Pascal Lefort et Jonathan Littell, "Nourriture et terreur en Sierra Leone", in S. Brunel (éd.), *Géopolitique de la Faim* (Paris, 1998).

53 Sergio Vieira de Mello, "OCHA: Visions, Priorities and Needs", 8 juin 1998.

54 Rapport C. Bruderlein, "Coping with the Humanitarian Impact of Sanctions: an OCHA Perspective", 2 décembre 1998.

qu'une sorte de suivi épidémiologique des effets des sanctions. De plus ce rapport, de Claude Bruderlein dénonce les difficultés particulières engendrés par les embargos régionaux ou d'origine régionale[55] et propose la création d'un Comité du Conseil aux Sanctions régionales.

b3) Enfin, plus récemment, sur le terrain, les agences humanitaires semblent s'être engagées dans la voie la plus prometteuse: un *moyen terme entre soumission et évasion*, dont deux affaires nous donnent l'exemple.

A propos de la *Libye*, l'OIT travaillait avec le gouvernement sur un programme de développement social. Face à l'embargo aérien, elle a arrêté le projet, mais n'a pas rapatrié les fonds qui lui étaient destinés, permettant ainsi à sa manière la continuation des activités.

Dans l'affaire d'*Irak*, le système des Nations Unies peut éprouver directement les effets de l'antagonisme de ses objectifs à court terme (chapitre VII) et à moyen terme (développement humain). En l'absence de la plupart des ONG, les Institutions spécialisées et les organismes subsidiaires sont les principaux acteurs de l'assistance humanitaire. Or, ils voient leur activité entravée par la lenteur de fonctionnement du "Comité 661". En mars 1999, le Groupe de Travail du Conseil de Sécurité sur les Questions humanitaires admit publiquement que l'embargo avait une certaine part de responsabilité dans la situation de l'Irak.[56]

Puis, en août 1999,[57] l'UNICEF s'est positionné discrètement et efficacement par un rapport donnant un tableau officiel des effets négatifs de l'embargo sur la situation humanitaire, après une enquête précise qui constitue une grande première. En effet, *l'UNICEF est venu apporter des éléments de connaissance objective* dans un débat obscurci par les passions. D'un côté, l'émotion sur les enfants d'Irak dont les médias montrent les images douloureuses; de l'autre, le thème quelque peu rajeuni d'un Saddam Hussein toujours dangereux qui échapperait encore et toujours aux contrôles et mènerait, désormais, la "guerre

55 Rapport disponible sur le site http:// www.reliefweb.int.ocha.

56 "Même si toutes les souffrances en Irak ne peuvent pas être imputées à des facteurs extérieurs, spécialement aux sanctions, le peuple irakien n'endurerait pas de telles privations en l'absence de mesures prolongées imposées par le Conseil de Sécurité et en l'absence des effets de la guerre"(CF/DOC/PR/1999/29).

57 L'enquête avait été menée de février à mai 1999. Cependant, à l'heure où s'est tenu le Colloque de Genève, les résultats n'en étaient pas encore publiés.

des sanctions" en manipulant l'opinion publique. Les résultats, contrôlés par un groupe d'experts indépendants, confirment la nocivité des sanctions sur la mortalité infantile,[58] dont la traduction serait un manque de 500.000 enfants de moins de cinq ans. Ils confirment aussi une situation désormais bien meilleure dans le Kurdistan[59] que dans le Centre et le Sud, où le taux de mortalité des "moins de cinq ans" est désormais presqu'égal à celui d'Haïti.[60] Au total, l'UNICEF conclut à l'existence d'une urgence humanitaire, sans sortir de ce qui est du cadre de son mandat, ni du respect qu'il doit aux organes principaux.

Le bureau régional de l'UNICEF a, pour cette enquête, fait preuve d'une grande autonomie. Il a également témoigné d'un grand pragmatisme en la conduisant avec les autorités respectivement en place dans le Sud et le Centre – le Gouvernement – et dans le Nord – les autorités locales kurdes. Et, fait significatif pour notre approche, il a bénéficié du support technique de l'OMS, laquelle a par là confirmé une liberté de manoeuvre qui s'était déja manifestée lorqu'elle n'a pas hésité à demander un avis consultatif sur les armes nucléaires.

Dès lors apparait, pour les agences (au sens large) humanitaires des Nations Unies, la possibilité d'échapper au rôle d'agent sanctionnateur. et de jouer, au contraire, un rôle positif, celui de rendre les sanctions compatibles avec les objectifs humanitaires.

Deux voies se dégagent. D'un côté, les mesures d'auto-régulation du système onusien, dont tout semble dire qu'elles semblent en cours de systématisation; mais qui doivent encore prouver leur efficacité. Et, de l'autre, un éventuel rejet des décisions de sanctions s'appuyant sur le statut des Institutions spécialisées, le traité les liant aux Nations Unies et le caractère d'ordre public de l'ensemble des "mandats" humanitaires des agences.

Il n'est pas interdit de rêver de la solution la plus souple, celle par laquelle les spécialistes humanitaires des Nations Unies façonneraient des sanctions d'un genre nouveau.

---

58 La mortalité dans la première année est passée de 47 à 108 pour mille, et la mortalité avant 5 ans de 56 pour mille à 131 pour mille entre la période 1984-1989 et la période 1994-1999 .

59 Dans le Nord, le taux de mortalité des moins de cinq ans est passé de 80 à 90 pour mille entre 1984-1989 et 1989-1994, puis est retombé à 72 pour mille dans la période 1994-1999.

60 Voir http/:www.unicef.org.

Techniquement, il s'agirait de passer d'un embargo peu filtrant à un embargo *ciblé et adaptable en fonction des effets.*

Juridiquement, cette voie nouvelle conduirait, *d'un mandat* seulement *susceptible d'être opposé* aux autorités sanctionnatrices, à un mandat *réellement exercé pour tempérer l'activité sanctionnatrice.*[61]

61 La démission du Coordinateur humanitaire pour l'Irak, M Van Sponek en février 2000, à l'heure où cet ouvrage est mis sous presse, interpelle. Elle fait suite à celle de son prédécesseur, Dennis Hallyday en septembre 1998. S'agit-il d'un signe avant-coureur de révolte des agents humanitaires dans le système onusien? Ou sera-t-elle sans lendemain.

13

UN SANCTIONS – THE ILO EXPERIENCE

Janelle Diller[■]

I INTRODUCTION

This commentary shifts our focus from United Nations (UN) sanctions under Chapter 7 of the Charter, and their effect on human rights and humanitarian assistance, to consider the approach of the International Labour Organization (ILO) to sanctions. My remarks will focus on two aspects: first, the ILO acting as a UN specialized agency in coordination with the UN and, second, the ILO acting *qua* ILO – a tripartite organization with roots squarely set in economic and civil society.

II ILO ACTING IN COORDINATION WITH THE UN

The Agreement between the International Labour Organization and the United Nations (Agreement) recognizes the ILO as a specialized agency under Article 57 of the UN Charter. The Agreement implies a presumption that the two organizations will cooperate in matters of mutual concern. Specifically, the ILO is committed to operate consistently with the purposes of the UN set forth in the UN Charter and, in particular, Article 55.

The Agreement further provides for ILO cooperation and participation, as necessary, in recommendations or actions decided upon by the Economic and

■ Legal Officer, Office of the Legal Adviser, International Labour Organization.

V. Gowlland-Debbas (ed.), *United Nations Sanctions and International Law*, p. 197-204.

Social Council or the General Assembly. Under the Agreement, the ILO is to cooperate with the Economic and Social Council, as requested, and to assist the Security Council in carrying out the latter's decisions concerning the maintenance or restoration of international peace and security.

In practice, since becoming the first specialized agency of the United Nations, the ILO has deferred to the UN in political matters. For example, the UN's determination of how a Member state is to be legitimately represented at the UN traditionally determines that same matter for the ILO. This approach has been the case recently in such political matters as the representation of Afghanistan (Rabani government); Cambodia; Somalia (no government); Zaire (Mobutu coup/Tshekedi); and the Federal Republic of Yugoslavia (successor to former Socialist republic 1993).

Under this framework, the ILO has respected the provisions of Security Council decisions relating to international peace and security which are relevant to its own activities. The following examples highlight the effects of this respect on the ILO's technical cooperation projects and even its diplomatic relations generally.

Libya. Following a Security Council Resolution barring the transfer of funds to Libya,[1] the ILO suspended a social security project, which had been funded by the Libyan government, and informed the Libyan government that the ILO could not return the funds to it. The ILO's interpretation of the Security Council Resolution was affirmed by the UN Sanctions Committee. Once the sanctions were suspended, the ILO reinstated the project and use of funds for that purpose.

Southern Rhodesia. In the case of Southern Rhodesia, when President Ian Smith issued a Unilateral Declaration of Independence (UDI), the Security Council condemned the action and refused to maintain contacts with the illegal government of Rhodesia.[2] The ILO followed suit in its decision to cut off all contacts with the Ian Smith government in 1965. Several years later, following relevant

1 SC Res. 883, UN Doc. S/RES/883, para. 12 (1993) (calling upon, *inter alia*, all international organizations to act strictly in accordance with resolution, notwithstanding existence of any rights or obligations conferred or imposed by any international agreement or any contract entered into or any licence or permit granted prior to resolution).

2 SC Res. 216, UN SCOR, Res. and Dec. at 8 (1965).

General Assembly resolutions,[3] the ILO withdrew all aid and cooperation for Southern Rhodesia, except that involving assistance through education to workers and employers organizations. When the independent government of Zimbabwe was declared, the ILO took immediate steps to establish relations and technical cooperation with that government.

Namibia. The case of Namibia represents the extreme length to which the ILO has gone in deferring to sanctions-based action of the UN. In 1978, the ILO admitted Namibia, then under governance of the UN Council for Namibia, over the objections of the Legal Adviser of the ILO, who asserted that Namibia did not have the attributes of statehood to be recognized as a state at that time. The International Labour Conference took the initiative to admit Namibia following the International Court of Justice's Advisory Opinion of 1971 recognizing that UN Member states should refrain from acts of support or recognition of the illegal presence of South Africa in Namibia, and a General Assembly resolution[4] requesting specialized agencies to grant full membership to the UN Council for Namibia as the legal Administering Authority for Namibia.

III ILO ACTING AS INNOVATOR TO BUILD PROMOTIONAL ELEMENT INTO UN SANCTIONS APPROACH

The ILO's action consistent with Security Council resolutions has not limited the Organization's action to the punitive dimension of certain such decisions. Rather, the promotional nature of the ILO's approach to international labour standards and the protection of workers rights is evident in the Organization's response to UN sanctions. The tripartite dimension of the Organization provides a unique strength and flexibility in respect to economic and diplomatic sanctions which strictly public organizations do not wield.

3 E.g., GA Res. 2326 (XXII), para. 8 (1967) (requesting all States, directly and through action in, *inter alia*, specialized agencies, to withhold assistance of any kind to regime of, *inter alia*, Southern Rhodesia until renouncing of "policy of colonial domination and racial discrimination"); GA Res. 2311 (XXII), para. 3 (1967) (recommending specialized agencies to, *inter alia*, extend all necessary aid to oppressed people of Southern Rhodesia).

4 GA Res. 32/9E (1977).

South Africa. In some respects, the ILO was ahead of the UN and others in taking concrete action against *apartheid* South Africa even while South Africa was still a member.[5] In 1964, the International Labour Conference adopted a Declaration and Plan of Action, which was subsequently revised several times,[6] responding to the governmental policy and practice of *apartheid.* The adoption led to action by the Organization characterized by both the punitive and promotional aspects discussed above. On the punitive side, South Africa was excluded from regional and other ILO meetings of which the composition was decided by the Governing Body of the ILO, its constitutionally-created executive organ. In addition, this was the first and only time to date that the Organization has called for disinvestment and a ban on further investment in a country, reflected in the commitments made respecting action by employers' organizations in the document.[7]

In the case of South Africa, the tripartite dimension of the ILO led to a vigorous debate, in which representatives of employers' organizations, as well as workers, supported a system in which their non-governmental involvement could affirmatively lead to change. The debate led to the creation by the International Labour Conference of a tripartite forum, the Committee on Apartheid, for reviewing the situation in South Africa and Namibia on a regular basis. Meeting annually, the Committee issued special reports on the implementation of sanctions and other actions against apartheid based on information from individual employers' and workers' organizations and governments. The Committee maintained a register of investment and divestment in South Africa, and acted in complementarity with other UN bodies and international organizations monitoring sanctions in South Africa.

Along with the above measures concerning South Africa, the ILO established an innovative platform for pursuing a wide range of technical cooperation

5 Shortly after the 1964 ILO Declaration, *infra,* South Africa notified the ILO of its intent to withdraw, which was made effective thereafter. South Africa's membership in the ILO was subsequently reinstated following the establishment of the post-*apartheid* government.

6 Declaration concerning the Policy of "Apartheid" of the Republic of South Africa and ILO Programme for the Elimination of "Apartheid" in Labour Matters in the Republic of South Africa, Geneva, 1964, revised June 1981; June 1988; June 1991; 1994.

7 Declaration concerning Action against Apartheid in South Africa and Namibia, Annex (Programme of Action against Apartheid), III (1)-(3) (Action by employers' organisations) (June 1988).

activities that involved workers' organizations and, to a lesser extent, employers' organizations, but obviously excluded the government. The programs included educational activities, technical assistance, small business development, and management training for independent workers' and employers' organizations. The training programs, which took place outside South Africa/Namibia, helped build the capacity of the trade union movement, which in turn became a key actor in the anti-apartheid struggle.[8] In so doing, the ILO contributed to building the capacity for a peaceful transition and laid key stones in the foundation of the economic and social infrastructure of South Africa today.

IV ILO ACTING THROUGH ITS OWN CONSTITUTIONAL MECHANISMS TO CONDEMN VIOLATIONS WHILE PROMOTING CHANGE

Commissions of Inquiry. The ILO has focused on achieving change in a situation of serious violations through a sanctions-based approach by means of commissions of inquiry, a mechanism established under the ILO Constitution (Articles 26 to 33). The constitutional process which leads to the establishment of a commission of inquiry is initiated by the filing of a complaint, by a government or workers' or employers' organization, or a combination of the same. If a commission of inquiry is deemed necessary, a commission of independent experts is appointed, which conducts an inquiry and prepares an independent report with findings as to the situation and recommendations to the government concerned for promoting change in a particular time frame. The government may choose whether or not to accept the recommendations contained in the report of the Commission and, if not, whether to refer the complaint to the International Court of Justice (ILO Constitution, Article 29(2)). In the Organization's follow up review of whether the government has implemented the recommendations of the Commission of Inquiry, the government is given an opportunity to be heard and may even request that a second commission of inquiry be established to confirm its compliance. If the government's implementation of the Commission of Inquiry's recommendations are not satisfactory, Article 33 of the Constitution, as revised in 1946, provides that, if the Member fails to carry out the recommendations within the time specified by the Commission, the Governing Body "may recommend to the Conference such action as it may deem

8 Since the mid-1980s, black South Africans had been allowed to join trade unions, thus channelling into the unions resources which would otherwise have gone into Black South African political activity, then banned.

wise and expedient to secure compliance" with the recommendations of the Commission of Inquiry.

The original Constitution of 1919 provided that, if a government failed to comply with the recommendations of a commission of inquiry, the Organization could impose measures of an economic character and the government concerned could resort to the then-established Permanent Court of Justice.[9] The provision was in effect (though unused) until 1946, when it was amended to delete the reference to measures of an economic character in light of the birth of the United Nations. The revised article provided, as noted above, that the Governing Body would recommend to the International Labour Conference "such action as it may deem wise and expedient to secure compliance [with the recommendations of the Commission of Inquiry]". During the process of revision,[10] the opinion was expressed that, under Article 103 of the UN Charter, it was no longer appropriate for the ILO to issue sanctions on its own given the new UN Charter structure and, in particular, Article 103's recognition of the primacy of the Security Council. In addition, the drafters explained that such a clause of general nature would permit latitude to adapt the Organization's intervention to the circumstances of each specific case, and to permit, if necessary, drawing

9 The original text read: "In the event of any Member failing to carry out within the time specified the recommendations, if any, contained in the report of the Commission of Enquiry, or in the decision of the Permanent Court of International Justice, as the case may be, any other Member may take against that Member the measures of an economic character indicated in the report of the Commission [a reference to the powers of commissions of inquiry under original Article 32] or in the decision of the Court [a reference to the Permanent Court of International Justice under Article 33] as appropriate to the case." During the period in which this article was in effect, no commissions of inquiry were established.

10 The deletion reflected the belief that the then-new International Court of Justice would defer to the Security Council, when necessary, to impose economic sanctions, if any, under Article 94 of the UN Charter. *Constitutional Questions, op. cit.,* para. 62. The legislative history further reflects a sense that it would be inappropriate for private members of a commission of inquiry to recommend the imposition of economic sanctions on Members. *Id.,* para. 63. See also W. Jenks, *The Prospects of International Adjudication* (London, 1964), pp. 696-97 (if economic measures were involved, "a question might arise as to how far such a recommendation by the Governing Body accepted by the International Labour Conference would justify a Member in taking action which might be inconsistent with other international obligations. Such a recommendation would not have the status of a decision of the Security Council which, in virtue of Article 103 of the Charter, would prevail over the obligations of the Member under any other international instrument.")

the attention of the Security Council to a Member's failure to comply. It was believed that the International Court of Justice, established at the time of the United Nations, would defer to the Security Council on such matters when necessary (see UN Charter, Article 94).

In practice, the past ten commissions of inquiry were created to investigate serious violations of fundamental labour rights. Follow up occurred through reporting and monitoring functions of the Organization, sometimes in the context of a change of government (e.g., Portugal in Angola; Chile; Nicaragua; Poland). Until this year, no follow up to any commission of inquiry involved invocation of Article 33 (although follow up in the case of Poland involved discussion of whether to invoke Article 33).

Invocation of Article 33: Myanmar. This year, following the work of a Commission of Inquiry involving Myanmar's obligations under the Forced Labour Convention, 1930 (No. 29), the Organization has placed an item on the agenda for the Governing Body meeting in November 1999 involving action to be recommended to the International Labour Conference under Article 33. A Commission of Inquiry, in a report published 2 July 1998, concluded that certain obligations under the Convention were violated in Myanmar in a systematic and widespread manner, and issued recommendations for the government to act on by 1 May 1999. In a report of the situation dated 21 May 1999, the Director of the ILO concluded that the government had failed to take the necessary steps to bring the relevant legislative texts into line with the Forced Labour Convention by 1 May 1999, as recommended by the Commission of Inquiry. In a move designed to highlight its concern with the situation in Myanmar and affirm the review to be undertaken under Article 33 by the Governing Body, the International Labour Conference adopted a resolution in June 1999 excluding Myanmar from regional and other meetings and restricting technical cooperation by the ILO to programs aimed at achieving compliance with the Commission of Inquiry's recommendations until such time as compliance is achieved.

V SUMMARY

In sum, the ILO's approach to sanctions provides a strikingly promotional dimension aimed at securing compliance and improvement on a road which would otherwise be primarily punitive in nature. This approach is made possible by the Organization's unique composition, an equal blend of public actors with the social partners, workers' and employers' organizations who work through civil society and private sector activity to achieve deep-rooted social and economic change. The amendment of the Organization's own constitutional sanctions permits its continuing coordination with UN Charter-based action while sustaining the ability to move beyond punishment to promoting change.

14

UN SANCTIONS – DILEMMAS FOR UNICEF

Karin Landgren[■]

Comprehensive economic sanctions have a devastating impact on those groups within a society which UNICEF is most committed to supporting. For UNICEF the dilemma posed by sanctions is immediate and acute. On the one hand, UNICEF is a subsidiary organ bound by resolutions of the Security Council, including in respect of sanctions. On the other, UNICEF's core role is to work for the most vulnerable of children and mothers.

The dilemma and tensions only deepen in the rare cases when sanctions are prolonged, such as in Haiti and, now, in Iraq. There are three additional points of tension, which underpin this primary dilemma. The first lies in how UNICEF's changing mandate will cause it to re-think its own role in situations where the rights of children are not respected. While the traditional UNICEF role emphasized the provision of goods and services such as immunisation and provision of clean water and education for children, the agency has now adopted an explicitly human rights-centred orientation. One consequence is to push the nature of UNICEF's response to children away from traditional motivations of charity and development towards emphasising states' own obligations to act to realize children's rights. This new emphasis on states' obligations, with its potential for conflict and confrontation with governments, is a departure from past practice and as such goes against the grain for some of its staff.

■ Chief, Child Protection, UNICEF. The author has served with the UN in numerous field assignments, including as UNHCR's Chief of Mission in Bosnia and Herzegovina in 1993. The views expressed here are hers alone, and do not necessarily represent those of UNICEF or of the United Nations.

V. Gowlland-Debbas (ed.), *United Nations Sanctions and International Law,* p. 205-210.

The second dilemma relates to popular expectations of UNICEF, led in part by its high media profile and deserved reputation as an advocate on behalf of children and mothers. Since its creation, UNICEF's profile has been largely positive and non-political. Its favourable media coverage is important not only for continued goodwill towards UNICEF in the countries where it operates, but also for securing the agency's financial base, as it relies heavily on voluntary funding and contributions from its National Committees in OECD countries for its operational activities. The perception of UNICEF as an agency which does good for children creates, reasonably, an expectation that where children are being harmed, UNICEF will help or at least speak out. So, where children are suffering as a clear consequence of a sanctions regime imposed by the Security Council there is an expectation, including inside the agency and amongst its supporters, that UNICEF will criticise sanctions and play a direct role in alleviating the plight of children. Reality rarely lends itself to this simplistic approach.

Finally, UNICEF has advocated a range of actions in situations where economic sanctions are imposed, namely, increased monitoring of the impact of sanctions on children, and more humanitarian exemptions to be granted under the sanctions regime. The risk here is that while these actions are likely to raise awareness of the harm being suffered by children, they may not, in themselves, alleviate the effects of sanctions. It may prove difficult for UNICEF to play its advocacy role and prescribe particular actions without becoming embroiled in the highly-politicised arena of sanctions. In the case of Iraq, every aspect of the debate is intensely politicised and polarized, to the point that any statement, however narrowly focused on the humanitarian situation, will resonate politically.

UNICEF approaches the issue of sanctions primarily from its humanitarian perspective, rather than the standpoint of international law. That said, UNICEF's mandate has, since 1996, been framed in a human rights perspective, that is a perspective based on international human rights law. According to its mission statement, the agency is mandated by the UN General Assembly to advocate for the protection of children's rights, to help meet their basic needs and to expand their opportunities to reach their full potential. The mission statement notes that UNICEF is guided by the Convention on the Rights of the Child and strives to establish children's rights as enduring ethical principles and international standards of behaviour towards children. UNICEF, it says, is committed to ensuring special protection for the most disadvantaged children, and responds in emergencies to protect the rights of children.

This orientation became at once more explicit and more practical in 1998, when UNICEF formally adopted a human rights-based approach to its activities. Establishing human rights (notably the Convention on the Rights of the Child and CEDAW) as UNICEF's principal frame of reference in operational activities encompasses both civil and political, and economic, social and cultural rights.

With respect to sanctions, the most recent and relevant guidance offered by a human rights body is the General Comment No. 8 of the Committee on Economic, Social and Cultural Rights, responsible for overseeing the implementation of the International Covenant on Economic, Social and Cultural Rights. In this Comment the Committee insists that the targeted state, along with the international community, must do everything possible to protect "at least the core content of the economic, social and cultural rights of the affected peoples", rights which are not nullified or diminished in any way by the imposition of sanctions, according to the General Comment.[1] The state is to take steps to the maximum of its available resources to minimise the impact on the most vulnerable, an obligation which the treaty body concerned is called on to scrutinise very carefully.

In some senses the Committee is stating the obvious: that the rights enjoyed by the citizens of a state party are not extinguished by the adoption of a sanctions resolution in the Security Council and that the obligations of the authorities in that country towards their citizens are similarly not diminished by the imposition of sanctions. However sensible this approach, it is clear that theory and practice diverge sharply when we look at the situation of vulnerable groups in states such as Iraq.

---

1 Implementation of the International Covenant on Economic, Social and Cultural Rights: General Comment No. 8 (1997), The relationship between economic sanctions and respect for economic, social and cultural rights (UN Economic and Social Council, E/C.12/1997/8, 12 December 1997). The General Comment also calls for effective monitoring and notes an obligation "to take steps, individually and through international assistance and co-operation, especially economic and technical", in order to respond to any disproportionate suffering experienced by vulnerable groups within the targeted country (para 14).

Since the early 1990s, UNICEF has recommended that a "child impact assessment" should be carried out when any type of sanctions are applied, with constant monitoring thereafter to gauge impact. This is consistent with the recommendation of the General Comment that economic, social and cultural rights be taken fully into account when designing an appropriate sanctions regime. UNICEF has been less visible as an advocate of greater action by the targeted State, however, where that State is believed not to be doing "everything possible" to protect the rights of children.

Popular expectations of UNICEF and the reality of sanctions create the remaining dilemmas. Economic sanctions hit children hard, both directly and indirectly. Direct effects include reduced immunisations against childhood diseases through vaccine non-availability and the breakdown of cold chains; increases in infectious diseases due to the breakdown of water and sanitation services; crises in families often accompanied by increases in psychological disorders; deterioration in the education system; and declines in food production and agriculture. Some of these effects can probably be addressed through exemptions to the sanctions regime and programmes such as the "oil for food" programme which Iraq belatedly accepted in late 1996. However, longer-term sanctions contribute to a broader and more general impoverishment and social degradation, which cannot be redressed piecemeal.[2] UNICEF can neither "fix the problem" nor, in the absence of any change to the underlying threat to international peace and security, as determined by the UN Security Council, can it call for the lifting of sanctions.

A further complication inherent to sanctions regimes makes it difficult for UNICEF to present a position which is at once strongly principled and easily

---

2 "The impact of sanctions, however, is perhaps most visible upon entering the households of affected families. Faced with higher prices for food, medicines and other essential items, sanctioned families are increasingly unable to cope. Unemployment, loss of income, and inflation make household survival even more difficult. Foodstores are quickly depleted, family possessions (including property) are sold, and loans are undertaken (sic) to provide much-needed income. In Iraq, 48% of households surveyed as early as September 1991 had already incurred heavy sanctions-related debts. Stress-related anxiety, depression and violence are other manifestations of a family's growing inability to cope with hardship. (...) Financial hardship led to child abandonment and increased begging. Other reports attest to the significant psychological impact of sanctions on children, the future impact of which is difficult to ascertain." *The Impact of Sanctions: A Study of UNICEF's Perspective*, Office of Emergency Programmes, Working Paper Series, February 1998, pp. 4-5.

understood. This is the impossibility of gauging which civilian hardship is directly attributable to sanctions, from that due to other factors, especially ongoing conflict and the human rights record of the regime in power. Targetted States, in campaigning for the lifting of sanctions, draw attention to the way their people are suffering, tending to blame all such suffering on sanctions. Images of this suffering can be a potent tool of foreign policy. Extensive use of such images and propaganda creates, reasonably enough, a concern that the authorities have little interest in lessening that suffering, even when they are in a position to do so.

Where children are suffering and a sanctions regime is in place, UNICEF has come under pressure from some media and from Non-Governmental Organizations for "not taking a stand on the issue" and for "putting politics before children". Governments without much enthusiasm for being urged to fulfil their obligations are nonetheless likely to seek UNICEF's help to do more to publicise the plight of children in the context of sanctions. It is clearly misguided to expect that UNICEF would be able to override both complex realities which lead to the imposition of sanctions, or to have a decisive impact on governments in this situation. However, the strength of the expectations underline UNICEF's vulnerability to perceptions of non-responsiveness, and place the agency under pressure to act or speak out against sanctions themselves.[3]

In January 1999, the President of the Security Council issued a Presidential Note[4] on strengthening the work of the sanctions committees. This included a provision for monitoring, throughout the sanctions regime, the humanitarian impact of sanctions on vulnerable groups, including children, and making required adjustments of the exemption mechanisms to facilitate the delivery of humanitarian assistance. The Executive Director of UNICEF, Carol Bellamy, welcomed this with a strong statement reiterating that "We must protect children from the effects of sanctions." In this Note, UNICEF obtained recognition of positions it had advocated for many years.

3 "There is the perception, and possibly the reality, that the sanctions, rather than the crises to which they respond, have created humanitarian emergencies." L.F. Damrosch, "The Civilian Impact of Economic Sanctions".

4 *Ie* a document agreed to by all members of the Council but without the binding character of Security Council resolutions.

Strengthening monitoring, and increasing humanitarian exemptions are likely to create a greater awareness among international decision-makers of the poor state of childrens' health, safety and well-being under sanctions. Where sanctions have been in place for some time, however, this unhappy state may reflect a deeper and more pervasive societal decline – families out of work, mental illness stemming from deprivation and despair, violence against and among children born of frustration, and reduced educational opportunities. This pall over society will not be redressed through humanitarian exemptions, as demonstrated by the impact of the "oil for food" programme in Iraq which has delivered impressive quantities of food and medicine, and is beginning to improve supplies of electricity and clean water, but cannot be expected to have much impact on other social and psychological impacts of sanctions.

There is no solution to the dilemmas which sanctions pose for UNICEF. The reality is that sanctions have been imposed only rarely by the Security Council and that comprehensive sanctions, such as are currently in place against Iraq and have previously been imposed against Haiti and South Africa, are even more unusual. On those rare occasions, UNICEF will need to remain at the forefront of helping to ensure that the Security Council is fully aware of the situation of the affected children; and that the targeted government is similarly aware of its own responsibilities.

15

UN SANCTIONS AND ICRC'S MANDATE

Michèle Kuhn▪

The following is an overview of ICRC's mandate and how it relates to sanctions, as well as the ICRC's attitude with regard to, and its response to economic sanctions.

Since the beginning of the nineties, the ICRC and the other components of the International Red Cross and Red Crescent Movement, through their field work, have increasingly had the opportunity to observe humanitarian consequences of sanctions, especially comprehensive trade sanctions.

In 1995, the International Red Cross and Red Crescent Conference adopted a resolution which addresses amongst other issues the humanitarian consequences of sanctions, encouraging states to consider the possible negative impact on the humanitarian situation of the civilian population when designing, imposing and reviewing economic sanctions, to consider assessing and monitoring the consequences of economic sanctions for the most vulnerable, and, for states subject to sanctions, to consider providing relief to the most vulnerable. The resolution calls on states to permit relief operations and calls on the components of the International Red Cross and Red Crescent Movement to contribute to the reduction of the undesirable side-effects in the humanitarian situation of the civilian population through assessing the impact and providing relief to the most vulnerable, in accordance with their respective mandates.

▪ Legal Officer, Division for Policy and Cooperation, International Committee of the Red Cross.

V. Gowlland-Debbas (ed.), *United Nations Sanctions and International Law*, p. 211-219.

I The ICRC's mandate

The ICRC is an impartial, neutral and independent organization whose exclusively humanitarian mission is to protect the lives and dignity of victims of war and internal violence and to provide them with assistance. It also endeavours to prevent suffering by promoting and strengthening international humanitarian law and universal humanitarian principles.

The ICRC's mandate has been conferred on it by the international community. This mandate has two legal bases: on one hand, it is enshrined in the Geneva Conventions of 12 August 1949 and their Additional Protocols of 8 June 1977. Since their origin, the ICRC has taken the initiative for and been closely associated to the development of these instruments of international humanitarian law. On the other hand, the ICRC's mandate is defined in its Statutes and the Statutes of the International Red Cross and Red Crescent Movement. The latter have been endorsed by the signatory states to the Geneva Conventions, together with the components of the International Red Cross and Red Crescent Movement, in their present version at the XXVth International Conference in 1986.

Some provisions of the Geneva Conventions give the ICRC explicit competencies, e.g. to carry out visits to Prisoners of War (Art. 126 GC III) or civilian internees (Art. 143 GC IV). Other provisions are related to tracing matters and to the application of the Geneva Conventions. A general right of initiative to carry out, subject to the parties' consent, humanitarian actions of protection and assistance in favour of the various categories of protected persons is contained in all four GC (Art. 9/9/9/10, Art. 81 AP I). All these provisions apply to international armed conflict. As to non-international armed conflict, Art. 3 para 2 common to all four Geneva Conventions states a right of initiative for these situations as well.

The conventional mandate is applicable in situations of armed conflict, whether international or non-international. It does not apply to situations of a lesser degree of violence such as internal disturbances or tensions.

In these situations, the ICRC's action is based on its statutory mandate, which is applicable in situations of conflict as well as in situations of a lesser degree of violence. It contains a right of initiative which is generally recognized by the states. Art. 5 paragraph 2 d) says that the role of the ICRC is

> "to endeavour at all times – as a neutral institution whose humanitarian work is carried out particularly in time of international and other armed conflicts or internal strife – to ensure the protection of and assistance to military and civilian victims of such events and of their direct results".

This provision covers not only situations where International Humanitarian Law is applicable, but also internal disturbances such as riots, isolated and sporadic acts of violence (as mentioned in Article 1 paragraph 2 of Additional Protocol II and explicitly excluded from its applicability).

In addition, Article 5 paragraph 3 of the Movement's Statutes provides a very general right of initiative to the ICRC which does not refer to a special type of situation:

> "The International Committee of the Red Cross may take any humanitarian initiative which comes within its role as a specifically neutral and independent institution and intermediary, and may consider any question requiring examination by such an institution."

The legal base of ICRC's interventions is therefore broader and stronger in situations of armed conflict, where it is based on international treaty law, than in situations of a lesser degree of violence.

The ICRC's mandate comprises protection and assistance. Both activities are closely linked. Protection and assistance means to prevent or put a stop to violations of law, to remedy the effects or limit the damage caused by such violations, and finally to repress the authors of such violations; however this last aspect is not within the competence of the ICRC.

In addition to the protection and assistance in favour of victims of conflict, Article 5 paragraph 2, c) of the Statutes gives the ICRC the task "...to work for the faithful application of international humanitarian law...". Articles 10/10/10/11 of GC I-IV provides that the ICRC may act as a substitute for a Protecting Power, whose task it is to co-operate in, and scrutinize the application of the Geneva Conventions. Article 97 of AP I states that amendments shall be made after consultation with the ICRC, and Article 98 gives the ICRC a right of initiative to revise Article I of the said Protocol (Regulations concerning the identification).

As International Humanitarian Law is applicable only in situations of armed conflict, in this regard again, the base of the ICRC's action is stronger in such situations than in situations of a lesser degree of violence. In these situations, the ICRC may refer to universal humanitarian principles. These are essentially identical with the hard core of human rights law from which no derogation is permitted. However, the ICRC has no mandate with respect to human rights law.

In the light of the above, the ICRC has no specific mandate with respect to sanctions. Sanctions may be imposed in times of peace or in times of conflict. The ICRC can respond to their consequences when they are imposed in a context which comes under its mandate. Sanctions imposed in times of peace come under the mandate of the National Societies of Red Cross or Red Crescent and their International Federation.

II THE ICRC'S ATTITUDE WITH REGARD TO, AND RESPONSE TO SANCTIONS

The ICRC is not generally opposed to sanctions, as they are permitted under Article 41 of the UN Charter as a measure of enforcement short of the use of force, in order to restore or maintain international peace and security. In the ICRC's view, however, there are limits to the extent of suffering which sanctions may legitimately cause. States and the UN are bound to observe the principles of international humanitarian law, human rights law and elementary considerations of humanity when designing, monitoring and reviewing a sanctions regime.

The ICRC is concerned about economic sanctions, particularly comprehensive trade sanctions, because they have the strongest potential of a negative impact on the situation of the civilian population. They may also adversely affect the delivery of humanitarian assistance. There are different ways in which the ICRC can respond to a sanctions regime.

It may respond to the needs of the civilian population through humanitarian assistance. It is not always easy to determine, however, which needs are caused by sanctions and which ones are a consequence of armed conflict.

For example in Iraq, the ICRC has been present since 1981, first in the context of the war between Iran and Iraq, then in the context of the second Gulf war and its aftermath, as well as of the conflict situation in the north of the country. Some of its activities, mainly in the North, are clearly linked to conflict. But the ICRC carries out a water and sanitation programme as well, which partly responds to the consequences of conflict, and partly to the consequences of economic sanctions: many installations have been destroyed during the Gulf war in 1991, others have fallen into disrepair due to the lack of maintenance. In 1999, the ICRC carried out a series of surveys of the medical infrastructure and set up an operation of support to medical structures. This action responds to the consequences of the economic sanctions.

The ICRC does not take a stand with respect to the reasons for the imposition of sanctions and of their likely effectiveness. These issues imply political considerations which may be controversial and on which the ICRC does not comment, in accordance with its principle of neutrality which prevents it from taking part in controversies of a political, religious, racial or ideological nature.

The ICRC may, however, take a stand – publicly or in its bilateral or multilateral contacts – in relation to the humanitarian situation under a sanctions regime, i.e. the suffering of the civilian population caused or exacerbated by economic sanctions. It may provide those involved in a particular sanctions regime – the sender state or states, the target state, the Sanctions Committee, the Security Council – with information regarding the humanitarian situation in the target state.

For example, the ICRC has regularly reported on the humanitarian situation in Iraq in its annual reports and appeals for funds, and in its high level contacts, mainly with the UN Security Council and the Sanctions Committee. In March 1999, the ICRC submitted a report to the Security Council's Panel II, which examined humanitarian issues in Iraq, on the humanitarian situation as it had observed it in its fields of expertise.

Furthermore, the ICRC can call – publicly or in its bilateral or multilateral contacts – for adequate humanitarian exemptions to the sanctions regime, which should be adequate in terms of the needs of the population and the requirements of International Humanitarian Law, Human Rights law and elementary considerations of humanity. It may enter into discussion with the responsible bodies (Sanctions Committees, states) to ensure that the exceptions function satisfactorily, enabling the ICRC and other humanitarian organizations to meet the needs of the population of the target state.

Former Yugoslavia is an example to show the manifold implications of sanctions implementation on the work of humanitarian organizations. When comprehensive economic sanctions were imposed on the FRY, and later on the Bosnian Serbs,

ICRC was carrying out an important operation for the victims of the conflict in Bosnia. Some problems arose then in the context of implementation of the humanitarian exemption.

First of all, I would like to state that these problems were not serious. The ICRC was in direct contact with the Sanctions Committee and with time, a relation of trust was built up. Never was an ICRC request turned down, and never was its action seriously hindered or stopped altogether by the implementation of the sanctions. The problems faced were of three kinds: lengthy and sometimes complicated administrative procedures and delays, lack of clear definitions, or too restrictive definitions, of the goods exempted for humanitarian purposes, and the need for the ICRC to import dual-use items and other goods that were not *a priori* humanitarian goods.

An important apparatus had been set up for the implementation of the sanctions in former Yugoslavia and Bosnia-Hercegovina, involving the EU and the WEU, the International Conference on Former Yugoslavia, the Sanctions Assistance Missions, as well as national customs authorities of the implementing states. As a consequence, clearances of sometimes multiple authorities were required. The procedures to be adopted were not always clear. A special situation arose when the FRY was at the same time target state of a sanctions regime, and implementing state of the sanctions imposed on the Serb-held territories of Bosnia-Hercegovina. The Yugoslav authorities wanted to comply very strictly with the sanctions resolutions and sometimes refused clearance although the sanctions committee had given it.

Regarding the humanitarian exemptions, the definition of food and medicine was at times very strict or lacked clear definitions. Moreover, the ICRC was running important water and sanitation programmes in Bosnia which required the importation of pumps and piping, generators and fuel. It needed as well office materials and computer logistics for its delegations and offices in Bosnia. For these items, the procedures were more complicated and could take up to three months.

Over time, the clearance procedure became smoother, and starting from February 1995, a kind of blanket exemption was obtained which required only a periodical notification of the goods to be imported.

Finally, the ICRC may, and in fact must, remind the international community and the actors involved in a sanctions regime that sanctions imposed during a time of armed conflict must comply with the relevant provisions of International Humanitarian Law: prohibition of starvation of the civilian population, the obligation of states party to the Geneva Conventions and their Additional Protocols to permit the supply of certain goods and to allow relief assistance.

The comments ICRC makes on the humanitarian situation must be based on its own observations in the field or on reliable and verifiable sources. It is not always possible, or advisable, to establish a link between the suffering of the civilian population and the sanctions, and the ICRC must always take care that its public comments do not negatively affect its operations in favour of the civilian population in the target state.

III THE ICRC'S RELATIONS WITH THE SECURITY COUNCIL AND THE SANCTIONS COMMITTEES

These relations must be seen in the light of the ICRC's legal status and international legal personality. The analysis of this complex issue goes beyond the framework of this presentation, therefore, just a few summary considerations shall conclude it.

The ICRC is an organization which cannot be clearly classified in a specific category and is widely recognized as an organization *sui generis*. It is not an international organization, as the generally recognized requirement of government participation is not fulfilled; quite to the contrary, in the interest of its independence, ICRC avoids any state representation within its bodies. Nor is it based on an international treaty, a criterion also widely recognized for the status of an international organization.

Formally, the ICRC resembles an NGO, as it is constituted as a private association under Swiss law. However, the ICRC acts in way fundamentally different from NGOs: it has a special link with the international treaties of International Humanitarian Law, that confer upon it an international mandate; many international organizations consider the ICRC, when giving it observer status, either as an entity different from the NGO group, or they assimilate it to an intergovernmental organization; and the ICRC's activities imply that it concludes headquarters agreements with states, that it maintains diplomatic relations with them, and that it participates in the revision or amendment of the humanitarian conventions.

It is generally recognized that the ICRC has an international legal personality because it is the direct addressee of provisions of public international law, and international law recognizes the ICRC's capacity to exercise rights and obligations on an international level. The ICRC has not all the rights and obligations which a state, as the classical subject of international public law, may have. Its rights and obligations are all related to the implementation of the mandate of the ICRC.

The headquarters agreement between Switzerland and the ICRC of 19 March 1993 recognizes explicitly its international personality and confirms its independence *vis-à-vis* the Swiss authorities.

Given its international personality, the ICRC treats with states and International Organizations on a level of co-ordination rather than subordination.

Regarding the ICRC's relations with the United Nations, the General Assembly has given it observer status. Its delegation in New York meets monthly with the chairman of the Security Council, and once a year, the ICRC President meets with the whole Security Council, to address humanitarian issues. On 12 February 1999, speaking about the protection of civilians in armed conflicts at the Security Council, the ICRC's President Cornelio Sommaruga addressed also the problem of the consequences of economic sanctions:

> "If the principles of humanitarian action are to be fully respected, aid workers must have access to people affected by conflicts. Where these people are also suffering from economic sanctions imposed on their country, caution must be exercised. Nothing can justify punishing an entire population for its government's misdeeds. It is not ICRC's place to comment on the use of economic sanctions per se; however, it is duty-bound – a duty which it has frequently carried out – to request exemptions to sanctions so that needy populations can receive humanitarian assistance. I am in full agreement with the Secretary-general of the United Nations, who has said that sanctions are known on occasion to have tragic consequences for civilian populations. The ICRC welcomes the fact that the Security Council has instructed

> its Sanctions Committees to examine the humanitarian impact of sanctions on the most vulnerable groups."[1]

As I have already pointed out, the ICRC also reports to the Security Council on the humanitarian consequences of particular sanctions regimes. The legal status of the ICRC allows it also to have direct access to the different Sanctions Committees, where it can advocate for the needs of the concerned civilian population, present its operational needs, and obtain clearances for the goods it needs for its operations.

1 "The Protection of Civilians in Armed Conflict", UN Security Council, 3977th meeting, Statement by Dr. Cornelio Sommaruga, President, ICRC (ICRC Ref. EXSO 99.02.12-ENG).

Sanctions and Humanitarian Law

Chair: *Christian Dominicé*
Honorary Professor, Graduate Institute of International Studies
Secretary-General, Institut de droit international

LA COMPATIBILITÉ DES SANCTIONS DU CONSEIL DE SÉCURITÉ AVEC LE DROIT INTERNATIONAL HUMANITAIRE

Djamchid Momtaz▪

Déjà, en 1919, l'obligation prévue dans le Pacte de la Société des Nations de rompre les relations commerciales avec l'Etat membre qui recourt à la guerre contrairement aux engagements pris était qualifié par le Président Woodrow Wilson de "remède terrible".[1] Depuis, avec l'interdépendance économique croissante des Etats, l'efficacité de cette arme n'a fait que croître.

Malheureusement, les sanctions économiques ont toujours des effets non intentionnels qui affectent sans discrimination combattants et population civile, plus particulièrement les groupes les plus vulnérables. Désormais, c'est la bonne réputation de la sanction économique, qualifiée longtemps d'"arme qui ne tue personne", qui est remise en cause. C'est pourquoi le CICR fut amené, dès la fin du premier conflit mondial,[2] à se préoccuper de ses effets néfastes. Il exprimait le vœu que les belligérants s'entendent pour prévoir des "exceptions humanitaires" aux sanctions et assurer ainsi une base juridique aux secours destinés aux civils les plus affectés par la rupture des relations économiques.

▪ Professeur de droit international public à l'Université de Téhéran. Associé à l'Institut du droit international. Membre de la Commission du droit international.

1 "Terrible Remedy", Cité par W. Michael Reisman et Douglas L. Stevick, "The Applicability of International Law Standards to United Nations Economic Sanctions Programme", (1998) 9 *EJIL*, p. 88.

2 Rapport du CICR à la treizième Conférence internationale de la Croix-Rouge (La Haye 1928) sur le rôle de la Croix-Rouge en cas d'application de l'article XVI du Pacte de la SDN.

V. Gowlland-Debbas (ed.), *United Nations Sanctions and International Law*, p. 223-232.

Des dispositions ont été ainsi prévues par la IVème Convention de Genève de 1949 relative à la "protection des personnes civiles en temps de guerre", complétées en 1977 par les Protocoles additionnels aux Conventions de Genève. Il ne fait désormais guère de doute que le Conseil de Sécurité est tenu de prendre en considération ces dispositions du droit international humanitaire lors de l'adoption de sanctions économiques. En vue d'assurer cette compatibilité et réduire les risques de dérapage lors de leur application, la mise en place d'un mécanisme s'est imposée.

I OBLIGATION DU CONSEIL DE SÉCURITÉ DE RESPECTER LES DISPOSITIONS DU DROIT INTERNATIONAL HUMANITAIRE RELATIVES À LA PROTECTION DE LA POPULATION CIVILE

On considère généralement que les dispositions du droit international humanitaire destinées à protéger la population civile des conséquences néfastes de l'interruption des relations économiques sont de nature *erga omnes*. L'obligation du Conseil de Sécurité de respecter ces dispositions lors de l'adoption des sanctions économiques et tout au long de leur application résulte de cette qualification.

A) Nature erga omnes des dispositions du droit international humanitaire relatives à la protection de la population civile

Conformément à l'article 23 de la IVème Convention de Genève, les Etats parties sont tenus d'accorder le libre passage de tout envoi de médicaments et de matières sanitaires destiné à la population civile de l'ennemi. Il en va de même des vivres indispensables, des vêtements, et des fortifiants réservés aux enfants de moins de 15 ans, aux femmes enceintes ou en couches. Sont considérés comme indispensables, entre autres, le lait, la farine, le sucre, la graisse, et le sel.[3]

Ainsi, la Convention de Genève ne vise à protéger que la catégorie la plus vulnérable de la population contre la famine pouvant résulter de l'interruption des relations économiques. L'article 54 §1 du premier Protocole additionnel aux Conventions de Genève, relatif à la protection des victimes des conflits armés internationaux, en énonçant la règle selon laquelle "il est interdit d'utiliser

3 *Cf.* Commentaire de la IVème Convention de Genève relative à la protection des personnes civiles en temps de guerre (Genève CICR, 1956), p. 194.

contre les civils la famine comme méthode de guerre",[4] étend cette protection à l'ensemble de la population civile d'un territoire occupé ou sous le contrôle d'une partie au conflit.[5] L'article 69 §1 de ce Protocole considère l'approvisionnement en vivres et en médicaments ainsi que la fourniture de vêtements, de matériel de couchage et de logements d'urgence comme étant essentiels à la survie de la population. Cette liste n'est pas exhaustive puisque cet article se réfère aux "autres approvisionnements essentiels". Dans la mesure où le caractère essentiel d'une denrée ou d'un bien peut aussi dépendre des conditions locales, cette approche se justifie.

Conformément à ces dispositions, l'obligation pour un Etat partie à la IVème Convention de Genève ou au Protocole additionnel I d'accorder le libre passage reste néanmoins subordonnée à la condition que l'action de secours parvienne bien aux catégories de civils concernées et qu'il n'en résulte pas un avantage manifeste pour les efforts militaires ou l'économie de la puissance ennemie; hypothèse pour le moins théorique, puisque, dans la plupart des cas, ces envois sont à peine suffisants pour répondre aux besoins les plus urgents de la population civile.

L'obligation d'assurer le ravitaillement des populations civiles affectées par un conflit armé en vivres et médicaments est le prolongement du droit à la vie, solennellement proclamé par l'article 3 de la Déclaration universelle des droits de l'homme et que l'article 6 du Pacte international relatif aux droits civils et politiques considère comme inhérent à la personne humaine et auquel l'article 4 de ce même Pacte n'admet aucune dérogation. C'est ainsi que l'article 1 §2 commun à ce Pacte et celui relatif aux droits économiques, sociaux et culturels déclare en des termes identiques que "en aucun cas, un peuple ne pourra être privé de ses propres moyens de subsistance". Cet interdit, corollaire du droit à la vie, est évidemment destiné à mettre les individus à l'abri de la faim, protection qualifiée de "droit fondamental" de l'homme par l'article 11 §2 du Pacte international relatif aux droits économiques, sociaux et culturels.[6]

---

4 L'article 14 du Protocole II additionnel aux Conventions de Genève, relatif à la protection des victimes des conflits armés non internationaux reprend en termes identiques cette disposition.

5 Cf. articles 69 et 70 du Protocole I.

6 Paul Tavernier, "Sanctions économiques et droits de l'homme", Journée d'études du Centre de recherches et d'études sur les droits de l'homme et le droit humanitaire (CREDHO) 2 mai 1992. Se référant à l'article 1 §2 commun aux deux Pactes, l'auteur remarque à juste titre que cette disposition ne semble pas avoir retenu l'attention de

Ainsi, les dispositions pertinentes du droit international humanitaire sont destinées à sauvegarder des règles concernant les droits fondamentaux de la personne humaine, règles qualifiées par le célèbre *dictum* de la Cour internationale de Justice dans l'affaire Barcelona Traction *d'erga omnes.*[7]

B) *Le respect par le Conseil de Sécurité des dispositions du droit international humanitaire relatives à la protection de la population civile*

Pour la Cour internationale de Justice, l'obligation de suspendre les relations conventionnelles pouvant résulter d'une résolution du Conseil de Sécurité ne peut affecter les dispositions relatives à la protection de la personne humaine contenues dans les traités de caractère humanitaire. Cette exception à la règle générale de l'extinction et la suspension des traités est prévue à l'article 60 de la Convention de Vienne sur le droit des traités. La Cour s'y est expressément référée, la qualifiant de règle codifiant le droit coutumier existant, à l'occasion de l'Avis consultatif rendu dans l'affaire du Sud-ouest africain.[8]

Dès lors, en cas de "conflits" entre les dispositions des sanctions économiques du Conseil de Sécurité et celles du droit international humanitaire relatives à la protection de la population civile, l'article 103 de la Charte des Nations Unies ne pourrait être invoqué pour obliger les Etats membres au respect des décisions du Conseil. En effet, cet article vise la prééminence du droit des Nations Unies sur le droit conventionnel et ne concerne nullement les obligations des Etats telles qu'elles résultent du droit international général, et plus particulièrement

---

ceux qui se sont penchés sur le problème des sanctions économiques, disposition qui met en valeur la contradiction entre les droits de l'homme et les sanctions décidées par l'ONU. *Cf.* dans le même sens les commentaires de Charles A. Allen, "Civilian Starvation and Relief During Armed Conflicts; the Modern Humanitarian Law ", (1989) 19 *Georgia Journal of International and Comparative Law*, plus particulièrement pp. 52 et suivantes.

7 Affaire de la Barcelona Traction Light and Power Company Limited *(Belgique c. Espagne),* CIJ Recueil, 1970, p. 32. *Cf.* G. Abi-Saab, "The Specificities of Humanitarian Law", in Christophe Swenarski (ed.), *Etudes et essais sur le droit international humanitaire et sur les principes de la Croix Rouge en l'honneur de Jean Pictet* (CICR, 1984), pp. 270 et suivantes.

8 Avis Consultatif du 21 juin 1971 sur les *Conséquences juridiques pour les Etats de la présence continue de l'Afrique du sud en Namibie (Sud-ouest africain) nonobstant la Résolution 276 (1970) du Conseil de Sécurité,* CIJ Recueil, 1971, p. 47. *Cf.* Commentaire de Vera Gowlland-Debbas sur l'étude de Nico Schrijver, "The Use of Economic Sanctions by the Security Council: an International Law Perspective" in *International Economic Law and Armed Conflict* (Dordrecht/Boston/London , 1994), pp. 171 et suiv.

celles qualifiées d'*erga omnes*. D'ailleurs, la question ne s'est jamais posée, puisque "le Conseil de Sécurité a toujours prévu l'exception humanitaire" dans ses résolutions imposant des sanctions économiques,[9] y compris dans celles concernant l'Irak.

Dans ce dernier cas, ce sont les conditions restrictives de recours à cette exception qui ont soulevé des difficultés. En effet, la Résolution 661 du 6 août 1990 du Conseil de Sécurité, contrairement à celle adoptée dans le cadre du conflit yougoslave, n'autorise l'acheminement des produits alimentaires que si "les considérations humanitaires le justifient". La résolution 666 du 13 septembre 1990 devait confier au Comité *ad hoc*, mis en place dans le cadre de la Résolution 661, la responsabilité de déterminer si de telles conditions existent, la décision du Comité sur la nécessité de fournir les denrées alimentaires devant, dans chaque cas, être entérinée par le Conseil de Sécurité.

Dans la mesure où le Conseil de Sécurité n'avait nullement l'intention d'utiliser la famine comme arme de combat contre l'Irak, cette condition restrictive ne se justifiait guère. En effet, tout envoi de vivres est par définition humanitaire. Telle est la position adoptée par quelques Etats[10] et le CICR. Ce dernier s'est d'ailleurs refusé de se plier à la procédure prévue par cette Résolution, se contentant de notifier au Comité compétent l'envoi des vivres.[11] Le CICR, à l'instar de la majorité de la doctrine, considère que le critère fixé par le Conseil de Sécurité n'était pas compatible avec le principe de libre passage des denrées alimentaires tel que prévu à l'article 23 de la IVème Convention de Genève.[12]

---

9 Rés. CS 253 du 29 mars 1968, adoptée lors de la crise rhodésienne. *Cf.* Rés. CS 257, 30 mai 1992, adoptée au cours du conflit yougoslave.

10 Pour l'Algérie, le §3 de la résolution 661 exclut de l'embargo les fournitures à usage médical et les produits alimentaires. Doc. NU S/21705 du 5 septembre 1990. D'après le projet de résolution soumis par Cuba au Conseil de Sécurité, l'approvisionnement en denrées alimentaires de base ainsi qu'une assistance médicale étaient considérés comme un droit fondamental de l'homme. Doc. NU S/21742 Rev.1 du 12 septembre 1990. Ce projet ne recueillit que trois voix, celles de la Chine, du Yémen et de Cuba. *Cf.* Martti Koskenniemi "Le Comité des sanctions (créé par la Résolution 661 du 6 août 1990 du Conseil de Sécurité)", (1991) XXXVII *AFDI* 126-127.

11 Jean-Philippe Lavoyer "Le CICR et le conflit du Golfe. Quelques aspects juridiques", in *Les aspects juridiques de la crise et de la guerre du Golfe* (Paris, 1991), pp. 201.

12 *Cf.* W.M. Reisman, *supra*, n.1, p. 132. Theodor Meron "Prisoners of War, Civilians and Diplomats in the Gulf Crisis", (1991) 85 *AJIL*, pp. 107-108; R. Provost "Starvation as a Weapon. Legal Implications of the UN Food Blockade against Iraq and Kuwait ", (1992) 30 *CJTL*, p. 609 et Luigi Condorelli "Le droit humanitaire dans la crise et la

Quoi qu'il en soit, l'application rigide des sanctions dans le temps a eu pour conséquence d'affamer les groupes les plus vulnérables de la population irakienne. C'est la conclusion à laquelle parvient le rapport du Secrétaire Général adjoint à l'administration et à la gestion de l'Irak et du Koweït, rendu public le 20 mars 1991.[13] Deux jours plus tard, le Comité de sanction décidait de secourir de toute urgence la population civile de l'Irak et de soumettre désormais l'acheminement de l'aide humanitaire à une procédure simplifiée et accélérée de notification et d'approbation tacite,[14] décision qui sera entérinée par la Résolution 687, adoptée le 3 avril 1991 par le Conseil de Sécurité.

L'expérience irakienne met ainsi en évidence les failles du système de sanctions des Nations Unies et la nécessité de mettre en place un mécanisme destiné à assurer un meilleur équilibre entre les exigences du maintien de la paix et le respect des normes du droit international humanitaire.

II Mécanismes assurant le respect des dispositions du droit international humanitaire relatives à la protection de la population civile par le Conseil de Sécurité

C'est le Secrétaire Général des Nations Unies qui prit l'initiative, dans son Supplément à l'Agenda pour la paix, d'attirer l'attention sur les imperfections du système des sanctions et de faire certaines propositions en vue de limiter ses incidences négatives sur le plan humanitaire.[15] Elles furent bien accueillies par le Conseil de Sécurité[16] et ses 5 membres permanents qui, à leur tour, soumettront un document officieux dans ce sens.[17] Il en va de même du commentaire préparé par le Conseil économique et social de l'Organisation des Nations Unies, plus concerné par les conséquences néfastes des sanctions sur les droits

"guerre" du Golfe", in *Les aspects juridiques de la crise et de la guerre du Golfe*, *supra*, n.11, p. 195.

13 Doc. NU S/22366 du 20 mars 1991.

14 Doc. NU S/AC 25/SR.36 du 22 mars 1991.

15 Supplément à l'Agenda pour la paix: rapport de situation présenté par le Secrétaire Général à l'occasion du cinquantenaire de l'Organisation des Nations Unies, (A/50/60 S/1995/1, 25 janvier 1995), §68 et 75.

16 Déclaration du Président du Conseil de Sécurité du 22 février 1995 (S/PRST/1995/9).

17 Document officieux des cinq membres permanents du Conseil de Sécurité sur les "incidences des sanctions sur le plan humanitaire", du 13 avril 1995 (S/1995/300).

économiques, sociaux et culturels auxquels se réfèrent la Charte et les Pactes.[18] Il convient de mentionner également la résolution de la 26ème Conférence internationale de la Croix-Rouge et du Croissant-Rouge, qui partagent les mêmes préoccupations.[19]

Dans l'ensemble de ces documents, deux idées force se dégagent: la nécessité d'évaluer l'impact potentiel des sanctions sur la population civile de l'Etat ciblé avant l'adoption de la sanction et tout au long de son application; ensuite, sur la base des informations ainsi recueillies, celle du contrôle de l'application des sanctions, suivi, le cas échéant, de leur ajustement en vue de s'assurer de leur conformité avec les dispositions pertinentes du droit international humanitaire.

A) L'étude d'impact des sanctions

L'expérience de ces dernières années montre clairement que le Conseil de Sécurité ne s'est généralement pas préoccupé, avant de prendre une décision politique, des conséquences des sanctions économiques sur la population civile. Le Secrétaire Général des Nations Unies recommande, dans son Supplément à l'Agenda pour la paix, que l'impact potentiel des sanctions soit évalué avant qu'elles soient imposées. Il est certain que pour mener à bien cette tâche, l'accès aux informations est primordial. Or, dans les cas où l'Etat sanctionné est un pays en voie de développement, ce qui a toujours été le cas au cours de ces dernières années, les statistiques sont souvent rares et peu fiables. Pour surmonter ces difficultés, l'aide du Département des affaires humanitaires de l'Organisation des Nations Unies, des Etats et des organisations non gouvernementales pourrait s'avérer fondamentale.[20]

Il est désormais établi que les sanctions économiques peuvent perturber gravement les circuits de distribution des produits de première nécessité et affecter leur qualité, entraînant de graves conséquences pour la santé de la population. Il s'agit en fait des effets indirects des sanctions sur l'économie du pays visé et de leurs conséquences sur l'approvisionnement de sa population civile.

18 Implementation of the International Covenant on Economic Social and Cultural Rights. General Comment n° 8 (1997) The Relationship Between Economic Sanctions and Respect for Economic Social and Cultural Rights, du 12 décembre 1997 (E/C12/1997/8).

19 Résolution n° 4 de la 26ème Conférence internationale de la Croix Rouge et du Croissant Rouge, Décembre 1995.

20 Document soumis par les 5 membres permanents du Conseil de Sécurité.

Quelle que soit l'exactitude de l'étude d'impact, elle doit permettre au Conseil de Sécurité de moduler dans chaque cas le régime de sanctions en fonction des ressources dont l'Etat visé dispose. Le Conseil de Sécurité pourra ainsi maximaliser les effets politiques recherchés et réduire au minimum les conséquences néfastes des sanctions sur la population civile de l'Etat concerné.

L'étude d'impact des sanctions devrait évidemment rester un impératif tout au long de la période pendant laquelle les sanctions sont en vigueur. En effet, l'expérience des dernières années a montré que les sanctions sont souvent appelées à durer. Dans ces conditions, à supposer que les dispositions d'une résolution imposant une sanction soient, lors de son adoption, conformes au droit international humanitaire, le prolongement de leur application risque de créer à la longue des situations et des souffrances humainement intolérables au regard du droit international humanitaire. Le suivi de l'application des sanctions s'impose donc de toute évidence.

On s'accorde généralement pour confier cette tâche de recherche et d'information aux Comités *ad hoc*, mis en place par le Conseil de Sécurité dans le cadre de chaque régime de sanctions et composés de tous ses membres, en vue d'assurer l'application effective des dispositions des résolutions. Il appartiendra à ces Comités, appelés plus communément Comités de sanctions, de s'employer sans relâche à obtenir des éléments d'information concernant l'impact humanitaire des sanctions et les disponibilités alimentaires dans les pays concernés. Pour ce faire, les Comités devraient s'entendre avec les organismes du système des Nations Unies et les organisations régionales en vue d'établir un réseau de communication adéquat et efficace. S'il s'avère nécessaire, les présidents des Comités devraient se rendre dans les pays concernés afin de réunir des données de première main sur l'impact des sanctions.[21]

Des doutes ont été exprimés sur l'impartialité et la capacité des Comités de sanctions de mener à bien de telles missions. Il a été suggéré de confier une telle responsabilité à la Commission internationale d'établissement des faits, mise en place dans le cadre de l'article 90 du Protocole additionnel I. On est en droit d'exprimer quelques réserves quant à la compétence de cette Commission, chargée plutôt d'enquêter sur tout fait prétendu être une infraction ou une violation grave aux Conventions de Genève et à ce Protocole. Par ailleurs,

21 Note du Président du Conseil de Sécurité sur les travaux des Comités de sanctions, du 29 janvier 1999 (S/1999/92).

un nombre limité des Etats parties à cet instrument ont accepté la compétence de la Commission. Par contre, on pourrait examiner avec plus d'attention la proposition tendant à confier cette tâche aux délégués du CICR présents sur le territoire de l'Etat concerné, ou, du moins, accorder plus de poids à leurs rapports. Il en va de même de la suggestion tendant à mettre en place un Comité de sanctions unique et permanent, doté d'un personnel spécialisé dans ce genre d'investigations.[22]

B) L'application des sanctions dans le temps

Les exceptions humanitaires prévues dans toutes les résolutions du Conseil de Sécurité imposant des sanctions ne peuvent suffire en elles-mêmes pour faire face aux situations d'urgence résultant de l'application des régimes de sanctions. Il faudrait aussi prévoir dans ces résolutions toutes dispositions nécessaires destinées à garantir le libre accès de l'aide humanitaire.

C'est ainsi qu'il serait opportun de prévoir, comme il a été suggéré,[23] dans les régimes de sanctions, des dispositions par lesquelles tous les Etats, y compris ceux visés, seraient tenus d'assurer l'accès sans entrave de l'aide humanitaire. Une telle obligation faciliterait grandement la mise en œuvre des nouvelles mesures d'exemption qui seront adoptées en cas de situation d'urgence humanitaire par le Conseil de Sécurité et le Comité de sanctions concerné.

Ces mesures d'exemption destinées à ajuster le régime de sanctions aux nouvelles conditions humanitaires font généralement suite aux demandes émanant des Etats visés par les sanctions ou d'organismes humanitaires. Ces demandes concernent évidemment l'acheminement des produits autres que les fournitures médicales et les denrées alimentaires, exemptées par définition de tout régime de sanctions. Elles visent plutôt les biens dont la pénurie pour l'économie et l'industrie du pays sanctionné aurait de graves répercussions sur le plan social et humanitaire. Dans ces cas, il a été suggéré que l'examen de telles demandes soit soumis à une procédure simple et expéditive et que les demandes émanant des organismes humanitaires soient traitées en priorité.[24]

22 Hans Peter Gasser, "Collective Economic Sanctions and International Humanitarian Law" (1996) 56 *Heidelberg Journal of International Law,* p. 903.
23 Document soumis par les 5 membres du Conseil de Sécurité.
24 Propositions du Secrétaire Général dans le Supplément à l'Agenda pour la paix.

Fort heureusement, le Conseil de Sécurité s'est engagé à exempter désormais des régimes de sanctions l'importation vers les pays ciblés des produits de base[25] nécessaires aux industries locales dans les secteurs pharmaceutique et agricole. Une telle restriction sera évidemment de nature à rendre moins fréquent le recours à des mesures d'exemption pendant la période d'application des sanctions et à garantir une plus grande compatibilité des résolutions du Conseil de Sécurité avec les dispositions pertinentes du droit international humanitaire.

Rappelant la nécessité de disposer d'un mécanisme tendant à rendre les sanctions moins brutales et plus efficaces, le Secrétaire Général se réjouit, dans son rapport à la 53ème session de l'Assemblée Générale, de voir les Etats appuyer la notion de "sanctions intelligentes"[26] Il est néanmoins d'avis que la communauté internationale ne devrait pas se faire d'illusions sur le résultat d'une telle démarche. Il n'est en effet pas facile de concilier la politique humanitaire et des droits de l'homme avec les objectifs d'un régime de sanctions. Instrument coercitif, la sanction économique est par nature préjudiciable.[27]

Dans la mesure où les sanctions sont destinées à modifier le comportement de l'Etat qui menace la paix et la sécurité internationale, la question se pose de savoir s'il y a lieu de les maintenir au cas où il s'avérerait que le but poursuivi ne pourra être atteint. En effet, prolonger indûment la période d'application des sanctions ne ferait qu'accroître leur coût humanitaire et engendrer des conséquences autres que celles prévues à l'origine, et ce aux dépens de la population civile de l'Etat visé. D'autre part, mettre fin, dans de telles conditions, au régime des sanctions, risquerait fort d'être perçu par les responsables d'Etats fauteurs de troubles comme un encouragement à utiliser leur propre population comme bouclier. En définitive, c'est l'efficacité du régime des sanctions qui mériterait d'être repensée et revue.

25 Doc. S /1999/92, *supra*, n.21.

26 Rapport du Secrétaire Général à la 53ème session de l'Assemblée Générale (A/53/1), §62.

27 *Ibid.* §64.

17

LA COMPATIBILITE DES SANCTIONS DU CONSEIL DE SECURITE AVEC LE DROIT INTERNATIONAL HUMANITAIRE - COMMENTAIRE

Luigi Condorelli[■]

La tâche qui m'a été confiée m'apparaît – je dois l'avouer – bien difficile après avoir écouté le Professeur Momtaz. L'organisatrice de ce colloque, en effet, m'a demandé de "discuter" le rapport qu'il vient de présenter, alors que je constate ne pouvoir rien discuter du tout, pour la simple raison que je suis fondamentalement d'accord avec lui. A la question de savoir si les sanctions économiques du Conseil de sécurité doivent respecter les principes des Conventions de Genève de 1949 et de leurs Protocoles additionnels de 1977, le Professeur Momtaz a répondu que oui, et cela est effectivement indiscutable pour moi aussi. Puis le Professeur Momtaz s'est attaché à montrer que les vrais problèmes concernent l'identification des voies, des manières, des procédures et des mécanismes devant être utilisés afin de réaliser une telle conformité; et là non plus je n'ai aucune remarque critique à formuler. En somme, je pourrais fort bien limiter mon intervention à trois mots: il a raison!

Cependant, si j'agissais ainsi je ne remplirais pas le contrat que j'ai passé avec mon amie et collègue Vera Gowlland, à laquelle j'ai promis de parler quelques minutes. Qu'il me soit permis alors de revenir sur le sujet de la présente session, mais non pas pour débattre du "comment" la compatibilité pourra être assurée, pour discuter des détails. En souvenir de ce qu'observait précédemment le Professeur Abi-Saab, concernant le penchant qu'ont les universitaires d'un certain type (ceux qui se targuent – comme c'est tant son cas que le mien – du titre de "généralistes") pour les aspects généraux et les réflexions fondamentales,

■ Professeur de droit international public, Université de Genève.

V. Gowlland-Debbas (ed.), *United Nations Sanctions and International Law*, p. 233-240.

je voudrais me poser, voire vous poser, deux questions, que j'appellerai celle du "pourquoi" et celle du "pour qui". La première consiste à déterminer pourquoi les principes et règles du droit international humanitaire lient le Conseil de sécurité et doivent être pleinement respectées par lui (comme d'ailleurs par tous les autres organes des Nations Unies), notamment lors de l'adoption et de la mise en œuvre de sanctions économiques. La seconde ("pour qui") vise à analyser le jeu de la responsabilité internationale en cas de violation du droit humanitaire par le Conseil et, plus spécialement, à établir qui doit être considéré l'auteur du fait illicite: est-ce la seule Organisation internationale qui engagera sa responsabilité dans un tel cas, ou bien les Etats membres aussi, dans la mesure où ils contribueraient à l'adoption et/ou à l'exécution de la décision illégale du premier ?

Commençons par le pourquoi. Le Professeur Momtaz nous a indiqué sa préférence pour l'une des réponses possibles: Le Conseil doit se conformer au droit humanitaire parce que les obligations que prescrit celui-ci sont *erga omnes.* Cette dernière affirmation quant à la nature des obligations humanitaires est effectivement indiscutable, mais est-ce une bonne explication en l'espèce? Le fait qu'il s'agit d'obligations à respecter à l'égard de tous ne nous dit pas, en vérité, pourquoi elles lient le Conseil: une chose est de déterminer à qui sont dues les prestations requises par une règle de droit, une toute autre est d'identifier le titulaire de l'obligation d'effectuer lesdites prestations.

De plus, on notera que les explications de ce genre (obligations *erga omnes,* normes de *jus cogens,* etc.), sur lesquelles je reviendrai d'ici peu, se rattachent à l'idée qu'au-delà de la dimension strictement conventionnelle (laquelle *per se* ne concernerait pas l'ONU, sujet international non lié par les instruments pertinents), le droit humanitaire révèle une dimension ultérieure qui s'impose tous azimuts, y compris aux Nations Unies. Or, il me semble que, avant de s'aventurer dans cet étage supérieur de l'analyse juridique, il convient avant tout de mettre en exergue les caractéristiques bien particulières du droit humanitaire, déjà d'après les dispositions mêmes des Conventions et Protocoles de Genève. Sans oublier de souligner que ces dispositions font l'objet d'une acceptation véritablement universelle, puisque – faut-il le rappeler? – pratiquement tous les Etats de notre planète sont parties aux Conventions de Genève: ils partagent tous, donc les conceptions que lesdites dispositions expriment et consacrent.

Quelles sont ces caractéristiques? Essentiellement, celles qu'exprime de manière très efficace l'art. 1 commun aux Conventions de 1949 et l'art. 1, alinéa 1, du Premier Protocole de 1977: une disposition – qui engage les Etats à "respecter et faire respecter" le droit international humanitaire "en toutes circonstances" – dont je ne me lasse pas depuis fort longtemps de rappeler l'importance bien singulière. Si le respect du droit humanitaire est dû "en toutes circonstances", ceci implique *a contrario* (l'*argumentum a contrario* est, ne l'oublions pas, l'un des outils fondamentaux de travail pour le juriste), que les Etats Parties – tous les Etats, en fait – partagent la conception d'après quoi aucune circonstance de quelque sorte que ce soit ne saurait justifier un comportement allant à l'encontre des prescriptions du droit humanitaire. Aucune des "circonstances excluant l'illicéité", admises normalement par le droit de la responsabilité internationale des Etats, ne saurait donc être légitimement invoquée ici: par exemple, ni la légitime défense, ni les contre-mesures, ni non plus – on peut sans doute l'inférer, mais on y reviendra – la qualité de membre des Nations Unies !

Comme nous le savons, dans les Conventions et les Protocoles de Genève cette idée fondamentale est développée et concrétisée au moyen de plusieurs dispositions spécifiques, dont je me limiterai à citer ici celle interdisant toute dérogation conventionnelle aux règles humanitaires, celle déniant au consentement des victimes la capacité de justifier les violations et celles, nombreuses, proscrivant les représailles contre les personnes et les biens protégés par les règles humanitaires. Autant dire que tous les Etats Parties aux instruments en question – c'est-à-dire pratiquement tous les membres des Nations Unies – sont convaincus qu'il faut toujours observer les règles humanitaires, que cette observation n'est pas soumise à une logique de réciprocité (ou de "donnant-donnant") et qu'aucune justification valable ne peut être invoquée en droit pour guérir l'illicéité de tout comportement contraire: même pas celle pivotant sur l'idée de la riposte proportionnée aux violations dont on a été la victime. Evidemment, puisqu'on parle pour l'instant du droit humanitaire en tant qu'ensemble de règles conventionnelles, il ne faut pas oublier de citer la confirmation que donne à ce sujet l'art. 60, par. 5, de la Convention de Vienne sur le droit des traités, qui proclame que face à une violation substantielle des dispositions à caractère humanitaire d'un traité on n'a pas le droit d'invoquer l'*exceptio inadimpleti contractus* comme cause d'extinction du traité en question.

Toutefois, la dimension conventionnelle n'est pas en soi décisive pour régler une fois pour toutes, et en termes absolus, la question des relations entre le droit de Genève et ce qu'on peut appeler le "droit de New York", avec à son sommet la Charte des Nations Unies. On sait, en effet, qu'une disposition de la Charte que l'on a déjà beaucoup citée ici, l'art. 103, assure la primauté des obligations découlant de la Charte sur celles prévues par d'autres traités. En théorie, donc, les Etats devraient respecter et exécuter les décisions du Conseil (comme le leur demande l'art. 24 de la Charte), sans pouvoir s'y refuser au nom d'obligations, contraires en hypothèse, prescrites par le droit de Genève. Autrement dit, toujours en théorie la Charte donnerait au Conseil le pouvoir de libérer les Etats, dans un cas déterminé, du respect du droit humanitaire, au moyen d'une décision imposant des sanctions.

Il faut noter tout de suite qu'une telle théorie serait en désaccord évident avec la pratique des Nations Unies, et du Conseil de sécurité en particulier: on ne compte pas le nombre de fois où les organes de l'Organisation ont, par le biais de recommandations ou décisions appropriées, rappelé aux Etats en conflit la nécessité d'observer les instruments humanitaires, voire lancé carrément des actions de diverses sortes, motivées par le souci de voir respectés les principes humanitaires, allant jusqu'au point – on le sait – de créer de toutes pièces des Tribunaux pénaux afin de pourvoir à la répression des violations graves de ces principes, de sorte à parer aux défaillances des Etats à ce sujet. Voilà déjà un constat en face duquel il apparaîtrait singulièrement étonnant, voir totalement contradictoire, d'imaginer que le Conseil pourrait demander aux Etats de ne pas respecter telle ou telle règle humanitaire en appliquant des sanctions!

Mais il y a bien plus: la théorie en question apparaît insoutenable dès que l'on songe à la conjonction de deux arguments juridiques essentiels: c'est que, *primo,* au-delà de la dimension conventionnelle, les principes humanitaires relèvent sans conteste du droit international général et lient de ce fait tous les sujets internationaux, y compris les Nations Unies (et, il va sans dire, le Conseil de sécurité); et c'est que, *secundo,* ces principes sont à qualifier d'"intransgressibles".

Quant au premier point, inutile d'entrer dans trop de détails: la très large correspondance entre droit conventionnel et droit coutumier en matière humanitaire fait l'objet d'un constat très largement répandu. Il suffira à ce sujet de rappeler, à titre d'exemple, ce que la CIJ a récemment trouvé l'occasion de relever dans son Avis consultatif de 1996 sur la licéité de la menace ou de l'emploi d'armes nucléaires: le *corpus* du droit international humanitaire, tel qu'il figure dans les grandes conventions qui le codifient, constitue pour l'essentiel du droit international général et coutumier. Ainsi, c'est au sujet d'un "grand nombre de règles de droit humanitaire" que la Cour observe (par.79): elles "... s'imposent ... à tous les Etats, qu'ils aient ou non ratifié les instruments conventionnels qui les expriment".[1] Plus loin (par. 82) la Cour parle, notamment à propos des Conventions de Genève de 1949, de règles conventionnelles qui étaient déjà devenues coutumières "dans leur grande majorité" lors de la codification. On n'oubliera pas non plus de mettre en relief ici qu'en 1986 la Cour, dans la célèbre affaire Nicaragua/Etats-Unis, avait déjà spécifiquement établi la nature coutumière du principe "respecter et faire respecter" consacré par l'art. 1 commun aux Conventions de Genève.[2]

Puisqu'il s'agit de principes et règles de droit international général, il va de soi qu'ils doivent être respectés par tous les sujets internationaux. Non seulement, donc, par les Etats, mais aussi par les organisations internationales dont l'activité tomberait, pour une raison ou une autre, sous la coupe du droit international humanitaire. Pour ce qui est de l'ONU, l'admission de la part de ses organes principaux que son action doit se dérouler dans le respect des principes humanitaires est chose courante: on en trouve l'expression, par exemple, spécialement dans les accords avec les Etats de provenance et avec les Etats de déploiement des forces des Nations Unies.[3] Certes, il est question ici d'actions ponctuelles sur le terrain, dans le cadre de situations à caractère conflictuel; mais il va de soi que de telles admissions ont une signification et des implications plus générales, puisqu'elles traduisent de toute évidence l'idée que les Nations Unies sont bien soumises au droit humanitaire toutes les fois où celui-ci est pertinent *in casu.*

Quant au second point, il faut se souvenir que dans son Avis consultatif de 1996, déjà cité, la CIJ, outre que de ranger les règles fondamentales du droit international humanitaire dans l'univers du droit international général, les a qualifiées d'"intransgressibles" (par. 79 de l'Avis). Il s'agit ici d'une innovation linguistique qui ne brille pas par sa clarté, d'autant plus que le texte de l'Avis exclut explicitement la possibilité d'assimiler *sic et simpliciter* l'expression

1 Recueil CIJ, 1996 (I), par.79.
2 Recueil CIJ, 1986, par.220.
3 Le 6 août 1996 a été publiée l'importante circulaire du Secrétaire général des Nations Unies sur le "Respect du droit international humanitaire par les forces des Nations Unies" qui, outre que confirmer l'applicabilité pleine à l'action de ces forces des "principes et règles fondamentaux du droit international humanitaire", pourvoit à une identification plutôt détaillée de ceux apparaissant davantage pertinents.

"normes intransgressibles" à celle de "normes impératives" (ou de *jus cogens*). On croit comprendre qu'une telle formulation relèverait d'un compromis concocté afin d'éviter que la moutarde ne monte au nez de certains juges qui notoirement ne tolèrent pas que l'on prononce devant eux les mots "*jus cogens*". Mais, quoi qu'il en soit de cette question, il semble bien que par cette terminologie la Cour entende justement mettre en évidence le concept fondamental d'après lequel aucune sorte de circonstance justificative ne saurait être alléguée afin d'exclure le caractère illicite des comportements contredisant les normes en question: en somme, le respect de celles-ci est dû à toute la communauté internationale, et non pas aux autres parties au conflit dans le cadre d'une relation synallagmatique.

Ce concept doit être appliqué, cela va de soi, à tous les destinataires des normes humanitaires: il s'ensuit donc, d'une part, que toute action de tout organe des Nations Unies doit toujours respecter, en toute circonstance, le droit humanitaire; et, d'autre part, qu'aucun Etat ne pourrait s'abriter valablement derrière une décision onusienne pour justifier une conduite contredisant les impératifs humanitaires. De plus, l'ONU se trouve elle aussi soumise au principe "intransgressible" établissant l'obligation de "faire respecter": par conséquent, non seulement elle ne saurait exempter aucun Etat dudit respect, mais au contraire elle a le devoir précis d'adopter les mesures capables d'assurer l'observation par les Etats des principes humanitaires.

J'ai ainsi mis au clair le "pourquoi". Il est temps maintenant d'en venir au "pour qui". Comme je l'ai dit au début, il s'agit de savoir qui doit endosser la responsabilité internationale pour fait illicite en cas de sanctions édictées par le Conseil qui seraient en contradiction avec les principes humanitaires. La constatation précédente, d'après laquelle ces principes sont indiscutablement applicables, outre aux Etats qu'à l'ONU, comporte comme corollaire évident qu'il n'y aurait dans ce cas fait illicite de l'Organisation, avec – bien entendu – toutes les conséquences qui peuvent en découler, en termes par exemple d'obligations de cessation et de réparation. Mais il y a bien un deuxième corollaire à souligner: les Etats qui s'associeraient à la décision illégale du Conseil de sécurité en l'exécutant (ou qui se conformeraient à une recommandation entachée du même vice) mettraient eux aussi en jeu leur responsabilité internationale pour fait illicite, sans pouvoir prétendre que joue à leur décharge, en tant que circonstance excluant l'illicéité, leur qualité de membre de l'ONU, astreint à respecter les dispositions de la Charte.

Ce que je viens d'affirmer concernant l'ONU vaut, c'est clair, pour toute organisation internationale dont l'action pourrait, d'une façon ou d'une autre, tomber dans la sphère d'application du droit humanitaire: bien sûr, les organisations régionales aussi, par exemple celles qui sont actives en matière de maintien et rétablissement de la paix, et l'OTAN au premier chef. On ne peut pas à ce sujet ne pas songer à l'OTAN ces temps-ci, vu le rôle important (et très discuté) que cette Organisation a pris en Ex-Yougoslavie, et au Kosovo en particulier: on doit réaffirmer l'obligation tant de l'OTAN que de ses Etats membres de respecter les règles humanitaires en cas d'engagement de leurs forces dans des situations conflictuelles, que ce soit avec ou sans l'autorisation préalable du Conseil de sécurité.

Le Juge Rosalyn Higgins nous a donné matière à réflexion lorsqu'elle a rappelé dans son intervention orale une argumentation proposée dernièrement par le Conseil du Canada devant la CIJ, lors des plaidoiries concernant l'affaire Yougoslavie/Etats membres de l'OTAN. D'après le Canada, nous a-t-elle dit, si l'action militaire de l'OTAN représentait vraiment une violation des principes humanitaires (en l'espèce, selon l'accusation de Belgrade, une violation de la Convention sur le génocide), c'est la responsabilité internationale de l'OTAN qui aurait été le cas échéant mise en jeu, et non pas celle des Etats membres dont les forces n'ont fait qu'exécuter les ordres reçus de l'organe de commandement intégré. J'espère que la Cour trouvera l'occasion de condamner un tel argument, qui pour moi, plus que faux, est franchement aberrant. Il mérite à mon sens à peu près le même accueil qu'on donnerait à la thèse faisant valoir, en droit pénal interne, que le membre d'une association de malfaiteurs n'a pas à être puni pour les méfaits commis par le groupe ... Par ailleurs, chacun sait qu'à l'OTAN toutes les décisions fondamentales sont toujours prises à l'unanimité des Etats membres: ceux-ci doivent donc assumer tous, en même temps que l'Organisation, la responsabilité des actes de leurs forces armées placées sous commandement unifié. On pourrait peut-être imaginer des exceptions dans des cas particuliers, s'il pouvait être prouvé qu'un éventuel comportement précis n'est imputable qu'à un seul sujet international pour des raisons spéciales. Mais la règle ne peut être à mon sens que l'engagement de la responsabilité solidaire tant de l'Organisation que de ses Etats membres.

Mutatis mutandis, le même principe doit être utilisé pour l'ONU, en cas de sanctions violant le droit humanitaire décidées par le Conseil de sécurité, à la différence près qu'outre la responsabilité internationale de l'Organisation sera mise en cause ici celle des seuls Etats membres ayant exécuté la décision en question.

Quelques remarques encore en songeant plus particulièrement aux actions militaires onusiennes (qu'elles soient d'ailleurs sanctionnatrices ou non), vues sous l'angle du respect du droit humanitaire. Il faut songer ici à la distinction entre, d'une part, les actions militaires réalisées par des Etats suite à l'autorisation du Conseil de sécurité et, d'autre part, celles se déroulant sous le commandement et le contrôle direct de l'Organisation.

Dans le premier cas, d'éventuelles violations des principes humanitaires constitueraient des faits illicites imputables de toute évidence aux Etats concernés, et non pas à l'Organisation. Mais j'ai déjà relevé que l'ONU incomberait alors l'obligation générale de "faire respecter" ces principes. De plus, il va de soi qu'une telle obligation serait ici encore davantage pertinente et astreignante, face à une action menée par les Etats, pourrait-on dire, pour son compte et dans son intérêt.

Dans le second cas, c'est-à-dire quand les forces armées sont sous commandement direct de l'Organisation, c'est la responsabilité de celle-ci qui jouerait lors de l'éventuelle violation du droit humanitaire dont ces forces pourraient se rendre coupables. Cependant, il ne faut pas oublier que lesdites forces sont formées de contingents militaires mis à disposition des Nations Unies par des Etats membres. Ceux qui les composent, tout en devenant des organes de l'Organisation (à laquelle de ce fait leurs actes seront imputables), continuent cependant de garder le *status* d'organes militaires de leur Etat d'appartenance et restent d'ailleurs soumis (tout au moins pour ce qui est de l'aspect disciplinaire) au commandement de l'Etat d'envoi au travers du "*contico*" (*contingent commander*). Dans une étude d'il y a quelques années, j'ai soutenu que ce double lien organique comporte inévitablement une double imputation des violations commises et, par conséquent, une double responsabilité internationale: celle encourue par les Nations Unies se cumule, en somme, à celle de l'Etat national du contingent.

SANCTIONS AND INTERNATIONAL HUMANITARIAN LAW – COMMENTARY

Marco Sassòli[■]

I INTERNATIONAL HUMANITARIAN LAW APPLIES TO ARMED CONFLICTS; SANCTIONS ARE NOT ARMED CONFLICTS

International Humanitarian Law, being the branch of international law protecting victims of armed conflicts and limiting the amount of violence used in armed conflicts to that necessary to overcome the military potential of the enemy, by definition applies to armed conflicts.[1] While military sanctions are armed conflicts to which International Humanitarian Law applies, economic sanctions are not armed conflicts. International Humanitarian Law can therefore only regulate them when they are directed against a party otherwise engaged in an armed conflict.

■ Dr. iur., Advocate, Registrar at the Swiss Supreme Court. The views expressed in this article are exclusively those of the author.

1 *Cf.* Art. 2 common to the four Geneva Conventions (Geneva Convention for the Amelioration of the Condition of the Wounded and Sick in Armed Forces in the Field, of 12 August 1949 (75 UNTS 31 - 83); Geneva Convention for the Amelioration of the Condition of the Wounded, Sick and Shipwrecked Members of Armed Forces at Sea, of 12 August 1949 (75 UNTS 85 - 133); Geneva Convention relative to the Treatment of Prisoners of War, of 12 August 1949 (75 UNTS 135 -285); Geneva Convention relative to the Protection of Civilian Persons in Time of War, of 12 August 1949 (75 UNTS 287 - 417) [hereafter: Convention IV], Art. 1 (3) and (4) of the Protocol Additional to the Geneva Conventions of 12 August 1949, and relating to the Protection of Victims of International Armed Conflicts, of 8 June 1977 (1125 UNTS 3 - 434) [hereafter: Protocol I], and Art. 1 of the Protocol Additional to the Geneva Conventions of 12 August 1949, and relating to the Protection of Victims of Non-International Armed Conflicts, of 8 June 1977 (1125 UNTS 609 - 699) [hereafter: Protocol II].

V. Gowlland-Debbas (ed.), *United Nations Sanctions and International Law,* p. 241-248.

II Rules of International Humanitarian Law protecting the right of the civilian population to humanitarian assistance

Starvation of civilians as a method of warfare is prohibited by International Humanitarian Law.[2] While this prohibition is clear, it is difficult to apply, because belligerents will always claim that their measures causing starvation among the civilian population are not directed against civilians, but against combatants, which would be lawful under International Humanitarian Law. Therefore, the detailed rules of International Humanitarian Law on relief are of great practical importance. Article 23 of Convention IV obliges each High Contracting Party – and not only belligerents – to allow the passage of medical and religious supplies intended only for civilians. This obligation also covers foodstuffs, clothing and tonics, but only if they are intended for children under fifteen, expectant mothers or maternity cases. Only when relief is intended for an occupied territory, Convention IV forsees a general obligation of the occupying power to agree to relief schemes and an obligation for all High Contracting Parties to permit free passage of such consignments.[3]

As in many other fields, Protocol I drastically improves this regime applicable to humanitarian assistance, which is clearly insufficient outside occupied territories. Its Article 70 prescribes that if a civilian population is not adequately provided with relief supplies, relief actions which must be humanitarian and impartial in character and conducted without any adverse distinction "shall be undertaken." It however subjects such relief actions to the consent of the parties concerned. Taking the right to food in International Human Rights Law[4] into account, this condition may however not be understood as a license for belligerents to refuse such supplies at will. It rather means that if all the conditions are satisfied, a party must give its consent.[5] Once there is consent of the party concerned, all High Contracting Parties must facilitate rapid and unimpeded passage of the relief consignments, even if they are destined for the civilian

---

2 *Cf.* Art. 54 (1) of Protocol I and Art. 14 of Protocol II.

3 *Cf.* Art. 59 of Convention IV.

4 *Cf.* Art. 25 of the Universal Declaration of Human Rights and Art. 11 of the International Covenant on Economic, Social and Cultural Rights.

5 In the *Case concerning Military and Paramilitary Activities in and against Nicaragua (Nicaragua v. US), Merits*, ICJ Reports, 1986, pp. 14 ff., para. 242, the International Court of Justice has ruled that there can be no doubt that the provision of strictly humanitarian aid to persons or forces in another country cannot be regarded as contrary to international law.

population of the adverse party. Under Convention IV and Protocol I those allowing the passage of relief consignments may however insist on guarantees that they will not be diverted, including by local supervision of their distribution. It is well known that authorities controlling the civilian population in need sometimes do not agree to such outside supervision. The result is a stalemate between three positions: the right of the civilian population to be assisted; the territorial sovereignty of the receiving State which makes relief actions on its territory against the will of its authorities practically impossible; and the right of any State allowing the passage of the consignments to insist on local supervision.

The described regime applicable to humanitarian assistance is that prescribed for international armed conflics. International Humanitarian Law applicable to non-international armed conflicts contains in Article 18 (2) of Protocol II a more rudimentary regime, expressing, however, the same principles.

III ABSENCE IN INTERNATIONAL HUMANITARIAN LAW OF RULES ON TRADE AND FINANCE ASPECTS OF SANCTIONS

The main humanitarian problems connected with sanctions do not generally arise because those sanctions prohibit the passage of relief consignments which International Humanitarian Law prescibes to be allowed to pass. The main problem is rather that the State under sanctions and its population are often in the long run unable to buy goods indispensable for the civilian population, because sanctions hinder the national economy from earning the necessary foreign currency through exports of goods and services. On the other hand, the population of countries of the size of Iraq or the Federal Republic of Yugoslavia could not possibly be fed and clothed exclusively through international assistance.

International Humanitarian Law, however, does not address exports by a belligerent country and contains no rules on those trade and finance aspects. It would also be difficult to request a belligerent to permit the adverse party to continue exporting goods and services at a peacetime level. Furthermore, the use of the money thus earned would be even more difficult to monitor than that of relief goods.

IV Application, by analogy, of the rules of International Humanitarian Law to sanctions outside armed conflicts

Even though International Humanitarian Law does not apply to economic sanctions outside armed conflicts, one could nevertheless apply it by analogy, as a minimum standard. Such an analogy could be based on a reasoning similar to that of the International Court of Justice in the *Corfu Channel Case*, when it applied a convention of the laws of war to a peacetime event because of "elementary considerations of humanity, even more exacting in peace than in war."[6] One may indeed well argue that if it is prohibited by international law to deprive the civilian population, even that of the adverse party, of essential relief supplies in wartime, this prohibition should even more so apply in peacetime relations. The present author would however suggest that in peacetime relations additional limits must apply, if only because of the right to food which fully applies in peacetime and contains also obligations for third states and for the international community.[7]

When United Nations sanctions are concerned, it should furthermore be taken into account that they are a form of law enforcement, while armed conflicts are by definition a basically anarchic situation to which International Humanitarian Law can only apply an insufficient minimum of humanity. In law enforcement, more restrictive limits of international legality, public interest and proportionality should apply, than those imposed on a belligerent. Specific rules applicable to UN sanctions are therefore desirable and International Humanitarian Law can only be a minimum standard.

V United Nations sanctions against a party to an armed conflict should respect International Humanitarian Law

The rules of International Humanitarian Law on humanitarian assistance discussed above limit economic sanctions taken against a party to an armed con-

6 *Cf. The Corfu Channel Case (Merits)*, ICJ Reports 1949, p. 22.

7 *See General Comment 12 (1999) 7 – The Right to Adequate Food (art. 11)* by the Committee on Economic, Social and Culural Rights (E/C.12/1999/5 of 12 May 1999), in particular para. 37, and its *General Comment No. 8 (1997) – The relationship between economic sanctions and respect for economic, social and cultural rights* (E/C.12/1997/8 of 12 December 1997), paras. 11-14.

flict. The question, however, arises whether this is also true if the sanctions have beeen decided by the UN Security Council.

a) Must UN Security Council resolutions comply with International Humanitarian Law?

First it has to be clarified whether the UN Security Council is itself bound to International Humanitarian Law. The UN is not a party to the treaties of International Humanitarian Law. Its Member States are, but it is doubtful whether a State obligation to comply with certain rules of behaviour also applies to the voting of that State in an organ of an international organization. The suggestion that the UN is at least bound by customary International Humanitarian Law would solve most practical difficulties, as the basic rules on humanitarian assistance are customary. Conceptually, however, this suggestion is not entirely convincing as the customary nature of a rule only overcomes the lack of a treaty link, but does not necessarily alter the active personal scope of application of that rule. It is therefore necessary to check, including through analysis of UN practice, whether those customary International Humanitarian Law rules actually apply to non-state actors like the UN or to States acting as organs of international organizations. It has been shown elsewhere in this book that at least as far as the actual practice is concerned, the answer is positive. UN economic sanctions have actually complied with the requirements of International Humanitarian Law.[8]

A further argument in favour of the applicability of International Humanitarian Law to UN sanctions against a party to an armed conflict can be derived from the distinction between *ius ad bellum*, i.e., the law regulating the legitimacy of the use of force, and *ius in bello*, i.e. the law regulating how armed conflicts must be conducted, in particular protecting their victims. *Ius in bello* must apply independently of *ius ad bellum*, i.e., independently of the legitimacy of the cause for which a belligerent is fighting.[9] Under Article 41 of the UN Charter, UN economic sanctions are decided to maintain or to restore international peace

8 *Cf.* also Hans-Peter Gasser, "Collective Economic Sanctions and International Humanitarian Law", (1996) 56 *ZaöRV* 888-894.

9 This fundamental distinction between *ius ad bellum* and *ius in bello* is recognized in preambular para. 5 of Protocol I and has already been underlined in the case *US v. Willhelm List and Others (The Hostage Case)*, by the US Military Tribunal at Nuremberg, reproduced in L. Friedman (ed.), *The Law of War, A Documentary History*, (New York, 1972), Vol. II, pp. 1313-1314. See also Christopher Greenwood, "The relationship between jus ad bellum and jus in bello", (1983) 8 *Review of International Studies* 221-234.

and security, i.e, to enforce *ius ad bellum*. International Humanitarian Law applies to any exercise of the *ius ad bellum*. It may therefore be presumed that a UN Security Council resolution applying sanctions to a party to an armed conflict wants those to be implemented in a way compatible with International Humanitarian Law, just as it has never been questioned that a UN Security Council Resolution authorising the use of force by Member States is no license to violate International Humanitarian Law in that use of force. This is even more so as the respect of human rights, which are detailed out for the specific threats posed by armed conflicts in International Humanitarian Law, is as much a purpose of the United Nations as the maintainance of international peace and security.[10] The UN therefore has to pursue the latter purpose while preserving the former.

b) States implementing UN economic sanctions are bound by International Humanitarian Law

Economic sanctions are mainly implemented by States. States are bound by International Humanitarian Law. Article 103 of the UN Charter certainly prescribes that in the event of a conflict between obligations under the UN Charter and those under any other international agreement, the former shall prevail. The International Court of Justice has decided that obligations under the UN Charter include those under UN Security Council resolutions.[11] One may however argue that Article 103 refers only to treaty obligations[12] and in any event not to obligations under *ius cogens*,[13] while the core of the obligations under International Humanitarian Law relating to humanitarian assistance is customary and belongs to *ius cogens*. The least one may affirm is that while implementing UN sanctions taken under *ius ad bellum*, States are bound to comply with *ius in bello*, except if the resolution explicitly states otherwise, which is never the case. Any UN sanctions regime must be interpreted as desiring to respect the limits of International Humanitarian Law.

10 *Cf.* Art. 1 (1) and (3) of the UN Charter.

11 See the Order of 14 April 1992 in the Case *Questions of Interpretation and Application of the 1971 Montreal Convention arising from the Aerial Incident at Lockerbie (Libyan Arab Jamahiriya v. US),* ICJ Reports, 1992, p. 126.

12 See Dissenting Opinion of Judge Bedjaoui to the Order of 14 April 1992 in the *Lockerbie Case, ibid.*, pp. 155-156, para. 29.

13 See Separate Opinion of Judge Lauterpacht in the *Case concerning Application of the Convention on the Prevention and Punishment of the Crime of Genocide (Bosnia and Herzegovina v. Yugoslavia), Provisional Measures, Order of 13 September 1993*, ICJ Reports, 1993, p. 440/441, paras 100 - 102.

VI OUTLOOK: FROM ECONOMIC SANCTIONS IN THE INTERNATIONAL SOCIETY TO CRIMINAL JUSTICE IN THE INTERNATIONAL COMMUNITY

Even when economic sanctions taken against a party to an armed conflict comply with International Humanitarian Law and even if those taken outside armed conflicts respect its limitations by analogy, they inevitably violate humanitarian principles and principles of justice. They inevitably have the consequences of a collective punishment;[14] they inevitably affect mainly the civilian population[15] and individuals who are neither responsible for – nor able to modify – the State action which has caused the sanctions. This is, however, inherent in the nature of an international society made up of States.

International law can today be described as composed of two layers. The first, traditional layer consists of the law of the international society regulating the co-ordination and co-operation between its members – essentially States and international organizations created by States. As any legal order, this law forsees sanctions, including economic sanctions, against its subjects in case they violate it. The second layer consists of the law of the international community consisting of six billion human beings. The relationship between those two layers is a very controversial, constantly developing subject.

In the first layer, sanctions must inevitably be directed against its subjects, i.e., States, and not against non-subjects, i.e., individuals. The main concern in imposing those sanctions cannot be how they will affect components of those subjects, i.e, human beings. Those sanctions were inevitable as long as the legislator of traditional international law, i.e. States – and in particular those States which complain most about the unjust and inhumane character of sanctions -, did not agree that international law enforcement mechanisms may pierce the corporate veil of the State and enforce international law directly against the individual responsible for a violation of international law – because in the end, despite all traditional concepts, only individuals can violate the law.

Today, however, the second layer, the law of the international community, is developing. One of its branches (containing also rules of the first layer), inter-

14 Prohibited by Art. 33 of Convention IV, Art. 75 (2)(d) of Protocol I, and Art. 4 (2)(b) of Protocol II.

15 Attacks directed at or indiscriminately affecting the civilian population are prohibited by Art. 51 of Protocol I and Art. 13 of Protocol II.

national criminal law, is directly addressed to individuals. This branch is also starting to have international enforcement mechanisms – international criminal tribunals. Those tribunals can take, in certain cases of violations of international law, sanctions against individuals. Such sanctions have, compared to sanctions against States, a greater preventive and stigmatising effect. Contrary to economic sanctions, they are decided in a formalized, fair procedure, without veto powers and much less influenced by political considerations than the decision-making process of the UN Security Council. Most importantly, punishment, contrary to sanctions, leads to the individualisation of responsibility and repression. It clarifies that the horrible crimes witnessed by our century were not committed by "the Serbs", "the Germans", "the Croats" or "the Hutus", but by criminal individuals. To cope with criminal individuals, not sanctions against their community are needed, but punishment. As long as the responsibility remains with a State or a people, there is, conversely, the germ for future wars.

As soon as international criminal justice will function effectively and everywhere, the international community can therefore abandon the archaic enforcement measure of economic sanctions, which is inevitably unjust and inevitably results in human suffering – and in practice leads to additional, unnecessary suffering. The creation of the two international criminal tribunals for the former Yugoslavia and Rwanda and the adoption of the Statute of the International Criminal Court in Rome on 17 July 1998, are extremely important and encouraging steps in this direction. Now the Statute of the International Criminal Court has to be universally accepted. In the meantime, it is worth constantly evaluating and finetuning economic sanctions, to minimize their inevitable negative consequences on the civilian population. The papers presented at the Colloquium have provided many worthy suggestions in this field.[16]

16 See also Gasser (*supra,* n. 8), pp. 897-904.

PART III

IMPLEMENTATION OF SECURITY COUNCIL SANCTIONS RESOLUTIONS

Sanctions and Private Rights

Chair: *Jean-Michel Jacquet*
Professor, Graduate Institute of International Studies

IMPLEMENTATION OF SECURITY COUNCIL RESOLUTIONS TAKEN UNDER CHAPTER VII IN GERMANY

Jochen A. Frowein▪

I INTERPRETATION OF SECURITY COUNCIL RESOLUTIONS

After the historical changes of 1989/90 the Security Council has moved into the center of United Nations activities and has adopted the role which was designed for it in 1945. The number of resolutions based on Chapter VII, almost negligible until 1990, is now very impressive indeed.[1] According to Article 24 of the Charter, Members have conferred on the Security Council primary responsibility for the maintenance of international peace and security and they have agreed that in carrying out its duties under this responsibility the Security Council acts on their behalf. While that provision was more or less a dead letter until 1990 it shows its overwhelming importance for public international law nowadays. Security Council Resolutions under Chapter VII are binding for every Member state. According to Article 25 the Members of the United Nations agree to accept and carry out the decisions of the Security Council in accordance with the present Charter. Under Article 41 the Council may impose economic boycotts and take all other decisions for a peaceful solution of international conflicts with binding force. Under Article 42 the Council may use military means.[2]

▪ Dr. jur., Dr.jur.h.c., M.C.L., Professor of International Law, Director of the Max-Planck-Institute for Comparative Public Law and International Law; former Vice-President of the European Commission of Human Rights.

1 Until 1990, the Security Council had adopted 11 resolutions with express reference to Chapter VII or one of its articles. Until March 1998, this number has risen to 147.

2 J.A. Frowein, "On Article 41" and "On Article 42", in Bruno Simma et al. (eds.), *The Charter of the United Nations* (Oxford, 1994), pp. 621 et seq., 628 et seq.

V. Gowlland-Debbas (ed.), *United Nations Sanctions and International Law*, p. 253-265.

It is not surprising that with this far-reaching power of decision the interpretation of Security Council resolutions acquires primary importance. Legal certainty which plays such a prominent role in national law is of equal importance in the international sphere. This is particularly so where the issue arises of what sort of obligations flow from a Security Council resolution for all Member states and primarily for the state against whom the Security Council is acting. Where the Council authorises the use of force against a Member state this issue of legal certainty may touch upon the question of existence of a sovereign state.

When the United Nations Security Council, for the very first time, authorised the use of armed force it did so in an extremely narrowly defined way. In Resolution 221 of 9 April 1966, the Security Council called upon the government of the United Kingdom, "to prevent by use of force if necessary" the arrival at Beira in Mozambique of vessels reasonably believed to be carrying oil destined for Rhodesia. It empowered the United Kingdom to arrest and detain the tanker known as the Joanna V upon her departure from Beira in the event her oil cargo is discharged there.[3] On the basis of that resolution the United Kingdom introduced a Navy control system along the coast of Mozambique. Force was used in some instances.[4] It was clear that all those concerned knew exactly what was authorised by the Security Council.

The interpretation of treaties is one of the eternal issues of international law. The Vienna Convention on the Law of Treaties has opted for the generally recognised rule that treaties shall be interpreted in good faith in accordance with the ordinary meaning to be given to the terms of the treaty in their context and in the light of its object and purpose. Adding the well-known subjective element, Article 31 para. 4 indicates that a special meaning shall be given to a term if it is established that the parties so intended. In the same way Article 31 para. 3 attaches great importance to the practice of the parties which may shed light on their understanding.[5]

---

3 Frowein, "On Article 39", *supra,* n. 2, pp. 605 *et seq.*, (pp. 615 *et seq.*); "On Article 42", *ibid.*, p. 633 *et seq.*

4 C. Rousseau, "Chronique des faits internationaux", (1967) 71 *RGDIP* 472 *et seq.*; Frowein, *supra,* n. 3.

5 R. Bernhardt, "Interpretation in International Law", in *id.* (ed.), *Encyclopedia of Public International Law*, Vol. II (North – Holland, 1995), p. 1416 *et seq.*

It should not be automatically assumed that Security Council resolutions should be interpreted in all respects in the same way as treaties.[6] It is certainly correct that, as for the interpretation of all legal instruments, the rule enshrined in Article 31 para. 1 of the Vienna Convention is also applicable here. The resolution must be interpreted in good faith in accordance with the ordinary meaning to be given to the terms of the resolution in their context and in the light of its object and purpose. However, much more care must be exercised when the importance of practice under a specific resolution is to be evaluated. The resolution is not based on the common will of all those concerned. It is based on the common will of the majority of the members of the Security Council, including the permanent members, at least by abstention. This means that states against whom the Security Council exercises its power under Chapter VII have not contributed to the formulation of the resolution. As far as they are concerned the resolution has the same sort of objective existence as laws or administrative acts in a specific legal system. Therefore, the objective view of the neutral observer as addressee must be the most important aspect for the interpretation. Subjective intentions of some members of the Security Council, particularly intentions covered by the formulation or hidden in specific wording can, at least in principle, not be seen as in any way decisive. The recent events concerning the interpretation of Security Council resolutions related to Iraq seem to be of special importance in that context.

II LEGAL STATUS OF THE UNITED NATIONS CHARTER WITHIN THE DOMESTIC LEGAL ORDER

Under German constitutional law all treaties which affect matters of legislation or concern the political relations of the Federal Republic need the formal consent of the Federal Parliament (Bundestag) by a specific law (Art. 59 para. 2 of the Constitution). The United Nations Charter has received that consent by legislation. Therefore, the Charter has the status of normal federal legislation in the domestic legal order.

The consent given by legislation before the ratification on the international level of a treaty is decisive for its rank and status in the domestic legal order. This does not mean, however, that the treaty is directly applicable in the national

6 See, in general, M.C. Wood, "The Interpretation of Security Council Resolutions", (1998) 2 *Max Planck Yearbook of United Nations Law* 73 *et seq.*

legal system. That will depend upon the specific nature of the individual treaty rules. It is in particular the wording and the context of specific provisions to which German courts refer when deciding whether or not they may be directly applied in the German legal systems. Sometimes the notion of "self-executing nature" is used in this context. It is quite possible that a treaty may contain several provisions which are considered to be self-executing while others are not. Where introductory or other clauses of a treaty show that the whole instrument should not be considered to be directly applicable in domestic law this will be decisive.[7]

It is clear that almost all provisions of the United Nations Charter are not self-executing. They refer to the obligations of states *vis-à-vis* the United Nations and to the specific competences of United Nations organs. It is, therefore, not surprising that decisions by municipal courts which discuss the question of the self-executing nature of parts of the United Nations Charter do not seem to exist at all. One could argue that Art. 2 para. 5 UN-Charter could, under certain circumstances, be seen as a self-executing rule which would prohibit state organs to grant any assistance to a state against which preventive or enforcement action is being taken by the Security Council. It is, however, much more likely that courts would in fact look to the specific implementing provisions, if available.

One could also argue that Art. 104 UN-Charter, according to which the organization shall enjoy in the territory of each of its members such legal capacity as may be necessary for the exercise of its functions and the fulfilment of its purposes, should be interpreted as a self-executing rule. In the same sense, according to Art. 105 of the Charter, the organization shall enjoy in the territory of each of its members such privileges and immunities as are necessary for the fulfilment of its purposes. Under German law, however, the issue of the direct applicability of these rules will not arise since the legal capacity of the United Nations as well as its privileges and immunities have been laid down by specific internal legal provisions.[8] This has been achieved in the following way: In the federal law giving consent to the treaty on privileges and immunities of the specialized agencies of the United Nations a mandate was given to the Federal Government to grant by regulation legal capacity and privileges and immunities

7 Comp. Jochen A. Frowein, "Federal Republic of Germany", in Francis G. Jacobs (ed.), *The Effect of Treaties in Domestic Law* (London. 1987), p.63 at 69.

8 See Ignaz Seidl-Hohenveldern and Karin Rudolph, "Art. 104", in Simma (ed.), *The Charter of the United Nations, supra*, n. 2 p. 1127 (para. 6).

to all those organizations to which Germany has become a member or where other reasons are available.[9] On the basis of this mandate the Federal Government has, by regulation, provided already before the admission of the Federal Republic to the United Nations for the legal capacity of the United Nations as well as for its privileges and immunities.[10]

It should also be mentioned that the nature of the United Nations played an important role in German constitutional law when Art. 24 para. 2 of the Constitution was interpreted by the Federal Constitutional Court in the case concerning the participation of German armed forces in United Nations (authorized) operations in the former Yugoslavia and Somalia. According to Art. 24 para. 2 the Federal Republic can participate in a collective security system. The Federal Republic, according to that provision, will accept restrictions of its sovereign rights for the establishment of a peaceful order among the peoples of Europe and the world. The Federal Government had argued that it could use German armed forces for United Nations authorized peacekeeping activities on the basis of this rule notwithstanding another rule in the constitution according to which the use of armed forces needed an explicit mandate in the constitution (Art. 87a para. 2). The Federal Constitutional Court confirmed that Art. 24 para. 2 is indeed a sufficiently clear provision on the basis of which German armed forces can be used for operations decided by collective security systems.[11]

III Applicability of United Nations Decisions in Domestic Law

According to Art. 24 para. 1 of the German Constitution the Federation may, by legislation, transfer sovereign rights to international organizations.[12] This provision exists since 1949 and it was of great importance for the integration of Europe. The European Communities were always seen as the main examples for international organizations to which specific sovereign rights have been transferred. It was Art. 24 para. 1 which was considered to be the constitutional basis for the direct applicability of regulations and decisions by the European

---

9 Federal Law of 22 June 1954, BGBl. 1954 II, 639 in the form of the Federal Law of 28 February 1964, BGBl. 1964 II, 187.

10 Regulation of 16 June 1970, BGBl. 1970 II, 669 *seqq.*

11 BVerfGE 90, 286, 349 *seq.*

12 "Der Bund kann durch Gesetz Hoheitsrechte auf zwischenstaatliche Einrichtungen übertragen".

Communities in the German legal order.[13] Since 1992 the amended Art. 23 is applicable for the European Communities.[14]

The general interpretation of Art. 24 para. 1 has always been that the transfer of sovereign rights under that article refers to the possibility of exercising jurisdiction with direct effect within the German territory. A transfer of sovereign rights does not take place where international organizations may (only) take measures which are binding for the Federal Republic as such without necessarily having direct effect in the German legal order itself. Therefore, it is so far almost generally agreed that Art. 24 is not applicable for the United Nations and that, although decisions taken under Chapter VII are binding for the Federal Republic as a state, they do not have direct effect on German territory or for persons under German jurisdiction.

It should be noted, however, that this view has now been challenged, at least with respect to "orders" which emanate from the International Criminal Tribunal for the former Yugoslavia.[15] It is true that the Federal Government has taken the position that the decisions of the Security Council which established the two International Criminal Tribunals for the former Yugoslavia and Rwanda and some of the activities of these Tribunals under the Statute "create immediately binding obligations at least for the Member states without further implementing measures by the national legislators" and these would constitute an exercise of sovereign rights in the sense of Art. 24 para. 1.[16] Nevertheless the Government has introduced legislation "to bring German law in accordance with the obligations for the state which derive from the resolutions and the Statute (of the Tribunal) and transfers of sovereignty and to enable a smooth fulfillment of these obligations".[17]

---

13 Albrecht Randelzhofer, "Art. 24" para 45", in Maunz/Dürig, *Grundgesetz Kommentar*, München (looseleaf).

14 Art. 23 para. 1: "Zur Verwirklichung eines vereinten Europas wirkt die Bundesrepublik Deutschland bei der Entwicklung der Europäischen Union mit, die demokratischen, rechtsstaatlichen, sozialen und föderativen Grundsätzen und dem Grundsatz der Subsidiarität verpflichtet ist und einem diesem Grundgesetz im wesentlichen vergleichbaren Grundrechtsschutz gewährleistet. Der Bund kann hierzu durch Gesetz mit Zustimmung des Bundesrates Hoheitsrechte übertragen. ..."

15 Christian Tomuschat, "Sanktionen durch internationale Strafgerichtshöfe", in *Verhandlungen des Sechzigsten Deutschen Juristentages,* Münster 1994, Bd. II/2, München 1994, Q 66 *seq.*

16 BT-Drs. 13/57, 6 *seq.* (Yugoslavia) and BT-Drs. 13/7953, 6 (Rwanda).

17 BT-Drs. 13/57, 6 *seq.* (Yugoslavia) and BT-Drs. 13/7953, 6 (Rwanda).

These ambiguous sentences, however, do not necessarily mean that "orders" or other acts by the International Tribunals would have direct effect in Germany without implementing legislation. Such a position is still very much an exception in legal doctrine and is subject to serious objections which mainly derive from the requirement of an informed parliamentary consent. In addition, there seem to be no court decisions which challenge the traditional view. In fact, several decisions by German courts have confirmed that Security Council decisions under Chapter VII have no automatic effect without being implemented. The Federal High Court for criminal matters, for example, decided on 21 April 1995 that decisions of the Security Council under Chapter VII have no immediate legal effects for the citizens of Member states. They only bind the Member states as such and need specific implementation.[18]

There is, however, one decision by the Federal Constitutional Court which could create some doubts as to this position. That is the decision according to which the North Atlantic Treaty Organization (NATO) is an international organization to which sovereign rights in the sense of Art. 24 para. 1 have been transferred.[19] This decision, however, has to be seen in its specific context. Although NATO is an organization which in principle does not exercise jurisdiction with direct effect on the territory of its Member states, the Federal Constitutional Court applied Art. 24 para. 1 because of the enormous impact specific decisions on the use of certain weapons, in particular the use of nuclear weapons, could have for the Federal Republic of Germany. The Court held that the President of the United States, when giving permission to use nuclear weapons stationed on German territory, would exercise jurisdiction transferred to NATO under Art. 24 para. 1 of the Federal Constitution.[20] This decision, however, can certainly not be interpreted to include the organization of the United Nations. Even a decision which is directly binding for the Federal Republic of Germany under Chapter VII of the United Nations Charter would not have a comparable direct effect for the federal territory without implementation by German decisions.

It is therefore reasonably clear that under German constitutional law decisions by the Security Council of the United Nations, even binding decisions under Chapter VII of the Charter, will not have direct effect within the German municipal legal order.

18 BGHSt 41, 127 (129 *seq.*).
19 BVerfGE 68, 1.
20 BVerfGE 68, 1 (92).

IV The Implementation of Security Council Decisions by the European Union

Security Council resolutions under Art. 41 which declare a partial or total trade boycott with a specific country are implemented for all the Member states of the European Union by specific normative acts of the European Union.

The normal procedure consists in the adoption of a joint position under Art. 15 of the Union Treaty which will then be implemented by the Council under Art. 301 of the EC Treaty by the adoption of a regulation under European Community law which immediately prohibits such trade which is outlawed by the decision of the Security Council.[21] The regulation is immediately effective within the German legal system and creates duties for all individuals under German jurisdiction. There are many examples for this sort of EC regulations: Regulations have been adopted for comprehensive trade boycotts as well as for specific decisions to block bank accounts or to impose air traffic restrictions as well as travel restrictions.[22]

There is one important exception which concerns the trade with weapons. The Security Council has in many cases imposed embargoes on all trade with weapons concerning specific countries. This started with Rhodesia and South Africa, then followed Iraq, former Yugoslavia, Somalia, Libya, Liberia, Haiti, Angola, Rwanda, Sierra Leone, the Federal Republic of Yugoslavia and Eritrea and Ethiopia.[23] The implementation of these sanctions also begins by the adoption of a joint position within the Common Foreign and Security Policy of the European Union. However, no EC regulations are adopted for the imple-

---

21 See Horst Krenzler, "Die Handelspolitik der Europäischen Gemeinschaft als Instrument der Friedenssicherung", in *Verhandlungen des Sechzigsten Deutschen Juristentages* Münster 1994, Bd. II/2, München 1994, Q 46 *seqq.*

22 See e.g. Council Regulation (EEC) 877/82 of 16 Apr. 1982, O.J. L 102/1 (Argentina); Council Reg. (EEC) 2340/90 of 8 Aug. 1990, O.J. L 213/1 and Council Reg. (EEC) 3155/90 of 29 Oct. 1990, O.J. L 304/1 (Iraq/Kuwait); Council Reg. (EC) 3274/93 of 29 Nov. 1993, O.J. L 295/1 and Council Reg. (EC) 3275/93 of 29 Nov. 1993, O.J. L 295/4 and Council Reg. 945/92 of 14 Apr. 1992, O.J. L 101/53 (Libya).

23 See SC Res. 232 (1966) (Southern Rhodesia); SC Res. 418 (1977) (South Africa); SC Res. 661 (1990) (Iraq/Kuweit); SC Res. 713 (1991) (Yugoslavia); SC Res. 733 (1992) (Somalia); SC Res. 748 (1992) (Libya); SC Res. 788 (1992) (Liberia); SC Res. 841 (1993) (Haiti); SC Res. 864 (1993) (Angola); SC Res. 918 (1994) (Ruanda); SC Res. 1132 (1997) (Sierra Leone); SC Res. 1160 (1998) (Federal Republic of Yugoslavia); SC Res. 1298 (2000) (Eritrea and Ethiopia).

mentation because Member states seem to be of the opinion that they have at least concurring jurisdiction in that regard under Art. 296 of the EC Treaty. Therefore, in that respect only national measures are being adopted.[24]

V NATIONAL DECISIONS TO IMPLEMENT CHAPTER VII RESOLUTIONS

German municipal law provides mainly for two techniques to implement Security Council resolutions under Chapter VII of the Charter which prohibit specific forms of trade. These techniques will first be explained without having regard to EC law.

The German Law on Foreign Trade contains a mandate for the Federal Government to prohibit by specific regulation the export of any goods which fall under a decision of the Security Council.[25] Such a regulation can be adopted immediately after the Security Council has decided. The second technique concerns goods which under German Law always need a specific authorisation to be exported. This is so for weapons which are usually used in armed conflicts (Kriegswaffen).[26] Since any export of these weapons needs a special authorisation such authorisations will simply be refused as a matter of administrative practice as soon as the Security Council has taken a decision which prohibits this export.[27] This technique has even been used in cases of doubt, such as whether the export of blueprints for submarines was prohibited by the arms

---

24 See "Völkerrechtliche Praxis der Bundesrepublik Deutschland", (1969) 29 *ZaöRV*, 135 *seqq.* (Southern Rhodesia); (1979) 39 *ZaöRV*, 597 and (1992) 52 *ZaöRV*, 946 and 1041 (South Africa); (1992) 52 *ZaöRV*, 944 *seq* and 982 *seq.* (Iraq and Kuweit); (1993) 53 *ZaöRV*, 1041 and 1083 *seq.;* (1994) 54 *ZaöRV*, 962 seq, (1995) 55 *ZaöRV*, 1197 *seq.* and 1230 *seqq.*, (1997) 57 *ZaöRV*, 1090 (Former Yugoslavia); (1994) 54 *ZaöRV*, 962, (1995) 55 *ZaöRV*, 1198, (1996) 56 *ZaöRV*, 1135 (Libya); (1996) 56 *ZaöRV*, 1135 (Haiti).

25 Sect. 2 para. 1 no. 2 of the the Law on Foreign Trade (Aussenwirtschaftsgesetz) provides that "as far as this law admits restrictions it can be prescribed by regulation that legal acts or acts in general either 1) require an authorization or 2) are prohibited". Sect. 5 provides that "legal acts or other acts in foreign trade can be restricted ... in order to comply with international agreements which have been ratified by the Federal Parliament". Sect. 7 para. 1 permits that "legal acts and other acts in foreign trade can be restricted to ensure the security of the Federal Republic of Germany".

26 Sect. 2 para. 2 of the Law on the Control of War Weapons (Kriegswaffenkontrollgesetz), BGBl 1990 I, 2506; concerning the practice see ZaöRV 53 (1993) 1041 *seq.* (South Africa).

27 See e.g. (1979) 39 *ZaöRV*, 597 *seq.;* 1993, 1041 *seq.*

embargo under Security Council Resolution 418 (1977) against South Africa.[28] The same procedure applies where visa requirements exist and the Security Council restricts travel for a specific country. In these circumstances no specific regulation is adopted but the competent authorities will not grant visas to the persons concerned.[29]

Although EC regulations are directly applicable in the German legal system it is nevertheless necessary that the German legislator create a separate legal basis for criminal or administrative punishment in case of violation of the prohibitions since, under German law, criminal or administrative punishment is only possible where a specific legal provision expressly authorises punishment. For the moment the EC has no jurisdiction to lay down such rules. Currently, the basis for the punishment under German law is laid down in Section 34 para. 4 of the Law on Foreign Trade.[30] According to that provision a person may be punished who violates a regulation issued under the Law on Foreign Trade or a regulation adopted by the European Communities which was published in the German Collection of Federal Statutes (Bundesgesetzblatt) or in the Federal Gazette (Bundesanzeiger) if those regulations concern the implementation of Security Council measures adopted under Chapter VII of the United Nations Charter. So far, however, EC Regulations have never been published in the Federal Collection of Statutes. They have, on the other hand, occasionally been published in the Federal Gazette.[31] In all other cases the export prohibitions already implemented by EC regulations are repeated separately to be the basis for possible punishments. This will be done in the specific regulation for foreign trade which is based on the Law on Foreign Trade.

Such provisions are usually worded in the following manner: "To ensure the punishment in case of violation of the respective provisions by the European Communities are prohibited: 1. The import of all products originating in or coming from ...".[32] Taken together, these rules mean that persons under German jurisdiction may inform themselves about the respective prohibitions by

---

28 (1989) 49 *ZaöRV* 531.

29 Information by the German Foreign Ministry, 3 February 1998.

30 See also judgments BGHSt 41, 127; BGH NStZ 1995, 550; BGH NJW 1996, 602.

31 See e.g. Bundesanzeiger 1993, 10938 (Council Regulation (EC) 3275/93 of 29. Nov. 1993, O.J. L 295/4 (Libya)).

32 "Zur Gewährleistung der Straf- und Bußgeldbewährung entsprechender Verbote der Europäischen Gemeinschaften sind verboten: 1. Die Einfuhr aller Erzeugnisse mit Ursprung in oder Herkunft aus ...", Sect. 69a of the Regulation on Foreign Trade.

following carefully the German statute books on regulations concerning foreign trade.

The Federal Court of Justice has discussed the relationship between the national and the European acts.[33] The Court held that although the separate German legislative acts were constitutive in some respects, in particular with regard to their being the basis for possible punishment, they were only declaratory insofar as they proclaimed and circumscribed the EC prohibitions which have direct effect in Germany. It is interesting to note that the Court also raised the question whether the German legislative acts should be regarded as constitutive in their entirety in case the EC Regulations were illegal or even void under EC law. Even if that were the case, however, the Court reasoned, the intention of the German legislator to merely enact declaratory prohibitions precluded an interpretation of them as being constitutive.[34]

The system adopted by the German legislature and as interpreted by the Federal Court of Justice has the strange consequence that under German law the EC regulation is, in practice, often without much importance. It is really the German Law on Foreign Trade and the specific rules of the German regulation which are based on the Law on Foreign Trade which are taken note of. This would only be different if the pertinent EC regulations would always be published in the Collection of Statutes or in the Federal Gazette.

VI IMPLEMENTATION OF SECURITY COUNCIL RECOMMENDATIONS

Where the Security Council has only recommended boycott measures it is within the discretion of Member states to decide whether they will follow that recommendation or not. They are, however, under an obligation to exercise that discretion *bona fide* and to consider the recommendation in that sense. When the Council recommended in Resolutions 566 (1985) and 569 (1985) economic boycotts against South Africa the EC adopted a resolution within the European political co-operation to respect that recommendation. The Federal Republic

33 BGH JZ 1994, 725

34 See Jochen A. Frowein, "Regionale Sicherheitssysteme und nationales Recht", in *Verhandlungen des Sechzigsten Deutschen Juristentages* Münster 1994, Bd. II/2, München 1994, Q 31.

of Germany adopted measures to implement the resolution.[35] German courts have held in several contexts that recommendations adopted by the Security Council may be of importance for the interpretation of German law or the application of specific measures in the German legal system. The Federal Court for Social Security Matters, for instance, has taken recommendatory Security Council resolutions into consideration for the purpose of interpreting the term "territory of the State of Israel"in the sense of a German-Israeli Social Security Agreement."[36]

VII Cooperation with the International Criminal Tribunals

The establishment by the Security Council of the International Criminal Tribunals for the former Yugoslavia and Rwanda required special implementing legislation by the Member states. In Germany, the Federal Parliament has passed two virtually identical "laws on cooperation" to that effect.[37] These laws establish a general duty of the German judiciary to cooperate with the International Criminal Tribunals, in particular to discontinue and transfer proceedings to those Tribunals at their request (arts. 1 and 2). In addition, the cooperation laws require that persons be arrested and transferred at the request of the Tribunals and and that members of the Tribunals, on the basis of a special request, be even permitted to independently collect evidence (arts. 2-4). The cooperation laws do, however, reserve the right to order and execute compulsory processes to the competent German authorities which, in such a case, must comply with the applicable German law (art. 4 para. 4). German courts must also determine independently whether the criminal proceedings or the person which the International Tribunal seeks to be transferred relate to crimes within that Tribunal's jurisdiction (art. 2 para. 3). It is questionable, however, whether these reservations can limit the power of the Tribunals to issue orders and their inherent power to determine the scope of their jurisdiction.[38]

---

35 See (1988) 48 *ZaöRV*, 279.

36 BSGE 66, 28 ((1991) 51 *ZaöRV*, 183).

37 BGBl. 1995 I, 485 (Yugoslavia Tribunal); the law on cooperation with the Rwanda Tribunal has not yet been published in the Federal Statute Book but the text can be found in BR/Drs. 139/98 of 13 Feb 1998.

38 See Jochen Abr. Frowein, Georg Nolte, Karin Oellers-Frahm and Andreas Zimmermann, "Investigating Powers of the International Criminal Tribunal for the Former Yugoslavia vis-à-vis States and High Government Officials", in (1997) 1 *Max Planck Yearbook of United Nations Law*, 349, 362 and 367.

VIII Security Council Resolutions concerning the Authorisation to use Armed Force

The authorisation given by the Security Council to use armed force may, under certain circumstances, have an immediate effect in German law. This is so since Art. 24 para. 2 of the German constitution refers to collective security systems. Where the Security Council authorizes the use of armed force and the German government with the consent of the Federal Parliament decides to participate in such an action the constitutional justification will exist in the decision taken by the Security Council together with Art. 24 para. 2 of the constitution and the specific German decisions. The Federal Constitutional Court has clarified, in the decision mentioned earlier, that such an effect of United Nations decisions is fully compatible with German constitutional law.[39]

39 BVerfGE 90, 286.

LES EFFETS JURIDIQUES DES RÉSOLUTIONS DU CONSEIL DE SÉCURITÉ SUR LES CONTRATS PRIVÉS.

Geneviève Burdeau▪

La question des effets juridiques des sanctions économiques décidées par les Etats sur les contrats privés a été abordée dans un certain nombre d'études mais en général de manière dispersée. En particulier les effets des embargos, des boycotts des gels d'avoirs étrangers décidés unilatéralement ont retenu l'attention des spécialistes de droit international privé soit de manière spécifique dans des études consacrées à ces questions, soit dans le cadre d'études générales concernant les lois de police ou l'ordre public.[1] Souvent la question est envisagée à propos des mesures décidées unilatéralement par certains Etats.[2]

S'agissant des effets des résolutions du Conseil de Sécurité sur les relations juridiques privées, la question n'a semble-t-il guère fait l'objet d'études systématiques.[3] Elle présente des spécificités notables et soulève des questions originales qui ont commencé à se poser en pratique essentiellement depuis 1990

▪ Professeur à l'Université de Paris I – Panthéon Sorbonne; Secrétaire générale de l'Académie de droit international de La Haye.

1 H. van Houtte; "The Impact of Trade Prohibitions on Transnational Contracts", (1988) no.2, *RDAI* 141-154; X. Dieux, "Questions relatives aux effets de la contrainte étatique sur les contrats économiques internationaux –un point de vue belge", (1987) *RBDI* 184.

2 *Cf.* par exemple H. Gherari et S. Szurek (ed.) *Sanctions unilatérales, mondialisation du commerce et ordre juridique international. A propos ds lois Helms-Burton et d'Amato-Kennedy*, Cedin Paris X (Paris, 1998).

3 B. Grelon et Ch. Gudin, "Contrats et crise du Golfe", (1991) *JDI* 643; G. Burdeau, "Les conséquences de la crise du Golfe sur les relations économiques privées", in *Les aspects juridiques de la crise et de la guerre du Golfe*, Cahiers de CEDIN (Paris, 1991).

V. Gowlland-Debbas (ed.), *United Nations Sanctions and International Law*, p. 267-288.

et de manière de plus en plus pressante et fréquente au fur et à mesure que le recours aux mesures de l'article 41 de la Charte s'amplifiait.

Avant d'entrer dans le vif du sujet, il est indispensable de circonscrire les données propres au problème ici posé: Quelles sont les caractéristiques des résolutions en cause? Quels sont les contrats affectés par ces résolutions? Enfin quels sont les effets de ces résolutions sur ces contrats?

QUELLES RÉSOLUTIONS?

Les résolutions du Conseil de Sécurité auxquelles on songe ici sont essentiellement celles adoptées sur la base de l'article 41 de la Charte des Nations Unies. Elles imposent à l'ensemble des Etats membres de l'Organisation de rendre obligatoires pour leurs ressortissants des mesures destinées à faire pression sur un ou plusieurs Etats directement impliqués dans une situation menaçant la paix et la sécurité, et elles invitent les Etats tiers à faire de même: à la différence des mesures décidées unilatéralement par les Etats, ces résolutions, obligatoires pour tous les Etats membres et invitant également les Etats non-membres à s'y conformer, ont une portée quasi universelle.

Il s'agit donc de mesures *décidées par le Conseil de Sécurité* et non par un Etat particulier. Ainsi les effets des sanctions décidées en vertu de l'article 41 sont liés aux caractéristiques même des résolutions du Conseil de Sécurité. On peut supposer que celles-ci soulèveront des problèmes différents de ceux posés par les lois étrangères de police ou d'application immédiate. En effet, quelle que soit la loi applicable au contrat, celle-ci devra en principe contenir nécessairement des dispositions transposant les interdictions édictées par le Conseil de Sécurité. A supposer même qu'il s'agisse d'un contrat sans loi, ces mêmes interdictions auront vocation à s'appliquer. Par son objet en effet, on peut avancer que la résolution fait partie de l'ordre public transnational.[4] Les problèmes de contrariété à l'ordre public national ne devraient donc logiquement pas se poser. Bien entendu la rédaction de la résolution a une importance cardinale à cet égard, de même que celle des textes nationaux (ou communautaires) d'application.

4 Ph. Kahn, "A propos de l'ordre public transnational: quelques observations" *Mélanges Fritz Sturm*, Ed. jur. de l'Université de Liège (Liège, 1999), pp. 1539-1550.

Il s'agit en outre de mesures à *portée universelle* ou quasi universelle ayant un caractère obligatoire pour tous les Etats. Enfin les effets des sanctions décidées en vertu de l'article 41 sont liés aux *caractéristiques même des résolutions du Conseil de Sécurité*:. Dès lors, on peut supposer que les griefs d'extraterritorialité qui ont parfois été adressés à certaines mesures unilatérales n'auront pas lieu d'être en l'occurrence.

Toute sanction décidée par le Conseil de Sécurité sur le fondement de l'article 41 a un *caractère temporaire*, puisqu'il s'agit intrinsèquement d'un moyen de pression provisoire sur un Etat déterminé afin de l'amener à modifier son attitude en matière de sécurité. L'application de la mesure est dominée par la perspective de sa levée dans un délai incertain. L'incertitude pesant sur la durée probable de la mesure est une source de difficulté, mais en cela il n'y a pas de différence fondamentale avec les sanctions économiques unilatérales qui, elles aussi, n'ont pas vocation à être définitives.

L'objectif de rétablissement de la paix et de la sécurité qui justifie la mesure d'interruption des relations économiques est un objectif considéré comme fondamental et primant les intérêts particuliers. Il en résulte une certaine tendance des juges et des arbitres à interpréter de manière rigoureuse les interdictions édictées par les résolutions, comme le montre par exemple la jurisprudence de la Cour de Justice des Communautés européennes.

Il convient ensuite de souligner *l'objet de plus en plus diversifié* des sanctions, ce qui va entraîner des conséquences de plus en plus variées sur toutes sortes de relations contractuelles. Certes les résolutions qui seront principalement prises en compte sont celles qui adoptent des sanctions économiques: interruption des relations commerciales, mais aussi gel des avoirs financiers, interdiction d'investir, interdiction de faire droit à des demandes en justice, interdiction de délivrer des visas. Mais d'autres résolutions que celles fondées sur l'article 41 peuvent avoir des effets sur les relations privées. Ainsi le déclenchement d'une opération militaire de rétablissement de la paix, telle que l'opération "Tempête du Désert" en 1990 sur le fondement de la résolution 678 a pu, par elle même, perturber la réalisation de certains contrats privés.[5]

5 La jurisprudence a eu ainsi à se prononcer sur les conséquences de l'annulation d'un voyage en conséquence du début de l'opération "Tempête du Désert" en 1991. Cf. Tribunal d'instance du 1er arrondissement de Paris, Jugement du 15 mars 1993, *Epoux Souriau c/ Société Mondoclub, Mondial Tours et Air France,* (1993) *Revue Française*

QUELS CONTRATS?

Il convient également de déterminer quels sont les *types de contrats* susceptibles d'être affectés par la mise en œuvre des résolutions du Conseil de Sécurité.

Il s'agira dans la majorité des cas de contrats entre parties privées. Les sanctions économiques apparaissent comme une entrave momentanée à la liberté des échanges économiques internationaux que l'on cherche par ailleurs à promouvoir. A cet égard, les sanctions sont ressenties comme une gêne par les opérateurs privés des pays non visés par les sanctions et ceux-ci ont parfois le sentiment que pèse spécifiquement sur eux un rôle d'auxiliaire de la Communauté internationale qu'ils n'ont pas sollicité. D'où la tentation sinon de violer délibérément les mesures restrictives du commerce, du moins d'en minimiser les effets ou de les contourner et de chercher à défendre leurs intérêts commerciaux.

Pourront également être affectés des contrats conclus par des autorités publiques, voire avec l'Etat cible ou avec des émanations de celui-ci. Dans cette dernière hypothèse se posera éventuellement la question de savoir si l'Etat cible peut invoquer les immunités de l'Etat souverain. On a soutenu que l'Etat visé par les sanctions, du fait des atteintes à sa souveraineté découlant des résolutions, ne serait plus vraiment souverain et ne pourrait plus invoquer ses immunités. Cette thèse a été récemment accueillie par la Cour de Cassation française dans un arrêt rendu le 15 juin 1999, dans des termes assez contradictoires et d'ailleurs peu convaincants. A propos d'une affaire dans laquelle une entreprise française cherchait à exécuter contre l'Etat Irakien une condamnation de payer le prix de fournitures résultant d'un contrat antérieur à 1990, La Cour de Cassation a paru considérer que les sanctions internationales entraîneraient des limitations de la souveraineté irakienne et que la disposition de la résolution 687 imposant à l'Etat irakien d'honorer scrupuleusement ses dettes empêcherait l'Etat irakien d'opposer son immunité d'exécution.[6]

Au delà de contrats assez variés (vente, prestation de services, transports, assurances, dépôt, etc...), ce sont aussi des situations juridiques diverses qui

---

de droit aérien et spatial, p. 351.

6 Cour de Cassation 1ère chambre civile, 15 juillet 1999, *Dumez c/Etat irakien et a.* (2000) *JDI*, p. 45, avec la note de M. Cosnard qui critique à juste titre l'interprétation que l'arrêt donne de la résolution 687.

peuvent se trouver affectées, comme la libre disposition des biens en cas de gel et donc certains aspects du droit de propriété.

QUELS EFFETS?

Les sanctions économiques soulèvent naturellement des problèmes d'application dans le temps. Affectant d'abord la mise en œuvre des contrats en cours dont elles visent clairement à paralyser l'exécution, elles influent également sur la conclusion de contrats postérieurs, mais avec des effets juridiques que la rédaction de la résolution du Conseil de Sécurité ne permet pas toujours de préciser: s'agit-il d'une interdiction de négocier, de conclure, ou seulement d'exécuter?

Par ailleurs il faut rappeler que les résolutions du Conseil de Sécurité s'adressent aux Etats et que, pour avoir un effet sur les relations juridiques privées, elles devront, selon des modalités définies par chaque droit national, se voir conférer un caractère obligatoire dans l'ordre interne. On a pu discuter du point de savoir si, par leur objet même, les interdictions décidées par le Conseil de Sécurité ne devaient pas être considérées comme directement obligatoires pour les opérateurs privés.[7] Sauf dans quelques Etats dont la Constitution reconnaît un effet obligatoire aux résolutions du Conseil de Sécurité, une transposition en droit interne sera sans doute nécessaire. Que cette transposition soit ou non requise par le droit national, il n'est pas rare qu'elle soit l'occasion d'ajouter des dispositions complémentaires. Les personnes privées pourront-elles alors contester les mesures internes dont l'objet dépasse les exigences de la résolution, en se fondant sur la violation de certains principes ou règles de droit interne tels que le respect du principe de la liberté du commerce ou du droit de propriété, ou de droit international tels que le respect des traités? C'est une question qui est susceptible de se poser de même que celle d'un éventuel contrôle de légalité des "ajouts" des textes d'application.

Dans une analyse très intéressante des résolutions imposant des sanctions[8], M. Cosnard souligne la double nature, à la fois normative et politique des résolutions: si leur aptitude à créer des normes directement obligatoires pour

7 Voir sur ce point les auteurs évoqués dans la note précitée de M. Cosnard et en particulier B. Conforti, "Cours général de droit international public", (1988) 212 *Recueil des Cours* 48s.

8 *Ibid.* p. 51.

les particuliers est problématique, en revanche elles s'intègrent dans une *situation politique* dont les opérateurs économiques doivent tenir compte.

Les questions soulevées ci-dessus laissent entrevoir la complexité des questions qui peuvent surgir à propos de l'incidence des sanctions économiques décidées par le Conseil de Sécurité sur les contrats privés. Cette incidence ne peut pas être envisagée uniquement d'un point de vue contentieux. En effet, les sanctions civiles, pénales ou administratives, qui sont d'ailleurs souvent assez illusoires en droit interne pour assurer le respect effectif des interdictions découlant des résolutions du Conseil de Sécurité, sont rarement mises en œuvre. Néanmoins les opérateurs sont, dans leur grande majorité, conscients de la nécessité de ne pas enfreindre les interdictions et ils doivent donc en connaître les contours qui ne sont pas toujours très aisés à déterminer. Afin d'étudier ces incidences, on s'efforcera donc de préciser successivement les effets des résolutions sur la formation des contrats, sur leur exécution et enfin sur le contentieux relatif aux contrats.

I Formation et Validité des Contrats[9]

S'agissant de la formation des contrats, la question des effets des résolutions du Conseil de Sécurité prises sur le fondement de l'article 41 ne paraît jusqu'à présent s'être posée que pour les contrats à venir. En effet les résolutions du Conseil de Sécurité imposant des interdictions d'importer ou d'exporter n'ont pas eu en général comme objet d'invalider expressément des contrats en cours mais seulement d'empêcher l'exécution de certains contrats par exemple en interdisant l'exportation ou l'exportation de certaines marchandises ou en empêchant la restitution de dépôts bancaires.

L'approche du Conseil de Sécurité est beaucoup plus macro-économique que juridique et beaucoup plus pragmatique que théorique: il s'agit de faire pression sur l'Etat cible en rendant quasi impossible l'ensemble des relations économiques de celui-ci avec l'extérieur, tant qu'il n'a pas obtempéré. Il ne s'agit donc pas de porter un jugement sur la validité de telle ou telle relation juridique particulière, ni sur son bien-fondé ou sur la situation pariculière du contractant étranger, mais de s'assurer que l'Etat cible sera privé de relations économiques

9 J. Combacau, *Le pouvoir de sanction de l'ONU. Etude théorique de la coercition non militaire* (Paris, 1974).

avec l'étranger et donc gêné dans sa vie économique, ce qui est censé l'amener à résipiscence. Le Conseil de Sécurité agit en décideur politique plus qu'en législateur. Ainsi, la nullité des contrats en cours ou l'interdiction de conclure des contrats pour le futur n'est pas manifestement sa perspective principale, d'autant qu'elle dépasse sans doute ses compétences. En général, c'est aux Etats membres que le Conseil s'adresse pour exiger qu'il soit mis fin de manière effective aux relations économiques avec l'Etat cible, laissant à ceux-ci le soin d'adopter les modalités juridiques appropriées en droit interne. La résolution indique l'effet pratique recherché, mais laisse en principe à l'Etat le choix des moyens juridiques.

Cependant, même si le Conseil de Sécurité vise essentiellement à paralyser les *effets* des contrats en cours, ses résolutions peuvent, par leur rédaction, soulever des questions de *validité* des contrats en cours ou à venir. On voit également apparaître dans certaines résolutions des éléments d'un *contrôle sur la conclusion* des contrats. Ce contrôle est destiné à permettre la mise en œuvre de certaines limites à l'isolement de l'Etat sanctionné, essentiellement pour des considérations humanitaires.

A) *Validité des contrats en cours*

Comme on vient de le dire, l'objectif du Conseil étant essentiellement pragmatique, la validité des contrats en cours n'est en principe pas affectée par les sanctions.

Les principes généralement admis de droit transitoire trouveront ici application: les situations légalement constituées en vertu d'un contrat conclu avant l'interdiction résultant de la résolution ne sont pas affectées. Ainsi, il n'y a pas eu de difficulté particulière pour les tribunaux à déclarer après 1990 qu'une entreprise irakienne était tenue de verser le montant du prix de marchandises livrées avant l'imposition de l'embargo en vertu de contrats antérieurs.[10]

A cet égard, il paraît difficile de se rallier à l'interprétation qui avait été avancée par J. Combacau à propos des résolutions 232 et 253 adoptées par le Conseil

10 Voir par exemple l'affaire précitée supra note 2 dans laquelle les juges du fond avaient déclaré la partie irakienne redevable du montant du contrat exécuté avant août 1990. Bien qu'il se fut agi du ministère de la Défense, le juge avait écarté l'immunité de juridiction eu égard au caractère commercial du contrat.

de Sécurité dans l'affaire de Rhodésie.[11] Celui-ci suggérait en effet que l'interdiction édictée dans ces résolutions "nonobstant tous contrats conclus ou toutes licences accordées avant la date de la présente résolution"

> "s'analyse comme une invitation faite aux Etats de prendre des lois ou des règlements rétroactifs puisque, allant au delà du principe d'application immédiate, ils devraient concerner non seulement les situations créées à partir du moment où la norme interne entrerait en application, mais aussi celles résultant de contrats antérieurs".[12]

Il semble bien qu'il n'y ait là, à proprement parler aucune rétroactivité, mais seulement l'application du principe classique de l'effet immédiat de la loi nouvelle habituellement admis dans le domaine des contrats[13] L'expression "nonobstant tous contrats conclus ou toutes licences accordées" fait obstacle à la mise en œuvre pour l'avenir de contrats déjà conclus, mais ne remet pas en cause les effets déjà acquis sur le fondement de ces contrats.[14]

Aucune résolution du Conseil de Sécurité ne paraît avoir mis en cause la validité de contrats en cours. Néanmoins la prolongation de certains embargos, en particulier celui décidé à l'encontre de l'Iraq en 1990 a parfois conduit le juge a admettre que l'embargo avait pu, compte tenu des particularités du mode de conclusion du contrat entraîner la résolution de celui-ci. Ainsi, dans une ordonnance de référé rendue le 31 octobre 1990, le Tribunal de commerce de Nanterre a accepté à la demande du vendeur de constater la résolution d'un contrat de vente matérialisé par des confirmations de commande, afin de permettre au vendeur de récupérer la marchandise en cours d'acheminement et non encore réglée.[15]

Cette solution s'explique plus par le souci pratique de protéger les intérêts du vendeur que par un raisonnement juridique très élaboré. Cette décision met néanmoins en lumière une question particulière à laquelle les résolutions n'apportent

---

11 Rés. CS 232 (1966) du 16 décembre 1966 et 253(1966) du 29 mai 1966.

12 *Supra*, n. 3, p. 270.

13 Roubier, *Le droit transitoire* (1959).

14 D'ailleurs le décret français du 23 août 1968 pris en application de cette résolution se borne à transposer l'interdiction d'exporter et d'importer, JORF 27 août 1968, p. 8216.

15 Tribunal de commerce de Nanterre, 31 octobre 1990, *S.A. Lesieur International c/Sté Norasia*, (1991) *AFDI* 895 et *Les Petites Affiches*, n°156, 28 décembre 1990. 21, note P.M. Martin in n° 15, 4 février 1994.

pas de réponse claire: quelle est la situation juridique de la marchandise en cours d'acheminement au moment où l'embargo entre en vigueur? Dans l'affaire précitée la solution a sans doute été facilitée par le fait que la marchandise était couverte par une clause de réserve de propriété au profit du vendeur. Tel n'est pas nécessairement le cas dans d'autres contrats. Mais en toute hypothèse, la solution consistant dans la résolution du contrat devrait être justifiée au regard des règles du droit gouvernant le contrat.

Les règlements communautaires reprennent clairement l'interdiction d'importer et d'exporter, mais également la formule ambiguë contenue dans les résolutions interdisant "d'exercer toute activité ayant pour objet ou pour effet de favoriser les activités visées"[16], qui pourrait, selon une interprétation extensive laisser penser que la conclusion de contrats pourra être englobée dans l'interdiction. Toutefois on pourrait soutenir que "l'exercice d'activités"vise des opérations matérielles et non pas la conclusion de contrats.

B) L'interdiction de conclure des contrats pour l'avenir. Formulation des interdictions

Comme on l'a déjà indiqué, la plupart des résolutions ne prévoient pas explicitement d'interdiction de conclure des contrats dans le futur. Cependant, l'interdiction de commercer avec l'Etat sanctionné a souvent été interprétée comme une interdiction de conclure de nouveaux contrats, à défaut de remettre en cause, pour les anciens, autre chose que leur exécution à venir.

Il n'est évidemment pas possible de répondre de manière générale à la question de la licéité de la conclusion de contrats postérieurement à la résolution du Conseil de Sécurité. Il faut en effet se référer dans chaque cas à la rédaction précise de la résolution pertinente, mais aussi aux textes nationaux de mise en œuvre qui, sur ce plan, peuvent parfois aller plus loin que la résolution elle-même.

En ce qui concerne les résolutions elles-mêmes, il faut noter une évolution dans les expressions employées. En effet si les premières résolutions (affaires rhodésienne[17] et iraquienne[18]) ont prévu essentiellement une prohibition des expor-

16 *Cf.* par exemple le règlement 2465/96 du 17 décembre 1996 concernant l'interruption des relations économiques et financières entre la Communauté Européenne et l'Iraq, JOCE n°L/337/1.

17 Rés. CS 253(1968) du 29 mai 1968.

tations ou des importations ou des "activités qui auraient pour effet de favoriser l'exportation ou le transbordement de tous produits de base ou de toutes marchandises en provenance" du pays sanctionné, certaines résolutions plus récentes tendent à interdire les "transactions", expression qui pourrait être entendue comme incluant les contrats eux-mêmes. Par ailleurs, il est courant que les résolutions instaurant une interdiction d'exportation prévoient également la prohibition de "toutes activité qui auraient pour effet de favoriser l'exportation".[19] Cette expression est assez ambiguë et pourrait être interprétée comme englobant la conclusion ultérieure de contrats.

C) Problème des contrats sous condition suspensive

L'ambiguïté de ces formules d'interdiction soulève naturellement la question de la validité de contrats postérieurs conclus sous condition suspensive de la levée de l'interdiction.

La question doit être envisagée au regard de la nature des mesures décidées par le Conseil de sécurité. En effet, bien que l'on utilise souvent, et même dans les ouvrages juridiques, le terme de "sanctions", la nature véritable des mesures de restriction des échanges fondées sur l'article 41 de la Charte de l'ONU est d'un autre ordre. Comme on l'a déjà souligné, le terme de "sanction" est inapproprié pour désigner une mesure qui n'a pas le caractère d'une punition définitivement infligée à un contrevenant mais un moyen de pression indirect destiné à obtenir un changement d'attitude de l'Etat visé. Cette analyse[20] qui

18 Rés. CS 661 du 6 août 1990.

19 Rés. CS 253 (1968) contre la Rhodésie, 661 (1990) contre l'Iraq, 757(1992) contre la Yougoslavie.

20 Combacau, *supra,* n.9, p. 17 *séq.*: "Le but de la sanction est la cessation d'une situation. Ce n'est ni une sanction civile ni une sanction pénale mais une voie d'exécution. (...) Il ne s'agit pas pour l'O.N.U de punir, mais de *faire cesser le trouble à l'ordre* que provoque la prolongation de la situation. Toute fondée qu'elle soit en droit sur la violation d'une prescription, la sanction réagit, non contre cet acte lui-même, mais contre la situation qui en résulte." Il précise un peu plus loin: "C'est une voie d'exécution qui ne correspond ni à une exécution d'office, ni à une exécution forcée, mais à une astreinte. Qu'elle soit économique, politique, militaire, il s'agit toujours, non de passer outre à la volonté de l'Etat, mais de faire pression sur elle, en lui proposant une alternative continue: ou bien la persistance de l'infraction et le maintien d'une situation défavorable, ou bien l'abandon de l'attitude illégale et l'abrogation de l'acte de sanction".

avait été présentée il y a longtemps par J. Combacau a été régulièrement rappelée par la doctrine depuis 1990.[21]

Dans ces conditions, la mesure restrictive n'est pas imposée pour elle-même, mais uniquement dans la perspective d'un changement d'attitude de l'Etat cible dans le domaine de la paix et de la sécurité. Dès lors il est juridiquement correct d'envisager qu'un jour futur, et, sous réserve d'un changement d'attitude de l'Etat cible, la reprise effective des échanges sera possible. Si donc la résolution prise en application de l'article 41 n'envisage, comme c'est le plus souvent le cas, que l'interruption effective des échanges et non l'interdiction de contracter, on ne voit pas ce qui conduirait à condamner la conclusion de contrats sous la condition suspensive de la levée des sanctions, sous réserve, bien entendu, que le texte national de mise en œuvre de la résolution ne soit pas plus restrictif.

La question de la validité des contrats sous condition suspensive a été discutée par des auteurs de droit privé, au regard de la lecture conjointe de résolutions du Conseil de Sécurité et de textes de mise en œuvre, notamment de règlements communautaires, dont la formulation était généralement plus large. La formulation de ces derniers textes internes étant généralement décisive, les argumentations sont assez prudentes. Ainsi, dans une des premières études parues après la crise du Golfe, B. Grelon et Ch.-E. Gudin[22], relèvent que les termes employés dans le règlement communautaire du 8 août visent expressément des actes juridiques "transaction commerciale", "vente", "fourniture" et non de simples actes matériels et qu'il "en résulte que la simple conclusion d'un contrat de vente ou de fourniture, même en l'assortissant d'un terme pour son exécution – la fin de l'embargo – est interdite dès lors que l'autre partie est une partie irakienne au sens du Règlement". Toutefois cette affirmation se trouve quelque peu tempérée par le paragraphe suivant dans lequel les auteurs écrivent:

> "Plus délicate est la question de savoir si la conclusion d'un contrat sous condition suspensive de la fin de l'embargo est, elle aussi, possible. Le doute est en effet

21 *Cf.* par ex. R. Higgins, *Problems and Process. International Law and how we use it* (Oxford, 1994), p. 166.

22 Grelon et Gudin, *supra*, n.3, pp. 633-678.

> permis dans la mesure où, tant que la condition est pendante, le contrat ne produit aucun effet".[23]

La validité du contrat sous condition suspensive est également avancée par Xavier Dieux.[24]

Cette position doit être approuvée: en effet la résolution n'a en vue que les effets immédiats du contrat.

Une question particulière pourrait surgir à propos de contrats conclus sous la condition suspensive de la levée des sanctions, dans l'hypothèse où, après l'intervention d'une résolution décidant de la levée des sanctions, la réglementation nationale du pays de l'exportateur maintiendrait l'interdiction.

D) Le contrôle de la conclusion des contrats par le Comité des sanctions
L'intervention du Comité des sanctions en vue d'autoriser la conclusion de certains contrats est devenue classique. Mais ses interventions se sont diversifiées et amplifiées. Toutefois il faut noter qu'il n'existe pas de contrôle systématique, le Comité n'ayant pas le pouvoir de se saisir lui-même. Il appartient donc aux Etats d'assurer le respect des restrictions aux échanges et de saisir le Comité des demandes de dérogation. Ainsi, certains contrats dont la compatibilité pouvait être discutée au regard des résolutions du Conseil de Sécurité ont pu être conclus dès lors que les Etats concernés n'ont pas jugé nécessaire de saisir le Comité.[25] Il est toutefois probable que ces cas sont restés limités.

En principe les parties au contrat sont libres d'établir le contenu de leur accord, l'intervention du Comité des sanctions se présentant comme un droit de regard emportant le pouvoir d'autoriser ou d'interdire l'opération. Toutefois, avec la résolution "Pétrole contre nourriture", le contrôle est poussé nettement plus

---

23 On ne suivra pas ces deux auteurs pour l'argumentation qu'il cherchent à tirer d'un parallèle avec la jurisprudence de la Cour de Cassation française relative à la validité de certains contrats conclu sous condition suspensive de l'autorisation administrative du contrôle des changes.

24 Dieux, op. cit., *supra*, n.1, p.195.

25 Il en est ainsi d'un contrat conclu le 21 mars 1997 avec l'Iraq pour 23 ans par l'entreprise pétrolière russe Lukoil pour le développement du champ de Qurna ouest qui n'a pas été soumis au Comité des sanctions.

loin puisque c'est le contenu même du contrat qui fait l'objet d'un contrôle et l'autonomie des parties contractantes s'en trouve réduite d'autant.

1) Le cas général: l'autorisation de conclure le contrat
Comme on le sait l'institution d'un Comité chargé de veiller à l'application des exceptions aux embargos en faveur des fournitures de biens de première nécessité ou de fournitures médicales, remonte à la première expérience du Conseil de Sécurité dans ce domaine, au moment de l'affaire de Rhodésie. La résolution 253 du 26 mai 1968 instaurait un mécanisme qui allait devenir systématique. Le Comité instauré par chacune des résolutions imposant des sanctions se voit confier la tâche d'une part d'examiner les rapports présentés par le Secrétaire général sur l'application de la résolution mais également de "solliciter de tous les Etats des informations complémentaires concernant les mesures qu'ils auront prises pour assurer l'application effective des dispositions de la présente résolution".

L'interprétation qui a été donnée de cette disposition a conduit a une pratique qui confère aux Comités des sanctions un droit de regard sur les contrats ou plus généralement sur les projets d'exportation de fournitures à usage médical et de produits alimentaires de première nécessité. En effet, même si la formulation généralement adoptée paraît indiquer que les exportations de produits médicaux sont autorisées de plein droit, alors que les exportations de produits alimentaires seraient soumises à une appréciation des circonstances les rendant nécessaires, en fait il s'est imposé comme une règle que toutes les exportations sont soumises de manière systématique par les Etats au Comité des sanctions[26] qui, dans le premier cas les autorise automatiquement et dans le second les soumet à un examen. Cette méthode au cas par cas, qui a été suivie faute pour les Etats de se mettre d'accord sur une liste de produits, introduit donc dans la conclusion des contrats une condition préalable d'autorisation délivrée par le Comité des sanctions sur demande des Etats.

26 Les résolutions autorisent en général "les fournitures à usage strictement médical et, dans les cas où des considérations humanitaires le justifient, les produits alimentaires". Sur le débat suscité par cette dernière expression, cf.M. Koskenniemi, "Le Comité des sanctions (créé par la résolution 661(1990) du Conseil de Sécurité)", (1991) *AFDI* 119-137; P. Conlon, "Lessons from Iraq: The Functions of the Iraq Sanctions Committee as a Source of Sanctions: Implemenation, Authority and Practice", (1995) no.3 *Va.J.Int'l L* 633-668; P. Conlon, "Legal Problems at the Center of United Nations Sanctions", (1996) 65 *Nordic Jorunal of International Law*.

A ce régime d'autorisation préalable s'ajoutent les difficultés liées au règlement financier des contrats commerciaux dont la conclusion est éventuellement admise. En effet une grande incertitude a plané sur l'impact sur de tels contrats du gel des avoirs financiers souvent introduit comme sanction complémentaire depuis 1990. De fait, la rédaction de la résolution 661 qui a inauguré cette mesure, était muette sur ce point. Jusqu'en 1992 l'autorisation d'exportation délivrée par le Comité des sanctions indiquait que l'Etat concerné était autorisé à lever le gel pour permettre le financement de l'opération. Cette pratique a cessé depuis lors, si bien qu'en dehors des fournitures de produits médicaux ou alimentaires par des organismes d'assistance, l'achat de tels produits par les Etats sanctionnés est devenue normalement impossible. Certains Etats comme la Jordanie ou la Suisse ont autorisé leurs banques à ouvrir des lignes de crédit avec la perspective que les crédits seraient remboursés après la levée des sanctions.[27] Ainsi le financement des contrats commerciaux, notifiés au Comité des sanctions (fournitures bénéficiant d'une exception de principe) ou autorisés par celui-ci, repose largement et de manière assez hypocrite sur la position individuelle des Etats plus ou moins tolérante en matière de règlement financier. Mais la tendance générale est de considérer que le gel des avoirs financiers s'oppose au financement des contrats par ailleurs considérés comme rentrant dans les exceptions et, de ce fait, les exceptions à finalité humanitaires se trouvent très largement privées de possibilité effective d'application.

Dans le cadre particulier de la résolution 986 du 14 avril 1995 dite "Pétrole contre nourriture", il est prévu que l'Iraq doit soumettre à l'approbation du Secrétaire Général un plan semestriel de distribution intégrant une liste des marchandises qu'il a l'intention d'acquérir. Ainsi l'objet des contrats est soumis à un contrôle préalable, ce qui n'empêche pas un contrôle strict au cas par cas par le Comité 661.[28]

27 La Jordanie ayant supprimé cette possibilité en 1996, l'Iraq s'est trouvé dans l'impossibilité de se faire ouvrir de nouvelles lignes de crédit auprès des banques jordaniennes. Cet élément, en renforçant la pression sur l'Iraq a contribué à l'acceptation par cet Etat de la résolution Pétrole contre Nourriture.

28 Les modalités d'application de la résolution 986 ont fait l'objet d'un Mémorandum d'accord détaillé signé le 20 mai 1996 entre le Secrétariat de l'ONU et le gouvernement irakien. Cf. (1996) *DAI* N°13, pp. 500-505.

2) Un cas extrême: le contrôle par le Comité des sanctions du contenu des contrats

Dans le cas particulier des contrats pétroliers conclus avec l'Iraq dans le cadre de la résolution 986, c'est la négociation et le contenu même des contrats qui se trouvent soumis à un contrôle du Comité 661.[29] Ce sont ainsi les détails concernant la fixation du prix d'achat, l'itinéraire suivi par les produits et la référence au paiement par lettre de crédit à l'ordre du compte séquestre qui sont imposés aux parties. Ce contrôle a priori tout à fait exceptionnel est de loin le plus poussé qu'ait exercé par le Comité des sanctions jusqu'à présent. Comme l'écrit un auteur il s'agit là d'une manifestation originale d'un ordre public international.[30]

II Exécution des Contrats

L'effet le plus évident des résolutions du Conseil de Sécurité décidant de "sanctions" économiques sur les contrats est d'interrompre les contrats en cours de validité. Cet effet immédiat sur les contrats antérieurement conclu n'a jamais été contesté. Ceci ne signifie pas qu'il ne soulève pas des problèmes pratiques délicats, tenant notamment au caractère difficilement prévisible de l'effet des sanctions.

A) Le principe de l'interdiction temporaire d'exécution

1) Portée de l'interdiction

L'interdiction temporaire d'exécution est habituellement déduite des mesures d'embargo ou d'interruption des relations commerciales. S'agissant de contrats de vente, la livraison des marchandises sera prohibée. De fait, c'est sous la forme d'une impossibilité d'exporter que cette prohibition se concrétisera, l'administration des douanes du pays exportateur empêchant la sortie des marchandises. Ainsi, dans l'hypothèse d'un contrat de fourniture conclu par un vendeur situé dans un pays donné mais portant sur une marchandise stockée dans n'importe quel pays membre de l'ONU, l'interdiction d'exporter sera appliquée par les douanes du pays où se trouve la marchandise. Une telle

---

29 Pour une analyse détaillée de ces contraintes, cf, A. Bencheneb, "Pétrole contre nourriture: L'ONU et les contrats internationaux d'assouplissement de l'embargo consécutif à la guerre du Golfe", (1997) *JDI* 945.

30 *Ibid.*

situation est évidemment totalement différente de celle d'un embargo décidé unilatéralement par un seul Etat.

Pour certains contrats, la suspension d'exécution est directement édictée. Ainsi, la résolution 748 du 31 mars 1992 à propos de la Libye prévoit que "Les Etats interdiront à leurs nationaux ou à partir de leur territoire, le paiement de nouvelles réclamations sur la base de contrats d'assurance en cours".

S'agissant du gel des avoirs financiers, c'est l'exécution des contrats de dépôt conclu avec des banques ou des institutions financières qui se trouvera paralysée.

Dans la pratique, l'articulation des mesures d'embargo et des mesures de gel n'est pas toujours assurée. Ceci tient souvent au fait que les mesures de gel des avoirs du pays sanctionné sont mises en œuvre par les Etats dans le cadre de législations diverses notamment relatives au contrôle des changes, dont la logique d'application est différente. Il en est résulté que l'on a pu voir surgir d'étranges débats à propos de l'immunité d'exécution de l'Etat iraquien, alors que l'exécution des condamnations pécuniaires auxquelles le juge était convié de prêter son concours, se heurtait manifestement au gel des avoirs financiers de l'Etat concerné.[31] Mais, compte tenu de la technique de réglementation des changes utilisée -au moins en France- le juge n'a pas les moyens juridiques d'appliquer le gel.[32]

31 *Cf.* l'arrêt de la Cour de cassation française cité *supra,* n. 4 dans lequel l'immunité d'exécution de l'Etat irakien a été écartée au motif que cet Etat ne serait plus vraiment souverain. Le juge belge a adopté une attitude opposée en affirmant que l'Etat irakien pourrait invoquer son immunité d'exécution pour s'opposer à une saisie de ses biens consécutives à un jugement le condamnant à payer une somme d'argent à un créancier. (CA Bruxelles 8ème ch, 10 mars 1993, *Rafidain Bank c/ Consarc,* J.T. 1994 787, note J. Verhoeven; (1996) *JDI* 444, note R.T.). Dans aucun des deux cas, l'impossibilité d'exécuter contre l'Etat irakien résultant du gel des avoirs irakiens n'a été invoquée. Il est vrai que le gel est censé être provisoire alors que l'immunité d'exécution de l'Etat souverain étranger, dès lors qu'elle est reconnue, a un caractère permanent. Mais en toute hypothèse, le juge n'est pas en mesure de donner effet *motu proprio* à la mesure de gel.

32 Le décret français du 2 août 1990 destiné à organiser le gel des avoirs iraquiens en France ne prévoit pas directement cette mesure. Rédigé à la manière d'une mesure de contrôle des changes, il prévoit que "Sont soumis à autorisation préalable du ministre chargé de l'Economie les opérations de change, les mouvements de capitaux et les règlements de toute nature entre la France et l'étranger effectués pour le compte de personnes physiques ou morales résidentes au Koweit ou en Irak ou de nationalité koweitienne ou irakienne. Sont également soumises à autorisation(...)la constitution

2) Question des sous-contrats

Lorsque l'exécution du contrat en cours est interdite, se pose un problème très délicat, celui des sous-contrats: la suspension du contrat principal entraîne-t-elle celle des sous-contrats liés à l'exécution du contrat principal? Il semble qu'il n'y ait pas à cet égard de solution générale et que les éléments de fait propres à chaque situation pourront conduire, selon les cas à considérer que la suspension s'étend ou non aux sous-contrats. Deux critères paraissent jouer un rôle important dans cette appréciation: d'une part l'objet du sous contrat et d'autre part la connaissance que le sous-contractant a pu avoir de l'existence du contrat principal. Ainsi, il sera plus facile au juge ou à l'arbitre de refuser d'allouer des dommages-intérêts à un sous-contractant si son contrat portait sur la fourniture de choses de genre plutôt que sur un corps certain et s'il n'était pas informé de l'existence du contrat principal.

Il y a eu peu d'exemples en jurisprudence, mais on peut citer une très intéressante sentence arbitrale du 20 juillet 1992 qui concernait, à propos de l'exécution d'un contrat principal conclu entre une entreprise italienne et un ministère irakien, le sous-contrat conclu par le fournisseur italien avec un sous-contractant italien. Le contractant principal, considérant que l'exécution du contrat principal était devenue impossible en raison des sanctions décidées à l'encontre de l'Iraq en août 1990, avait décidé de suspendre l'exécution du sous-contrat et naturellement, le sous-contractant a estimé qu'il était injuste de lui faire supporter le charge de l'inexécution du contrat principal. Dans cette sentence arbitrale, les arbitres ont considéré que le sous-contrat avait bien été affecté en prenant en compte la rédaction extrêmement large du règlement communautaire du 8 août 1990 qui applique la résolution 661. Les arbitres ont également tenu compte du fait que le sous-contractant avait connaissance de la destination finale de la marchandise et que, par conséquent, il était informé du fait que la marchandise allait en Iraq. Finalement, les arbitres ont estimé qu'il y avait une certaine équité dans ces conditions à faire partager au fond le poids de l'inexécution entre le contractant principal et le sous-contractant.[33]

Mais, naturellement, les circonstances de l'espèce pourraient être tout à fait différentes. On pourrait imaginer des hypothèses de sous-contrats dans lesquels le sous-contractant n'aurait pas eu connaissance de la destination de la mar-

---

et la liquidation d'investissements d'origine koweitienne ou irakienne en France."

33 Sentence de la Chambre d'arbitrage de Milan du 22 Juillet 1992 (1993) YCA 80.

chandise et par conséquent, dans lesquelles il n'y aurait pas lieu de lui faire supporter la charge de l'inexécution.

B) Le sort des contrats paralysés

A propos de l'exécution des contrats se pose naturellement la question du sort des contrats dont l'exécution est paralysée par la décision du Conseil de sécurité, notamment en cas de prolongation des sanctions. En d'autres termes, ces contrats vont-ils être simplement suspendus ou, passé un certain délai, pourront-ils être considérés soit comme résolus, soit comme terminés.

Il y a eu sur ce point des prises de position de la part de la jurisprudence. Ici encore, la jurisprudence n'est pas très abondante, mais il y a tout de même des décisions qui ont considéré, notamment à propos de l'affaire irakienne, qu'au bout de deux ans on devait considérer qu'il n'y avait plus de chance de pouvoir exécuter le contrat. Par conséquent, si la loi applicable au contrat prévoit que l'impossibilité absolue d'exécuter entraîne la terminaison du contrat, le contrat doit être terminé. C'est la position qui a été avancée par les arbitres dans la sentence italienne précitée du 20 juillet 1992. Dans cette affaire en effet, le sous contrat était régi par le droit italien. qui prévoit que, lorsqu'il y a l'impossibilité absolue d'exécuter, le contrat est terminé. Les arbitres ont admis l'invocation de la clause *rebus sic stantibus* en considérant qu'au bout de deux ans, la mesure d'embargo pouvait être considérée comme n'étant plus provisoire.[34]

Certaines décisions, se fondant sur les circonstances particulières de l'espèce, ont pu considérer qu'il y avait eu résolution du contrat.[35] On pourrait en ce sens citer certaines décisions concernant la question délicate des garanties à première demande.[36]

---

34 A cet égard, l'invocation de la théorie de la force majeure selon le droit français, de la frustration admise dans les droits anglo-saxons, de l'*Unmögligkeit* selon le droit allemand ou d'autres théories analogues arrivent à des résultats pratiques similaires.

35 Tribunal de commerce de Nanterre, 31 octobre 1990, *S.A. Lesieur International c/Sté Norasia,* (1991) *AFDI.*895 et *Les Petites Affiches,* n°156, 28 décembre 1990. 21, note P.M. Martin in n° 15, 4 février 1994.

36 *Cf.* par exemple Cour d'appel de Paris, 1ère chambre, section B, 23 juin 1995, *S.A. Butec c/ Union des banques arabes et françaises "UBAF" et a.*, *J.C.P.*, éd. Entreprises, 1995 (n° 43), n° 735 avec note Bachir Georges Affaki; (1997) *JDI,* p. 441 avec note André Jacquemont. Sur la même affaire, voir également Cour de cassation, 1ère chambre civile, 24 février 1998, n° 357, *Société Rafidain Bank et Société State Establishment for*

C) La levée des sanctions

Jusqu'à présent, la levée des sanctions ne paraît pas avoir soulevé de difficultés particulières, mais dès lors qu'il n'est pas question de revenir sur les effets des sanctions pendant la période d'application de ces dernières, des difficultés pourraient surgir à propos de la délimitation précise de ces effets.

III CONTENTIEUX DES CONTRATS

L'imposition de sanctions par le Conseil de Sécurité a pu avoir certaines incidences sur le mode de règlement des litiges concernant les contrats privés. Deux questions notamment se sont posées: l'existence d'une résolution du Conseil de sécurité décidant les sanctions a une incidence sur le mode de règlement normal des litiges relatifs aux contrats affectés par les sanctions économiques. Par ailleurs le Conseil de Sécurité, depuis l'affaire irakienne a adopté des dispositions spécifiques destinées à interdire de faire droit à des demandes contentieuses émanant du pays sanctionné. Ces dispositions, que l'on a pu retrouver à propos d'autres pays finissent par apparaître comme un type nouveau de mesure prise en vertu de l'article 41 de la Charte.

A) Sanctions décidées par le Conseil de Sécurité et soumission des litiges entre contractants au mode de règlement normal

Le premier effet observable des sanctions sur le mode normal de règlement des litiges concerne la question de savoir si les sanctions n'ont pas pour effet de soustraire le litige à la compétence du juge ou de l'arbitre. La question a été discutée à plusieurs reprises tant en ce qui concerne le règlement judiciaire que le règlement arbitral. En ce qui concerne le règlement arbitral, on a soutenu, notamment devant le Tribunal fédéral suisse, que l'intervention d'une résolution du Conseil de sécurité aurait pour conséquence de rendre le différend non arbitrable. Le requérant soutenait en l'espèce que l'embargo décidé par le Conseil de Sécurité empêchait de faire valoir des prétentions découlant de contrats passés

pipelines dite "SEP" c/ S.A. Butec et Union des banques arabes et françaises dite "UBAF", (1998) *JDI*, p. 963 avec note André Jacquemont. *Cf* également dans le même sens, l'affaire *Endecco Barazzuol J.V. c/Banca Nazionale del Lavoro et Banca Commerciale Italiana* qui a donné lieu à un jugement du Tribunal civil de Padoue du 1er octobre 1993.

avec l'Iraq et rendait par conséquent le litige inarbitrable.[37] Cette argumentation a été rejetée à juste titre par le Tribunal fédéral suisse dans un arrêt de 25 juin 1992, mais, en tout cas, c'est une idée qui a été avancée.

En ce qui concerne le règlement judiciaire, on retrouve ici la question des immunités. La question s'est en effet posée de savoir si, en cas d'inexécution d'un contrat, l'Etat défendeur visé par les sanctions, pouvait invoquer son immunité. La question a été plaidée devant les juridictions belges qui ont résolu à vrai dire la question en s'appuyant sur la théorie de l'immunité restreinte, c'est-à-dire en considérant que le contrat était un contrat à caractère économique conclu dans des conditions analogues à celles qu'utilisent les opérateurs privés, et que par conséquent, l'immunité de juridiction ne pouvait pas être invoquée par l'Etat.[38] De manière extrêmement contestable, la Cour de Cassation française, comme on l'a déjà mentionné, a paru considérer que l'Iraq, eu égard aux obligations qui lui sont imposées par le Conseil de Sécurité, ne serait plus un Etat souverain et qu'il ne pourrait plus, par conséquent se prévaloir de son immunité d'exécution.[39]

B) Dispositions spécifiques destinées à faire échec aux demandes de l'Etat sanctionné

Enfin, à propos du contentieux, il faut signaler que, depuis l'affaire irakienne[40], un certain nombre des résolutions contiennent des dispositions spécifiques qui

---

37 Trib. Féd. Suisse 23 juin 1992, *Fincantieri-Cantieri Navali c/M, Rev.arb.* 1993, n°4, p. 691, note F. Knoepfler. Le Tribunal affirme, dans un ordre assez discutable: "Les mesures commerciales prises à l'encontre de la République d'Irak soulèvent certes la question de la validité des contrats conclus avant leur adoption, voire celle de l'impossibilité subséquente d'exécution desdits contrats; mais il n'apparaît pas- et les recourantes ne le démontrent en tout cas pas- que cet état de choses doive déboucher sur la constatation de l'inarbitrabilité des prétentions déduites de ces contrats (...) On ne voit pas, en particulier, quels principes juridiques fondamentaux établiraient un monopole de la juridiction étatique pour régler les différends portant sur des prétentions de nature civile influencées par des règles de droit international public.

38 *Cf.* arrêt cité *supra,* n. 23.

39 Voir *supra,* n. 4.

40 Rés. CS 687 du 3 avril 1991, article 29. La même disposition a été reprise dans le paragraphe 8 de la Rés. CS 883 du 11 novembre 1993 à l'encontre de la Libye. Cette mesure a été mise en œuvre par le règlement (CE) n° 3275 du Conseil du 29 novembre 1993. JOCE L 295/4.

sont destinées précisément à faire obstacle à des demandes contentieuses émanant du pays sanctionné. La première de ces dispositions est très connue. C'est celle du paragraphe 29 de la Résolution 687 contre l'Irak. La même formule a été reprise à l'égard de la Libye dans la Résolution 883. Elles prévoient que les Etats prendront les mesures nécessaires pour qu'il ne puisse être fait droit à aucune réclamation présentée par un ressortissant ou une société de l'Etat sanctionné résultant d'un contrat ou d'une opération dont l'exécution a été affectée par les mesures d'interruption des relations économiques. Ainsi, les parties originaires des Etats cible ne pourront pas obtenir de compensation pour la non-exécution des contrats affectés par les sanctions, et ce, même si, comme ce fut le cas en Iraq, la législation de l'Etat sanctionné impose à ses propres juges de considérer comme fautive la suspension des contrats affectés par les sanctions.[41]

Pour terminer, il convient de soulever une question qui n'a pas été évoquée, qui est celle de la charge finale du coût des sanctions. Les sanctions ont un coût pour les opérateurs économiques: lorsque les contractants voient un contrat remis en cause, inexécuté à cause des sanctions, ceci leur est évidemment préjudiciable. Et on peut se demander s'il est normal que ce coût économique des sanctions pèse de manière assez aléatoire sur tel ou tel opérateur économique qui va se trouver frappé brusquement par les effets indirects des mesures décidées par le Conseil de sécurité, ou si dans ce domaine, il ne serait pas approprié de prévoir une certaine socialisation du risque. Ce sont en effet les Etats qui sont responsables du maintien de la paix et de la sécurité internationales, et non les entreprises commerciales. Alors, cette idée a naturellement suscité des réclamations qui ont été présentées par des entreprises contre des Etats pour obtenir une indemnisation sur la base de la rupture d'égalité devant les charges publiques, mais en général sans succès, les tribunaux ayant en général considéré que l'effet des sanctions n'était pas véritablement spécial mais affectait de nombreuses entreprises étrangères aux Etats cible Jusqu'à présent donc, ce genre de demande n'a pas beaucoup prospéré et on remarque que les opérateurs d'ailleurs n'ont pas réclamé grande chose, ce qui peut paraître un peu étonnant. On peut imaginer, si les sanctions se multiplient, des mécanismes d'assurance

41 Loi iraquienne n°57 de septembre 1990. La solution indiquée au texte s'impose à l'abitre ou au juge national de tout Etat membre de l'ONU en verteu de l'ordre public transnational, même si le contrat est régi par la loi iraquienne. Néanmoins il faut réserver la situation du juge iraquien qui se considérera sans doute comme tenu d'appliquer sa loi nationale d'ordre public.

contre les impacts des sanctions décidées par le Conseil de sécurité, mais ceux-ci se heurteraient sans doute à quelques problèmes de principe.

Special Problems for Implementing States

Chair: *Erik Suy*
Emeritus Professor of International Law,
Catholic University of Leuven

REGIONAL INTERFACE BETWEEN SECURITY COUNCIL DECISIONS AND MEMBER STATES IMPLEMENTATION: THE EXAMPLE OF THE EUROPEAN UNION

Daniel Bethlehem▪

Within the general scheme of an examination of special problems arising from the implementation of Security Council decisions imposing economic sanctions, the focus of the present paper is the European Union (EU) as a "regional interface" between the Security Council and those Members of the United Nations which are also Member states of the EU.[1] This formulation implies an ap-

---

▪ Practising Barrister, Deputy Director of the Lauterpacht Research Centre for International Law and Fellow of Clare Hall, University of Cambridge.

1 The description "European Community" (EC) refers to the arrangements first established by the Treaty of Rome Establishing the European Economic Community (EEC) of 1957, as amended by various acts of accession and treaties of amendment including, most recently, Title II of the Maastricht Treaty on European Union (TEU) and the *Treaty of Amsterdam*. The description "European Communities" refers to the three communities: the European Community, the European Coal and Steel Community (ECSC) and the European Atomic Energy Community (EAEC). The description "European Union" refers to the arrangements established by the *TEU*, as amended by the *Treaty of Amsterdam*. By Article 1 of the *TEU*, the European Union "shall be founded on the European Communities, supplemented by the policies and forms of cooperation established by this Treaty". The "policies and forms of cooperation" referred to include, in particular, those relating to the common foreign and security policy (Title V) and police and judicial cooperation in criminal matters (Title VI). In contrast to the European Community, the European Union does not have legal personality. The form of cooperation that characterises the Union is therefore largely inter-governmental. While a formal distinction must be made between acts of the EU and acts of the EC, it is increasingly the case, particularly in the area of the implementation of international economic sanctions, that these acts are inextricably intertwined. This matter is discussed further in the body the present paper. For further consideration, see Kapteyn and Verloren van Themaat, *Introduction to the Law of the European Communities* (3rd ed., London, 1998), at pp.45-76.

V. Gowlland-Debbas (ed.), *United Nations Sanctions and International Law*, p. 291-305.

preciation that the EU is in fact an interface between the Security Council and the Member states in question; that the obligations created for the Member states as a result of binding decisions of the Security Council imposing economic sanctions are in some way addressed by the EU on behalf of its Members.

While the EU invariably does act to ensure implementation of Security Council decisions imposing economic sanctions within its Member states, and there is therefore a measure of truth in the proposition that the EU is an interface between the Security Council and EU Member states, the proposition does not accurately reflect the often complex regime of sanctions implementation within the EU. Nor does it accurately describe the legal dimension of the EU's role in these matters.

I THE "EUROPEAN UNION", "EUROPEAN COMMUNITY" AND "EUROPEAN COMMUNITIES"

Before turning to consider these matters further, a preliminary note of explanation is required. As has already been observed in footnote 1 above, a distinction must be drawn between the "European Union", the "European Community" and the "European Communities". Although there is an overlap in the membership of these arrangements, and the terms "European Union" or "European Community" are often used loosely to describe the over-arching political arrangements encompassing those states that are parties to the three principal agreements constituting the European Communities, the formal distinction between these entities remains centrally important to an accurate appreciation of the legislative basis and modalities of EU sanctions implementation.

Until the entry into force of the *TEU* on 1 November 1993, competence to act in implementation of UN sanctions was based on the terms of the ECSC Treaty, the EAEC Treaty and the EEC Treaty distinctly. Thus, for example, the principal basis of competence relied upon by the EEC in implementing sanctions was Article 113 of the EEC Treaty dealing with the common commercial policy,[2] the measures in question invariably taking the form of Council Regulations. In contrast, insofar as measures were required to be taken under the aegis of

2 Now Article 133 of the EC Treaty, as renumbered by the *Treaty of Amsterdam*.

the ECSC or EAEC, distinct acts were required. Thus, for example, in the case of sanctions against Iraq, in addition to various Council Regulations adopted on the basis of Article 113 of the EEC Treaty,[3] sanctions were also implemented by a *Decision of the Representatives of the Governments of the Member states of the European Coal and Steel Community, Meeting within the Council.*[4] As a matter of formality, therefore, in the period prior to the entry into force of the *TEU*, sanctions were implemented at Community[5] level by distinct acts of the various Communities. Within these arrangements, the principal focus of sanctions implementation, given the scope of the various treaties, was by the EEC. As a matter of practical significance, discussion of Community competence to implement United Nations sanctions thus took the form of a discussion of the competence of the EEC in this matter.[6]

The entry into force of the *TEU* introduced important additions into the process of sanctions implementation at Community level. Whereas prior to the *TEU* sanctions implementation was a matter for the EEC, through its institutions – the Council, the Commission and, on occasion, the Parliament – the *TEU* provisions on a Common Foreign and Security Policy (CFSP) gave the newly established European Union an important role in this field. Thus, pursuant to Article J.8 of the *TEU*, "the principles of and general guidelines for the common foreign and security policy" were to be defined by the European Council. More specifically, Article J.2 provided *inter alia* that "the Council shall define a common position" on any matter of foreign and security policy of general interest. Article J.3 went on to lay down procedures for adopting "joint action" in matters covered by the foreign and security policy. Pursuant to these articles, EU Member states were required to ensure that their policies and activity conformed to the decisions reflected in the relevant common position or joint action.

3 See, for example, *Council Regulation (EEC) No.2340/90 preventing trade by the Community as regards Iraq and Kuwait*, 8 August 1990 (OJ No L 213/1, 9 August 1990 and Corrigendum at OJ No L 216/28, 11 August 1990).

4 *Decision No.90/414/ECSC of the Representatives of the Governments of the Member states of the European Coal and Steel Community, Meeting within the Council, preventing trade as regards Iraq and Kuwait*, 8 August 1990 (OJ No L 2313/3, 9 August 1990 and Corrigendum at OJ No L 216/28, 11 August 1990).

5 For ease of reference, the term "Community" is used in this paper as a generic term to describe the supranational arrangements applicable in one form or another to the fifteen Member states which comprise the EU, EC, ECSC and EAEC.

6 In keeping with this focus, the discussion of competence that follows will also be limited to that of the competence of the EEC and that of its successor, the EC.

In the light of these provisions – subsequently amended by the *Treaty of Amsterdam* – sanctions implementation at Community level thus took on two forms: action by the European Union pursuant to the CFSP provisions of the *TEU* and action by the European Community pursuant to specific legislative powers in the EC Treaty.[7] Action by the EU invariably took the form of the definition of a common position. Action by the EC took the form of the adoption of legislative measures, invariably Council Regulations, enacting specific measures of sanction. These measures in turn would create obligations within the domestic legal orders of the various EC Member states on the basis of such established principles of Community law as direct application, direct effect and the supremacy of Community law over national law. Linking these two forms of action was the requirement, introduced by amendment as Article 228a of the EC Treaty, that where it is provided, in a common position or joint action adopted under the CFSP provisions of the *TEU*, for action to be taken by the Community "to interrupt or to reduce, in part or completely, economic relations with one or more third countries, the Council shall take the necessary urgent measures". Action by the EC imposing economic sanctions pursuant to Article 228a of the EC Treaty thus became conditional on action being first taken by the EU under the CFSP provisions of the *TEU*.

It is against this background that the question of whether the EU/EC is to be regarded as an interface between decisions of the Security Council imposing sanctions and the obligations of EU Member states must be addressed.

II THE EU/EC AS AN INTERFACE BETWEEN THE SECURITY COUNCIL AND EU MEMBER STATES

The EU/EC is not a Member of the United Nations. Subject to any discussion of the obligations of non-Members of the UN to comply with decisions of the Security Council on the basis of general international law, the EU/EC does not, therefore, itself have an obligation as a matter of treaty law to give effect to decisions of the Security Council imposing economic sanctions. If the EU/EC has an *obligation* to act at all in relation to such measures, the obligation is a derivative obligation based on the obligation of EU/EC Member states in respect

7 By Article G.A(1) of the *TEU*, the term "European Economic Community" was to be replaced by the term "European Community".

of Security Council decisions and the transfer of competence in respect of such matters from the Member states to the EU/EC.

In contrast to the position of the EU/EC, EU Member states, as Members of the United Nations and parties to the UN Charter, have a direct obligation to comply with decisions of the Security Council imposing economic sanctions pursuant to Articles 25 and 48(1) of the Charter.[8] Furthermore, pursuant to Article 103 of the Charter, in the event of a conflict between their obligations under the Charter and their obligations under the EC Treaty or the *TEU*, their obligations under the Charter will prevail.[9] As a matter of their obligations under the UN Charter, therefore, EU Member states are required to take such action as may be necessary to carry out the decisions of the Security Council imposing economic sanctions notwithstanding any commitments to the contrary that might be contained in the EC Treaty or the *TEU*.

Article 103 of the UN Charter, establishing a hierarchy of treaty obligations with obligations under the Charter at the pinnacle, is to some extent mirrored by Article 307 of the EC Treaty.[10] This provides as follows:

> "The rights and obligations arising from agreements concluded before 1 January 1958 or, for acceding States, before the date of their accession, between one or more Member states on the one hand, and one or more third countries on the other, shall not be affected by the provisions of this Treaty.
>
> To the extent that such agreements are not compatible with this Treaty, the Member state or States concerned shall take all appropriate steps to eliminate the incompatibilities established. Member states shall, where necessary, assist each other to this end and shall, where appropriate, adopt a common attitude.

---

8 Article 25 provides: "The Members of the United Nations agree to accept and carry out the decisions of the Security Council in accordance with the present Charter." Article 48(1) provides: "The action required to carry out the decisions of the Security Council for the maintenance of international peace and security shall be taken by all the Members of the United Nations or by some of them, as the Security Council may determine."

9 Article 103 of the Charter provides: "In the event of a conflict between the obligations of the Members of the United Nations under the present Charter and their obligations under any other international agreement, their obligations under the present Charter shall prevail."

10 Ex Article 234 of the EEC Treaty.

> In applying the agreements referred to in the first paragraph, Member states shall take into account the fact that the advantages accorded under this Treaty by each Member states form an integral part of the establishment of the Community and are thereby inseparably linked with the creation of the common institutions, the conferring of powers upon them and the granting of the same advantages by all other Member states."

As regards fourteen of the fifteen EU Member states that became Members of the United Nations prior to becoming Member states of the EC,[11] the UN Charter creates rights and obligations that antedate their rights and obligations under the EC Treaty. Pursuant to Article 307 of the EC Treaty, rights and obligations under the UN Charter will therefore prevail over rights and obligations under the EC Treaty. Only for Germany, which became a Member of the United Nations in 1973, do the rights and obligations created by the EC Treaty predate those of the Charter.

While, in view of the obligations of the EU Member states under the UN Charter, the implementation of binding resolutions of the Security Council by EU Member states has not proven to be particularly problematic, the scope and operation of Article 307 of the EC Treaty remains of importance to the extent that it is relevant to the division of competence between the Member states and the EC in respect of the implementation of such measures. This arises from the interplay of three factors: the obligations of UN Members in respect of decisions of the Security Council under Articles 25 and 48 of the Charter; the division of competence between the EC and its Member states in respect of the subject-matter of the sanctions in question; and the twin principles of EC law that Member states of the Community are in general precluded from acting in areas of Community competence and may not adopt measures implementing directly applicable measures of EC law. Also of relevance to a consideration of these factors is the controversy and fluidity that is sometimes associated with the question of the division of competence between the EC and its Member states on matters relating to international trade, external relations and the CFSP.

---

11 The dates of UN and EC membership respectively in the case of the EU Member states is as follows: Austria – 1955, 1995; Belgium – 1945, 1958; Denmark – 1945, 1973; Finland – 1955, 1995; France – 1945, 1958; Germany – 1973, 1958; Greece – 1945, 1981; Ireland – 1945, 1973; Italy – 1955, 1958; Luxembourg – 1945, 1958; Netherlands – 1945, 1958; Portugal – 1955, 1986; Spain – 1955, 1986; Sweden – 1946, 1995; United Kingdom – 1945, 1973.

In the light of these provisions, the implementation of Security Council decisions imposing economic sanctions by EU Member states is an often tangled amalgam of three forms of action as follows: (a) action by individual EU Member states, within the limits of their own municipal law, pursuant to their obligations under the UN Charter; (b) action by the EU, in the form of a common position under the CFSP provisions of the *TEU*, with which Member states must comply; and (c) action by the EC, in the form of binding legislative measures, which give rise to directly applicable obligations of Community law.

A number of conclusions emerge from these factors. First, the EU/EC is not obliged to act, as a matter of international law, in implementation of Security Council sanctions decisions. Second, to the extent that it does so, it acts in fulfilment of a derivative obligation of its Member states under the UN Charter and a transfer of competence in respect of the matters in question from the Member states to the Community. Third, notwithstanding EU/EC competence in these matters, EU Member states remain under an obligation, as a result of their membership of the UN, to carry out the decisions of the Security Council imposing economic sanctions. Fourth, pursuant to Article 103 of the UN Charter, the obligations of the EU Member states under the Charter prevail over any inconsistent obligations that might arise under the EC Treaty or the *TEU*. Fifth, the subsistence of obligations under the Charter is recognised by Article 307 of the EC Treaty (although there may be special problems in this regard for Germany). Sixth, in practice, given the derivative competence of the EU/EC in these matters but the direct obligations and residual competence of the Member states, the EU/EC and the Member states frequently act in parallel in the implementation of sanctions.

In the light of these conclusions, while it is clear that, in many instances, the EU/EC will be an "interface" between the Security Council and the EU Member states in respect of sanctions implementation – in the sense of acting as a conduit for the implementation of sanctions within the Community legal order[12] – this will not always be the case. In particular, notwithstanding action by the EU/EC in such matters, as EU Member states remain under a direct obligation to carry out the decisions of the Security Council, and to the extent that, in fulfilment of this obligation, they consider that there is an independent

12 See further D. Bethlehem, "International Law, European Community Law, National Law: Three Systems in Search of a Framework", in M. Koskenniemi (ed.), *International Law Aspects of the European Union* (The Hague, London, etc., 1998), at pp.169-196.

requirement to act, EU Member states will frequently act independently of any action by the EU/EC.

III The EU/EC Implementation Process

As the preceding discussion suggests, the sanctions implementation process in EU Member states is potentially convoluted. Leaving aside the various processes of national implementation – which fall outside the scope of this paper – key features of the EU/EC implementation process are as follows.

As has already been noted, the principle basis of competence relied upon by the EEC in implementing sanctions was Article 113 of the EEC Treaty[13] dealing with the common commercial policy. As described in paragraph 1 of this Article, the common commercial policy

> "shall be based on uniform principles, particularly in regard to changes in tariff rates, the conclusion of tariff and trade agreements, the achievement of uniformity in measures of liberalisation, export policy and measures to protect trade such as those to be taken in the event of dumping and subsidies."

Pursuant to Article 113(2) of the EEC Treaty, the *Commission* was required to submit proposals to the Council for the implementation of the common commercial policy. The Council was required to act on these proposals by a qualified majority.

In addition to Article 113 of the EEC Treaty, the Community was also competent to act in implementation of UN economic sanctions under other provisions of the EEC Treaty. Thus, for example, pursuant to Article 75 of the EEC Treaty, the Council was required to act, by qualified majority (in the period after 1966), on a proposal from the Commission in respect *inter alia* of "common rules applicable to international transport to or from the territory of a Member state or passing across the territory of one or more Member states".

Distinct from Article 113 of the EEC Treaty, and other similar provisions, was Article 224 of the EEC Treaty.[14] This provided:

13 Now Article 133 of the EC Treaty, as amended by the *Treaty of Amsterdam*.
14 Now renumbered as Article 297 of the EC Treaty pursuant to the *Treaty of Amsterdam*.

> "Member states shall consult each other with a view to taking together the steps needed to prevent the functioning of the common market being affected by measures which a Member state may be called upon to take in the event of serious internal disturbances affecting the maintenance of law and order, in the event of war, serious international tension constituting a threat of war, or in order to carry out obligations it has accepted for the purpose of maintaining peace and international security."

As will be apparent, this provision – perhaps the most obvious constitutional basis for giving effect within the Community to decisions of the Security Council imposing sanctions – left the matter of the measures to be taken to the *Member states*. The *Community* had no direct role to play.

For some years, no doubt with a view both to guarding their competence in such matters and because Article 224 recommended itself as the logical provision on which to base measures of economic sanction, the approach adopted by the Member states was to act pursuant to Article 224.[15] Article 224 was, for example, the principal basis on which the Member states acted in implementation of the UN sanctions imposed against Rhodesia.

This practice notwithstanding, for reasons, it would seem, of both competence and efficiency, the preferred legislative basis for Community sanctions measures shifted over time towards Article 113 of the EEC Treaty and other similar provisions. While the effect of this was to enable the *Community* to act, and perhaps to ensure a degree of harmonisation of sanctions across the Community Member states, the consequence of this was also to move sanctions implementation into the arena of "normal" Community trade measures. The result was to limit the scope for Community action to the areas in which the Community, as opposed to the Member states, was competent to act. While the adoption of measures in implementation of the common commercial policy fell clearly within the scope of Community competence, the imposition of restrictions in respect of, for example, the movement of capital, did not.

For the purpose of filling in this gap in Community competence, the Maastricht Treaty amended the EEC Treaty by adding Articles 73g and 228a. These pro-

15 See, for example, the discussion by P.J. Kuyper in "Sanctions Against Rhodesia: The EEC and the Implementation of General International Legal Rules", (1975) 12 *CMLRev* 231.

visions, now respectively renumbered by the *Treaty of Amsterdam* as Articles 60 and 301 of the EC Treaty, provide as follows:

> "*Article 60*
>
> 1. If, in the cases envisaged in Article 301, action by the Community is deemed necessary, the Council may, in accordance with the procedure provided for in Article 301, take the necessary urgent measures on the movement of capital and on payments as regards the third countries concerned.
>
> 2. Without prejudice to Article 297 and as long as the Council has not taken measures pursuant to paragraph 1, a Member state may, for serious political reasons and on grounds of urgency, take unilateral measures against a third country with regard to capital movements and payments. The Commission and the other Member states shall be informed of such measures by the date of their entry into force at the latest.
>
> The Council may, acting by a qualified majority on a proposal from the Commission, decide that the Member state concerned shall amend or abolish such measures. The President of the Council shall inform the European Parliament of any such decision taken by the Council."
>
> "*Article 301*
>
> Where it is provided, in a common position or in a joint action adopted according to the provisions of the Treaty on European Union relating to the common foreign and security policy, for an action by the Community to interrupt or to reduce, in part or completely, economic relations with one or more third countries, the Council shall take the necessary urgent measures. The Council shall act by a qualified majority on a proposal from the Commission."

As will be evident, Article 60 establishes a Community competence in respect of sanctions relating to capital movements and payments. Article 301 establishes a more general Community competence in respect of economic sanctions where this is required in a common position or in a joint action adopted in accordance with the CFSP provisions of the *TEU*.[16]

16 For further discussion of these matters see MacLeod, Hendry and Hyett, *The External Relations of the European Communities* (Oxford, 1996), at chapter 19.

Three aspects of the new arrangements warrant comment. First, on the basis of these measures, the Community now has a virtually all-embracing competence in the field of economic sanctions.[17] Second, as has already been observed, the Community's competence in this area is now tied fundamentally to the CFSP framework established by the *TEU*. Third, one consequence of this linkage of the Community's competence in respect of sanctions to the CFSP arrangements under the *TEU* has been to shift the initiative in respect of sanctions, albeit within certain constraints, back to the Member states. This follows from the fact that, under Article 13(1) and (2) of the *TEU*, it is the *European Council* that shall "define the principles of general guidance for the common foreign and security policy" and "decide on common strategies to be implemented by the Union in areas where the Member states have important interests in common".[18] Further, by reference to these principles, general guidelines and common strategies, it is the *Council* that "shall take the decisions necessary for defining and implementing the common foreign and security policy",[19] that "shall recommend common strategies ... and shall implement them, in particular by adopting joint actions and common positions"[20] and that "shall adopt joint actions".[21] The locus of competence in respect of sanctions implementation, at least in respect of the initiation of measures, has thus reverted to the Member states acting within the Council.[22]

---

17 Given that Article 301 refers to "economic relations", it has been argued that it could not be relied upon to impose an arms embargo or to sever amateur sporting or cultural ties. See MacLeod, Hendry and Hyett, *ibid*, at p.356.

18 The "European Council" is described in the following terms in Article 4, paragraph 2, of the *TEU*: "The European Council shall bring together the Heads of State or Government of the Member states and the President of the Commission. They shall be assisted by the Ministers for Foreign Affairs of the Member states and by a Member of the Commission. The European Council shall meet at least twice a year, under the chairmanship of the Head of State or Government of the Member state which holds the Presidency of the Council."

19 Article 13(3) of the *TEU*.

20 Article 13(3) of the *TEU*. Pursuant to Article 15 of the *TEU*, "[t]he Council shall adopt common positions. Common positions shall define the approach of the Union to a particular matter of a geographical or thematic nature. Member states shall ensure that their national policies conform to the common positions."

21 Article 14(1) of the *TEU*.

22 Given the changes brought about by the *TEU*, and the evident and abundant reliance on the CFSP provisions by the Council in the case of sanctions implementation, the question may be posed as to whether there is any residual competence to act in respect of sanctions under Article 133 of the EC Treaty. More particularly, are there any circumstances in which the Commission will retain an independent competence to initiate

IV Special Problems Arising From Implementation

Independent of any problems of a substantive nature to which sanctions measures may give rise, the broad framework of sanctions implementation at Community level itself raises certain difficulties. One of the most significant of these difficulties emerges from the fact that, in many cases, sanctions are implemented in parallel by both the EU/EC and the Member states in terms which often create overlapping obligations cast in slightly different terms. So, for example, in the case of sanctions against Yugoslavia based on Security Council Resolution 757 (1992), the EEC (as it then still was) adopted various measures, including Council Regulations 1432/92[23] and 990/93,[24] which prohibited exports to Serbia and Montenegro. In parallel to these measures, the United Kingdom enacted various Orders in Council, including the *Serbia and Montenegro (United Nations Sanctions) Order 1992*, which covered broadly the same ground.

While in most instances these overlapping measures did not give rise to practical difficulties, issues of legal certainty, particularly in the context of criminal prosecutions based on these measures, are apparent.[25] Questions have also arisen as to the respective obligations to act in implementation of sanctions by the Community and its Member states and, in the event that both act, the relationship between the two sets of measures.[26] In *R v. Searle and Others*,[27] for example, the English Court of Appeal concluded that, pursuant to Article

---

sanctions under Article 133 of the EC Treaty, or some similar provision, notwithstanding Articles 60 and 301 of the EC Treaty and the CFSP provisions of the TEU?

23 Council Regulation (EEC) No 1432/92 of 1 June 1992 prohibiting trade between the European Economic Community and the Republics of Serbia and Montenegro (OJ No L 151, 3.6.92, p.4); as amended by Council Regulation (EEC) No 2015/92 (OJ No L 205, 22.7.92, p.2) and Council Regulation (EEC) No 3534/92 (OJ No L 358, 8.12.92, p.16).

24 Council Regulation (EEC) No 990/93 of 26 April 1993 concerning trade between the European Economic Community and the Federal Republic of Yugoslavia (Serbia and Montenegro) (OJ No L 102, 28.4.93, p.14).

25 For a judicial consideration of the issues that arose as a result of the overlapping nature of these measures see the Judgment of the English Court of Appeal in *R. v. Searle and Others* [1995] 3 CMLR 196.

26 See, for example, Case C-124/95, *R. v. HM Treasury and Bank of England,* ex parte *Centro-Com Srl* [1997] 1 CMLR 555; also *R. v. HM Treasury*, ex parte *Centro-Com Srl* (English High Court) [1994] 1 CMLR 109.

27 *Supra*, n. 25.

234 of the EEC Treaty (as Article 307 of the EC Treaty was numbered prior to amendment by the *Treaty of Amsterdam*),

> "the U.K. had a duty to act directly to implement the United Nations Resolution. What was necessary to be done was a matter for the national authorities to decide. There is no question of the [UK] Order being incompatible with the [EC] Regulations or seeking to disapply them. Article 234 operates to prevent the Community from impeding the United Kingdom's performance of its obligations under the Charter."[28]

A more nuanced treatment of the effect of Article 234 was given by the European Court of Justice in Case C-124/95, *R. v. HM Treasury and Bank of England,* ex parte *Centro-Com Srl.*[29] In this case, the Court concluded *inter alia* that

a although EC Member states retained their competence in matters of foreign and security policy, this had to be exercised in a manner consistent with EC law. In particular, Member states could not treat national measures imposing sanctions as falling outside the scope of the common commercial policy on the ground that they had foreign and security objectives;[30]

b where Community rules implement the necessary measures of sanction, national measures covering the same ground cannot be justified;[31] and

c the purpose of Article 234 of the Treaty was to ensure that application of the Treaty did not affect the commitment of a Member state to respect the rights of non-Member states under an earlier agreement and to comply with its corresponding obligations. Where a prior agreement allowed, but did not require, the Member state to adopt a measure which appeared to be contrary to Community law, the Member state had to refrain from doing so.[32]

The relationship between national and Community measures implementing UN sanctions was also addressed by the European Court in Case C-177/95, *Ebony Maritime SA and Another v. Prefetto Della Provincia di Brindisi* concerning

---

28 At paragraph 59.
29 *Supra,* n. 26.
30 At paragraphs 24-30.
31 At paragraphs 44-49.
32 At paragraphs 56-60.

the obligation of Member states to implement penalties in respect of the breach of EC Regulations imposing sanctions.[33] In this case, the Court accepted that national measures prescribing a sanction in the event of a breach of a Community measure were not only permitted but, in some circumstances, were required in order to guarantee the effectiveness and application of Community law.

Other issues that arise from the broad framework of sanctions implementation at a Community level include the following:

a in contrast to national implementation regimes which generally identify a competent authority which is able to licence transactions that may otherwise appear to come within the scope of the sanctions, sanctions implementation at Community level has not generally included such arrangements with the result that it has been relatively inflexible. The absence of a Community licensing authority also poses potential difficulties in circumstances in which national and Community legislation operate in parallel and a licence is issued by the relevant national authority in respect of a transaction that may be covered by both sets of measures;

b notwithstanding the extension of Community competence in respect of sanctions as a result of Article 60 and 301 of the EC Treaty, questions remain about the scope of Community competence in such matters. By way of illustration of this matter, Article 301 is cast in terms of "economic relations" and would seem, therefore, to exclude competence on the part of the Community to adopt measures restricting activity such as sporting ties, cultural exchanges and diplomatic links, all of which have been the subject of Security Council sanctions in the past;[34]

c questions may also arise about the *vires* of EC Regulations giving effect to Security Council decisions in circumstances in which the Regulations go beyond the terms of the Resolution. The question, in such circumstances, is whether there are any constraints on the scope of legislative action by the Community purportedly in implementation of decisions of the Security Council as there are under the laws of at least some of the Member states.[35] By way of example, EEC Regulation 1432/92 prohibiting trade

33 [1997] 2 CMLR 24.

34 See, for example, Security Council Resolution 757 of 30 May 1992 imposing sanctions against the Federal Republic of Yugoslavia (Serbia and Montenegro).

35 See, for example, the *United Nations Act, 1946* of the United Kingdom.

between the EEC and Serbia and Montenegro in accordance with the requirements of Security Council Resolution 757 (1992) prohibited *inter alia* "the provision of non-financial services whose object or effect it is, directly or indirectly, to promote the economy of the Republics of Serbia and Montenegro".[36] An examination of Resolution 757 (1992), however, indicates no decision by the Security Council on the matter of non-financial services. In such circumstances, what, if any, are the legislative constraints on the Community?

V CONCLUDING OBSERVATIONS

In the light of the preceding discussion, a number of concluding observations may be expressed. First, the EU/EC is both an interface between the Security Council and EU Member states, acting as a conduit in the implementation of economic sanctions, and operates in parallel with Member state implementation. Second, in the light of recent jurisprudence of the European Court of Justice, it is, however, apparent that where Community rules implement the necessary measures of sanction, national measures covering the same ground will not be justified. Third, despite this attempt to introduce a measure of clarity into the sanctions implementation process, it seems likely, at least in some circumstances, that both the Community and the Member states will continue to act in tandem in implementation of Security Council decisions. This follows from the fact that Member states remain under a direct obligation, pursuant to the UN Charter, to carry out the decisions of the Security Council and that, notwithstanding recent amendments of and refinements in the Community implementation process, sanctions implementation at Community level is relatively less flexible and potentially more limited in scope than that at national level. In many cases, the effectiveness and application of Community law will also require the enactment of national enforcement measures. Fourth, sanctions implementation at Community level involves various elements – the adoption of common positions or joint actions by the Council pursuant to the CFSP provisions of the *TEU*; the adoption of legislative measures by the EC pursuant to some or other legal basis in the EC Treaty, generally likely to be Article 301; and, where necessary and appropriate, the adoption of distinct measures pursuant to the terms of the ECSC and/or EAEC Treaties.

36 Regulation 1432/92, *supra*, n. 23, at Article 1(d).

ENFORCING THE ECONOMIC EMBARGO AT SEA

Alfred H.A. Soons[■]

I INTRODUCTION

This contribution[1] examines some of the legal questions which have arisen as a result of actions taken at sea by States in attempts to enforce economic embargoes ordered by the UN Security Council under its powers as provided in Article 41 of the UN Charter.

The Security Council used its powers under Article 41 for the first time in 1966 against Southern Rhodesia[2] and again in 1977 against South Africa.[3] Although Article 41 was used only twice during the first forty-five years of the existence of the United Nations, in the subsequent ten years, since August 1990 (the Iraq/Kuwait Crisis) it has been used 12 times: against Iraq (1990-), the territory of the former Yugoslavia (1991-1996), Libya (1992-), Somalia (1992-), Liberia (1992-), the Federal Republic of Yugoslavia (Serbia and Montenegro; hereinafter referred to as FRY; later extended to the Bosnian Serbs) (1992-1996),

■ Professor of Public International Law, Utrecht University.

1 An earlier version of this paper was published as "A 'New' Exception to the Freedom of the High Seas: the Authority of the UN Security Council", in T.D. Gill and W.P. Heere (Eds), *Reflections on Principles and Practice of International Law* (Dordrecht, 2000), pp. 205-221.

2 Resolution 232 of 16 December 1966. The sanctions against Southern Rhodesia were lifted in December 1979.

3 Resolution 418 of 4 November 1977. The arms embargo against South Africa was terminated in May 1994.

V. Gowlland-Debbas (ed.), *United Nations Sanctions and International Law*, p. 307-324.

Haiti (1993-1994), Angola/UNITA (1993-), Rwanda (1994-), Sudan (1996-),[4] Sierra Leone (1997-), and again the FRY over the situation in Kosovo (1998-). As will be seen, the issue of maritime enforcement of these mandatory sanctions was specifically raised in only six out of the total of 14 cases: Southern Rhodesia, Iraq, the territory of the former Yugoslavia, FRY, Haiti, and Sierra Leone.

When the Security Council decides on mandatory sanctions under Article 41 of the UN Charter (hereafter referred to as embargoes), all Member states are under a duty to comply with such a decision (Art. 25 of the Charter). Embargoes can be limited to certain materials, such as arms and oil, or can be comprehensive, covering all economic activities, usually with certain exceptions for humanitarian purposes. Import from and/or export to the target State of such materials is then prohibited. Part of these materials, perhaps a large part, depending on the location of the target State, is normally transported by sea, even in the case of land-locked target States. Therefore, the Security Council resolutions imposing sanctions usually explicitly call upon States to prevent shipment of the prohibited materials by vessels flying their flag.

The supervision of the implementation of embargoes, as far as shipment of prohibited materials is concerned, is usually carried out in ports. This alone, however, has proved to be insufficient to prevent attempts to breach an embargo. Ships may already be underway when the embargo is established or may change destinations at sea; in some ports supervision is inadequate; fraud and corruption may occur. As a result, for a really effective embargo, additional supervision may be necessary at sea, in particular in areas near the ports of the target state, or, if the target state is land-locked, the ports in neighboring states used for transshipment. Such supervision at sea may involve interception of vessels and verification of whether they are proceeding to or from ports in the target state or transshipment points and whether they are carrying embargoed materials. If necessary, for the purpose of verification, the vessel may be boarded and inspected, and finally, if the vessel is found to be in contravention of the embargo, it may be diverted to another destination or arrested.[5] Apart from

---

4 The sanctions against Sudan were never actually implemented. They were restricted to air transportation.

5 Upon arrival in a port, the vessel and/or her cargo may be impounded and/or confiscated according to the law of the port state. These issues will not be discussed in this contribution.

such organized forms of maritime interdiction it is possible that in particular cases of suspected attempts to violate an embargo action may be required against the ship involved.

Such actions to enforce a UN embargo at sea raise a number of questions. May these actions be taken only by the flag state of the ship in question or with the consent of the flag state? What if the flag state is also the target state? If states other than the flag state may take such actions, which other states may do so? Which means may be employed for taking action? What measures may be taken if a foreign ship does not voluntarily cooperate for this purpose? With respect to which categories of foreign ships may such actions be taken? In which maritime jurisdictional zones may such enforcement action be undertaken? These questions will be discussed in the subsequent sections of this contribution. It should be stressed that this discussion does not pretend to be exhaustive: some issues can only be touched upon here and further analysis will be necessary before definitive conclusions can be drawn.

Before dealing with these questions on the basis of the practice of the Security Council and the Member states of the United Nations, in particular in the recent cases since 1990, first a brief review will be given of the Southern Rhodesia case, the Security Council's first experience with an embargo and its enforcement at sea.

II THE FIRST EXPERIENCE OF MARITIME ENFORCEMENT: SOUTHERN RHODESIA

In 1965, the white minority regime of Southern Rhodesia unilaterally declared independence for this British colony. The United Nations General Assembly and Security Council both immediately adopted resolutions strongly condemning the unilateral declaration of independence.[6] Shortly thereafter, on 20 November 1965, the Security Council adopted Resolution 217 calling for an embargo, particularly of arms and oil, against Southern Rhodesia. There can be no doubt that Resolution 217 was recommendatory in nature; it was not a mandatory

6 See J.E.S.Fawcett, "Security Council Resolutions on Rhodesia", (1965-1966) *BYIL* 103-121; J.W.Halderman, "Some Legal Aspects of Sanctions in the Rhodesian Case", (1968) 17 *ICLQ*, 672-705.

decision under Article 41 of the Charter.[7] This fact is important when reviewing the legal position of the initial actions for enforcement at sea of the recommended measures.

The United Kingdom in particular was asked to enforce these measures, and it wanted to prevent the transshipment of embargoed materials, in particular oil, to Southern Rhodesia through the Mozambique port of Beira. Mozambique was then a Portuguese colony and Portugal was not willing to implement the (non-binding) sanctions, invoking rights of access to the sea for land-locked countries. The United Kingdom government took the position that, under these circumstances, it could only act against foreign ships attempting to reach Beira for unloading cargo destined for Southern Rhodesia with the prior consent of the flag State.[8] Thus the British Navy, which had warships present in the area, did not actually prevent a Greek tanker, the *Joanna V*, suspected of carrying oil for Southern Rhodesia, from entering the port of Beira in early April 1966. It had previously requested the captain of the vessel not to enter the port, but the captain had refused to comply. Greece did not allow action against its ships unless authorized by the Security Council. Another Greek tanker, the *Manuela*, also suspected of carrying oil for Southern Rhodesia, was underway.[9]

There was then a debate in the Security Council in which differing opinions were expressed on whether or not the United Kingdom was allowed under Resolution 217 to take action against foreign ships without permission of the flag State. In the Security Council, the Soviet Union and the African members (Mali, Nigeria and Uganda) took the position that the United Kingdom was entitled to take action. Other members, notably the United Kingdom, the United States, France, and the Netherlands, took the position that it was not allowed to do so in the absence of a clear legal basis to override the jurisdiction of the flag state.[10] The United Kingdom had therefore presented a draft resolution explicitly authorizing the taking of action against foreign vessels. The final result of the debate was that on 9 April 1966 the Security Council adopted the draft

---

7 Fawcett, *supra*, n.6, p. 120. Halderman, *supra*, n.6, p. 685. V.Gowlland-Debbas, *Collective Responses to Illegal Acts in International Law. United Nations Action in the Question of Southern Rhodesia* (Dordrecht/London/Boston, 1990), p. 400.

8 SCOR, 21st Year, 1276th Meeting, pp. 5 *et seq.*, April 9, 1966.

9 See H.L. Cryer, "Legal Aspects of the Joanna V and Manuela Incidents, April 1966", (1966) *Australian Yearbook of International Law* 85-98.

10 Gowlland-Debbas, *supra*, n.7, pp. 402-406.

as Resolution 221, by 10 votes to none with 5 abstentions.[11] Paragraph 5 of Resolution 221 reads:

> "5. *Calls upon* the government of the United Kingdom to prevent, by the use of force if necessary, the arrival at Beira of vessels reasonably believed to be carrying oil destined for Southern Rhodesia and empowers the United Kingdom to arrest and detain the tanker known as the *Joanna V* upon her departure from Beira in the event her oil cargo is discharged there."

Thus the Security Council specifically authorized the United Kingdom to act. It took immediate action, and the *Manuela* was stopped and diverted by a British warship. The *Joanna V,* after leaving Beira some time later, was allowed to proceed after inspection because it had not unloaded the oil at the port.[12] It should be added that, by the time they were intercepted by the British Navy, both ships had lost their Greek flag, and the *Manuela* had even lost another nationality (Panamanian) that it had for a few days in between.[13] Consequently, they were ships without a flag, and the United Kingdom did not need the authorization in these cases after all.[14]

The debate on what exactly was the legal basis of Resolution 221 still continues.[15] It most probably was Chapter VII of the Charter, but it is not clear which article. According to some, it would have been Article 42,[16] which is very unlikely. Article 42 deals with measures involving the threat or use of force. The confusion here arises from the fact that the resolution uses the term "force" *("to prevent, by the use of force if necessary"),* but that was not, it is submitted, meant to constitute the armed force that Article 42 refers to. The "force" referred to in this resolution is to be regarded more like police force,

---

11 *Id.*, p. 403.

12 Consequently the question under which rules of *national* law the British warship would have been entitled to arrest and detain a foreign vessel in the high seas did not arise.

13 Cryer, *supra,* n.9, pp.85-86, 90.

14 Ships without a flag may be subjected to the jurisdiction of any State. *Cf.* Article 6, paragraph 2 of the 1958 Geneva Convention on the High Seas, reflecting customary international law.

15 See O. Scholz, *Die Durchsetzung von Zwangsmassnahmen nach Art. 41 der Satzung der Vereinten Nationen, insbesondere mit militaerischen Mitteln* (Frankfurt am Main, 1999), pp. 51-52.

16 E.g., J.Bayliss, "Remarks" in *Contemporary International Law Issues: Opportunities at a Time of Momentous Change* (Dordrecht/Boston/London, 1994), p.341. Cryer, *supra,* n.9, p. 93.

the means of coercion exercised on behalf of governments that has been used by warships when they enforce law against individuals. Perhaps the legal basis of the resolution was Article 41, but that would be remarkable because the embargo resolution itself (Resolution 217), which Resolution 221 was supposed to help enforce, was not based on Article 41: it was not a mandatory resolution. Resolution 221 may therefore be regarded as having been based on some implied power of the Security Council under Chapter VII of the Charter at that time.[17]

This unclear situation changed a few months later, however, when the Security Council on 16 December 1966 adopted Resolution 232, by which the embargo became mandatory under Article 41. This constituted the first time that this Charter provision was applied. Subsequently, Resolution 217 could be seen as supplementing this mandatory embargo, and both resolutions were based on Article 41.[18]

For the next ten years, the United Kingdom conducted its so-called *Beira Patrol* under both resolutions until the sanctions against Southern Rhodesia were lifted in 1979. It once used the threat to employ force, authorized by Resolution 221, in December 1967 against a French tanker, the *Artois*, which refused to stop. The British warship on patrol fired warning shots and the tanker indeed stopped.[19]

The question of the right of States other than the United Kingdom to take action in the high seas against foreign ships suspected of attempting to break the embargo against Southern Rhodesia was not raised during this period.[20]

17 Fawcett, *op.cit.* n.6, pp. 120-121. Gowlland-Debbas, *supra*,n.7, pp. 416-419.

18 It is interesting to note that the Security Council did not deem it necessary to issue a new authorization to the United Kingdom after the adoption of Resolutions 232 (and later 253) extending the scope of the embargo.

19 Gowlland-Debbas, *supra*, n.7, p.406.

20 Under SC Res. 217 the British Navy did not have the authority to take action against foreign ships which had violated the embargo after they had left the port of Beira. In such circumstances only the flag state could undertake proceedings, enforcing its national law.

III THE SUBSEQUENT PRACTICE OF THE UN SECURITY COUNCIL AND THE MEMBER STATES

A) *Requirement of authorization*

This was the experience up to 1990. The embargo against South Africa was not enforced at sea but only in ports: an organized operation off the coasts of South Africa apparently was not practicable and politically not acceptable. Then on 2 August 1990, Iraq invaded and occupied Kuwait. On 6 August, the Security Council adopted Resolution 661, containing a comprehensive mandatory embargo covering Iraq and Kuwait. On 12 August the United States and the United Kingdom governments, at the request of the Kuwaiti government, started to enforce the embargo against Iraqi vessels and, if necessary, foreign flag vessels in the Persian Gulf and Red Sea. The authority to do this was disputed by Iraq and several other states – notably Libya, Sudan, Yemen, and Jordan – and led to a debate in the Security Council. The United States and the United Kingdom claimed to be acting under Article 51 of the Charter, in collective self defense assisting Kuwait.[21] The essential difference with the Southern Rhodesia case indeed was that in the case of Iraq having invaded Kuwait a situation of armed conflict was in existence where the right of (collective) self defense could be exercised. In the exercise of this right a maritime blockade against Iraq could be instituted under the traditional law of maritime warfare.[22]

No attempt was made by the United States and the United Kingdom to base their actions on Resolution 661 itself. Should this be interpreted to the effect that the US and the UK were of the opinion that even a mandatory embargo in itself is not automatically a sufficient basis for enforcing it against foreign-flag ships? Eventually the Security Council decided that a specific authorization from it for these actions should be given (as being preferable over relying on

21 E. Lauterpacht *et. al.* (eds), *The Kuwait Crisis: Basic Documents*, vol. I (Cambridge, 1991), pp.245-248. See also C.C.Joyner, "Sanctions and Compliance in International Law: Reflections on the United Nations' Experience Against Iraq", (1991) 32 *Virginia Journal of International Law* 14.

22 H.B. Robertson, "Interdiction of Iraqi Maritime Commerce in the 1990-1991 Persian Gulf Conflict", (1991) *Ocean Development and International Law*, p. 295. On the U.S. activities see R.E. Morabito, "Maritime Interdiction: Evolution of a Strategy", (1991) *Ocean Development and International Law*, pp. 301-311.

Article 51)[23] and adopted Resolution 665 on 25 August 1990.[24] The operative paragraph 1 of that resolution reads as follows:

> "1. *Calls upon* those Member states cooperating with the government of Kuwait, which are deploying maritime forces to the area, to use such measures commensurate to the specific circumstances as may be necessary under the authority of the Security Council to halt all inward and outward maritime shipping in order to inspect and verify their cargoes and destinations and to ensure strict implementation of the provisions related to such shipping laid down in Resolution 661."

There has also been much discussion about the legal basis of this resolution.[25] Although the maritime interdiction activities carried out at that time were akin to a blockade in the sense of Article 42, that provision need not necessarily have been the legal basis. Although the reference to "measures" was generally understood to include the use of force as necessary, it is submitted that the basis of this resolution still was Article 41, an implied or inherent power of the Security Council to authorize states to enforce an embargo against foreign ships in order to enhance the effectiveness of the embargo. At the same time, the resolution left intact the possibility of using military force if necessary by coalition forces against Iraqi warships and other government ships, in the exercise of the right of (collective) self defense. After the ending of the hostilities in April 1991, Article 51 ceased to be a basis for enforcing the embargo. From then on, only Resolution 665 based on Article 41 remained.

The phrase used in Resolution 665 quoted above became standard language for cases where the Security Council wanted to explicitly authorize States to

23 Relying exclusively on Article 51 would mean that only States which had publicly announced that they were assisting Kuwait in the exercise of its right of self defense would be entitled to enforce the embargo against foreign-flag vessels.

24 The resolution was adopted by a vote of 13 to none, Cuba and Yemen abstaining.

25 R. Lavalle, "The Law of the United Nations and the Use of Force, under the Relevant Security Council Resolutions of 1990 and 1991, to Resolve the Persian Gulf Crisis", (1992) *Netherlands Yearbook of International Law* 16-30; T.D. Gill, "Legal and Some Political Limitations on the Power of the UN Security Council to Exercise its Enforcement Powers under Chapter VII of the Charter", (1995) *Netherlands Yearbook of International Law*, pp. 98-99; Bayliss, *supra*, n. 16, pp. 339-340; N. Schrijver, "The Use of Economic Sanctions by the UN Security Council: an International Law Perspective", in H.H.G. Post (ed.), *International Economic Law and Armed Conflict* (Dordrecht/London/Boston,1994), pp. 152-154; Robertson, *supra*, n.22, pp. 294-297. Scholz, *supra*, n.15, pp. 52-53.

enforce an embargo at sea. It was used subsequently in Resolutions 787 (16 November 1992)[26] and 820 (17 April 1993),[27] which cover the arms embargo against the territory of the former Yugoslavia and the embargo against the FRY, and in Resolutions 875 (16 October 1993)[28] and 917 (6 May 1994)[29] on Haiti. In these three cases, however, there was no situation of armed conflict between the enforcing States and the target state(s), and there was no alternative for Article 41 as the basis of the resolutions.

It should be noted that in the case of the territory of the former Yugoslavia a kind of maritime supervision had already started shortly after the arms embargo had been ordered by the Security Council, but before the adoption of Resolution 787. Warships from both the NATO and WEU Member states operating in the Adriatic Sea had begun to inspect ships flying their own flags, and in cases of foreign ships suspected of breaking the embargo notifications were sent to the flag state.[30]

---

26 Paragraph 12 of SC Res. 787 reads:
"Acting under Chapters VII and VIII of the Charter of the United Nations, *calls upon* States, acting nationally or through regional agencies or arrangements, to use such measures commensurate with the specific circumstances as may be necessary under the authority of the Security Council to halt all inward and outward maritime shipping in order to inspect and verify their cargoes and destinations and to ensure strict implementation of the provisions of resolutions 713(1991) and 757(1992);"

27 Paragraph 29 of SC Res. 820 reads:
"*Reaffirms* the authority of States acting under paragraph 12 of resolution 787(1992) to use such measures commensurate with the specific circumstances as may be necessary under the authority of the Security Council to enforce the present resolution and its other relevant resolutions, including in the territorial sea of the Federal Republic of Yugoslavia (Serbia and Montenegro);"

28 Paragraph 1 of SC Res. 875 was superseded by paragraph 10 of Reslution 917.

29 Paragraph 10 of SC Res. 917 reads:
"*Acting* also under Chapter VIII of the Charter of the United Nations, *calls upon* Member states cooperating with the legitimate government of Haiti, acting nationally or through regional agencies or arrangements, to use such measures commensurate with the specific circumstances as may be necessary under the authority of the Security Council to ensure strict implementation of the provisions of the present resolution and earlier relevant resolutions, and in particular to halt outward as well as inward maritime shipping as necessary in order to inspect and verify their cargoes and destinations and also to ensure that the Committee established pursuant to resolution 841(1993) is kept regularly informed;"

30 F. Pagani, "Le misure di interdizione navale in relazione alle sanzioni adottate dall'ONU", (1993) LXXVI *Rivista di Diritto Internazionale* 726-727.

In Resolution 1132 (8 October 1997) on Sierra Leone a different language was used. Paragraph 8 of that resolution reads as follows:

> "8. *Acting also* under Chapter VIII of the Charter of the United Nations, *authorizes* ECOWAS, cooperating with the democratically-elected Government of Sierra Leone, to ensure strict implementation of the provisions of this resolution relating to the supply of petroleum and petroleum products, and arms and related *matériel* of all types, including, where necessary and in conformity with applicable international standards, by halting inward maritime shipping in order to inspect and verify their cargoes and destinations, and *calls upon* all States to cooperate with ECOWAS in this regard;"

In this resolution the Security Council uses the term "authorize" rather than "call upon". No indication has been found for the reason for using this different terminology.

The practice of adopting specific authorizations, in combination with the persistent abstention of Member states to enforce mandatory embargoes against foreign ships at sea where the Security Council has not adopted specific authorizations – South Africa, Libya, Somalia,[31] Liberia, Angola/UNITA, Rwanda, and FRY (over Kosovo) – could lead to the conclusion that enforcement actions against foreign ships at sea, without the consent of the flag state, are only allowed with explicit Security Council authorization. In that view it can no longer be argued that a mandatory embargo in itself is sufficient for this purpose.

It should be added here that, apart from the actions by NATO and WEU during the period preceding the adoption of Resolution 787, also no instances are known of actions taken by states against foreign-flag ships with the consent of the flag state, or against their own ships, at sea to enforce an UN embargo in the cases where there were no specific authorizations from the Security Council for enforcement at sea.

31 Paragraph 16 of SC Res. 794 called upon all States to take all necessary measures to ensure the strict application of the arms embargo against Somalia, but did not explicitly refer to halting maritime traffic as in the other cases. When in February 1993 the Greek vessel *Bana I* with a cargo of arms destined for Somalia, via Mombasa, approached the area, the American authorities, when they became aware of the voyage, did not intervene but requested the assistance of the flag State and the port State. Pagani, *supra*, n.30, p. 722.

However, it is also possible to arrive at a somewhat different conclusion. An alternative view could be that the Security Council's practice of explicit authorization always involved cases of "organized" interdiction activities, where the initiative was taken by a coalition or organization of "willing and able" states and there was a need to make clear that the interdiction activities, including using means of coercion, were approved by (and under the final authority of) the Security Council. In this view the explicit authorization was not necessary from a strictly legal point of view, but was provided for political purposes: to enhance the legitimacy of the operation. The question then remains whether it would be lawful for a state to enforce a mandatory UN embargo against a foreign-flag vessel beyond the territorial sea without the consent of the flag state in a case where there is no explicit authorization in a prior Security Council resolution ("incidental" or *ad hoc* action as contrasted to the cases of "organized" interdiction operations, as conducted so far).[32]

It is possible to envisage a situation where a government is confronted with the situation that one of its warships would be in a position to take action against a foreign ship with respect to which there are reasonable grounds to believe that it is violating a mandatory embargo (but without there being a Security Council authorization to enforce). In such a case the government would obviously first ask permission of the flag state to act, and the flag state would be expected to give permission. But if it does not (for example, the flag state is also the target state) or if there is no time to ask permission it could be argued that the warship would not be acting unlawfully if it boarded and diverted the ship (and used means of coercion if necessary for that purpose) under the provisions of the UN Charter and general international law.[33] The government would have to report on its action immediately to the Security Council. It appears unlikely that the Security Council would subsequently disapprove of such action

32 It should be pointed out, however, that SC Res. 787 (Yugoslavia) and 917 (Haiti) explicitly authorize also States acting *nationally*. This undermines the alternative view presented here, and could be regarded as underlining the necessity of having an explicit prior authorization also in cases of *ad hoc* action as mentioned in this paragraph.

33 All Member states must comply with decisions of the Security Council, and since in this case the flag state is not complying the action of the intercepting warship may be regarded as a lawful countermeasure (alternatively, the principle of necessity might be invoked).

Finally it should be pointed out that the above discussion could be seen in a completely different light if a mandatory embargo ordered by the Security Council would constitute the basis for exercising universal jurisdiction by all Member states over sanction violators, comparable to for example the jurisdiction with respect to piracy in the high seas. In that case, all states would be entitled to act to enforce their national sanctions legislation against foreign ships also on the high seas even without prior explicit authorization by the Security Council. At present, however, that is not the situation.[34]

B) Entities authorized to enforce

The next question to be addressed is which states or other entities are authorized to enforce the embargo. Obviously the answer to this question may differ substantially according to the view adopted on the issue discussed in the preceding section. If the alternative view mentioned above would be adopted, all states would in principle be entitled to enforce the embargo. This section, however, will address the situation under the assumption that explicit prior authorization is indeed required.

It appears that not all Member states of the United Nations may automatically enforce an embargo under such circumstances. This issue is determined by the text of the authorizing resolution, and these resolutions have used different language.[35] For instance, the Southern Rhodesia resolution (221) refers only

34 In this connection, SC Res. 820 (on Yugoslavia) contained an interesting provision in paragraph 25, reading as follows:
"*Decides* that all States shall detain pending investigation all vessels (...) and cargoes found in their territories and suspected of having violated or being in violation of resolutions 713 (1991), 757 (1992), 787 (1992) or the present resolution, and that, upon a determination that they have been in violation, such vessels (...) shall be impounded and, where appropriate, they and their cargoes may be forfeited to the detaining State".
In the case of a vessel having been intercepted in the high seas and brought into port, the application of such measures (e.g., forfeiture) to such ship and cargo could in fact be regarded as an exercise of universal jurisdiction, on the express authorization of the Security Council. An example of such situation is provided by the case of the *Lido II*, a ship flying the Maltese flag, intercepted in the Adriatic Sea by a Dutch warship, boarded and brought into the port of Brindisi and subsequently forfeited by an Italian court. See Court of Justice of the European Communities, Case C-177/95, *Ebony Maritime SA and Loten Navigation Co. Ltd. v. Prefetto della Provincia di Brindisi and others*. Judgment of 27 February 1997. *European Court Reports* 1997, p. I-1111.

35 See also Article 48 of the UN Charter which stipulates that the Security Council decides which Member states should carry out its decisions.

to the United Kingdom. The Iraq resolution (665) refers to those Member states cooperating with the Government of Kuwait that are deploying maritime forces to the area. In the subsequent four cases, the Security Council's decisions on maritime enforcement were all taken also under Chapter VIII of the Charter. Resolutions 787 and 820 on the territory of the former Yugoslavia and the FRY refer to "states", not "Member states", acting nationally or through regional agencies or arrangements.[36] As a consequence, also non-UN Members were authorized. In Resolutions 875 and 917 on Haiti, there is again a reference to "Member states" cooperating with the legitimate government of Haiti, acting nationally or through regional agencies or arrangements.

In Resolution 1132 on Sierra Leone, only ECOWAS (the Economic Community of West African States) is authorized. This presumably means that actions may only be undertaken under the ECOWAS command structure established for this purpose (ECOMOG: the Military Observer Group of the Economic Community of West African States).[37] This would exclude individual actions of the various Member states of ECOWAS, not operating under this command.[38] It is not clear if the last phrase in paragraph 8 of this resolution, viz. "calling upon all States to cooperate with ECOWAS in this regard", was intended to involve other States in the interdiction activities, or merely to invite the assistance of flag states.

C) Means employed for enforcement

The various resolutions do not specifically address the question which means may or must be employed by the States (or organization) authorized to take

36 In practice, the interdiction activities were conducted under the auspices of WEU and NATO. For a brief overview see the (third and) *Final Report of the Security Council Committee established pursuant to resolution 724 (1991) concerning Yugoslavia* (UN Doc. S/1996/946 of 15 November 1996, Annex), p.32.

37 There is little information available on the actual enforcement at sea by ECOMOG. Apparently ECOMOG operations have been handicapped by lack of serviceable ships to effect the blockade by sea, but aircraft have contributed significantly. However, merchant ships have continued to enter Sierra Leone ports to discharge their cargoes in violation of the sanctions. See *First Report of the Economic Community of West African States Committee of Five on Sierra Leone to the Security Council made pursuant to resolution 1132 (1997)* (UN Doc. S/1997/895 of 17 November 1997, Appendix), pp. 13, 15-16. See also the *Report of the Security Council Committee established pursuant to resolution 1132 (1997) concerning Sierra Leone* (U.N. Doc. S/1998/1236 of 31 December 1998), which does not mention any maritime interdiction activities.

38 It is interesting to note that, in contrast to the resolutions concerning Yugoslavia and Haiti, SC Res. 1132 does not refer to States acting *nationally*.

action. There can be no doubt that warships and military aircraft may be employed, as these have traditionally been the means used by States for law enforcement at sea. However, there is no indication that other categories of government ships and aircraft normally used for law enforcement are excluded. The United States has employed Coast Guard vessels both in the Iraq/Kuwait Crisis and in the case of Haiti for embargo enforcement measures.[39] Italy used Coast Guard vessels in the Adriatic sea interdiction activities.

It would seem that the general requirements applicable to vessels and aircraft engaged in law enforcement activities at sea must be complied with. Consequently, any such vessels and aircraft must be clearly marked and identifiable as being on government service and authorized to that effect.[40]

D) Authorized measures

Another question concerns the measures that may be taken if a foreign ship does not cooperate voluntarily. Resolution 221 on Southern Rhodesia is the only case where there has been an explicit reference to the use of force. The phrase used in the cases of Iraq, the territory of the former Yugoslavia, FRY and Haiti is "*measures commensurate to the specific circumstances as may be necessary* under the authority of the Security Council" (emphasis added). Practice indicates that these include the whole range of actions mentioned above as necessary for effective enforcement of an embargo at sea: interception, and radio requests for information about destination and nature of cargo (which does not in itself affect flag state jurisdiction); boarding and inspection if necessary; and diversion or arrest, again if necessary.[41]

The use of force is also allowed as a last resort, according to the "rules of engagement" that have usually been coordinated among the states participating in the interdiction activities (as the enforcement of an embargo is generally referred to). Usually there is first a warning that force may be used. If that is not heeded, warning shots may be fired, and finally disabling shots, if at all possible without risk to human lives. The fact that the Security Council oversees

39 U.S. Coast Guard vessels have the status of warships. However, other states (e.g., the Netherlands) have not accorded this status to their Coast Guard vessels.

40 *Cf.* Article 110, paragraph 5 of the UN Convention on the Law of the Sea.

41 After an arrest and the bringing into port, ship and/or cargo can be seized and/or forfeited, as was done several times by Italian courts during the period of the embargo enforcement in the Adriatic Sea. See note 35 above. See also Pagani, *supra*, n.30.

these measures, according to the phrase "measures commensurate to the specific circumstances that may be necessary *under the authority of the Security Council*" (emphasis added) through reports that the Member states have to submit to the Security Council, gives the Security Council an opportunity to see if what actually is being done is adequate, commensurate to the specific circumstances in the various situations. Warning shots were fired in the Iraq/Kuwait Crisis on a number of occasions,[42] and at least once in the Adriatic Sea in enforcing the embargo against the FRY. No instances are known of disabling shots having been fired, but in some cases boarding parties on intercepted ships have had to employ physical force.[43]

As stated above, the "force" used in such cases may not necessarily be assimilated to the (military) use of force in international relations as intended in Article 2(4) of the UN Charter. It is submitted that such measures of coercion could better be compared with the civilian measures used by warships when they enforce national law at sea, usually referred to as "police force".[44] However, it is recognized that such a distinction may not be easily made within the context of the UN Charter and deserves further reflection.[45]

In the case of Sierra Leone, a different formulation was used. ECOWAS was authorized to ensure strict implementation of the embargo, "including, *where necessary and in conformity with applicable international standards*, by halting inward maritime shipping in order to inspect and verify their cargoes and destinations" (emphasis added). Here there is no reference to "measures", but to "applicable international standards" that have to be complied with. Two interpretations are possible here. One is that the applicable international standards include the same measures that have become international standards through

42 M. Voelckel, "Le navire et les situations internationales de crise. Rapport general", in *Société francaise pour le droit international. Colloque de Toulon. Le navire en droit international* (Paris,1992), p. 202; Scholz, *supra*, n.15, pp. 38-41; Bayliss, *supra*, n.16, p.342.

43 Scholz, *supra*, n.15, pp. 43-47.

44 This is without doubt the case when a warship takes action against a ship of its own nationality (and perhaps against ships without a nationality, depending on the national law of the warship). The same would apply if the action could be undertaken in the exercise of universal jurisdiction (see end of Section 3.1).

45 Note that Article 41 specifically refers to "measures not involving the use of *armed* force", which reinforces the view that coercion exercised for embargo enforcement is in principle more like police force.

the practice of implementing the previous Security Council resolutions on maritime enforcement of embargoes. Another interpretation would be that this phrase was intended to exclude measures of coercion against foreign ships (the use of force in last resort). The actual practice of ECOMOG does not shed any light on this question.[46]

E) Ships subject to enforcement

The next question to be addressed concerns with respect to which categories of foreign ships such actions may be taken. Here a distinction should be made between (1) ships flying the flag of the target State; and (2) other foreign-flag ships.[47] With respect to the latter category, practice indicates that only merchant ships and government ships used for commercial purposes may be subject to these measures under the present text of the resolutions. The French texts of the relevant resolutions are more explicit, by using the phrases *"tous les navires marchands"* and *"tout traffic maritime commercial"*. Ships entitled to sovereign immunity, such as government ships exclusively used for non-commercial purposes and warships, are not subject to these measures.

As far as ships flying the flag of the target State are concerned, it would seem logical that in principle they would all, irrespective of their status, be subject to enforcement measures.

F) Maritime areas covered by authorization

The final question to be raised concerns in which maritime jurisdictional zones the measures may be taken. But first it is important to note here that the relevant resolutions all in a somewhat indirect way seem to limit the area where the interdiction operations may be undertaken: by referring to halting "inward and outward maritime traffic" supposedly these areas must be located somewhere in the vicinity of the target State. Depending on the circumstances this can still be a vast area. However, this could be interpreted as excluding action against a ship on the other side of the world.

It is clear that measures may in any case be taken in all sea areas not subject to the sovereignty of a coastal State, i.e. the areas beyond the territorial sea, including the EEZ of any coastal State, and the high seas proper. These are the areas where the freedom of navigation operates.

---

46 See the Reports mentioned in note 37 above.
47 And ships without a nationality.

From the practice of the Security Council it follows that they are not permitted in the territorial sea of the target State unless they have been explicitly authorized by the Security Council. An example is Resolution 820 on the FRY, which in its paragraph 29 explicitly permits the maritime forces there to enforce the embargo in the territorial sea of Serbia and Montenegro.[48] Previous to the adoption of this resolution this was not allowed, and enforcement of the arms embargo in the territorial sea of Slovenia and Croatia remained permissible only with the consent of the coastal state. In the case of Iraq, there has not been such authorization and no enforcement action has been undertaken in its territorial sea.[49] In the case of Haiti, however, US vessels also operated within the territorial sea of Haiti by virtue of permission from the legitimate government of Haiti.[50] A similar situation could apply to Sierra Leone.

In the territorial sea of a third state, measures can be taken only with the explicit permission of the coastal state. In the Iraq/Kuwait Crisis, agreements were made by the coalition forces with most coastal states in the Gulf area that allowed the forces employed there to actually enforce the embargo in their territorial seas.[51] In the case of the Yugoslavian embargo, in the Adriatic Sea, Albania expressly consented to the exercise of enforcement actions in its territorial sea.[52]

A totally different matter, of course, is the enforcement of a UN embargo against foreign ships in passage in the territorial sea by the coastal state itself. It would seem beyond doubt that the coastal state would not be acting unlawfully if it took action against foreign ships violating the embargo while they are in in-

48 See note 27 above. Paragraph 29 should be seen in the light of the preceding paragraph 28, which prohibited all commercial maritime traffic from entering the territorial sea of the FRY.

49 It could be argued that until the hostilities ended in April 1991 enforcement action could be undertaken in the territorial sea of Iraq by virtue of the law of armed conflict. See L.E. Fielding, "Maritime Interception: Centerpiece of Economic Sanctions in the New World Order", (1993) *Louisiana Law Review*, pp. 1223-1224.

50 Other States (e.g., the Netherlands) did not operate in the territorial sea of Haiti.

51 Except Iran. Voelckel, *supra*, n. 42, p. 197. Additional problems were caused in this region by disputed claims to territorial sea areas by some of the coastal States.

52 Pagani, *supra*, n.30, p. 744.

nocent passage in its territorial sea or in transit passage through an international strait,[53] even if this would occur in locations very distant from the target state.

IV CONCLUSION

In all cases mentioned above of actual maritime enforcement of UN embargoes (except in the case of Sierra Leone), the resolution authorizing maritime enforcement was adopted after the establishment of the mandatory sanctions in preceding resolutions. This was the result of the initial uncertainty about the way in which the embargoes were to be enforced, in particular the actual need for enforcement at sea and the means that would be available from states able and willing to act.

However, based upon the experience so far, it should now be possible to include such authorization immediately in the resolution imposing sanctions (as was done in the case of Sierra Leone). Even in cases where there is no immediate need seen for concerted action by states to organize maritime interdiction activities it might be helpful if the authority to act is given in advance to individual states or collectivities of states confronted with a situation of attempted violation of an embargo where they happen to have the maritime enforcement means at their disposal in the area. Perhaps some standard phrase to this effect could be included in all future Security Council resolutions establishing an embargo. Obviously, a duty to report to the Security Council on actions taken would be an important element of such standard provision.

53 *Cf.* Article 27 of the UN Convention on the Law of the Sea, which does not prohibit such actions. They would also not be incompatible with Article 24, stipulating that innocent passage may not be hampered by the coastal State. This issue was briefly discussed during the Third UN Conference on the Law of the Sea (Second Committee).

CONSULTATION UNDER ARTICLE 50 OF THE UNITED NATIONS CHARTER: THE EXPERIENCE OF THE MIDDLE EAST

Bisher H. Al-Khasawneh[▪]

The conclusion of the Cold War and the emergence of a unipolar world has led to the reinvigoration of the United Nations' Security Council and extensive usage and action by the Council based on Chapter VII of the Charter. After the Iraqi invasion of Kuwait on 2 August 1990, it has been correctly stated that powers of a coercive nature vested by the Charter in the Security Council were rediscovered after seeming for decades a dead letter owing to the deadlock that overshadowed the deliberations of the Council and hindered its action during the Cold War era as a result of the extensive threat or actual use of the veto.[1] The early 1990's marked the resurrection of an active and effective Security Council. In the 45 years of the Council's existence prior to the Iraqi invasion of Kuwait in 1990, the Council passed 659 resolutions. In the last nine years since the invasion, the Security Council has passed over 400 resolutions. What is more significant for the purpose of this brief study, is that the Security Council has used mandatory sanctions since then in relation to at least half a dozen countries.[2]

▪ Former Legal Advisor, Jordanian Ministry of Foreign Affairs; currently attached to the Jordanian Embassy in Egypt.

1 See Dapo Akande, "The International Court of Justice and the Security Council; Is there Room for Judicial Control of the Decisions of the Political Organs of the United Nations", (1997) 46 *ICLQ*, p. 309

2 Prior to the Iraqi invasion of Kuwait in 1990 the Security Council had ordered mandatory sanctions only twice (comprehensive sanctions against Rhodesia and an arms embargo against South Africa). After the Iraqi invasion of Kuwait the Council imposed comprehensive sanctions on Iraq (Res. 661(1990)). Comprehensive sanctions were also ordered by the Council on the Federal Republic of Yugoslavia (Serbia and Montenegro)

V. Gowlland-Debbas (ed.), *United Nations Sanctions and International Law*, p. 325-334.

There is a consensus that resolutions passed by the Security Council under Chapter VII are mandatory in nature. Hence, States are obliged to comply, respect and act in accordance with such resolutions.[3] Since the Security Council was reactivated at the inception of the 1990's and as it has been resorting extensively to the weapon of imposing mandatory sanctions, which states are legally bound to carry out, it is very significant to explore the means and avenues available for states that are affected by the enforcement and compliance with sanctions imposed by the Security Council on a particular state. This study aims at briefly examining the means available within the Charter of the United Nations for such states. The focus of this brief study will be the case of sanctions ordered by the Council against Iraq in order to demonstrate how the enforcement of such sanctions affected certain countries severely and the means available for such countries to seek redress.

The imposition of sanctions against Iraq and Kuwait in 1990 marked a systematic and broader application of Article 50.[4] Twenty-three countries invoked Article 50 after the Security Council adopted resolution 661 imposing sanctions

---

(Res.757 (1992) and 787(1992) and 820(1993)), Haiti (Res.841 (1993), 861(1993), 873(1993) and 917(1994)), parts of the Republic of Bosnia and Herzegovina controlled Bosnian Serbs (Res.820(1993) and 942(1994)) and the then Areas protected by the United Nations in the Republic of Croatia (Res. 820(1993)). Partial sanctions were also imposed on Libya (Res.748 (1992) and 883(1993)) and the Sudan (Res. 1054(1996) and 1070(1996)). Partial sanctions were also imposed on the territories of Angola controlled by the UNITA rebel movement (Res. 864(1993)). Arms embargoes were ordered in respect of Liberia (Res. 788(1992)), Somalia (Res. 733(1992)), Rwanda (Res. 918(1994), 1011(1995)) and the whole of the territory of the Former Yugoslavia (Res. 713(1991)).

3 There is a general debate over the nature and binding quality of resolutions passed and adopted by the Security Council outside the scope of Chapter VII. The arguments regarding such resolutions are that they are, on one hand, non binding as a result of not have been adopted under Chapter VII and on the other that, on the basis of Article 25 of the Charter, all Security Council resolutions are binding. Article 25 stipulates that "The members of the United Nations agree to accept and carry out the decisions of the Security Council in accordance with the present Charter". According to this reading, the proponents of the view that all Council decisions carry and command the same legal force, argue that Art 25 made no distinction whatsoever between decisions based on Chapter VII and other Council decisions and resolution. Hence, they contend that all Security Council Resolutions are equally binding on Member states.

4 Prior to the Gulf Crisis, Article 50 had only been applied in connection with sanctions imposed against Rhodesia, as the only other instance at which sanctions were ordered was the imposition of an arms embargo against South Africa. The imposition of the arms embargo did not involve the invocation by countries of Article 50.

against Iraq and Kuwait.[5] These applications by affected *bona fide* third countries are entirely consistent with the objective of the measures taken by the Security Council under Article 41 of Chapter VII. There is a consensus on the fact that the measures adopted by the Security Council under Article 41 aim at restoring international peace and security, and when such measures manifest themselves in the form of comprehensive economic sanctions against a particular country, it must be clearly understood that they are intended to be coercive and directed against the country that has committed a threat to peace, breach of peace or act of aggression, and they should be designed to bring about a return of legality. There could also be, arguably, a punitive element to sanctions and a protective one sometimes.[6] In all cases, though, sanctions are not designed to harm countries other than the one that has committed a threat to peace, breach of peace, or act of aggression as determined by the Security Council. However, it is clear that when countries act in accordance with Security Council resolutions adopted under Chapter VII by imposing sanctions against a particular state, such countries may be affected and face special economic problems. Accordingly, Article 50 was designed to bring about a mechanism by which such countries would have a right to consult the Council with regard to finding a solution to these problems.

---

5 Bangladesh (9/10/1990), Botswana (27/9/1990), Bulgaria (12/9/1990), Czechoslovakia (13/9/1990), India (5/9/1990), Jordan (20/8/1990), Lebanon (31/8/1990), Mauritania (24/9/1990), Pakistan (14/9/1990), Palestine (16/10/1990), Philippines (5/9/1990), Poland (21/9/1990), Romania (27/8/1990), Seychelles (27/8/1990), Sri Lanka (5/9/1990), Sudan (6/11/1990), Tunisia (24/8/1990), Uruguay (13/9/1990), Vietnam (21/9/1990), Yemen (9/9/1990) and Yugoslavia (24/8/1990).

6 See D. Bethlehem, *The Kuwait Crisis: Sanctions and their Economic Consequences*, Part 1 (Cambridge, 1993), p. XXXV. It is argued that sanctions are primarily designed to bring about a return to legality. Daniel Bethlehem correctly argues that in the case of Iraq, there was a punitive element to sanctions that became more evident after the termination of hostilities and the adoption of the cease fire resolution 687. That resolution introduced a continuation of the sanctions imposed against Iraq until Iraq meets certain disarmament requirements that were laid out in that resolution along with other obligations that were of a punitive nature. Bethlehem also makes the point that resolution 661 and its imposition of sanctions against Iraq and Kuwait masked a fundamental difference in the objectives for imposing the sanctions. He correctly states that as far as Iraq was concerned, the sanctions were coercive in nature and designed to deter Iraq, while in the case of Kuwait the very same measure was protective aiming at guaranteeing that the Iraqi Government would not be able to have access to the Kuwaiti funds and assets.

The drafters of the United Nations' Charter foresaw the potential problems arising for countries due to their compliance and enforcement of sanctions imposed by the Security Council under Chapter VII. Thus, Article 50 was included in the United Nations' Charter as a safeguard and as a means of redress for those countries. Article 50 states that "If preventive or enforcement measures against any state are taken by the Security Council, any other state, whether a member of the United Nations or not, which finds itself confronted with special economic problems arising from the carrying out of those measures shall have a right to consult the Security Council with regard to the solution of those problems". It is clearly understood that Article 50 is restricted in clear terms to measures taken by the Security Council under Chapter VII.[7] Article 50 confers a right to consult with the Security Council not only to Member states but also non-members of the United Nations. The logic for such an extension of the right to consult is a manifestation of the reality that non-members must not become innocent victims of United Nations measures, in addition to inducing non-Member states to voluntarily participate in United Nations measures as did the Federal Republic of Germany in the case of sanctions imposed against Rhodesia and as did Switzerland and the Republic of Korea in the case of sanctions imposed on Iraq.[8]

A reading of Article 50 clearly suggests that countries faced with special economic problems emanating from their compliance with Security Council imposed sanctions have a right to *consult* the Council. This right to consult precludes, indeed, the country against which sanctions were being taken. It has been suggested that, on the basis of the reading of Article 50 and its legislative history, it could be conclusively asserted that affected states merely have a right to consult the Council without any corresponding duty on the part of the Security Council to provide a specific remedy.[9] However, it has been maintained that, in theory at least, it can be adduced that the Council has the competence under Article 50 to exempt certain states who do suffer from serious economic problems as a result of enforcing and applying sanctions against a state from their duty to participate in the implementation and enforcement of sanctions. The competence of the Council to grant such an exemption, it was maintained,

7 See comments on Art 50 by Prof. Brun-Otto Bryde in B. Simma (ed.), *The Charter of The United Nations: A Commentary* (Oxford, 1994), pp. 659-661

8 *Ibid.*

9 *Ibid.*

emanates from "Its monopoly right to lift sanctions".[10] It was suggested that another way by which the Security Council may choose to assist a country applying for consultations under Article 50 was through ordering payments to such a country/countries out of United Nations funds.[11] A third course of action for the Council would be to restrict itself to calling upon other United Nations members and specialised agencies to assist countries invoking Article 50.

The practice of the Security Council clearly suggests that the course of action adopted by the Council when certain countries invoke Article 50 has been restricted to calls of assistance made by the Council to other countries and specialised agencies. In the case of sanctions imposed against Iraq by resolution 661, the Security Council entrusted the committee established by the resolution with the task of assessing requests for assistance made under Article 50.[12] The recommendations of this committee regarding such requests were, with the exception of that concerning Jordan, formulated in the same terms. The operative paragraphs of each did provide that the Sanctions Committee

> "3. *Appeals* to all states on an urgent basis to provide immediate technical, financial and material assistance... to mitigate the adverse impact on its economy of the application ... of sanctions pursuant to resolution 661(1990)
> 4. *Invites* the competent organs and specialised agencies of the United Nations system, including the international financial institutions and the regional development banks, to review their programme of assistance to...with a view of alleviating its special economic problems arising from the application of sanctions against Iraq pursuant to Security Council resolution 661(1990).
> 5. *Requests* the Secretary General, on a regular basis, to seek information from states and the concerned organs and agencies of the United Nations system on action taken to alleviate the special economic problems of... and to report thereon to the Security Council."[13]

---

10 *Ibid.*, p. 660

11 See Advisory Opinion on *Certain Expenses of the United Nations*, ICJ Reports, 1962, pp. 151, 196. It must be noted however that from a practical point of view it is inconceivable that the Security Council would do so. Additionally, it is common knowledge that the United Nations has not been in a financial position to enable it to follow such a course of action.

12 See SC Res. 669 (1990)

13 Quoted in Bethlehem, *supra*, n.6, p. XIV. In the Case of Jordan, the Sanctions Committee made the following recommendation on 18 September 1990 (UN Doc. S/21786): "4. *Requests* the Secretary General to undertake expeditiously, in co-operation with the Government of Jordan, a full with suggestions for appropriate remedies to the problems

Despite these recommendations by the Sanctions Committee, including the ones relating to Jordan, that were by all counts much more elaborate, sympathetic and comprehensive than other recommendations, significant assistance was not forthcoming. Twenty-one countries, including Jordan dispatched a joint letter to the President of the Security Council on 25 March 1991.[14] The letter was formulated in the following terms

> "4. The problems affecting these countries persist, and in certain respects have been aggravated, while the appeals launched pursuant to the recommendations of the Security Council Committee and addressed to all concerned by the Secretary General, have not evoked response commensurate with the urgent needs of the affected countries.
> 5. Assistance to the affected countries in accordance with Article 50 of the Charter would reaffirm international solidarity and unity.
> 6. The 21 States launch a collective appeal, particularly to all donor States, to respond urgently and effectively in providing assistance to the affected countries by allocating additional financial resources both through bilateral channels and by supporting the actions of the competent organs and specialised agencies of the United Nations system.
> 7. The 21 States most seriously affected believe that it is essential that all Member states, as well as the United Nations, the specialised agencies and other international organizations of the United Nations system, take all appropriate action to cooperate with them in the field of trade, employment, economic assistance and other areas, in order to alleviate the difficult economic problems facing them.

---

resulting from measures assessment has undertaken to comply with resolution 661(1990), including especially the question of supply of petroleum and its derivatives

5. *Appeals,* based on this assessment, to all States on an urgent basis, to provide immediate technical, financial, and material assistance to Jordan to mitigate the consequences of the difficulties faced by Jordan as a result of this crisis.

6. *Requests* the Secretary General to develop methods for the purpose of receiving information from States about the contribution which they have or are prepared to make to alleviate the longer term hardships confronting Jordan as a result of its application of economic sanctions against Iraq.

7. *Calls upon* the Agencies, organs, organizations and bodies of the United Nations system to intensify their programmes of assistance in response to the pressing needs of Jordan and to report to the Secretary General what they are doing or are prepared to do.

8. *Requests* the Secretary General to appoint a special representative to co-ordinate assistance being given to Jordan by agencies in the United Nations system, humanitarian organizations and States which are prepared to participate in this effort, taking into account bilateral assistance being provided by States to Jordan".

14 See Security Council document S/22382, 25 March 1991.

> 8. The affected Countries believe that, given the magnitude of the difficulties they face, the Security Council should give renewed attention to these problems with a view to finding quick and effective solutions."

It is evident from this letter that all twenty-one states felt that the recommendations of the Sanctions Committee fell short of their needs and expectations and failed to provide remedies that significantly mitigated their special economic problems. This remained the general feeling of most states that applied for consultations under Article 50. The response of the Security Council in establishing a Sanctions Committee by resolution 661 and entrusting it to recommend means by which countries that are suffering from special economic problems as a result of applying and enforcing sanctions can mitigate these problems, fell short of providing a tangible remedy for such countries. It further supports the proposition that the right to consult with the Council under Article 50 does not trigger a corresponding duty by the Security Council to provide a specific remedy and consolidates the interpretation that a right to consult is not tantamount to a right to assistance. The wording of the recommendations of the Committee concerning applications made by states to consult under article 50 does not suggest or connote any commanding or binding language for states, specialised agencies and other organizations within the United Nations system to provide assistance. The recommendations were always cast in terms of *invites, appeals, calls upon* etc. Furthermore, the recommendations were never part of an explicit Security Council Resolution and were merely recommendations of a Committee created by the Council. This further confirms the view suggesting that the Council is under no legal duty whatsoever to provide specific remedies for countries invoking Article 50.

It must be mentioned at this point that Jordan was granted an exemption by the Council to continue its importation of petroleum supplies from Iraq. This grant that was given to Jordan, albeit conditional, supports the proposition that was made earlier regarding the competence of the Security Council to exempt a state or states partially or fully from applying and enforcing sanctions against a certain country that is adduced from the monopoly of the Council to impose and lift sanctions.[15]

---

15 See *supra*, n. 10.

Another interesting yet complicated issue regarding Article 50, is that of the type of economic losses that are incurred by states. Would states invoking Article 50 have a right to consult regarding economic losses that emanate directly from their participation in the enforcement and application of sanctions? In other words, is the right to consult restricted to economic losses that are a direct consequence of the imposition of sanctions, such as the loss of export markets, frustration of contracts etc? Or would states invoking Article 50 be able to include losses incurred owing to the perpetration of a threat to peace, breach of peace, or an act of aggression that in turn triggered the imposition of sanctions such as the increase in oil prices, loss of remittances of workers, loss of debts etc? Answering these questions requires a careful reading of Article 50. This reading would suggest that consultations must be restricted to losses emanating from "the carrying out of preventive and enforcement measures", which introduces a concept of causation into Article 50.[16] Yet an examination of the extensive state practice during the Kuwait crisis suggests that states invoking Article 50 tend to apply for consultations on the basis of both the losses that emanate directly from their participation in the preventive and enforcement measures, and those incurred as a result of the outbreak of hostilities. The recommendations of the Sanctions Committee seem to address both types of losses.[17]

However, this debate regarding the scope of losses that are included within the ambit of Article 50 remains academic. Losses that are directly incurred by states from their participation in the enforcement of sanctions have not, so far, been adequately met. States invoking Article 50 during the Kuwait crisis were practically never compensated either fully or significantly, for the losses incurred by them due to their participation in the application and enforcement of sanctions, needless to mention other broader losses. Additionally, the establishment by the Security Council of a Compensation Commission in the case of the Kuwait crisis would suggest that losses incurred as a result of the invasion itself

16 See D. Bethlehem, *supra*, n.6, p. XIIV.

17 *Ibid.* In the collection edited by Daniel Bethlehem, it is evident that states invoking Article 50 included in their application to consult under that article both direct and indirect losses. It is interesting to note that the recommendations of the Sanctions Committee did sometimes address economic difficulties that are not directly related to the participation of a state invoking Article 50 in the application and enforcement of the measures. The recommendations of the Committee regarding Jordan support this contention. For full text of the Committee's recommendations regarding Jordan, see Bethlehem, *supra*, n.6., p. 730 *et seq.*

are not within the limits of Article 50 but are rather addressed through this Commission. Practice is still undeveloped, and limited in this regard to the Kuwait crisis. Only future practice will determine the scope of losses to which Article 50 applies.

Article 50 consultations were used extensively for the first time by many states during the Kuwait crisis. The response of the Security Council to the applications for consultation under Article 50 by states facing special economic problems from carrying out preventive and enforcement measures prescribed by the Council in this crisis did not seem to have mitigated the problems of those countries. The Council predominantly restricted itself to asking Member states, specialised agencies and other organizations within the United Nations system to support countries facing special economic problems. The Security Council did not adopt any resolution to the effect of considering the losses incurred by states applying for consultation under Article 50 as an expense of the organization to be covered by the United Nations. Nor did the Security Council resort to absolving a country from applying and enforcing sanctions with the exception of allowing Jordan to continue importing petroleum from Iraq until it found an alternative. This militates in favour of the dominant point of view that suggests that the right to consult does not trigger a corresponding duty by the Security Council to provide an adequate remedy. Having said that, one must not lose focus of the reality that for economic sanctions to work, they have to receive the genuine support of the majority of states. Any prospects for future success for the imposition of sanctions is going to be influenced by the effectiveness of the solutions found for the hardships that were suffered by states during the Kuwait crisis. As the response to those problems was not all too effective, serious and detailed consideration should be given to providing adequate relief for countries facing special economic problems and invoking Article 50. Only through devising effective relief for those countries, would they willingly and fully participate in applying and enforcing Security Council imposed sanctions in the future.

THE POSITION OF STATES SPECIALLY AFFECTED BY SANCTIONS IN THE MEANING OF ARTICLE 50 OF THE UNITED NATIONS CHARTER – THE EXPERIENCE OF CENTRAL AND EASTERN EUROPE

Wladyslaw Czapliñski▪

I GENERAL PROBLEMS

The regulation concerning the effects of sanctions upon third states was present from the very beginning of the drafting of the Charter. It was included into the Dumbarton Oaks draft (Chapter VIII Part B No.11). During the San Francisco Conference the wording of this article was modified in order to make clear that no state-target of the sanctions could invoke any right formulated in Art. 50. The scope of these rights is in no way clear. From the wording of the provision it can be concluded that economic difficulties which justify the addressing by the specific state to the Security Council need not necessarily be directly connected with the sanctions, contrary to the formula used in Art. 49 of the Charter which obligates the states to cooperate in the implementation of measures decided by the Council. The rights amount exclusively to a consultation that excludes any obligation on the part of the Security Council except to advise on how to cope with the situation; in particular the wording of the provision excludes *prima facie* a duty to grant *any form* of economic assistance (although it is not forbidden).[1] The expenses granted should therefore be

▪ Titular Professor of International Law, Institute of Law Studies, Polish Academy of Sciences.

1 Commentators are unanimous that once granted the expenses of this kind will constitute "expenses of the UN" within the meaning of the Advisory Opinion on *Certain Expenses of the United Nations (Article 17, paragraph 2, of the Charter)*", ICJ Reports, 1962, p. 150 ff – see e.g. Bryde, "Article 50", in B.Simma (ed.), *Charta der Vereinten Nationen Kommentar* (München, 1991), p. 614; P.M. Eisemann, "Article 50", in J.P.Cot et A.

V. Gowlland-Debbas (ed.), *United Nations Sanctions and International Law,* p. 335-347.

covered from the financial sources of the UN. It cannot also be excluded that the Security Council, after having considered the circumstances of the case, will release the specific state from its duty to implement the sanctions. The implementation of Art. 50 is therefore subjected to a political decision and political configuration within the Council.

The rights under art.50 are not limited to the Member states of the UN, but are granted also to the non-Members. This is a logical consequence of Art. 2(6) – if such states can be involved in all activities aimed at the preservation of world peace and international security, including the policy of obeying sanctions, they must also obtain a right to remedies which enable them to cope with negative effects of the possible sanctions. At the present stage, the membership of the UN is practically universal, and it is not probable that any non-Member state might invoke these rights; however, in the past, several non-Members (both German States and Switzerland) participated in the sanctions on a voluntary basis, and there was no reason to exclude them.

II THE PRACTICE OF ARTICLE 50 BEFORE 1990

The practice of application of Art. 50 has not been very rich. In fact, it was invoked in connection with the economic sanctions against Rhodesia by nearly all neighbouring states (except South Africa). Security Council Resolution 253 (1968) which imposed a general trade embargo on Southern Rhodesia contained also a provision inviting the Members of the UN, Specialised Agencies and other agencies of the UN system to assist in resolving Zambia's economic difficulties. However, the following resolutions of the Council avoided any reference to Art. 50 of the Charter, and even situated the issue within Art. 49.[2] Similar pretensions were made by other States of the region – Portugal (on behalf of its province of Mozambique), Botswana and Malawi. Also in those cases, relevant Security Council resolutions did not invoke Art. 50, instead making an appeal to all the Member states to grant economic, financial, technical and

---

Pellet, *Charte des Nations Unies. Commentaire article par article* (Paris, 1991), pp. 763-764.

2 The Security Council sent a special mission to Zambia in order to evaluate the needs of the country – SC Res.327(1973) of 2 February 1973; in the same resolution the Council congratulated the government of Zambia for its decision to break all economic and commercial relations with Southern Rhodesia.

substantive aid to the states concerned because of their difficulties arising from the implementation of decisions of the Security Council aimed against an illegal regime in Southern Rhodesia.[3]

The same conclusion can be drawn from the action brought by Lesotho in connection with the measures taken against her by the Republic of South Africa because of the implementation of the UN policy of non-recognition of Transkei. The Security Council in a series of resolutions asked the Member states to grant an aid to Lesotho recognizing that her politics constituted an important contribution to the realization of the UN aims in Southern Africa.[4]

The appeals by the Security Council were not specially successful, and they were several times repeated by the UN agencies including the General Assembly. The response of the international community was however insufficient.

III THE CONTEMPORARY PRACTICE IN THE CASES OF IRAQ AND YUGOSLAVIA – ISSUES OF FACT

The issue of possible detrimental effects of the sanctions was considered during the Gulf War in respect of the specific economic situation of Jordan. The Jordanian economy depended to a large extent upon trade with Iraq, and the embargo upon the trade with that State caused important disturbances. In fact, these difficulties were resolved in an informal way, as Jordan was entitled to sell certain quantities of petrol of Iraqi origin; however, no data on the commerce are available and there is no supervision by the UN agencies on possible uses and abuses of this exceptional right. Certain measures were proposed also by the UN specialized agencies (like UNIDO or UNEP) to some other states affected by the sanctions and subsequently the military action against Iraq: Syria, Lebanon, and the group of four neighbouring States – Jordan, Kuwait, Bahrain, and Saudi Arabia.

3 See SC Res. 386 of 17 March 1976 and 411 of 30 June 1977 concerning Mozambique, and SC Res. 403 of 14 January 1977 and 406 of 25 May 1977, concerning Botswana.

4 *Cf.* in particular SC Res. 402 of 22 December 1976, SC Res. 407 of 25 May 1977; as well as the resolutions of the UN GA: 32/98 of 13 December 1977, 33/128 of 19 December 1978, 34/130 of 14 December 1979 and following.

The situation existing in the Gulf area and the developments in the former Yugoslavia led the UN Secretary General Boutros Ghali to include the issue of possible application of Art. 50 into the Agenda for Peace.[5] The instrument emphasizes a specific right of the states concerned not only to address their special needs to the Security Council but also to get their problems resolved; it recommended also to the Council to devise measures, in co-operation with the financial institutions and other international organizations mechanisms, to render the rights under Art. 50 effective. The same view was presented by the General Assembly in its resolutions on Agenda for Peace and Supplement to an Agenda for Peace (Resolutions 47/120B of 20 September 1993, and 51/242 of 15 September 1997, respectively).

The problem of implementation of the provisions of the UN Charter concerning aid to third States affected by sanctions presented itself to a much more important degree within the UN agencies in 1992-1993 in connection with the UN activities against "new" Yugoslavia. The issue was brought to the attention of the UN by a group of East European states including Bulgaria, Ukraine, and Romania, supported by certain non-aligned states like Lebanon, Jordan, and Uruguay. The group sponsored a number of the UN GA resolutions dealing with the issue;[6] it also played an important role within the Committee on the Charter of the United Nations and on the Strengthening of the Role of the Organization. The States concerned interpreted Art. 50 of the Charter broadly and maintained that the provision granted the States affected by sanctions and suffering important economic perturbation not only a right to a consultation on all decisions taken in connection with the sanctions imposed upon a perpetrator State but also a right to economic aid, compensation and other financial facilities. Such a position was generally rejected by Western states, including EU members, and the USA which found the claims of the group insufficiently founded on the UN Charter.

The situation was modified in a way in the mid-1990s when the Russian Federation supported actively the claimant states and became rapidly one of the leaders of the group.

It is interesting that a group of these States (Bulgaria, Ukraine, Romania, Macedonia, Albania and others) presented – mostly in 1993-1994 but also at a later

5 UN Doc. A/47/277 – S/24111 of 17 June 1992.
6 E.g. GA Res. 50/51, 51/208, 52/162, 53/107, 54/107.

stage – short documents concerning the evaluation of losses suffered by them in connection with the sanctions against Yugoslavia. The documents were in fact rejected by the UN agencies and sharply criticised in particular by the USA, France and Germany, not to mention other states. The representative of France, for example, stated during the 1994 session of the Special Committee of the UN Charter in a particularly sharp and even non-diplomatic way that if the states claiming compensation on the basis of Art. 50 had any illusions that they might obtain any financial redress, they should abandon these illusions as soon as possible. The group of claimant states have lately modified their position. Although the most active states still sponsor resolutions concerning Art. 50 and its role in mitigating the effects of sanctions for the third States, they do not claim direct financial compensation. When the present author tried to obtain information on these documents through diplomatic channels, he was informed by the responsible officials of the ministries of foreign affairs of the states concerned that no documents of that kind were officially presented.

IV The Fundamental Legal Issues Arising from the Possible Application of Article 50

All the activities were conducted through three channels:

- Special Committee on the Charter of the United Nations and on the Strengthening of the Role of the Organization;
- Second Committee of the General Assembly, dealing with the economic matters;
- Open Working Group on the Agenda for Peace, and in particular its committee on UN sanctions.

The analysis of the relevant documents shows the most important problems dealing with the application of Art. 50 of the UN Charter. At the present stage of research we shall refer to some instruments only, which however are representative of the totality of activities of the UN in this field.[7] The usual sequence of events is that the UN Secretary General on the inspiration of the GA resolution prepares his Report on implementation of provisions of the Charter related to assistance to third States affected by the application of sanctions. A similar report is prepared on the basis of the Report of the Secretary General

7 It is useful to refer here to the documents elaborated during the 54th Session of the UN GA in 1999: Doc.A/54/383, A/54/614, and Res. 54/107.

and other relevant instruments by the 6th Committee of the General Assembly. Finally, the General Assembly takes the results of the work into account and passes a respective resolution indicating the most important steps to be taken in order to make the rights of the states affected by sanctions effective.

Resolution 52/162 of 15 December 1997 adopted without vote and entitled "Implementation of the provisions of the Charter of the UN related to assistance to third States affected by the application of sanctions" invited the Secretary General to convene the meeting of the expert group the task of which was to elaborate a methodology of assessment of the losses incurred by states as a result of UN sanctions. The meeting took place in New York on 24-26 June 1998, and its results were presented in the Report by the UN Secretary General of 27 August 1998.[8] The group deliberated on the basis of two studies presented by M. Doxey and G.C. Hufbauer. The final report dealt with different aspects of economic, financial and social losses suffered by the States concerned, as well as with some costs of secondary nature, stemming indirectly from the application of sanctions. It stressed that the readiness of members of the international community to grant specific kinds of aid to the states affected by sanctions was not necessarily connected with notions of justice, burden-sharing and equal distribution of costs, but was strictly related to the idea of a strict implementation of sanctions. The forms and dimensions of the aid were connected with the evaluation of possible costs of military operations against the target State, and should be considered and assessed by the Security Council in advance before the imposition of sanctions. The remedies granted to the states specially affected by sanctions should necessarily correspond with the nature of the disadvantages and difficulties met by those States. The most important role in respect of coping with the problems should be played by international financial institutions including *inter alia*, the IMF, the World Bank, and regional development banks, as the most experienced bodies; financial measures should be accompanied by non-financial measures supporting international trade (arranged e.g. by the WTO and UNCTAD). However, other specialized agencies and institutions of the UN system, and in particular UNDP, UNICEF, FAO, ILO, WHO and UNHCR, should support the solutions proposed. All measures should be decided upon the basis of assessments made by special missions of the organizations to the third states concerned. The report of the meeting was endorsed by the Economic and Social Council in its resolution 1999/59 of 30 July 1999.

8 Doc. A/53/312.

The Report by the Secretary General of 23 September 1999 referred to two important questions: the opinions of certain governments presented upon invitation made by the expert group mentioned above, and information on the measures adopted by specialized agencies and organizations with a view to resolving the specific problems of the third states affected by sanctions. The opinions were presented by Belarus, Poland, the Russian Federation, Ukraine and Slovakia. They supported the ideas of sanctions targeted against the governing elites of the state concerned, in order to avoid important burdens against the entire population. It is important that the costs of the sanctions regime should be shared by all Member states, and therefore the elaboration of the burden-sharing mechanism is of utmost importance. The evaluation of costs and possible relief measures to third states should be necessarily made by the Security Council before the imposition of sanctions. As to the second part of the Report, it referred to a number of measures undertaken by the UN agencies and specialized programmes, regional economic commissions and regional development banks, but also other organizations like the European Union and the OECD.

On the basis of the report by the Secretary General, the 6th Committee of the General Assembly discussed a draft resolution introduced by Bulgaria, Russia and Ukraine. The resolution proposed to the major UN agencies to continue their activities (within their competence) to establish an effective system of aid to states affected by the sanctions. The Security Council was requested to introduce a system of mechanisms and procedures for early consultation with the states concerned, the special tasks to be implemented in particular by the sanctions committees (the work of which should be more effective and transparent). The Secretary General should implement the relevant resolutions of the General Assembly and establish a competent unit within the Secretariat to provide information on international assistance available; he should also elaborate a special report devoted to the practical implementation of the proposals by the expert group. The aid should be mobilised and monitored by the General Assembly and the Economic and Social Council. Finally, the organizations of the UN system, international financial institutions, other international organizations, regional organizations and Member states should address all problems of the states affected by sanctions in order to render their assistance more effective. The Report by the Special Committee on the Charter of the UN and on the Strengthening of the Role of the Organization at its 2000 session should address all the relevant issues in a detailed and exhaustive way.

V THE POSITION OF POLAND TOWARDS THE SECURITY COUNCIL SANCTIONS AND THE ROLE OF ARTICLE 50

Finally we would like to refer here briefly to the position of Poland on the problems of implementation of the Security Council sanctions in general, and application of Art. 50 in particular, as the evolution in this respect is characteristic for the Central European States and spectacular because of certain political issues.

A) Position of international law, including acts of international organizations, within the Polish legal order

Like all recent constitutions of the region, the Polish Constitution of 2 April 1997 contains relatively detailed provisions regulation concerning the relationship between international and domestic law.[9]

The constitutional provisions dealing with the relationship between international law and Polish domestic law starts with Article 9. It states that the Republic of Poland respects international law binding on it. The provision is of purely declaratory nature; it is situated in the chapter of the constitution dealing with the principles of the political, social and legal system of Poland. It has often been referred to as a possible basis of validity in the municipal legal order of these norms which have not been indicated in the remaining provisions of the constitution as sources of Polish domestic law: i.e. customary law,[10] non-

9 Among numerous publications dealing with the issue we mention: A.Wyrozumska, "Legal Bases of the Polish External Competence", (1998) 36 *AVR* 386; S.Biernat, "Constitutional Aspects of Poland's Future Membership in the European Union", *ibid.*, p.398; A.Wasilkowski, "International Law and International Relations in the New Polish Constitution of 2 April 1997", (1997-1998) 23 *PolYBIL* 7; J.Barcz, "Membership of Poland in the European Union in the Light of the Constitution of 2 April 1997. Constitutional Act of Integration", *ibid.*, p.21.

10 The only decision of a Polish court dealing with customary law concerned the state immunity (Supreme Court, 15 May 1959, OSPiKA 1960, Item 2). Customary rules can be applied on the basis of renvoi by specific municipal acts (like maritime law, aerial transportation law etc.). We would like, however, to quote the regulation of the Minister of Foreign Affairs of 17 June 1998, Dz.U. 1998, No.78, Item 512, on the rules of granting visas to diplomatic representatives according to which visas should be granted in accordance with domestic acts in force, binding international agreements, and existing international customs. The regulation introduces therefore customary law into municipal law without any specific constitutional basis.

ratified treaties and covenants, unilateral obligations, and binding norms elaborated by international organizations (if any).

Article 87 of the Constitution opens Chapter III concerning sources of law. According to it, international agreements duly ratified constitute the source of Polish law. There are two kinds of ratified treaties. Certain treaties can be ratified by the President directly on the basis of his personal prerogatives. The other categories of agreements can be ratified exclusively after the prior approval by the Parliament expressed in the form of so-called ratification law (Art. 89.1 of the Constitution). The Constitution extends the competence of the Parliament upon: treaties dealing with peace, alliances, political and military treaties; treaties concerning fundamental freedoms, rights and duties defined in the Constitution; membership in international organizations; treaties imposing important financial burdens upon the state budget; and international agreements reserved for the regulation by the laws of the Parliament.

The position of ratified international agreements in the Polish legal order has been regulated in Art. 91(1) of the Constitution. According to this provision, ratified treaties upon their publication in the Official Journal of the Polish Republic form part of the domestic legal order and are directly applicable unless their application is dependent upon the adoption of an act of Parliament. There is a doctrinal dispute between the partisans of the concept of transformation and those of incorporation as to the meaning of these provisions; in our opinion, from the theoretical point of view ratified international agreements are incorporated into the municipal law rather than transformed into domestic law.

The position of other international agreements in the Polish domestic legal order remains unclear. In theory, the agreements of this kind should not be directly applicable and should not concern issues listed in Art. 89(1); according to the Constitution, they do not constitute a source of Polish domestic law and they are not directly applicable, so that the agreements concluded in simplified form are binding exclusively upon the state administration, they are of internal nature and require an implementation by specific domestic act, i.e. either by statute enacted by the Parliament or by governmental regulation according to a pattern adopted in domestic law.

The Constitution invokes international law not only in the context of sources of law but also by some other occasions. So, for example, Art. 42.1 proclaims the rule *nullum crimen sine lege*, and states that this principle does not exclude punishment of perpetrators of crimes under international law. The provision can cause important difficulties in connection with the possible entry into force of international instruments on crimes against peace and humanity when the judges will be forced to decide whether specific acts do constitute a crime of aggression or other acts prohibited directly under customary international law. Difficulties connected with the application of customary law within the Polish municipal legal order would be multiplied by the necessity to interpret the international rules themselves (like the question whether specific activities can constitute aggression without being qualified as such by the UN Security Council).

B) Position of the legal instruments enacted by international organizations

Anticipating future membership in the European Union, the fathers of the Constitution proposed the introducing of provisions dealing with the transfer of certain competencies of the state powers to international organizations and international organs, as well as with the implementation of law enacted in the framework of international organizations in the Polish legal system. This problem has become actual under the current international obligations of Poland, in particular as far as it concerns resolutions of the UN Security Council (decisions within the meaning of Art. 25 of the UN Charter which are based upon Chapter VII), decisions of the Council of OECD and of the Council of the GATS. The latter are addressed to the Member states (decisions of the Council of the OECD are based on Art. 5.2 and leave to the Member states the choice of measures of municipal law to implement them, Art. 6.3; the same applies to acts adopted on the basis of GATS). As to the decisions of the Security Council, they were implemented in the following way:[11] the government passed resolutions or enacted regulations addressed to respective competent ministers requiring them to take necessary measures to implement the UNSC resolutions, and subsequently the ministers adopted these measures taking into account the requirements of municipal law. Except for one act, the said instruments did not invoke the UNSC resolutions but referred to municipal acts (statutes) as their bases. They were published in *Dziennik Ustaw* (Official Gazette) or in *Monitor Polski* (promulgation organ of the rank lower than Dziennik Ustaw). In some aspects, the solution applied was abused – let us quote the announcement by the Council of Ministers of 27 May 1994 that : limitations upon arms commerce with Yugo-

11 *Cf.* P.Daranowski, "The Resolutions of the Security Council of the United Nations Aimed at Maintenance or Restoration of International Peace and Security and the Polish Legal Order. The Practice of Implementation and Its Prospects", (1994) 21 *PolYBIL*, p.55 ff.

slavia was introduced in implementation of the Security Council resolution, without having published any resolution itself and without specifying the state agency which enacted the ban on arm exports or the legal basis of this ban under municipal law.

This practice cannot be upheld under the new Constitution in particular when the UNSC resolutions – even if addressed to the Member states – include provisions dealing with the status of individuals. They can contain provisions requiring the state agencies to act in a way contrary to constitutional norms. Art. 55 forbids for example an extradition of Polish nationals. Such a solution is fully compatible with international law. On the other hand, UNSC resolution 748(1992) dealing with the *Lockerbie* case demanded Libya to surrender her nationals and to subject them to the jurisdiction of foreign courts. The same is true as to the Yugoslavia tribunal. As long as there is no control of legality of the acts of UN agencies (the ICJ consequently rejected such a possibility in the *Namibia* [1971] and *Lockerbie* [1992] decisions), Poland can be confronted with the problem of implementation of UN instruments as a constitutional issue. The catalogue of sources of domestic law is exhaustive, and it does not provide for the enactment of regulations in order to implement international agreements (although one could suggest that these regulations could be treated as remaining within the scope of international agreements duly ratified by the Parliament, and therefore the constitutional requirement of defining the scope of regulations by law is fulfilled) – not to say that questions related to the status of individuals can under the new Constitution be regulated exclusively by the acts of Parliament. It seems necessary therefore either to implement UN SC resolutions by Parliamentary statutes (which would not necessarily be fully effective but would be "proper" from the legislative point of view) or to pass a law allowing the government to act in order to implement the Security Council's decisions. Neither solution of course is adequate in the case of instruments conflicting with constitutional provisions.

It is worth noting that at least some of the recently passed laws contain provisions concerning possible sanctions imposed either by Security Council resolutions or by other international organizations. For example Art. 2, 6(1)(19), 22(1)(9) of the law of 11 December 1997 on the administration of international commerce with goods and services[12] allows the Council of Ministers to intro-

12 Dz.U. 1997, No.157, Item 1057.

duce limitations upon the said commerce if the national interest or fundamental economic interest of the State so require, in accordance with the WTO regulations, or if it is necessary in order to meet the obligations of Poland deriving from the UN Charter in the field of international peace and security. The instrument provided for the implementation of these provisions is an ordinance *(rozporzadzenie)*. The same solution was adopted in Art. 19 of the law of 18 December 1998 on foreign currency.[13] The provision states that the Council of Ministers can enact ordinances in order to implement resolutions of the UNSC imposing limitation upon the payments or financial relations with specific states. These regulations are compatible with the Constitution of 1997. Generally the Constitution does not allow the enactment of executive measures by the Council of Ministers to implement international obligations. It is possible to enact such measures exclusively on the basis of specific provisions of a law (act of parliament), in the framework indicated by the law. Under these circumstances it seems necessary for the ministers to act on the basis of domestic acts.

In some cases, the resolutions of the Council of Ministers ordered the competent ministers to use their right of legislative initiative in order to amend specific laws, the application of which might be necessary or useful for the implementation of the SC sanctions. Such a solution was applied, for example, with respect to penal sanctions introduced by the Security Council; the Minister of Justice was requested to propose amendments to the criminal code concerning the criminalisation of acts punishable under the resolutions.

A specific solution was applied with respect to Resolution 986(1995) of 14 April 1995 establishing the UN Compensation Commission. The resolution defined the principles governing claims for damages suffered by UN Member states, corporations and individuals as a result of the invasion of Kuwait by Iraq. The Polish state, companies, and individual persons brought claims against the Iraqi government amounting to USD 187 mio. The resolution was not implemented within the Polish legal system properly speaking; no information on the resolution and its consequences was published in the Official Journal *(Dziennik Ustaw* or *Monitor Polski)*. All information concerning the measures applicable to the claims was disseminated exclusively by press and electronic media. All documentation concerning claims should have been sent by the persons concerned directly to the UNCC. A special agency within the Ministry

13 Dz.U. 1998, No.160, Item 1063.

of Economy was created; however, its task was exclusively to transfer the documents to Geneva without adding any sheet of paper. In fact, therefore, Resolution 986 became directly effective within the Polish legal order.

C) *Opinion of the Advisory Board by the Ministry of Foreign Affairs as to the position of the Security Council resolutions.*

The opinion of 10 May 1999 states in general terms that the Security Council resolutions are not directly applicable within the Polish legal order. They must be transformed into domestic acts. Some laws of the parliament contain delegation for the competent ministers to enact legislation concerning the implementation of these resolutions (commerce of goods and services, arms, finances, limitation on air transport). The advisory committee emphasises that the solution mentioned above is not universal. It is necessary therefore either to enact the resolution or ordinance by the Council of Ministers including a respective passage of the resolution, the act of domestic law being based directly upon Art. 24 and 25 of the UN Charter, or to pass a general law by the parliament concerning the implementation of the Security Council resolutions. The former solution would be in fact *contra* (or at least *infra*) *legem*; it would amount to an amendment of the constitutional gap; but on the other hand it would be a logical solution allowing rapid implementation of the Security Council decisions. Examples of modifications of the Constitution by constitutional practice can be found in the Polish legal system, and it should be not excluded in the context of the UN sanctions.

As to the *position of Poland towards the application of Art. 50*, an important evolution can be observed. At the very beginning of the Yugoslav conflict Poland supported the claims by the states concerned and even sponsored several resolutions on the topic. However, because of political reasons the Polish view was gradually modified. Two factors influenced this evolution. Firstly, the attitude of the claimant States became more and more aggressive and led to confrontation with the Western states. Secondly, the leadership of Russia complicated the situation of Poland, because of the notoriously bad mutual relations. The danger occurred that the states concerned would be dominated by Russia which would have been politically difficult. The government decided therefore to withdraw its support for the claims of particular states, and at the same time to continue (to a much lesser extent) a policy of formulating certain general rules governing the implementation of Art. 50. Such a stance corresponds with the policy of Western European states and the USA.

25

IMPLEMENTATION OF SANCTIONS – THE EXPERIENCE OF AFRICA

Tunguru Huaraka[▪]

I Introduction

Africa, in recent years, has spawned more situations of threat to international peace and security than any other region. The majority of these conflicts are internal conflicts which are fanned largely by competition for control of natural resources, in particular diamond mines. The exception to this general pattern is the war between Ethiopia and Eritrea. The war in the Democratic Republic of the Congo though involving five African countries – Angola, Namibia, Rwanda, Uganda and Zimbabwe – is basically an internal conflict involving several Congolese factions battling to overthrow the Government. But here again the control of natural resources has also sparked fighting among those forces opposed to the central Government. These factions seem to be united only in their opposition to the central authority but divided as far as who is to control the natural resources.

The Security Council decisions on sanctions in regard to these conflicts in Africa are, therefore, basically aimed at minimizing the intensity of the conflict and

▪ LL.B (Hons) Accra, LL.M London, PH.D Geneva. Special Advisor to the Minister, Ministry of Justice; First Ambassador Extraordinary and Plenipotentiary/Permanent Representative of the Republic of Namibia to the United Nations (1991-1996); Former Human Rights Officer (Secretary of the Committee of Racial Discrimination (CERD) United Nations Centre for Human Rights). Founder and Secretary-General of the African Association of International Law. The views expressed in this study are solely those of the author.

V. Gowlland-Debbas (ed.), *United Nations Sanctions and International Law*, p. 349-360.

the suffering of the ordinary people. Sanctions in situations of internal conflicts further aim at forcing the opposing groups to seek negotiated settlement and thus they are hardly aimed at punishing the violator of international peace and security.

It should be noted that the effectiveness of Security Council sanctions against UNITA (Angola) is also affected by poor infrastructures and communications of the countries of Southern Africa. Added to this are the problems caused by long and poorly controlled borders as well as traditional customs. The ethnic bondage and customs binding the various ethnic groups which straddle across the border, in these cases between Namibia and Angola, and Zambia and Angola, though divided by the colonial boundaries have never been broken or extinguished by such boundaries. For example, the border between Angola and Namibia is about 1,200 kilometers and cuts across several ethnic groups. Marriages and movement of persons and goods across the border are taken as normal and traditional. It is difficult to prevent constant cross border movements when uncles and aunts are separated from their nephews and nieces. However, it should be emphasized that these movements are not likely to violate sanctions against UNITA for what is transported are mostly for domestic use or performance of ethnic rituals.

But when smuggling involves diamonds it can easily be carried out without the knowledge of the central Government. However, such smuggling, if at all, will be on a very minor scale which can be dealt with by domestic jurisdictions as an ordinary criminal offense.

II SECURITY COUNCIL SANCTIONS AGAINST UNITA

The first sanctions against UNITA were imposed on 15 September 1993 following on UNITA's refusal to accept the result of the United Nations supervised elections in 1991 and instead restarting the war.

Security Council Resolution 864 (1993) of 15 September 1993 states:

> "19. Decides, with a view to prohibiting all sale or supply to UNITA of arms and related materiel and military assistance, as well as petroleum and petroleum products, that all States shall prevent the sale or supply, by their nations or from their territories or using their flag vessels or aircraft, of arms and related materiel of all

types, including weapons and ammunition, military vehicles and equipment and spare parts for the afore-mentioned, as well as of petroleum and petroleum products, whether or not originating in their territory, to the territory of Angola other than through named points of entry on a list to be supplied by the Government of Angola to the Secretary General."

Subsequently, the list was extended to include "motorised vehicles or watercraft or spare parts for such vehicles, or ground or waterborne transportation services" (Resolution 1173 of 12 June 1998).

Other measures were subsequently imposed against UNITA in 1997, by Resolution 1127 of 28 August 1997, including a strict travel ban on UNITA senior officials. Paragraph 4 of the said resolution reads:

"*Decides* that all States shall take the necessary measures:

(a) To prevent the entry into or transit through their territories of all senior officials of UNITA and of adult members of their immediate families, as designated in accordance with paragraph 11 (a) below, except those officials necessary for the full functioning of the Government of Unity and National Reconciliation, the National Assembly, or the Joint Commission, provided that nothing in this paragraph shall oblige a State to refuse entry into its territory to its own nationals;

(b) To suspend or cancel all travel documents, visas or residence permits issued to senior UNITA officials and adult members of their immediate families, ...;

(c) To require the immediate and complete closure of all UNITA offices in their territories".

In the hope of making them effective five years after the imposition of the first measures, they were tightened once again. This time the Security Council imposed financial restrictions. Resolution 1173 (1998) of 12 June 1998, *inter alia* states:

"11. *Decides* that all States, except Angola, in which there are funds and financial resources...of UNITA as an organization or of senior officials of UNITA or adult members of their immediate families..., shall require all persons and entities within their own territories holding such funds and financial resources to freeze them and ensure that they are not made available directly or indirectly to or for the benefit of UNITA as an organization or of senior officials of UNITA or adult members of their immediate families …

12. *Decides also* that all States shall take the necessary measures:

…

(b) to prohibit the direct or indirect import from Angola to their territory of all diamonds that are not controlled through the Certificate of Origin regime of the GURN".

These three broad types of measures the Security Council imposed against UNITA are far reaching; they could have achieved the desired results and significantly curtailed UNITA's capacity to wage war, had they been rigorously implemented.

III The Legal Basis

All the African States are Member states of the United Nations. Thus by the terms of Article 103 of the United Nations Charter:

> "In the event of a conflict between obligations of the Members of the United Nations under the present Charter and their obligations under any other international agreement, their obligations under the present Charter shall prevail".

Furthermore, the sanctions against UNITA are imposed by the Security Council under Chapter VII of the Charter of the United Nations. Therefore all the Member states are under obligations to implement such measures.

It will be observed in passing that with regard to the sanctions against UNITA, as far as it could be ascertained, no African state has indicated problems arising from the carrying out of such measures as provided for in Article 50 of the Charter.

Again, at the regional level, either within the OAU or SADC, African States always defend the UN actions, in particular the Security Council sanctions aimed at resolving African conflicts.

For instance the Final Communiqué of the 1998 SADC Summit of Heads of State or Government (Grand Baie, Mauritius 13-14 September) stated, inter alia:

> "The Summit urged Member states to ensure tight regulations and improved control of airports and airspace to ensure effective implementation of the UN sanctions against UNITA."[1]

If at all, what hampers effective implementation is not so much the lack of legal mechanisms but invariably the constraint of under-development, particularly of the infrastructures. This research has not yet revealed domestic courts judgments on United Nations sanctions. Given the provisions of Article 103 of the Charter of the United Nations, quoted above, it is very unlikely that a court in any African country, particularly countries of the SADC region with their strong adherence to the rule of law, will *challenge* the legal authority of the decisions of the Security Council on sanctions.

IV THE SITUATION UNDER DOMESTIC LAW

The starting point is that none of the SADC countries have felt it necessary to enact special laws to make Security Council sanctions against UNITA enforceable domestically. It is thus reasonable to assume that the national courts of those countries of SADC if called upon to decide the enforceability of Security Council sanctions will rule in their favour.

The Security Council sanctions against UNITA, as the UN Panel of Experts on Violations of Security Council Sanctions against UNITA found, are made ineffective as a result of smuggling. The Report of the Panel[2] found that petroleum and petroleum products are flown illegally from airfields in South Africa and over the airspace of Botswana and/or Namibia without these countries being able to detect such illegal flights. Moreover, diamonds from UNITA controlled areas are traded illegally in these countries.

Namibia is in many ways unique. Her history during the last century was the historical evolution of the role of the United Nations in decolonization.[3] As a result, the Constitution of the Republic of Namibia consecrates the primacy

1 UN Doc. S/1999/915.
2 UN Doc. S/2000/203 of 10 March 2000.
3 See Tunguru Huaraka, *Namibia by Resolution: A Legal Analysis of International Organizations' Attempts at Decolonization* (Unpublished Doctoral Thesis, Graduate Institute of International Studies, University of Geneva), 1979.

not only of international treaties, which includes the Charter of the United Nations, but equally principles of international law over domestic law. In this respect, the Namibian Constitution is very much more advanced than most constitutions in Africa.

Article 96 of the Namibian Constitution states:

> "The State shall endeavour to ensure that in its international relations it:
> ...
> (b) promotes international co-operations, peace and security
> (d) foster respect for international law and treaty obligations".

Obviously these are principles of state policy with great persuasive force upon the courts of the country.

That is not all. The Namibian Constitution is also specific as regards the legal force of international agreements.

Article 144 states:

> "Unless otherwise provided by this Constitution or Act of Parliament the general rules of public international law and international agreements binding upon Namibia under this Constitution shall form part of the law of Namibia."

Once Namibia ratifies or accedes to an international agreement, that agreement becomes automatically the law of Namibia. Under the Namibian Constitution international treaties to which Namibia is a party are self-executing. All that is needed, in certain cases, is to publish such treaties in the Government Gazette.

This means that decisions of the Security Council taken under Chapter VII of the Charter have a force of law in Namibia. In this respect, the sanctions imposed on UNITA by the Security Council in Resolution 864 (1993) on 15 September 1993 and all other subsequent resolutions are thus enforceable in Namibia. Although the matter has not been tested in Namibian courts, it is, however, evident that the Constitution is the supreme law of the land.

Further, other laws in Namibia which deal, for instance, with smuggling could be resorted to. For example, the Arms and Ammunition Act, 1996 (Act No. 7 of 1996) provides:

> "Section 22 (1).... No person shall, except on behalf of the State, import into or export from Namibia any arms or ammunition, including any arms or ammunition in transit through Namibia to any place outside Namibia".

The Diamond Act, 1999 (Act No.13 of 1999) by Part VI "Control Measures in Relation to Unpolished Diamonds" prohibits the possession of unpolished diamonds, sale or disposal of unpolished diamonds, receipt or purchase of unpolished diamonds, export or import of unpolished diamonds. All these activities can be carried out only by authorized persons; and the licenses to undertake such activities are granted only by the Minister of Mines and Energy of the Government.

The Panel of Experts on Violations of Security Council Sanctions Against UNITA reported that "UNITA personnel make use of Namibian territory to carry out UNITA related activities – without the knowledge of the Government of Namibia. These activities include diamond smuggling..."[4] The activities of UNITA in Namibia are thus purely criminal acts which the domestic laws should deal with effectively. The two laws stated above could effectively deal with smuggling of diamonds and arms and ammunition. The problem may be that of detection.

V Sanctions Busting: UNITA

The ineffectiveness of the Security Council sanctions against UNITA is basically due to two factors. In the first place, UNITA's control of some of the most lucrative diamond mines in Angola has assured it with huge sources of finance; secondly, the insatiable demand of the rich for diamonds makes smuggling of diamonds, particularly across such long and poorly controlled borders, inevitable.

In December 1998 when finally the Lusaka Protocol of November 1994 collapsed and full scale war resumed, the international community was shocked to note the types and quantity of arms UNITA had acquired despite the UN sanctions. UNITA is heavily armed even with heavy and modern weapons such as tanks and ground to air-missiles.

The question is how did UNITA acquire all these arms and related materiel despite the UN arms embargo?

4 UN Doc. S/2000/203, para. 46.

In this respect, the Security Council by Resolution 1237 (1999) of 7 May 1999 established the independent Panel of Experts to investigate violations of Security Council sanctions against UNITA. The Panel of Experts was asked to inform the Council on (a) how the sanctions against UNITA were being violated, (b) who was violating them, and (c) what could be done to make sanctions more effective.[5]

As far as arms are concerned, the Panel of Experts found that the major suppliers were mainly Ukraine and Bulgaria. The arms were paid in diamonds. The Panel of Experts further established that the Democratic Republic of Congo, then Zaire under the late President Mobutu, was the main transit point. With the change of Government in the DRC, Burkina Faso and Togo became the transit points.[6] The Report of the Panel of Experts also established that these countries issued false end-user certificates.[7]

With regard to supply of petroleum and petroleum products, the same countries were also found to have supplied UNITA with these products in violation of Security Council sanctions. Congo (Brazzaville) under former President Pascal Lissouba was also implicated in sanctions violations. The Panel of Experts also found that petroleum was smuggled across the border from Zambia, but probably without the support of Zambian Government officials.[8]

The leaders of the countries mentioned as having violated sanctions against arms and petroleum were allegedly paid by UNITA in diamonds. The Presidents of Burkina Faso, Blaise Compaore and of Togo, Eyadema, were specifically mentioned in this regard. The same countries allowed diamonds deals to be transacted in their countries. Rwanda is also reported to allow diamond transactions to be carried out openly. Diamond smuggling is also apparently carried out in Namibia, South Africa and Zambia, but without the knowledge of the authorities of these countries.[9]

The ease with which UNITA diamonds can be sold to diamond traders and polishers in Antwerp (Belgium) makes sanctions against diamonds difficult to

5 See UN Doc. S/2000/203 of 10 March 2000.
6 *Ibid.*, paras. 39-43.
7 *Ibid.*, para. 51.
8 *Ibid.*, para. 69.
9 *Ibid.*, paras. 84-86.

control. The Panel of Experts found that the Belgian authorities have failed to establish an effective import identification regime with respect to diamonds.[10]

The Panel of Experts found with regard to UNITA representation and travel that Burkina Faso serves as a *de facto* base of operations for UNITA's external activities in Africa. Togo too is said to provide a safe haven for Savimbi's family and for other senior officials. Togo is reported to have provided passports to many senior UNITA officials.[11]

UNITA is said to maintain "unofficial" representation in a number of European countries, such as France, Portugal and Switzerland as well as in the United States. Belgium on the other hand "is regarded by UNITA as an important representation center because of the country's role as a center for the diamond trade as well as being a place of contact for international arms dealers."[12]

The Panel of Experts further found that although UNITA does not maintain a representative in Namibia, apparently UNITA personnel use Namibian territory to carry out UNITA related activities. A similar situation is said to take place in South Africa.[13]

These findings of the Panel of Experts had earlier been reported by authoritative sources, for example the London weekly, *The Economist*, in its issue of May 29th – June 4th 1999, which noted that UNITA's network runs deep: "Zambia is now its main route for getting its diamonds out and bringing in quantities of guns and ammunition from Ukraine and elsewhere." The weekly further observed in an article entitled "Rocks that kill" that diamonds are so easily smuggled, and so ridiculously valuable, that enforcing a trade ban is extremely difficult

A London based non-governmental organization, Global Witness, published in 1998 a detailed report on diamond smuggling from Angola entitled "A Rough Trade – The Role of Companies and Governments in the Angolan Conflict". Global Witness reported that "Zambia's importance as a diamond route for

---

10 *Ibid.*, paras. 87-90.
11 *Ibid.*, paras. 141, 151.
12 *Ibid.*, para. 140.
13 *Ibid.*, paras. 146 and 149.

UNITA increased with the fall of Mobutu and the incursion of Angolan army troops into the DRC which initially closed off the traditional and major route from UNITA territories through DRC to Kinshasa". Global Witness further reported that the Zambian Ministry of Mines and Geological Survey "are not only happy to provide false Certificates of Origin but are clear that 'basically all diamonds here are Angolan'". Once this is done, the illegal diamonds are turned into a legal commodity and thus exportable under the terms of the United Nations Security Council embargo. The diamonds are then easily exported to countries such as USA, Britain, the Netherlands, Belgium, South Africa and Israel.

All these were thus collaborated by the findings of the Panel of Experts.

The Panel of Experts made a number of recommendations, one of which is of special importance for this Study. It recommended that the Security Council should apply the following measures against Governments found to have been intentionally breaking sanctions: – (i) formally declaring the offending countries to be sanctions breakers; (ii) discouraging Member states from supporting the candidacies of nationals from listed countries for senior positions within the United Nations system until the listed countries are declared to be complying with the sanctions; (iii) a ban on the holding of United Nations conferences in the listed countries until they are declared to be complying with the sanctions; (iv) discouraging other international organizations from holding conferences or meetings in the listed countries, or electing the country concerned as Chairman in office of any organization.[14]

This study has stressed the point that the ineffectiveness of the implementation of sanctions in the SADC countries was partly due to underdeveloped and poor infrastructures. To overcome this defect the Panel of Experts recommended that the international community should assist SADC countries to establish mobile radar systems that can be rapidly deployed in the sub-region for the purpose of detecting illegal flight activities across national borders.[15]

14 *Ibid.*, para. 179.
15 *Ibid.*, para. 170.

VI CONCLUSION

Zambia has persistently denied that it is assisting UNITA to evade Security Council sanctions. The allegations of arms and ammunition, petroleum and petroleum products passing through Zambia to UNITA held areas in Angola has strained the relationship between the two countries to a breaking point.

However, in mid 1999, through the auspices of the SADC Inter-State Defence and Security Committee the tension was diffused. Furthermore SADC put in place information-sharing arrangements on sanctions violations to assist members in implementing the sanctions against UNITA.[16]

It will be observed that the establishment of the Panel of Experts on Violations of Security Council Sanctions against UNITA is a novel procedure in implementation mechanisms of sanctions. Judging by their first report, which is very candid, it appears that the use of independent experts has made a substantial difference. It is very likely that similar independent panels of experts will be used in the future in similar situations. There is no doubt that Article 41 of the Charter empowers the Security Council to resort to such other measures to give effect to its decisions.

Many countries, in particular those that were mentioned as having violated the sanctions against UNITA were caught by surprise.

In its latest action on the matter of 18 April 2000, the Security Council by Resolution 1295 (2000) reconstituted a similar monitoring mechanism composed of up to five experts for a period of six months. This time it is a monitoring mechanism and not an investigating one. The Member states that were specifically mentioned by the Panel of Experts as having violated sanctions against UNITA will have a second chance to exonerate themselves.

After the expiration of six months, stipulated in the said resolution as 18 October 2000, the new monitoring mechanism of five experts will make a final report. It is expected that the Security Council will then take concrete measures against those countries which are confirmed to have violated sanctions against UNITA.

---

16 See UN Doc. S/1999/829, para. 12.

Meanwhile, the Security Council by the same resolution encourages the convening of a conference of experts to devise a regime for curbing the illegal supply of petroleum and petroleum products into UNITA controlled areas, including physical inspection.

With regard to the lack of capacity of the countries of SADC emphasized in this study, the Security Council by the same resolution invited SADC to make known what assistance SADC required in implementing sanctions against UNITA and strongly urged states and international organizations to consider the provision of financial and technical assistance to SADC in this regard.

It seems that henceforth the implementation of Security Council sanctions will take a different pattern.

MISE EN ŒUVRE PAR UN ETAT NON MEMBRE DES NATIONS UNIES – LE CAS DE LA SUISSE

Mathias-Charles Krafft[■]

La Suisse n'est pas (encore) membre des Nations Unies. Elle a en outre le statut d'un Etat neutre à titre permanent, statut qu'elle entend maintenir et qui comporte un certain nombre de droits et d'obligations fixés dans les Conventions de la Haye de 1907 concernant les droits et les devoirs des puissances et des personnes neutres en cas de guerre sur terre et en cas de guerre maritime, ainsi que dans le droit international coutumier. Le domaine d'application du *droit de la neutralité* est limité: il régit essentiellement le comportement de l'Etat neutre durant les conflits armés interétatiques. Quant à la *politique de neutralité,* elle regroupe toutes les mesures que prend l'Etat neutre à titre permanent, en temps de paix, pour préserver la crédibilité de sa neutralité.

Il est intéressant de relever à ce propos que, dans son dernier rapport en date du 7 juin 1999 à l'Assemblée fédérale sur la politique de sécurité de la Suisse, le Gouvernement de ce pays note que "le maintien de la neutralité permanente devra, même avec la meilleure utilisation possible de la marge de manœuvre qu'offre le droit de la neutralité, être soumis à l'avenir à la question critique de savoir si cet élément de notre stratégie en matière de politique de sécurité sera suffisant pour offrir, au XXIe siècle également, la meilleure perception possible des intérêts de la Suisse en matière de politique extérieure et de politique de sécurité".

■ Professeur à l'Université de Lausanne; Ancien Ambassadeur de la Confédération Suisse.

V. Gowlland-Debbas (ed.), *United Nations Sanctions and International Law*, p. 361-368.

Lorsqu'on examine l'attitude de la Suisse à l'égard des sanctions décrétées par le Conseil de sécurité des Nations Unies au titre du Chapitre VII de la Charte, il est nécessaire de bien distinguer la période avant 1990 et celle qui suit l'adoption des sanctions contre l'Irak.

I

S'agissant tout d'abord de la Rhodésie, le Conseil fédéral suisse relève, dans son message du 21 décembre 1981 concernant l'adhésion de la Suisse à l'Organisation des Nations Unies, que les sanctions décrétées par le Conseil de sécurité contre la colonie britannique ne sont pas demeurées sans conséquences pour la Suisse, "bien que notre pays, n'étant pas membre de l'ONU, ne fût pas tenu juridiquement d'appliquer les décisions du Conseil de sécurité". Le Gouvernement suisse ne manque toutefois pas de rappeler que l'article 2, paragraphe 6, de la Charte oblige l'Organisation à faire en sorte que les Etats qui ne sont pas membres des Nations Unies agissent conformément aux principes de la Charte dans la mesure nécessaire au maintien de la paix et de la sécurité internationales. Le Secrétaire général de l'ONU s'étant adressé à la Suisse, à plusieurs reprises, pour lui demander de participer à l'application des sanctions contre la Rhodésie, ce pays a jugé, étant donné le poids que l'unanimité de ses membres conférait alors à l'organisation mondiale, qu'il ne pouvait pas ignorer simplement ces appels. En particulier, la Suisse n'a pas été insensible à l'argument, relevant de la *politique de neutralité,* selon lequel, en restant à l'écart de l'action de l'ONU, elle pourrait servir de plaque tournante pour des opérations triangulaires (concernant, par exemple, des marchandises ne touchant à aucun moment le territoire suisse, mais faisant l'objet de transactions dans lesquelles étaient impliquées des personnes ayant leur domicile ou leur siège en Suisse) destinées à éluder les sanctions contre la Rhodésie et risquerait ainsi de favoriser l'une des parties au conflit.

C'est pourquoi la Suisse décida d'introduire à l'égard de la *Rhodésie*, entre autres mesures prises dans le cadre de sa *politique de neutralité*, la pratique du "courant normal" (stabilisation du volume des échanges au niveau moyen d'une période de référence – ordinairement triennale – antérieure à l'adoption des sanctions), à laquelle elle avait déjà eu recours lors de la seconde guerre mondiale. Elle a pris soin toutefois de relever qu'elle prenait ces mesures en vertu du pouvoir d'appréciation inhérent à sa politique de neutralité et que leur adoption ne pouvait pas être interprétée comme la reconnaissance d'une obligation juridique à la charge d'un Etat non membre de participer à des sanctions économiques. C'est donc de manière *autonome* que la Suisse prit les mesures en question.

Quant aux sanctions contre *l'Afrique du Sud*, elles n'ont occasionné aucune difficulté à la Suisse du point de vue de sa *politique de neutralité*. En effet, lorsque le Conseil de sécurité décréta, dans sa résolution 418 (1977), un embargo sur les armes contre ce pays en raison notamment de la présence continue de l'Afrique du Sud en Namibie (ancien territoire sous mandat de la Société des Nations), la Suisse appliquait déjà cette mesure de manière autonome, conformément à sa pratique de ne pas livrer d'armes dans des régions en proie à des tensions politiques. La résolution ordonnait aussi la cessation de toute coopération en ce qui concerne la fabrication d'armes nucléaires; or la Suisse, toujours selon le Conseil fédéral, n'entretenait aucune collaboration avec l'Afrique du Sud dans ce domaine, car elle est partie au Traité sur la non prolifération des armes nucléaires, qui lui interdit d'aider les Etats à se doter d'armes de ce type. Enfin, l'obligation de renoncer à octroyer des licences pour la fabrication d'armes n'avait pas de conséquences pratiques pour la Suisse, étant donné la retenue qu'elle s'imposait déjà dans ce domaine.

II

Le début des années 1990, avec l'adoption des sanctions décrétées par le Conseil de sécurité contre l'*Irak* comme suite à l'invasion du territoire de l'Etat du Koweït, devait entraîner un tournant dans la politique de la Suisse dans ce domaine. Le 7 août 1990, le Conseil fédéral adopta une ordonnance qui interdisait notamment toute activité commerciale avec la République d'Irak. Le Département fédéral des affaires étrangères chargea le Professeur *Dietrich Schindler*, de l'Université de Zurich, de procéder à une analyse détaillée de la compatibilité de la neutralité avec le système de sécurité collective des Nations Unies. Dans ses conclusions, l'éminent professeur releva, d'une part, que, selon la doctrine et la pratique, il y avait lieu d'admettre que le *droit de la neutralité* ne s'appliquait pas aux sanctions décrétées par le Conseil de sécurité sur la base de l'article 41 de la Charte, et que, d'autre part, l'étude de la pratique du Conseil de sécurité et de la jurisprudence de la Cour internationale de justice (avis consultatif de 1971 sur les conséquences juridiques pour les Etats de la présence continue de l'Afrique du Sud en Namibie) démontrait que les Etats non membres des Nations Unies étaient tenus de collaborer à la mise en œuvre des sanctions ordonnées par le Conseil de sécurité.

En ce qui concerne le premier point, le rapport du Conseil fédéral sur la neutralité joint à son rapport du 29 novembre 1993 sur la politique extérieure de la Suisse dans les années 90 confirme la thèse selon laquelle la participation d'un Etat neutre aux sanctions de l'ONU décrétées en vertu du chapitre VII de la Charte n'est pas en contradiction avec le *droit de la neutralité*. En revanche, sur le deuxième point, le Conseil fédéral a continué à déclarer qu'il appliquait de *manière autonome* les sanctions ordonnées, par exemple, contre l'*Irak*, la *Libye,* l'*Ex-Yougoslavie*, la *Somalie* et le *Liberia.* Sa position a été résumée dans les termes suivants dans son rapport du 1er juillet 1998 sur les relations entre la Suisse et l'Organisation des Nations Unies:

- La pratique du Conseil fédéral est d'appliquer de manière autonome les mesures décidées par le Conseil de sécurité dans l'intérêt de la paix et de la sécurité internationales.
- Se fondant sur la doctrine dominante en droit international, le Conseil fédéral soutient qu'une participation de la Suisse aux sanctions de l'ONU, même en tant qu'Etat non membre, est compatible avec son statut de neutralité permanente, lorsque les sanctions sont appliquées par une grande majorité des Etats de la communauté internationale.
- Des sanctions ne sont pas un acte de guerre; elles constituent au contraire un moyen légitime de rétablir une situation conforme au droit lorsqu'elles sont adoptées à l'encontre d'un Etat qui a violé le droit international.
- La neutralité est un moyen d'atteindre les buts politiques que sont l'indépendance, la paix et la sécurité. Elle ne peut donc pas être contraire à des sanctions qui ont pour seul objectif la paix et la sécurité.

III

L'adoption par le Conseil de sécurité de la résolution 827, le 25 mai 1993, concernant la création du Tribunal *ad hoc* chargé de juger les crimes de guerre commis en ex-Yougoslavie a donné l'occasion au Conseil fédéral d'affiner sa position lorsqu'il décida, le 2 février 1994, d'appliquer cette résolution à titre autonome. Voici l'essentiel de son argumentation:

Aux termes de l'article 34 de la Convention de Vienne sur le droit des traités, du 23 mai 1969, les traités ne lient pas les Etats tiers sans leur consentement.

Du point de vue juridique, ni la Charte des Nations Unies, ni les décisions obligatoires prises par le Conseil de sécurité de l'Organisation dans le cadre du chapitre VII de la Charte n'engagent donc la Suisse. L'article 2, paragraphe 6, de la Charte ne contredit aucunement cette affirmation. Cette disposition se borne en effet à stipuler que "l'Organisation fait en sorte que les Etats qui ne sont pas membres des Nations Unies agissent conformément [aux principes de l'Organisation] dans la mesure nécessaire au maintien de la paix et de la sécurité internationales". L'Organisation s'acquitte de cette obligation, qui pèse sur elle et non sur les pays qui n'en sont pas membres, en déclarant la résolution 827 applicable "aux Etats". Le fait que la Charte ne met aucune obligation à la charge des pays non membres ne signifie pas, toutefois, que ces derniers ne puissent pas consentir à assumer des devoirs dans le cadre de la Charte.

La Suisse, qui n'est pas membre des Nations Unies, s'est associée à plusieurs reprises à des résolutions du Conseil de sécurité à titre autonome, c'est-à-dire volontairement, pour des motifs d'ordre éthique et politique: solidarité avec la communauté des Etats en vue de maintenir la paix et la sécurité internationales; désir d'éviter que des sanctions prises en vertu du chapitre VII ne soient tournées par des opérations triangulaires impliquant la Suisse; lutte contre le terrorisme international.

La résolution 827 s'inscrit dans le cadre du chapitre VII et vise ainsi à restaurer et à maintenir la paix. Cette raison devrait à elle seule suffire pour amener la Suisse à appliquer ce texte à titre autonome.

IV

L'ordre juridique interne suisse est traditionnellement moniste. En effet, comme le Conseil fédéral et le Tribunal fédéral suisses l'ont souvent rappelé, les règles du droit international (conventionnelles, coutumières ou unilatérales) font en Suisse, à partir de leur prise d'effet pour ce pays, partie intégrante de l'ordre juridique suisse. Pour les justiciables, l'invocabilité en justice de dispositions de droit international suppose que celles-ci soient, considérées dans leur contexte et à la lumière tant de l'objet que du but de ces dernières, inconditionnelles et suffisamment précises pour produire en effet direct et s'appliquer comme telles à un cas d'espèce et constituer le fondement d'une décision concrète. Enfin, les organes de la Confédération ont, conformément à la doctrine dominante en Suisse, reconnu et confirmé à maintes reprises le principe de la primauté du droit international.

En adoptant, à titre autonome, des mesures pour mettre en œuvre des sanctions décrétées par le Conseil de sécurité des Nations Unies, le Conseil fédéral a eu principalement recours à une disposition de la constitution fédérale, l'article 102, chiffre 8, qui le charge de "veiller aux intérêts de la Confédération au dehors". Cette disposition habilite en effet le Gouvernement suisse à adopter des ordonnances et des décisions fondées directement sur la constitution, lorsque ces mesures sont nécessaires pour protéger les intérêts de la Confédération au dehors. La nouvelle constitution fédérale mise à jour adoptée le 18 avril 1999 par la majorité du peuple et des cantons contient un article 184, dont le paragraphe 3 prévoit que: "Lorsque la sauvegarde des intérêts du pays l'exige, le Conseil fédéral peut adopter les ordonnances et prendre les décisions nécessaires. Les ordonnances doivent être limitées dans le temps". Cette disposition est intitulée de manière générale: "Relations avec l'étranger".

A côté de cette norme constitutionnelle, l'ordre juridique suisse comporte des dispositions spécifiques insérées, en particulier, dans la loi fédérale du 30 juin 1972 sur le matériel de guerre, dont l'article 11, 2e alinéa, lettre a, prévoyait qu'aucune autorisation d'exportation ne sera délivrée "à destination de territoires où des conflits armés ont éclaté ou menacent d'éclater ou dans lesquels règnent des tensions dangereuses". Ces critères étaient généralement remplis dans les pays touchés par des sanctions. La nouvelle loi fédérale du 13 décembre 1996 sur le matériel de guerre contient un article 25, aux termes duquel "pour tenir compte des décisions prises par la communauté internationale, le Conseil fédéral peut décider qu'aucune autorisation ne sera accordée pour un pays déterminé ou pour un groupe de pays".

De même, l'article 6, 2e alinéa, de la loi fédérale du 13 décembre 1996 sur le contrôle des biens utilisables à des fins civiles et militaires et des biens militaires spécifiques prévoit que "les permis concernant les biens militaires spécifiques sont [...] refusés lorsque les Nations Unies ou certains Etats qui, comme la Suisse, participent à des mesures internationales de contrôle des exportations, interdisent l'exportation de tels biens, et si les principaux partenaires commerciaux de la Suisse s'associent à ces mesures d'interdiction".

Il convient en outre de rappeler que l'article premier de la loi fédérale du 25 juin 1982 sur les mesures économiques extérieures donne au Conseil fédéral, lorsque des mesures prises à l'étranger ou des conditions extraordinaires régnant à l'étranger ont, sur le trafic des marchandises, des services ou des paiements de la Suisse avec l'étranger, des effets tels que des intérêts économiques suisses essentiels s'en trouvent affectés, la compétence, en particulier, de surveiller l'importation, l'exportation et le transit des marchandises, ainsi que le trafic des services, de les soumettre au régime de l'autorisation, de les limiter ou de les interdire.

Enfin, il est intéressant de relever que si le Conseil fédéral a pu, en s'appuyant sur l'article 102, chiffre 8, de la constitution fédérale, décider d'appliquer à titre autonome la résolution 827 du Conseil de sécurité des Nations Unies, ainsi que le Statut du Tribunal international chargé de juger les personnes présumées responsables de violations graves du droit international humanitaire commises sur le territoire de l'ex-Yougoslavie depuis 1991, il a jugé opportun de faire adopter par le Parlement un arrêté fédéral relatif à la coopération avec les tribunaux internationaux chargés de poursuivre les violations graves du droit international humanitaire, arrêté qui porte la date du 21 décembre 1995.

L'application par la Suisse à titre autonome des sanctions décrétées par le Conseil de sécurité au titre du chapitre VII de la Charte des Nations Unies n'a pas occasionné de difficultés particulières autres que celles rencontrées par les Etats membres de l'Organisation. Ces problèmes ont trait, en particulier, aux exceptions prévues dans certaines des résolutions pour les marchandises exportées à des fins médicales ou humanitaires, aux cas de rigueur, ainsi que, dans le domaine financier notamment, à l'imprécision de certains termes utilisés par ces résolutions. Si la Suisse s'est tenue, d'une manière générale, aux dispositions adoptées par les Nations Unies, elle s'en est écartée, par exemple dans le cas de la Libye, lorsqu'il s'est agi d'autoriser à titre exceptionnel des paiements prélevés sur des comptes bloqués et des transferts de valeurs en capital bloquées, et ceci pour protéger des intérêts suisses. En outre, des problèmes ont pu surgir en ce qui concerne l'identification de certaines personnes et entreprises visées par des sanctions.

La collaboration avec les Nations Unies a été assurée de manière adéquate. C'est ainsi, par exemple, que l'ordonnance du 1er juillet 1998 instituant des mesures à l'encontre de la République fédérale de Yougoslavie prévoit, à ses articles 6 et 7, une collaboration avec les Nations Unies notamment pour la transmission des renseignements nécessaires aux autorités compétentes en matière d'exécution, de contrôle, de prévention et de poursuite judiciaire. La fourniture de renseignements aux Nations Unies est subordonnée à un certain nombre de conditions ayant trait, en particulier, au secret de fonction.

En ce qui concerne, enfin, la répression des infractions commises, les dispositions pénales contenues dans les ordonnances du Conseil fédéral prévoient soit une amende de 500'000 francs au plus, soit une peine d'arrêts ou une amende. Une peine d'emprisonnement devrait être prévue dans une loi au sens formel. L'élaboration d'une loi cadre concernant la mise en œuvre des sanctions est envisagée par les autorités fédérales.

PART IV

THE FUTURE OF SANCTIONS

Chair: *Ismat Kittani*
Special Adviser to the Secretary-General
of the United Nations in Geneva

THE IMPACT OF UNITED NATIONS SANCTIONS ON ECONOMIC DEVELOPMENT, HUMAN RIGHTS AND CIVIL SOCIETY

A. Amir Al-Anbari[■]

I THE EXISTING REGIME OF SANCTIONS

1. Economic sanctions are generally conceived as peaceful measures preferable to the use of force. In reality, however, economic sanctions are by no means peaceful and quite often are deadlier and more destructive than military action.

As President Woodrow Wilson of the United States put it, economic sanctions "provide a peaceful, silent and deadly remedy". In quoting President Wilson on sanctions, the report on World Disasters 1998 prepared by the IFRC and RCS, compared the impact of economic and military sanctions by emphasising that "one of the basic tenets of the laws of war makes the distinction between the combatant and the civilian." As far as civilians are concerned, the report noted that, according to the laws of war, they "should not be a target. Weapons should be designed and used so that they can be targeted at the combatants and avoid unduly harming civilians." In contrast the Report noted that "economic sanctions are proving to be no cruise missile. Practice has shown that they are not surgical strikes but extraordinary messy weapons, the economic equivalent of blanket bombing."[1]

■ Ph.D. in international law, Harvard Law School. Former Ambassador of Iraq to the UK, the USA, the UN and UNESCO.

1 International Federation of the Red Cross and Red Cross Societies. Report on World Disasters, 1998, pp. 92-93.

V. Gowlland-Debbas (ed.), *United Nations Sanctions and International Law*, p. 371-380.

2. Another problem that enables the Security Council to impose economic sanctions that could be the equivalent of blanket bombing is that although Article 41 of the Charter specifies certain non-military measures such as "complete or partial interruption of economic relations and of rail, sea, air ... and other means of communication ..." in principle, however, that Article leaves it to the discretion of the Security Council to impose whatever non-military measures it might choose. This is contrary to the general principle of criminal law in all Member states namely that no crime and no punishment may be imposed unless it is specified by law. It is true that Article 39 of the Charter requires the Council to make a determination as to "the existence of any threat to the peace, breach of the peace or act of aggression" before making its recommendations or decisions as to "what measures shall be taken in accordance with Articles 41 and 42 ..." Such a determination is equivalent to a judgement that an international crime has been committed, but the punishment to be imposed is left totally to the discretion of the Council which in practice means the five permanent members.

It may be argued that the Council being an organ of the United Nations is required to abide by Article (1) of the Charter which defines the purpose of the United Nations including acting in settling disputes 'in conformity with the principles of Justice and international law ...' In practice, however, the Council does not consider whether a particular sanction is prohibited by the principles of Justice and international law.

In effect the Council seems to think that any action it takes is consistent with these principles by virtue of its own approval.

Indeed, Article 41 of the Charter does not even require that sanctions should not violate the United Nations Charter or the Human Rights Convention and the Geneva Conventions and their Protocol concerning the treatment of civilians in time of armed conflicts.

3. Consequently, economic sanctions imposed on states or governments degenerate to a collective punishment of the people. It is almost a cliché to hear that the suffering of the civilians particularly children and women is a collateral or unintended side effects. Be that as it may, when the main victim of the sanction is the civilian population then the sanctions have to be terminated or modified in such a way as to ensure the safety and human rights of the civilian population. Under the present Charter there is no such requirement.

4. Following the collapse of Communism in the Soviet Union and Eastern Europe, new and dangerous ideology is being articulated and promoted, namely, the conflict of civilisations including religions and languages. Of course a policy influenced by such ideology will never be expressly cited but it could be the motive for the imposition of sanctions under one pretext or another.

5. Finally it must be recognised that the basic provisions of the United Nations Charter including Chapter VII, were drafted more than 50 years ago to accommodate the interests of the victorious five countries and to insure that world peace and order is maintained to protect and not to prejudice the interests of these countries. In the meantime the structure of the International Community has radically expanded and new international problems and issues require solutions and measures which cannot be implemented under the present Charter. It is of course difficult to revise the Charter but such a revision, particularly Chapter VII must be made. The end of the Cold War must help facilitate such a revision.

II New Regime of Sanctions

It will be recalled that for the first time in the history of the Security Council, a working session was held on 31 January 1992 at the level of heads of states or governments. One of the main decision the Council Summit adopted was calling on the Secretary-General to prepare and present to the Council an

> "analysis and recommendations on ways of strengthening and making more efficient within the framework and provisions of the Charter the capacity of the United Nations for preventive diplomacy, for peacemaking and for peace-keeping".[2]

The Secretary-General presented his reports entitled "An Agenda for Peace" and "Supplement to an Agenda for Peace"[3] which were discussed with general support by the Council, the General Assembly and Member states. In this Report the Secretary-General highlighted the quantitative and qualitative changes in United Nations activities since the end of the Cold War.

---

2 UN Doc. s/23500.

3 UN Doc. A/47/277 – S/241111, 17 June 1992 and A/50/60-S/1995/1, 3 January 1995, respectively.

In addition to the issues of preventive diplomacy and peacemaking, peace-keeping and post-conflict peace building and disarmament, the Secretary-General in his reports, found it pertinent and necessary to tackle the problem of sanctions. Referring to Article 41 of the Charter, which authorises the Security Council to call upon Member states to apply measures not involving the use of armed force in order to maintain or restore international peace and security, the Secretary-General concluded that such measures are based on a legal provision of the Charter. Accordingly "the purpose of sanctions is to modify the behaviour of a party that is threatening international peace and security and not to punish or otherwise exact retribution."[4] But in practice sanctions have actually been used as a collective punishment or to achieve objectives other than those for which sanctions were initially imposed. Such manipulation of sanctions takes place particularly when the objectives of the sanction are not clear or practically unattainable, and because of the lack of monitoring their application, impact and unintended effects.

As far as the objectives are concerned, the report raised the problem of the lack of clarity in the objectives of the sanctions, which as time passes are sometimes changed into different or additional objectives. Consequently, the report concludes that "This combination of imprecision and mutability makes it difficult for the Security Council to agree on when the objectives can be considered to have been achieved and sanctions can be lifted."[5]

Indeed even when the objectives are clearly defined and fully implemented they sometimes are taken as a basis for the imposition of new sanctions to achieve different objectives. To give one critical illustration, when the Council adopted resolution 661 (1990) following the entry of Iraqi armed forces in Kuwait, it specified two clear objectives, notably the withdrawal of the Iraqi forces to their pre August 2, 1990 positions and the return of the Kuwaiti Government to power. Both of these objectives were realised in early March 1991. Yet the Council, referring to the same resolution and other related ones but without making a new determination that a threat to peace existed, imposed new sanctions for the implementation of new and vague, indeed unattainable, objectives under resolution 687 (1991) which after more than eight years remain as they were imposed in 1991.

---

4 "Supplement to an Agenda for Peace", p. 16.

5 *Ibid.*

In addition to the lack of clarity of objectives which prolong or perpetuate sanctions, economic sanctions "raise the ethical question of whether suffering inflicted on vulnerable groups in the target country is a legitimate means of exerting pressure on political leaders whose behaviour is unlikely to be affected by the plight of their subjects."[6] Here there is a unique dilemma, which sheds doubt about the morality, legitimacy and effectiveness of the present regime of sanctions. For one reason or another sanctions are imposed more often than not on developing countries whose regimes are authoritarian or which, as noted by the Secretary-General, do not change their behaviour as long as it is the vulnerable groups, rather than the political or military elites, which suffer most under sanctions. If that is the case, imposition of sanctions in their present system, could arguably be considered as a crime against humanity since changing the behaviour of such regimes is futile whilst the deprivation of the lives and human rights of vulnerable groups is certain and predictable.

Of no less importance, the Secretary-General referred to the impact of sanctions on the development objective of the United Nations and the long-term damage to the productive capacity of the sanctioned country. Indeed as early as 1968, the International Conference on Human Rights convened by the General Assembly, held in Tehran, adopted Resolution XVII entitled 'Economic Development and Human Rights' which included the following paragraphs:

> *The International Conference on Human Rights,*
> *Believing* that the enjoyment of economic and social rights is inherently linked with any meaningful enjoyment of civil and political rights and that there is a profound inter-connection between the realisation of human rights and economic development.
>
> *Noting* that the vast majority of mankind continues to live in poverty, suffer from squalor, disease and illiteracy and thus leads a sub-human existence.

The "inherent correlation between the enjoyment of human rights and economic development is now universally recognised." Furthermore, economic development is no longer measured only by the growth of per capita income and the national domestic product; it is the quality of life, which a national society achieves that reflects its sustainable development. Accordingly, sustainable economic development calls for a healthy, educated and free nation with effective civil society institutions and democratic public authorities, independent

6 *Ibid.*

judiciary and uncorrupted business community. Thus any type of economic sanctions is bound to impair one or all aspects of sustainable development.

On the other hand, severe economic sanctions are bound to impoverish the majority of the population, cause hyperinflation, retard the agricultural, industrial, educational and health systems while spreading crime and corruption. The governing elite, however, increases its power in co-operation with a minority of collaborators who enrich themselves through smuggling and black marketeering.

In a recent article in the May/June 1999 issue of *Foreign Affairs* magazine two American Professors, John Mueller and Karl Mueller argued that "as cold war threats have diminished, so-called weapons of mass destruction – nuclear, chemical, and biological weapons and ballistic missiles – have become the new international bugbears".

The irony, they argued, is that "the harm caused by these weapons pales in comparison to the havoc wrecked by a much more popular tool: economic sanctions". The authors make a startling but well established conclusion that the atomic bombings of Hiroshima and Nagasaki killed more than 100, 000 people, while some 80, 000 were killed by chemical weapons in World War I, and 400,000 other people died because of intentional or accidental use of biological weapons and ballistic missiles.

In conclusion, they argue that "if the UN estimates of the human damage in Iraq are even roughly correct … it would appear that … economic sanctions may well have been a necessary cause of the deaths of more people in Iraq than have been slain by all so-called weapons of mass destruction throughout history."[7]

One could cite many other considerations that call for reforming the existing regime of economic sanctions, but what was mentioned above is sufficient to show that the existing regime of sanctions is indefensible, and unsustainable.

In his "Supplement to an Agenda for Peace", the Secretary-General made five proposals calling for: assessment of the impact of sanctions on the target country

7 *Foreign Affairs*, May/June 1999, p. 51.

and third countries before the imposition of the sanctions; monitoring the application of the sanctions; measuring the effects of the sanctions with a view to maximising their political impact and minimising collateral damage; ensuring the delivery of humanitarian assistance; and assisting states suffering collateral damage.

One could add to the above suggestions other measures including:

1. No sanctions should be imposed indefinitely. A suitable time limit must be included in the resolution imposing the sanction. Once the time limit is exhausted sanctions must automatically be terminated even if the objectives sought have not been achieved despite the imposition of the sanction during the period fixed in the resolution. Otherwise, indefinite sanctions are more likely to become a unilateral political instrument in the hands of one of the veto invested permanent members of the Council to realize its own political agenda in the name of international legitimacy and the authority of the Security Council.

2. The Security Council whose main responsibility is to maintain or restore international peace and security is by no means above the Charter of the United Nations nor is it immune of the rules and commitments provided for in the Charter and other collective international conventions which constitute the core of the international public order such as the Geneva Conventions and their protocols regarding the treatment and protection of civilian population in case of armed conflict as well as the Convention on the Prevention and Punishment of the Crime of Genocide of 1951. In this respect it should be noted that Article 103 of the Charter applies only to Member states. It is, indeed, *well established* that no international organ established by an international convention could be conceivably above international law and basic international conventions. Yet the Security Council, particularly the permanent members, quite often act as the victorious powers of World War II. But the rest of the international community which comprises more than 180 Member states were not defeated in that war nor could they be treated as colonies of defeated powers once they obtained their independence and became sovereign members of the United Nations on whose behalf the Security Council acts in maintaining international peace and security.

Accordingly no sanctions should violate such legal rules and commitments required by the UN Charter and other international conventions, which, despite the absence of a hierarchical system in the international legal order, are generally considered as the core of the international public order, which the Security Council must abide by in all its decisions. To insure that, UN imposed sanctions, be they economic and / or military, must be qualified by a *proviso* that such sanctions should not be interpreted or applied in violation of the Geneva Conventions, and their Protocols, the Universal Declaration of Human Rights and other basic conventions of humanitarian law. It is most frustrating for international jurists who believe in collective security under the rule of law, that the Security Council quite often indulges in vague, loose, even contradictory expressions while virtually authorising the use of force. The most glaring example of this is resolution 678 of November 29th 1990, authorising the American-led coalition to take "all necessary measures ... to uphold and implement" resolution 661 (1990) and other relevant subsequent resolutions. Since there were no qualifications relating to such measures it could arguably be interpreted as to authorise the use of nuclear weapons and other mass destruction weapons. Indeed, the American airplanes and missiles as well as British forces did use thousands of uranium-depleted warheads.

It follows that if any sanction imposed by the Council violates initially or eventually any convention or rule that is part of the international public order it should to be considered null and void. There is of course a problem as to who is to decide that a particular decision or sanction is null and void. The International Court of Justice should assume such jurisdiction.

The forthcoming permanent International Criminal Court could likewise assume such jurisdiction. In the meantime, individual Member states of the United Nations should have the power to declare that the enforcement of a particular sanction is in violation of the international public order and consequently it is free from adhering to it. The decision of the African Unity Organization not to abide by the Security Council sanction against air flights to or from Libya is an important precedent, which the Council should keep in mind so as to maintain its credibility and integrity in the future.

3. The enforcement of sanctions should not be entrusted to a sanctions committee which is a subsidiary organ of the Security Council but acts as if it is a super Security Council, disregarding explicit decisions and instructions of the Council as long as one member of the Committee withholds its approval or vetoes any decision supported by the rest of the members of the Sanctions Committee.

Thus the President of the Security Council addressed a letter on behalf of the Council's members,[8] requiring it to follow six measures in order to improve its actions and procedures, yet because of the action of one or more members of the Committee, the spirit and letter of the instructions of the President of the Council are often disregarded.

It is submitted that if the Council decisions imposing sanctions are to be implemented to achieve the objectives for which the sanctions were imposed, the enforcement of such decisions should be entrusted to a sanction committee acting not by unanimity but by a simple majority. Alternatively, the enforcement of such sanctions and/or the monitoring of their implications should be entrusted to the Inter-Agency of the United Nations specialised organizations including UNICEF, WHO and other humanitarian agencies. A third alternative would be to entrust the implementation of sanctions to Member states of the United Nations and their regional organizations.

It must be recognised, however, that most modern sophisticated weapons, including so called smart bombs, inevitably wound or kill civilians and civilian institutions. The use of depleted uranium warheads in the Gulf War is one of the most dangerous modern weapons. On impact, such warheads release nuclear radiation polluting land, water, and air, as well as agricultural and animal resources, causing as time passes, widespread cancerous and other terminal diseases. International scientists, particularly from Germany and Austria as well as Britain, now acknowledge that such nuclear radiation would last millions of years and spread throughout the region. Had the Security Council or its military committee been in charge of the use of force in the Gulf War it would certainly have refrained from using such warheads. Thousands of human lives as well as domestic and wild animals would have been saved now as well as in future generations.

Surprisingly, the International Atomic Agency (IAEA) has done nothing about the tragic consequences of spent uranium in the Gulf Region even though it keeps taking water and soil samples from various parts of Iraq. Its negative stance in this respect seems to rely on the argument that it is beyond its mandate to document and report on the tragic consequences of the weapons used during the Gulf War. Consequently it is the regions' countries that should take the

8 UN Doc. S/1995/234.

initiative and launch an international campaign regarding the use and consequences of the uranium depleted warheads and their remedies if any.

Given the provisions of the current UN Charter, the Security Council whenever enforcing sanctions against any member country should call upon the IAEA, WHO, UNICEF, UNESCO and other humanitarian Specialised Agencies as well as the ICRC, to monitor and report to the Council on the consequences of the use of such sanctions on civilian life and the environment and make necessary recommendations.

The above proposals would certainly reduce the illegal application of sanctions, but it is submitted that the only way to ensure the respect of Humanitarian International Law is to outlaw economic sanctions. While sanctions have to be applied against governments that threaten international peace and order or commit international aggression, such sanctions should be limited to the political and diplomatic spheres, including suspension of membership in the UN and other organizations and severance of diplomatic relations. Should such sanctions prove to be ineffective or impractical, the use of force according to Article 42 of the Charter should be resorted to. However, the use of force in such a case should be carried out by and/or under the strict supervision of the Security Council, so as to ensure first the proportional use of force and second, that no illegal weapons affecting civilians or destroying the environment be allowed to be used.

Horrible as it is, the use of force if controlled by the Security Council and monitored by the Specialised Agencies is in my view less destructive than economic sanctions, which victimise the innocent vulnerable civilians, and destroy life and environment in the targeted country.

ALTERNATIVES TO ECONOMIC SANCTIONS

Christine Chinkin■

I INTRODUCTORY COMMENTS

Considering the merits of non-coercive alternatives to economic sanctions inevitably risks the charges of idealism and naïvete. However a number of speakers in this conference have raised considerable doubts about the efficacy of sanctions: even on their own terms sanctions rarely work and the material costs to non-targeted states and the implications for human rights make their justification problematic, even when they can in some sense be said to have worked. It therefore makes sense at least to give consideration to some non-coercive alternatives, either in conjunction with sanctioning policies or separate from them. The other alternative is the use of force, which raises a host of other legal and moral considerations that are beyond the subject of this paper.

The question of sanctions, and alternatives to them, bring together three main areas of international law and the relationship between them:

1 the maintenance of international peace and security;
2 compliance with the international rule of law;
3 peaceful settlement of international disputes.

There are tensions between these areas. Compliance with an international rule of law suggests a vertical legal order while dispute settlement remains predicated

■ Professor of International Law, London School of Economics and Political Science.

V. Gowlland-Debbas (ed.), *United Nations Sanctions and International Law*, p. 381-391.

upon the consent of sovereign and equal states in a horizontal order. Further, measures imposed for the maintenance of international peace and security are not necessarily directed at resolving the underlying dispute and may even exacerbate it, thus giving rise to further non-compliance.

It is also necessary to address the purposes of sanctions. We cannot determine whether sanctions have been successful except against their function, nor weigh alternatives except against the ends we are trying to achieve. Further, their legal and moral justification rests upon the objectives sought. Of course sanctions have a number of purposes, some of which are expressed while others remain unexpressed. Under the UN Charter collective sanctions ('measures not involving the use of armed force') should only be imposed as part of the Security Council's strategy to respond to a threat to international peace and security.[1] In reality other motives often merge with, or displace, that primary objective. These include: to put an end to a state of affairs; to stop or induce change in behaviour; to achieve a particular objective; to ensure respect for and compliance with what the sanctioning body perceives as norms of international law; to limit potential damage (arms embargoes); to warn of further coercive measures to come; to serve as a rallying point in condemnation of certain behaviour; to assure domestic audiences that a response is being made to some behaviour presented as unacceptable (with the added advantage that the cost of this response is unlikely to be heavy for that domestic audience); to maintain the credibility of the sanctioning institution; to punish. These purposes and objectives may be mixed among protagonists and may vary at different times in the application of sanctions giving rise to lack of clarity in purpose and disagreement as to when the objective has been achieved.

If the major objective is punitive there may be no basis to seek alternatives, although there are important questions about their conformity with international law and their duration: how long is an appropriate 'sentence' in international law? If other purposes are paramount, especially those relating to behavioural change and compliance, useful insights might be gained from work in these areas. Theories of compliance and conformity with international law have moved beyond the punitive/positivist model to encompass other approaches. For example, Professor Kingsbury has pointed out that compliance is not a free-standing concept but rather that it derives its own meaning and utility from

1 UN Charter, articles 39 and 41. Unilateral sanctions (countermeasures) are also introduced for a range of purposes, and are subject to a separate legal regime.

different theories of law.[2] Nor can there be a simple binary distinction between compliance and non-compliance as international practice is fluid, variable and contextual.[3] Concepts of compliance depend upon understandings of the relations between law, behaviour, objectives and justice. It might also be useful to consider whether new perspectives can be gained for international relations from studies of sanctioning behaviour within domestic law, for example from criminology, behavioural sciences, including organizational behaviour, and evolving theories of alternative dispute resolution (ADR).

Compliance in the context of sanctions has two aspects: compliance (by all states) with the terms of the sanctions themselves and compliance (by the sanctioned state) with the underlying norms of law in question. With respect to the first, it may be that compliance is simply not appropriate for either the sanctioned state or others who must take major economic and political losses at the instance of the Security Council. To maximise the likelihood of compliance all states (or at least a sufficient number) must perceive the sanctions in Professor Franck's terms as legitimate and fair.[4] Regardless of their legal justification, if the imposition of sanctions is not so considered, compliance will be less forceful and may cease if sufficient states consider their duration to be excessive. Lack of transparency in Security Council decision-making and accountability for those decisions may undermine the perception of sanctions as legitimate and fair. With respect to the second, it is necessary that the sanctioned state shares the belief in the legitimacy of the norm to be enforced. Otherwise while there might be a pragmatic short-term expedient response, there is unlikely to be any long-term attitudinal change. Harold Koh has pointed to the role played by internal legitimation of norms[5] and if this is not present sanctions are unlikely to be an effective instrument for change. International law is of course a universally applicable system – current globalisation trends both appear to strengthen this appeal to universality and undermine it through an assumption of the globalisation of values. If values are not in fact shared – and sanctions are imposed for violation of norms based upon those values – then there is unlikely to be compliance. Sanctions will then be perceived as tools of the power-

2 B. Kingsbury, "The Concept of Compliance as a Function of Competing Conceptions of International law", (1998) 19 *Michigan Journal of International Law* 345.

3 *Ibid.* at 346.

4 T. Franck, *The Power of Legitimacy among Nations* (1990).

5 H. Koh, "Why Do Nations Obey International Law?", (1997) 106 *Yale Law Journal* 2599.

ful states to establish and enforce standards to which weaker states must conform. The pre-eminent role of the United States both in imposing sanctions unilaterally and in championing collective sanctions through the Security Council feeds into this perception and threatens states' commitment to upholding the legal authority of the Security Council.

Internalisation of norms is especially problematic in the context of human rights. Sanctions have been increasingly imposed for humanitarian violations with adverse consequences for human rights. Further, violations of human rights are rarely straight-forward but bring together complex issues of political and cultural self-determination, economic restructuring and long histories of various forms of intervention which all compromise commitment to universal standards. Methods such as the world travelling notion advanced by Isabelle Gunning,[6] or the cross cultural dialogue advocated by Abdullah An-Naim,[7] that rest on mutual communication in an attempt to achieve understandings of the root problems may in the long term be more effective than sanctions. Strategies for advancing the objectives of integrating human rights throughout the work and agencies of the United Nations, co-ordination between the human rights bodies and other UN agencies, and the allocation of adequate resources for human rights monitoring and implementation all require increased attention.

Leaving the issue of legitimacy, the imposition of sanctions too often assumes a positivist approach to the violation of a rule (or rules) of international law and a belief that the punishment of wrongdoing actors will induce changed behaviour. The greater use of international sanctions coincides with an especially punitive trend in domestic policies, most notably in the United States, that is seen in the growing prison population, longer custodial sentences, greater use of the death penalty and punishments designed to humiliate. The assumption that punishment and humiliation induce compliance is open to question. First, research suggests that it is not punishment that leads to compliance but the likelihood of sanctions being imposed. If a wrongdoing state knows that it can rely upon support within the Security Council, or that proposed sanctions against

6 I. Gunning, "Arrogant Perception, World Travelling and Multicultural Feminism: the Case of Female Genital Surgeries", (1991-2) 23 *Columbia Human Rights Law Review* 189.

7 A. An-Naim, "State Responsibility to Change Religious and Customary Laws", in R. Cook (ed.), *Human Rights of Women: National and International Perspectives* (1994) 167 at 178-181.

it will be vetoed, it is more likely to continue its behaviour. This both weakens the normative order and fosters a climate of non-compliance. If, on the other hand, it is recognised that certain acts will have inevitable consequences then forbearance is more likely. Some of the rhetoric of 'zero tolerance' could be valuable here. This also relates back to the moral imperative of sanctions. The expectation that wrongdoers will be treated alike lies at the heart of the legitimacy of any criminal justice system. This is severely compromised in the international system where some wrongdoers act with impunity.

There is perhaps a feeling that the current international legal order is threatened by lawlessness, that chaos is threatening and that sanctions must be imposed to reassert authority and order in the terms of the disciplining agency. But punitive measures alone rarely work and law-breaking behaviour continues. It is perhaps comparable to disciplining a child for repeated naughty behaviour – a not infrequent response from adults that indicates frustration and anger, but does not invariably lead to change. It is also worth remembering that:

> Those international lawyers who represent the current period in world history as one of order threatened by chaos ... represent only one perspective: that of those who had a stake in the old world order. This story ... does not describe the experience of many groups.[8]

For those who do not have such a stake – states that see themselves as disadvantaged by the existing order, marginalised groups, rebels challenging the internal authority of the state – sanctions will have little or no effect.

Changing perspectives to explore other theories of behavioural change for their relevance to international affairs could be attempted. One example is Braithwaite's work on restorative justice,[9] with its emphasis on methods of reintegration. Despite the obvious dangers of transplanting domestic theories into the international arena, some thought to the underlying philosophies could be given. Technical assistance programmes of the human rights bodies, or approaches such as those of the International Labour Organization discussed in this book could be viewed in this light.

---

8 A. Orford, "The Politics of Collective Security", (1996) 17 *Michigan Journal of International Law* 373 at 400.

9 J. Braithwaite, *Crime, Shame and Reintegration* (Cambridge, New York, etc., 1989).

Other theories of compliance are those based upon rational choice, that those subject to sanctions will make rational responses based upon economic realities, and the institutional management model developed by Chayes and Chayes in the influential book *The New Sovereignty*.[10] Such models require identification of the linkages that motivate economic choices and the leverage that can be used on actors. However they depend upon the assumption that targeted actors will perceive their self-interest in objective rational terms and remove from the equation the apparently irrational behaviour and messy attributes of international disputes such as nationalism, historical attachment to land etc. Nevertheless the work on compliance elsewhere in international law, such as procedures introduced under environmental treaties, should be examined by the Security Council. Environmental compliance procedures have been worked out to operate within an institutional framework and aim at providing both inducements for compliance and sanctions for non-compliance, thus combining the 'carrot and stick' approaches. There is a danger of the Security Council becoming compartmentalised and isolated from changing directions in other areas of international law to the detriment to its own capacity to seek innovative approaches.

II Some Non-Coercive Alternatives to Sanctions

Bearing in mind some of these questions of behavioural change, inclusion and participation, some alternative approaches will be briefly mentioned. None of the processes are new; rather existing processes have been adapted and moulded to changing circumstances. It is noticeable that the more frequent imposition of sanctions since 1990 has been accompanied by growing attention to devising flexible regimes for peaceful dispute settlement, which involve the participation of the alleged wrongdoer in seeking a solution to the situation. There has also been some limited greater recourse to adjudicatory methods, for example to the contentious jurisdiction of the ICJ and the reference of two disputes to the International Tribunal for the Law of the Sea.

The desirability of pre-emptive action was raised in *An Agenda for Peace* 1992 and its 1995 *Supplement* and has been reiterated by the current Secretary-General in his 2000 Report. Preventive deployment requires taking a long-term

10 A. Chayes & A. Chayes, *The New Sovereignty: Compliance with International Regulatory Agreements* (Cambridge, MA, etc.,1995).

view through data collection and collation to provide an early warning of situations with the potential for crisis. There is also the need for proper analysis of the data, integrated preventive strategy and the political will of the Security Council to act responsibly upon the basis of the information received. Despite the evident sense of this, states remain unwilling to take pre-emptive measures to reduce the likelihood of a subsequent threat to international peace and security, that in terms of expended resources, would be cost-effective. An example is Kosovo where events in 1989 and then in Bosnia served as warnings of the humanitarian violations that were to come. The West's need for Milosevic to be a party to the Dayton Agreement in 1995 and the subsequent lifting of sanctions against Yugoslavia all fed into the continuation of the humanitarian abuses that eventually culminated in NATO's actions in 1999 and the international presence in Kosovo for the foreseeable future.

A holistic view of preventive action is needed that looks at the symptoms of insecurity, including further work on the understanding of what constitutes a threat to international security. It is a truism that 'the hidden agenda' for peace and security is that more attention and effort must be given to pressing economic, social and environmental problems.[11] To this end the Security Council must both seek and be open to receipt of information from such bodies as ECOSOC, the Specialised Agencies and human rights institutions and then feed such information into its decision-making. A welcome innovative step was the attendance of the Secretary-General's Special Adviser on Children in Armed Conflict before the Security Council to give a graphic account of his work. So too has been the interaction between the Security Council and regional organizations. In turn, other agencies, including the financial institutions, must take account of the security (understanding security in this extended sense) aspects of their agendas.

An example of such a preventive measure is the establishment of the High Commissioner for National Minorities within the OSCE.[12] The position is a manifestation of the commitment of the OSCE to the peaceful settlement of disputes in post Cold War Europe. It sees the threat to security in Europe in wide terms. The mandate of the High Commissioner is to serve as 'an instru-

11 B. Urquart. 'The UN and International Security after the Cold War', in A. Roberts & B. Kingsbury (eds), *United Nations, Divided World* (Oxford, 1993), p. 81 at 97.

12 The Foundation on Inter-Ethnic Relations, *The Role of the High Commissioner on National Minorities in OSCE Conflict Prevention* (The Hague 1997).

ment of conflict prevention at the earliest stages.' The High Commissioner operates independently of all parties, carries out on-site investigations and offers preventive diplomacy in an attempt to promote dialogue, confidence and co-operation. He acts as a "trip wire" to alert members to areas where threats to security cannot be contained. The OSCE has also agreed a Court of Conciliation and Arbitration. Although it can be justifiably noted that these innovations have not prevented grave conflict in Europe (and that the Court has not yet been used) they should not be discounted. Other institutions, notably the International Court of Justice, have suffered long periods of under-utilisation but nevertheless have survived to make a substantial contribution.

Preventive measures merge into processes for the peaceful settlement of disputes that are emphasised in the UN Charter, and through the concept of peacemaking, in an *Agenda for Peace*. The methods listed in Article 33 conform with what in domestic law have become known as ADR processes. Advocates of ADR find much common ground with the Chayes and Chayes model of international law compliance, pointing to the benefits of co-operative problem solving in which those involved explore options for settlement. Such processes represent a progression as UN Charter, chapter 6 merges into the coercive measures of chapter 7. However they should not be seen in a linear development with disputants moving from one process to another as the previous one fails. Rather they are all instruments in an armoury upon which disputants can draw separately, or in conjunction with each other, as the circumstances warrant.

In domestic arenas a great deal of work and training goes into enhancing the effectiveness of ADR methods. This includes work on seeking the appropriate process for particular types of dispute; determining the role and methods of third party facilitators; equipping third party intermediaries with skills to assist the parties in resolving their own disputes and seeking options for mutual gain. In international disputes this is all much more haphazard. International states-man, diplomats and those employed as third party facilitators may be naturally born and gifted mediators. They also may not be. Some people in these positions may have little understanding of the dynamics of ADR processes and how their potential can be harnessed. Training in the process and skills acquisition is becoming regarded as essential in domestic mediation but is apparently dispens-able in international disputes. Training of potential third party facilitators and debriefing on previous attempts at dispute settlement and crisis containment should become routine so that lessons can be learned and experiences shared. A data bank of good practice developed from the work of regional and global institutions, diplomatic staff and individuals who have acted as mediators or facilitators in international disputes should be maintained, publicised and used.

Institutionalisation (global and regional) of preventive and dispute resolution mechanisms can enhance legitimacy, expertise and resources, but the demands of the institution may impede the flow of the necessary interaction. The good offices role of the UN Secretary-General has both a preventive and dispute resolution function. While seeing it as one of the most important functions of the UN in its bringing together of investigative and mediatory techniques under the auspices of the UN, Professor Franck has noted the limitations caused by the separate political decisions of the Security Council.[13] These restrict the Secretary-General's freedom of manoeuvre and the inherent independence and flexibility of the process. Affording the third party leverage can increase the likelihood of success but raising that leverage to the level of threats of force if the settlement is not accepted (as at Rambouillet) also undermines the separate nature of the process. More attention to the ever more sophisticated analyses of ADR processes needs to be undertaken by international lawyers to identify the factors conducive to success.

Another aspect of ADR is the need to ensure maximum participation by those involved in a negotiatory process. Broad participation may however raise other tensions. For example there is the dilemma of international negotiations with an alleged violator of international law, such as a person indicted by a war crimes tribunal. Just as the ethical downside of sanctions has been addressed in this conference so too must that of non-coercive alternatives. Such negotiations, while expedient, may pave the way for further violations of international law. Further, the focus upon states in international disputes may leave out many layers of the issue. Negotiations that do not include all participants, including appropriate non-state actors, may discount important information, knowledge and relevant factors and assume a level of state control over those actors that does not exist. Any agreement reached without their participation may be practically unworkable, but state elites may be unwilling to legitimate the claims of such actors by consenting to their participation. Other issues relate to the representativeness and accountability of such non-state actors. In any given situation these questions will need addressing.

---

13 T. Franck, *Fairness in International Law and Institutions* (Oxford, 1995).

Similarly, the Security Council continues to perceive the state as a unitary and monolithic entity. Sanctions are directed against the state (or occasionally at a faction within the state) with the assumption that this is the way to change the behaviour of those in control. Liberal theorists however argue that this is too simplistic and prefer to present the state as disaggregated, as comprising many different sources of power and influence from professional networks to civil society that in turn operate across state boundaries in the various manifestations of international civil society. "The autonomy of the state in the face of international military and capital structures and of connections between transnational and local interests has long been put in question ... the integrated study of a wide variety of norms and actors is long overdue."[14] This is equally applicable to the imposition of sanctions and to alternatives to them. Strategies should be sought that draw upon the networks that are being created and the methods that are being devised on the ground.

Attempts to locate dispute resolution closer to the arenas of dispute so as to include local perspectives and initiatives may also be beneficial. One example is that of the African Women's Committee on Peace. This Committee is to be involved at all levels in the work of the institutions and mechanisms of the OAU for conflict prevention, management and resolution. The proposal envisages an autonomous committee comprising 16 women – 6 government representatives, 5 members from NGOs and 5 selected in their personal capacity – to co-ordinate with peace movements at national, regional and local levels. It is intended to ensure women's participation in all African peace initiatives, including those involving fact-finding, negotiation and mediation. It will also promote women at high decision and policy-making levels to provide information on localised issues. This vision recognises the importance of regional organizations, local knowledge and commitment. It also extends participation to ensure the inclusion of women's voices that are most frequently excluded. It surely makes sense to bring crucial decision-making back to the zones of conflict where there is the highest stake in their settlement and a practical understanding of the obstacles. It is not suggested that any of these alternatives provide the answers, nor that they should exclude other methods, including sanctions. What is suggested is that they are worth exploring to extend the range of options for dealing with threats to international peace and security.

---

14 B. Kingsbury, *supra*, n. 2 at 371.

This conference has demonstrated the distinctive features of sanctions and examined their place in national and international legal orders. It has demonstrated that further work is needed on how these distinctive features fit into theories of compliance and behaviour change. This raises numerous other questions, some of which have been alluded to throughout the conference and which also require further research and analysis: *inter alia* are sanctions efficient; are sanctioning institutions efficient; what is meant by efficiency, and is efficiency the appropriate measure of sanctions; how do decision-making processes in the Security Council impact upon sanctioning regimes; what is the balance between internal and external factors in ensuring the effectiveness of sanctions; how do international institutions tap into those domestic factors? In considering such questions the place of non-coercive alternatives should also be scrutinised.

CONTRAINTE LÉGALE ET VIOLENCE ILLÉGALE EN DROIT INTERNATIONAL: FONDEMENTS DE LA DISTINCTION

Monique Chemillier-Gendreau[▪]

Les sanctions, innomées dans la Charte bien que largement présentes, constituent le mécanisme clef du droit international. La crise de ce mécanisme illustre, si elle est avérée, une crise du droit international comme tel. Mais la problématique est alternative: est-ce seulement une crise de fonctionnement que la société internationale serait capable de dépasser? Dans cette hypothèse il faut réfléchir aux conditions nécessaires à une sortie de crise. C'est à quoi s'emploie majoritairement la doctrine du droit international. Ou bien n'y a-t-il pas une crise plus structurelle, tenant aux fondements incertains du droit international et qui, une fois ouverte, ne se refermerait pas si facilement ? C'est cette seconde hypothèse que je me propose d'explorer. Mais alors il faut tenter d'aller au plus intime des relations entre la violence et le droit bien que ces relations restent en partie énigmatiques ou irrationnelles.

Il est banal mais nécessaire de rappeler que le droit est un substitut à la violence. La norme a pour fonction d'organiser les situations sociales à partir de certaines valeurs communément partagées. Au nom de ces valeurs, le droit fonctionne comme contrainte sur les comportements. Mais cette contrainte n'est ni arbitraire, ni sans contrepartie. Elle est imposée selon une logique qui garantit en échange un certain équilibre social. Et l'on évalue le droit à sa capacité à réduire les désordres et à juguler les violences les plus débridées. Il crée ainsi, c'est en tout cas ce que l'on attend de lui, des espaces de liberté, de démocratie, éventuellement de progrès social et de paix.

▪ Professeur à l'Université Paris VII, Denis Diderot.

V. Gowlland-Debbas (ed.), *United Nations Sanctions and International Law*, p. 393-401.

Si l'on me suit jusque là et si l'on jauge le droit international à cette aune, les résultats sont piteux. Dans les relations internationales la violence, qu'elle soit militaire ou qu'elle prenne d'autres formes, ne cesse de se répandre et les inégalités de se renforcer. La violence militaire, celle qui menace la paix internationale, ayant atteint pendant la première moitié du siècle un étiage insoutenable, le droit des Nations unies avait tenté un saut qualitatif considérable. En effet, en dépit des théories de la guerre juste, le droit positif n'avait jusque là rien su faire d'autre qu'un peu d'humanisation de la guerre avec les Conventions de La Haye. Il n'y avait rien là-dedans qui se rapprochât des rapports qu'entretiennent le pouvoir et le droit dans les sociétés internes, rien qui fût comparable au discours sous-jacent à tout pouvoir national et qu'il est possible d'illustrer par la formule suivante: j'étends sur vous la violence (légitime) de ma loi souveraine et vous l'acceptez car cela vous protège de violences pires encore.

Or sans l'outil de la loi, et sans souveraineté à leur profit, les Nations Unies ont tenté d'atteindre le même résultat par convention. L'échange qui est au cœur de la Charte est bien celui-là: tous les Etats renoncent à l'un des attributs les plus forts de la souveraineté, le droit de faire la guerre. Mais en contrepartie, chacun est assuré de bénéficier de la sécurité collective, c'est-à-dire du fait que toute situation d'atteinte ou de menace à sa propre sécurité serait sanctionnée par des organes ayant reçu cette compétence de la collectivité. Sans sous-estimer les quelques cas dans lesquels le mécanisme des sanctions a été mis à l'épreuve avec une relative efficacité, on conviendra que le bilan global du système n'est pas bon. L'équilibre entre contrainte légale et violence illégale n'est pas réalisé, tout simplement parce que la contrainte légale est informe. Cela tient à l'oubli dans lequel sont tombées les dispositions centrales de la Charte, à savoir ses articles 43 à 46. La contrainte légale manque tout autant de rigueur lorsqu'il s'agit de sanctions économiques. La manipulation des procédures par la résolution 687 et celles qui ont suivi sur l'Irak, résolutions à travers lesquelles on a mené sans débat un processus de substitution de cause à la sanction imposée, en sont l'illustration éclatante. Il apparaît aujourd'hui sans ambiguïté possible que ces manœuvres procédurales ont conduit à des violations substantielles des droits de l'homme et à un mépris affiché du droit humanitaire.

Par ailleurs, la ligne qui sépare violence légale et illégale, difficile à tracer en soi, a été brouillée par l'impossibilité de plus en plus radicale à distinguer des situations internationales dans lesquelles il y a conflit ou différend entre deux ou plusieurs Etats et des situations beaucoup plus complexes où la ligne entre questions nationales et internationales s'est transformée en une zone aux contours indéfinis. Ainsi la question de la violence et du droit ne peut plus être posée de manière distincte dans le cadre de chaque société étatique et dans le cadre de la société internationale. La réflexion critique que je propose ici plonge ses racines dans une analyse des rapports de la violence et du droit dans les systèmes internes. Elle s'appuie sur cette part grandissante des conflits agitant la société internationale qui proviennent d'une contestation du découpage en Etats. Or, ce découpage en Etats était jusqu'ici la base même de la société internationale. Les limites d'efficacité du droit des peuples à disposer d'eux-mêmes comme norme sont atteintes dans les Balkans, mais aussi dans plusieurs parties de l'Afrique et à un moindre degré partout où pointe un risque de dislocation de l'Etat. Mais une autre part des conflits ou tensions naît de nouvelles formes d'hégémonie de nature transnationale qu'elles soient militaires, agro-alimentaires, financières, énergétiques, communicationnelles, etc. Elles sont le fait de pouvoirs qui surpassent les Etats, les ignorent ou les contraignent. Elles s'exercent dans un espace libéré à leur profit: l'espace mondial. Les Etats se trouvent ainsi menacés à la fois par des forces infra-étatiques et d'autres, supra-étatiques. La longue histoire de la souveraineté comme pouvoir exclusif s'exerçant dans un espace maîtrisé est en voie de s'achever. Mais, ce qui est rendu visible de ce fait, c'est la complexité de la crise de la souveraineté.

Il y a crise comme espace de pouvoir, mais aussi comme nature du pouvoir. Il est vrai que, à la sortie de la féodalité et au fil de plusieurs siècles, les Etats monarchiques et religieux européens s'étaient lentement constitués dans leurs frontières. Le principe *"chaque Prince est empereur en son royaume"* est alors décisif. Lorsqu'au XVIIIè siècle, s'esquisse une tentative de sécularisation du pouvoir, la souveraineté est déplacée du chef du roi sur celui du peuple, mais en réalité le déplacement aboutira sur le corps de la Nation avec la mise en œuvre de la représentation nationale. Voulu comme une libération, ce mouvement ne le sera qu'en partie, car il n'y a aucune rupture avec l'ordre marchand et la puissante logique qui l'anime.

Bien plus tard, dans le courant du XXè siècle, les tentatives de libération sociale prirent deux formes distinctes en dépit des liens qu'elles eurent parfois: la lutte des classes dans le cadre des mouvements communistes et les luttes de libération nationale contre le colonialisme et dans certains cas contre l'impérialisme, principalement en Amérique latine. Mais ces luttes ne remirent pas en cause le modèle de l'Etat et sa souveraineté. Les sociétés gérées pendant des décennies par le marxisme s'y rallièrent. Et l'Etat et son pouvoir souverain cristallisaient le désir et le point d'aboutissement des luttes de libération nationale. Mais tous comptes faits, en notre fin de siècle, ni les unes ni les autres de ces luttes ne remirent en cause l'ordre de la production et des échanges. Celui-ci poursuivit sa course à travers ces événements. La déposition du colonialisme juridique à peu près partout, puis la déposition du socialisme réel là où il s'était implanté, ont laissé la place à l'Etat et à l'économie de marché comme des concepts universels. Mais, devenu universel, c'est-à-dire généralisé à toutes les sociétés humaines comme modèle d'organisation politique et de centralité du droit interne, l'Etat échoue en même temps à être une figure de l'universel social du groupe humain qu'il prétend représenter. Il est aux prises avec l'exclusion. Il poursuit la chimère de la réintégration de tous, sans être en mesure d'y parvenir. Il apparaît ainsi que la théorie juridique de la souveraineté qui est au cœur de notre discipline est devenu factuellement inexacte. La souveraineté ne correspond plus à sa propre définition puisqu'elle n'est plus l'exclusivité des compétences sur un territoire. Les pouvoirs régaliens sont amputés chaque jour davantage. Dire cela n'est pas énoncer un jugement de valeur. Il ne s'agit ni d'approuver, ni de regretter, attitude qui revient aux politiques. Dire cela est seulement formuler un jugement de réalité.

Il faut revenir au fait que nous avons à la fois crise de l'espace du pouvoir et crise de la nature du pouvoir. En effet, il y a deux questions en une et cette dualité de la question donne à voir l'artifice de la frontière entre le droit interne et le droit international. Le concept de souveraineté n'est plus efficient comme pensée de la nature et des fondements du pouvoir et il peine à organiser la distribution du pouvoir entre les territoires. Selon la formule du philosophe Gérard Mairet, il est devenu un concept inerte.[1] L'une des erreurs de la théorie classique a été de sous-estimer le lien entre la maîtrise du marché intérieur et des échanges extérieurs d'une part et le pouvoir souverain de l'Etat de l'autre. On a méconnu l'importance, pour la cohérence entre la théorie et la pratique, de la maîtrise directe ou indirecte (cela dépendait des choix politiques) des fonctions sociales ou économiques. Aujourd'hui des fonctions essentielles en matière de finances, de communication, de contrôle de l'alimentation ou de l'environnement, de protection de la santé, se sont déterritorialisées, internationalisées. Elles ont perdu leur "traçabilité" à l'image des produits alimentaires suspects ... Mais dans le même temps, elles sont l'objet d'un encadrement juridique international extrêmement réduit.

1 Gérard Mairet, "Le *principe de souveraineté. Histoire et fondements du pouvoir moderne*" (Paris, 1997).

La crise de la souveraineté est en même temps une crise de la loi nationale. Cette loi interne résultait jusqu'à ce siècle, d'une alchimie par laquelle la violence était maîtrisée au sein d'une société aux contours délimités. Il y a la violence fondatrice du droit. Elle donne naissance au pouvoir constituant qui émerge souvent de convulsions sociales. Il y a force de la loi qui prolonge la première violence, la domestique, la transforme pudiquement en "contrainte". Elle préside à la contingence du juste. En effet, la balance imposée entre toutes les revendications des acteurs sociaux est de nature contingente. On lui demande seulement de produire une situation sociale pacifiée. Il y a là-dedans un aspect de fable car la loi souveraine appuyée sur l'énigme première de la souveraineté, plus ou moins authentifiée par des mécanismes de démocratie institutionnelle, masque toujours une dose d'inégalité irréductible.

Une zone d'indifférenciation persiste ainsi nécessairement entre la violence et le droit. Pendant longtemps, elle a été occultée, effacée par la haute figure de la souveraineté à partir de laquelle il était possible d'affirmer: cette violence-là est répréhensible, celle-là ne l'est pas car elle est le fait de la loi. Ce à quoi nous assistons, avec la montée en puissance d'une économie et d'une communication mondialisée, c'est à l'affaissement, difficilement réversible, de la souveraineté des Etats et de leurs droits internes. Dès lors, la zone d'indifférenciation entre la violence et le droit s'élargit, devient visible. Nombreux sont les Etats qui n'ont plus la maîtrise de zones d'exclusion sociale souvent considérables. Le droit qu'ils édictent n'y pénètre pas. Parfois, ils ne sont pas en mesure d'en édicter. Les souverainetés épuisées produisent de plus en plus de situations d'abandon social qui sont en elles-mêmes de la violence et qui en produisent plus encore en réponse.

Le cadre spatial d'application de la loi a éclaté. Mais en même temps, la souveraineté comme concept engendrant la loi a montré ses limites.[2] Est-ce à dire que par une translation spatiale, l'équilibre créé dans le champ national serait reproductible sur un espace plus vaste? Non, car, imparfaite et hasardeuse, l'articulation ébauchée dans la Charte des Nations unies entre emploi légal de la force (le mécanisme désigné sous le terme de sanctions) et violence illégale laisse proliférer cette dernière. Elle atteint dans ses formes militaires comme dans ses formes autres que militaires, des dimensions tragiques. Le monde est en communication intense et extensive, alors qu'il ne forme pas une société,

---

2 Voir Marcel David, *"À propos de la souveraineté: deux relectures de Carl Schmitt"*, *RDP*, (1999) no. 3, p. 661 *sq.*

car les rapports entre la violence et le droit n'y ont pas été pensés, ni rendus possibles de manière à engendrer la paix sociale attendue.

Les carences sont de plusieurs ordres. Le droit dans la pensée moderne (il s'agit ici du droit en général, c'est-à-dire principalement du droit interne), en tant que système lié à la démocratie, permet de dégager de l'objectivité à partir des subjectivités qui s'affrontent. Le désaccord des sujets crée une tension en termes de valeurs. Dire la norme, c'est choisir entre des valeurs opposées. Mais pour que ce choix ne soit pas arbitraire, le droit (et là est sa nature profonde) met en place des procédures. Celles-ci sont le filtre des valeurs. La substance énoncée dans la norme ou ensuite mise en action sur le terrain est soutenue par la rigueur des procédures qui est le gage de l'objectivité. Il n'y a pas de droit sans respect des procédures. En droit international, les contre-mesures (explosions des subjectivités et négation du droit) et le débat à leur propos témoignent de l'impasse conceptuelle dans laquelle on est entré. Le droit qui est contrainte, doit résulter d'un minimum de différenciation d'avec la force. Il faut justifier pour quelles raisons et par quels moyens la violence qu'il impose est supérieure à la violence brute. Or nous sommes en difficulté sur les énoncés premiers du droit international et à nouveau en difficulté sur les procédures d'application. Le droit international est un droit quasi-exclusivement contractuel. Le respect de la souveraineté externe de l'Etat a conduit à construire le droit international sur la base du volontarisme. Aujourd'hui le poids et la force des acteurs privés les mènent à leur tour à favoriser la forme contractuelle dans le champ international. La question: peut-il y avoir droit sans une articulation entre un échelon législatif et un échelon contractuel, est ignorée. Cependant, les contrats, indispensables à la vie sociale, laissent le rapport de forces entre les partenaires à l'état brut. La loi est d'une autre nature. Liée à l'énigme de la souveraineté et du pouvoir, elle est en démocratie la forme que prend l'expression de la volonté générale, la manière de mesurer quelles sont les valeurs partagées. Elle permet de réduire le pouvoir de certains au bénéfice des autres. Elle pose les limites de la liberté contractuelle des sujets. La chose qui manque le plus dans la construction inachevée du droit international, c'est un équivalent législatif qui marque les limites substantielles à la liberté de contracter. Les catégories du droit impératif général et de la coutume peinent à remplir cette fonction. Quant aux traités multilatéraux généraux, les Etats savent bien se souvenir qu'ils sont de nature contractuelle pour y faire des réserves, leur ajouter des déclarations interprétatives, ou tout simplement se soustraire aux obligations qui en découlent. Le Conseil d'Etat français dans l'arrêt Sarran du 13 octobre

1998, en donne un exemple.[3] Il s'agissait du décret organisant la consultation des populations de la Nouvelle-Calédonie. Ce texte était contesté sur la base de certaines dispositions du Pacte international sur les droits civils et politiques. Le Conseil d'Etat, dans une raideur toute jacobine, a refusé d'admettre la suprématie des traités internationaux sur la Constitution dans l'ordre interne. N'est-ce pas refuser toute efficacité réelle au droit international? La déliaison sociale qui apparaît en de si nombreux points de la planète, n'est pas sans rapport avec la carence d'un équivalent législatif à l'échelle internationale. La réduction de la violence ne se négocie pas. Elle ne peut se consolider dans la transaction. Cette réduction n'est possible qu'à travers l'autorité et la généralité de la loi. Les critères pour distinguer la violence légale de la violence illégale doivent être fixés par avance et en des termes applicables de la même manière à tous les sujets de droit. Les outils dont nous disposons dans ce sens sont trop imprécis et trop incomplets. Les grands principes de la Charte, ceux du droit humanitaire, l'ensemble des normes à valeur coutumière ou impérative universelle auxquels aucun Etat ne saurait déroger, ces principes-là sont très largement insuffisants. Il ne peuvent présider au classement précis dont nous avons besoin entre les actes licites et les actes illicites.

Mais objectera-t-on, peut-il y avoir loi ou équivalent législatif sans une autorité pour la dire? Et cette autorité doit-elle être souveraine? C'est toute la question des procédures. Il faut un organe en charge de dire la loi. Il n'est pas nécessairement souverain. Il ne peut plus l'être dans le monde actuel inéluctablement ouvert, puisque souveraineté veut dire exclusivité de l'autorité alors que l'ouverture entraîne des compétences concurrentes. Mais cette autorité doit être légitime, ce qui est différent. Le chemin est donc étroit si l'on veut éviter une centralisation accélérée de la société internationale qui ne ferait que réduire la diversité du monde et accroître les inégalités. Deux organes ont la compétence et la légitimité nécessaires pour nous permettre de perfectionner le droit international en parant aux écueils mentionnés. Il s'agit d'abord de la Cour internationale de justice. Elle prendrait son envol si sa juridiction devenait obligatoire (réforme qui est décisive) et si elle acceptait d'assurer le contrôle de la légalité internationale à tous égards. L'autre organe qu'il faut faire sortir de l'ombre, c'est l'Assemblée générale des Nations unies qui devrait retrouver une place beaucoup plus importante dans le processus de confirmation de la coutume.

3 Voir Denys Simon, "L'arrêt Sarran: dualisme incompressible ou monisme inversé?" *Europe*, (Mars 1999) no. 3, p. 4 *seq.*

Si le droit était plus clair et bénéficiait de plus d'autorité, il y aurait moins d'hésitations sur les comportements auxquels doit s'appliquer la violence légale. Resterait la question de son exercice. À cet égard, tout est à reprendre. Il faut revenir à l'application rigoureuse de la Charte sans négliger l'option de la révision de la Charte. Il y a eu violation de la Charte, dès qu'il y a eu délégation de son pouvoir d'entreprendre des actions armées opérée en aveugle par le Conseil de sécurité en direction des Etats. Or l'article 42 emploie le terme "entreprendre" qui ne peut pas être interprété comme déléguer. La meilleure preuve se trouve dans les termes de l'article 46 soigneusement passé aux oubliettes: *"Les plans pour l'emploi de la force armée sont établis par le Conseil de sécurité avec l'aide du Comité d'Etat-major"*. Il n'y a pas là la plus petite ouverture vers une délégation. Il était alors normal que cet abus d'interprétation, véritable violation de la Charte, conduise à l'instrumentalisation du Conseil de sécurité auquel nous assistons. On est même passé de la délégation donnée avant les opérations militaires (guerre du Golfe) à la délégation reconstruite *a posteriori* (guerre du Kosovo). Cela est venu à l'origine de l'absence de moyens militaires dans laquelle se sont trouvées les Nations unies. Mais les raisons qui avaient empêché d'appliquer l'article 43 de la Charte ne peuvent-elles désormais être dépassées? Pourquoi aucun gouvernement et guère de juristes ne posent cette question? Pour enrayer la dérive actuelle, il est urgent d'y revenir car de la réponse qu'on y apporte dépendent l'objectivité et la généralité des moyens d'action de l'Organisation. Les Etats membres, ceux de l'OTAN comme les autres, doivent mettre par avance des forces armées à la disposition des Nations unies et laisser ces dernières gérer ces forces selon tous les éléments de procédure édictés par le chapitre 7 de la Charte. La sécurité collective sera radicalement liquidée (et elle est en passe de l'être) si l'on ne revient pas à une gestion commune de forces internationales dont l'Organisation doit pouvoir disposer par avance, en dehors de tout conflit.

Ce point est central. Il correspond tout simplement à une stricte application du texte de la Charte. Mais nous butons alors sur la question du veto. Que faire si, à supposer des forces mises à la disposition permanente du Conseil, celui-ci se trouve à propos de leur usage, paralysé par un veto? Le problème n'est pas nouveau. Mal réglé dans la Charte, il l'était cependant d'une manière feutrée par l'article 12. Ses termes permettent d'aller plus loin qu'un recours tout-à-fait exceptionnel à l'Assemblée générale. Si le Conseil ne remplit pas ses fonctions, l'Assemblée peut faire des recommandations. Toute la querelle doctrinale autour de la résolution 377, ne s'était-elle pas soldée dans le sens d'une coutume interprétative de ce texte dans le sens de sa plus large application? D'où vient que l'on ne l'évoque plus si ce n'est parce qu'il n'a été utilisé que lorsque l'Assemblée générale était supposée être docile à certains et qu'elle ne l'est plus? Mais alors le droit a été confisqué par la politique...

Certains ne manqueront pas de faire remarquer qu'un organe collégial aussi lourd que l'Assemblée générale ne peut que bien exceptionnellement gérer un conflit dans sa durée et dans toutes ses dimensions. Nul n'en disconvient et cette solution est un pis aller. Mais si le Conseil de sécurité reste installé dans un jeu de vetos permanent, alors il faut regarder courageusement la nécessité de la réforme du Conseil de sécurité. Et la seule qui serait efficace, serait celle qui irait jusqu'à la suppression de la catégorie des membres permanents. Le propos parait encore à beaucoup iconoclaste. Pourtant, il faudra inéluctablement en venir là. L'Occident prône dans le monde entier non sans une certaine assurance, la démocratie institutionnelle comme un système politique modèle. C'est, dit-on, la meilleure réalisation de la liberté car dans ce cadre chaque peuple peut choisir ses dirigeants, ceux qui incarneront sa représentation, et lui imposeront une norme commune. Comment pouvons-nous continuer d'accepter que dans la société internationale, le peuple des Nations, ne choisisse pas régulièrement, librement et pour une durée limitée, toutes celles d'entre elles qui le représenteront?

Pour en avoir trop mal usé, le Conseil de sécurité dans sa composition actuelle, notamment pour ce qui concerne les membres permanents, n'est plus l'autorité capable d'appliquer la contrainte légale contre la violence illégale. En droit interne, je l'ai rappelé, la crise de la souveraineté rend de plus en plus fragile la différenciation entre la violence et le droit. Dans la société internationale, l'absence d'une souveraineté est en réalité une chance que nous devons saisir pour refonder le système. Allant au-delà de l'énigme qui a jusqu'ici flotté sur la séparation entre la violence et le droit, nous pouvons enfin rapprocher modestement le droit de la raison en en faisant un outil de la démocratie internationale. C'est l'avenir que je souhaite aux sanctions.

PART V

ANNEXES[■]

■ Available electronically.
Prepared by Hassiba Hadj Sakraoui.

LIST OF DOCUMENTS

I SECURITY COUNCIL

A. Security Council Resolutions relating to sanctions (Select list)

(See http://www.un.org/documents/scres.htm)

Southern Rhodesia:

- S/RES/216 (1965) of 12 November 1965
- S/RES/217 (1965) of 20 November 1965
- S/RES/232 (1966) of 16 November 1966
- S/RES/253 (1968) of 29 November 1968
- S/RES/277 (1970) of 18 March 1970
- S/RES/460 (1979) of 21 December 1979

South Africa:

- S/RES/418 (1977) of 4 November 1977
- S/RES/421 (1977) of 9 December 1979
- S/RES/919 (1994) of 25 May 1994

Iraq:

- S/RES/661 (1990) of 6 August 1990
- S/RES/665 (1990) of 25 August 1990
- S/RES/666 (1990) of 13 September 1990
- S/RES/670 (1990) of 25 September 1990
- S/RES/678 (1990) of 29 November 1990
- S/RES/687 (1991) of 3 April 1991
- S/RES/706 (1991) of 15 August 1991
- S/RES/712 (1991) of 19 September 1991

- S/RES/778 (1992) of 2 October 1992
- S/RES/986 (1995) of 14 April 1995
- S/RES/1111 (1997) of 4 June 1997
- S/RES/1153 (1998) of 20 February 1998
- S/RES/1284 (1999) of 17 December 1999

Former Yugoslavia:

- S/RES/713 (1991) of 25 September 1991
- S/RES/724 (1991) of 15 December 1991
- S/RES/757 (1992) of 30 May 1992
- S/RES/787 (1992) of 16 November 1992
- S/RES/820 (1993) of 17 April 1993
- S/RES/827 (1993) of 25 May 1993
- S/RES/942 (1994) of 23 September 1994
- S/RES/943 (1994) of 23 September 1994
- S/RES/992 (1995) of 11 May 1995
- S/RES/1021 (1995) of 22 November 1995
- S/RES/1022 (1995) of 22 November 1995
- S/RES/1074 (1996) of 1 October 1996
- S/RES/1160 (1998) of 31 March 1998
- S/RES/1199 (1998) of 23 September 1998
- S/RES/1244 (1998) of 10 June 1999

Libya:

- S/RES/731 (1992) of 21 January 1992
- S/RES/748 (1992) of 31 March 1992
- S/RES/883 (1993) of 11 November 1993
- S/RES/1192 (1998) of 27 August 1998

Somalia:

- S/RES/733 (1992) of 23 January 1992
- S/RES/751 (1992) of 24 April 1992

Liberia:

- S/RES/788 (1992) of 19 November 1992
- S/RES/985 (1995) of 13 April 1995

Haiti:

- S/RES/841 (1993) of 16 June 1993
- S/RES/861 (1993) of 27 August 1993
- S/RES/873 (1993) of 13 October 1993
- S/RES/875 (1993) of 16 October 1993
- S/RES/917 (1994) of 6 May 1994
- S/RES/940 (1994) of 31 July 1994
- S/RES/944 (1994) of 29 September 1994

Rwanda:

- S/RES/918 (1994) of 17 May 1994
- S/RES/997 (1995) of 9 June 1995
- S/RES/1011 (1995) of 16 August 1995
- S/RES/1013 (1995) of 6 September 1995
- S/RES/1161 (1998) of 9 April 1998

Angola:

- S/RES/864 (1993) of 15 September 1993
- S/RES/1127 (1997) of 28 August 1997
- S/RES/1173 (1998) of 12 June 1998
- S/RES/1221 (1999) of 12 January 1999
- S/RES/1237 (1999) of 7 May 1999

Sudan:

- S/RES/1054 (1996) of 26 April 1996
- S/RES/1070 (1996) of 16 August 1996

Sierra Leone:

- S/RES/1132 (1997) of 8 October 1997
- S/RES/1156 (1998) of 16 March 1998
- S/RES/1171 (1998) of 5 June 1998

B. Other Security Council documents

1- S/1995/234 of 29 March 1995: Note by the President of the Security Council
2- S/1995/300 of 13 April 1995: Letter dated 13 April 1995 from the permanent Representatives of China, The Russian Federation, The United Kingdom of Great

Britain and Northern Ireland and the United States of America to the United Nations Addressed to the President of Security Council

3- S/1995/438 of 31 May 1995: Note by the President of the Security Council

4- S/1996/54 of 24 January 1996: Note by the President of the Security Council

5- S/1998/1016 of 30 October 1998: Note by the President of the Security Council

6- S/1999/92 of 29 January 1999: Note by the President of the Security Council: Work of the Sanctions Committee

II Supplement to an Agenda for Peace (excerpts):

7- Position paper of the Secretary-General on the occasion of the Fiftieth Anniversary of the United Nations
A/50/60-S/1995/l, 3 January 1995

III General Assembly Resolutions:

8- A/RES/48/210 of 21 December 1993: Economic Assistance to States Affected by the Implementation of the Security Council Resolutions Imposing Sanctions Against the Federal Republic of Yugoslavia (Serbia and Montenegro)

9- A/RES/50/51 of 11 December 1995: Implementation of Charter Provisions Related to Assistance to Third States Affected by the Application of Sanctions

10- A/RES/51/193 of 10 February 1997

11- A/RES/51/242 of 15 September 1997: Supplement to an Agenda for Peace

12- A/RES/53/107 of 20 January 1999: Implementation of the Provisions of the Charter of the United Nations Related to Assistance to Third States Affected by the Application of Sanctions

13- A/RES/54/107 of 25 January 2000: Implementation of the Provisions of the Charter of the United Nations related to Assistance to Third States Affected by the Application Sanction

IV Other Documents:

14- Resolution of the 26th International Conference of the Red Cross and Red Crescent. Resolution 4: Principles and Action in International Humanitarian Assistance and Protection, 1 January 1996

15- E/C.12/1997/8 of 12 December 1997: Committee on Economic, Social and Cultural Rights, General Comment N° 8 (1997): The Relationship between Economic Sanctions and Respect for Economic, Social and Cultural Rights

16- ICTY, Tadic (IT-94-1): Prosecutor v. Dusko Tadic a/k/a “Dule”, Decision on the Defence Motion for Interlocutory Appeal on Jurisdiction, 2 October 1995 (excerpts)

17- ICTY, Milosevic & Others case (IT-99-37): Prosecutor v S. Milosevic, M. Milutinovic, N. Sainovic, D. Ojdanic & V. Stojiljkovic, Decision on Review of Indictment and Application for Consequential Orders, 24 May 1999

18- “A Peace and Security Agenda for Children”, by Carol Bellamy, Executive Director of UNICEF, 12 February 1999 (excerpts)